Puritans in the New World

Frontispiece. Captain Thomas Smith (d. 1691), self-portrait, Boston, Mass. The verses under his hand are quoted in the headnote on Anne Bradstreet (chap. 12). Courtesy of the Worcester Art Museum, Worcester, Mass.

Puritans in the New World

A Critical Anthology

EDITED BY

David D. Hall

PRINCETON UNIVERSITY PRESS

PRINCETON AND OXFORD

Published by Princeton University Press, 41 William Street, Princeton, New Jersey 08540
In the United Kingdom: Princeton University Press, 3 Market Place, Woodstock,
Oxfordshire OX20 1SY

Library of Congress Cataloging-in-Publication Data
Puritans in the New World: a critical anthology / edited by David D. Hall.
p. cm.
Includes bibliographical references and index.
ISBN 0-691-11408-0 (cl.: alk. paper) — ISBN 0-691-11409-9 (pb.: alk. paper)
1. Puritans — New England — History.   2. Puritans — New England — History — Sources.
3. Puritans — New England — Biography.   4. New England — History — Colonial period,
ca. 1600–1775.   5. New England — History — Colonial period, ca. 1600–1775 —
Sources.   6. New England — Church history.   7. New England — Church history —
Sources.   I. Hall, David D.
F7.P986 2004
285′.9′0974 — dc22
2003065495

British Library Cataloging-in-Publication Data is available

This book has been composed in Sabon

Printed on acid-free paper. ∞

www.pupress.princeton.edu

Printed in the United States of America

10   9   8   7   6   5   4   3   2   1

Contents

Introduction

Puritans in the New World: A Critical Anthology tells the story of a remarkable culture that emigrants from England transported to New England in the seventeenth century, and it does so in the words of these Puritans themselves. We hear them giving thanks that so many have crossed the Atlantic safely, that in their new home "all things" are being done "righteously [and] religiously," and, as the years unfold, worrying whether the second-generation colonists will remain faithful to the "errand" of the founders. We hear other voices as well, for Puritanism was no monolith, and the colonists did not have the land to themselves; Native Americans had long been present in the new world. We hear the radical Roger Williams as he begins to plead for liberty of conscience; we hear the charismatic Anne Hutchinson defying the magistrates and ministers; and we hear the same words Native Americans heard, listening to missionaries bringing them the Christian message or going to war instead. The purpose of *Puritans in the New World* is to present, in all its richness, the lived experience of being a Puritan in the strange, contested, and hopeful setting of the New World.

Who were the Puritans? The short answer to this question is that they were reformers in a national church, the Church of England, which did not fully embrace the Protestant Reformation of the sixteenth century. After Henry VIII renounced the authority of the pope and made himself head of the Church in the 1530s, England became nominally Protestant. Some within the Church, including several of its bishops, called for more sweeping change. Instead, the Church reverted to Catholicism during the brief reign of Henry's daughter Mary (1553–1558). But when Elizabeth I (1558–1603) came to the throne, Protestantism returned — a Protestantism held in check, however, by a monarch who rejected the demands of the reformers. Not only in her reign, but also during those of her successors James I (1603–1625) and Charles I (1625–1649), conflict persisted in Church and Parliament, and in scores of towns and cities, over the nature of the true church, with one party, nicknamed "Puritans," pursuing an agenda that owed much to the Calvinist (or Reformed) tradition as it arose in Europe.[1] When, quite unexpectedly, war broke out between Parliament and king in 1642 and the parliamentary forces under Oliver Cromwell gained the upper hand, Puritan-minded reformers found to their surprise that they did not agree among themselves on how to rebuild the Church. The restoration of the monarchy in 1660, following a decade in which England had been ruled as a commonwealth under Cromwell and others, brought a century of conflict to a close, for those who continued to insist on reform were thereafter excluded from the Church as "Dissenters" or Nonconformists.[2] Only in New England did the reformers have their way. Here alone, civil and religious leaders shared the same goals; here alone among the English settlements in the Western Hemisphere Puritanism became the dominant culture.

The name Puritan was not of the reformers' choosing. As William Bradford remarked in *Of Plymouth Plantation*, it arose as a term of mockery loosely connected with a controversy in the Christian church in the fourth century C.E. but expanded into caricature in popular theater of the late sixteenth century: the Puritan as a zealous busybody. To this day it remains a term of caricature. Eventually some seventeenth-century English men and women embraced it as a positive term designating their commitment to obey the will of God as fully as possible.[3] Doing so meant that these people lived in ways that were distinctive: observing the Sabbath more strictly than most others did, relishing sermons, "godly" books, and the Bible, and preferring the fellowship of other "godly" people like themselves even if doing so had the practical consequence, as it did for the future emigrant John Trumbull, of being "disgrace[d] in streets and threaten[ed]" by his former friends (see below, chap. 11). Yet we must not assume that every person in England lined up on one side or the other. Many preferred the middle to either extreme; some were Puritans in one respect but not in others, for the Puritan movement had its conservatives or moderates as well as its radicals. At the local level, where Puritanism gained the support of some gentry and urban elites despite the opposition of the monarch, the movement was able to train and sponsor ministers who became expert in preaching the "practical divinity" that we encounter in part II.[4]

Recognizing this diversity is what makes *Puritans in the New World* a

[1] A useful guide is Menna Prestwich, ed., *International Calvinism, 1541–1715* (New York, 1985). Broadly speaking, the colonists were Calvinist in their theology (see pt. II), accepting in 1648 and again in 1680 the Westminster Confession as their standard of orthodoxy (see Walker [1893]). They also owed their "two kingdom" theory of church and state to the Reformed tradition.

[2] See Michael Watts, *The Dissenters* (New York, 1978).

[3] The contested uses of the term are reviewed in Christopher Hill, *Society and Puritanism in Pre-Revolutionary England* (New York, 1964), chap. 1.

[4] Bremer (1997); Collinson (1982, 1983); and on the fashioning of a distinctive ministry, Haller (1938), Hall (1972), Webster (1997), and Staloff (1998).

"critical anthology." Yet our awareness of the movement's complexity must not stand in the way of grasping its core principles and practices. Foremost among these principles was the insistence that Roman Catholicism distorted the nature of the church and the doctrine of salvation by grace. Puritans were at one with Protestants of the sixteenth century in declaring that the salvation of sinners was entirely God's doing. Emphasizing the sovereignty of God no less strongly than John Calvin did before them, Puritan preachers described saving grace as a free, unmerited gift to sinners. Puritans also derided the Catholic sacramental system as "idolatry." Saints and saints' days, relics and pilgrimages — these and many other aspects of Catholicism were "superstitions," not, as Catholics believed, intermediaries that embodied the sacred. Puritans especially denounced the superstitions they encountered in worship, characterizing as superstitious or a human "invention" any practice for which no specific authority existed in the Bible. Again, they were reiterating a basic Protestant principle. But the more radical wing of the movement carried this principle to an extreme by declaring that the Bible contained rules for worship and the organization of the church that had the binding force of law. To those in the Church of England who argued otherwise, Thomas Hooker replied in 1633, the year he emigrated to New England, that the Christian church "must deliver the laws which she hath received from her King, not dare to make laws."[5] This way of thinking lay behind the reluctance or outright refusal of many English clergy and laypeople to participate in acts of worship that the Church of England had inherited from Catholicism.

To its determination to uphold the sovereignty of God and purify the church the Puritan movement added the goal of elevating the standards for being a Christian. A characteristic device of Puritan preaching was to contrast the figure of the "sincere" or "real" Christian with that of the temporizer who refuses to acknowledge the full burden of being a sinner and hesitates to undergo the transformation that Puritans referred to as the "new birth" or "conversion." Asking themselves the question, what constitutes authentic Christianity? Puritans answered it by raising the bar. How they did so can be observed in those sections of this book (parts III and VI) where laypeople describe their quest for saving grace. At a time in English history when many of the "lower orders" comprehended but little of Christian doctrine and spirituality, the fluency of these men and women is remarkable. For them the sovereignty of God and the burden of "original sin" were not abstract propositions but powerful truths that bore directly on how they were to live

[5] Williams et al. (1975), 327. See also Coolidge (1970), chap. 1; and for the broader context, Carlos M. N. Eire, *War against the Idols: The Reformation of Worship from Erasmus to Calvin* (New York, 1986).

and die. For them too the Bible embodied the living, vital presence of the Holy Spirit, a "mirror" in which they could gaze upon their true selves and find lessons pertinent to almost every life situation.

Puritans also raised the bar for how Christians were to behave in everyday society. Like other Protestants of their day, they harped on the tension between "flesh" and "spirit" or, as they put it using metaphorical language, between the "world" and the "pilgrim." The Puritans did not renounce the "world" or things of the flesh as insistently as some ascetics have done in the longer sweep of Christian history. Indeed, they celebrated the order and beauty of the created world as the handiwork of God and, in everyday life, were far from being prudes or killjoys. What they wanted was that Christians practice an ethic of self-denial — using time wisely for God's ends and obeying the duties or laws that God commanded. Puritans were realists who expected every Christian to falter in this self-discipline, but they insisted on its importance nonetheless. How this ethic was internalized may be seen in Mary Rowlandson's fretting that she had become careless about the Sabbath and in her concluding evocation of the transiency of earthly things (chap. 26).

In yet another respect the Puritans followed in the steps of the Protestant Reformers of the sixteenth century by endorsing the goal of "social discipline" or a "reformation of manners." It is easy to exaggerate the scope of this campaign and to distort the reasons why Puritans in England undertook it.[6] It is also tempting to assume that in New England, where Puritans were in charge, the campaign for discipline was fully effective. Indeed, as emigration was under way in the 1630s, excitement ran high that a new kind of society was being created, a community without "the unclean conversation of the wicked," as Thomas Weld reported to his former parishioners in England (chap. 2). All too soon, the colonists were finding plenty of examples of sinfulness in their midst. Yet expectations remained high[7] long after the excitement of the early years had subsided, as the litany of complaints of the "Reforming Synod" of 1679–1680 indicate (chap. 19).

Puritanism in New England changed over time. So do all religious movements in response to social and political circumstances, and as they work through their own internal contradictions. The colonists faced three major problems, each of which had long-term consequences for their culture. The first was whether to exclude or tolerate their fel-

---

[6] See Wrightson and Levine (rev. ed., 1995) and, for a more nuanced understanding of this campaign, David Underdown, *Fire from Heaven: Life of an English Town in the Seventeenth Century* (New Haven, Conn., 1992).

[7] Expectations that were persistently borne out in certain social indices, such as the low rate of bastardy. Thompson (1986).

low Puritans who challenged the emerging system of church, state, and theology. The most publicized confrontations were those with radicals such as Roger Williams and Anne Hutchinson or, in later years, the Baptists and the Quakers (see part V), but conservatives also weighed in against the "New England Way."[8] The second was how to reconcile de facto independence with the authority of the English government, a task that became increasingly difficult after Charles II was restored to the monarchy in 1660. Eventually Massachusetts had to accept a new charter (1691) that imposed a limited version of toleration and replaced a locally elected governor with one appointed by the Crown. The third was how to deal with those in their midst who did not meet the high standards for piety that the founders had institutionalized in the "Congregational Way" (see chap. 4). Puritans in England were working within a Church that included everyone, disciplined or not. But from the beginning, the churches in New England were selective in their membership. What should be done about those on the outside? And, once it became clear in the 1650s that the second-generation colonists were hanging back from becoming "full" members, what should be done about them and their children? Not without much resistance, the majority of ministers and laity eventually decided to retain as many people as possible within the church, using the sacrament of baptism for this purpose. The consequence of doing so was a kind of doublespeak: the bar remained high, with a "new birth" in grace as the goal, yet the bar was also reset to validate baptismal membership.[9]

All this is to say that the transfer of Puritanism from the Old World to the New was charged with strains and stresses, some of them expected, some unexpected. Other strains arose during the course of the seventeenth century, strains recorded in William Bradford's lament about the loss of community (chap. 1), in ongoing confusion about prosperity, and in efforts to define New England's "errand into the wilderness" (part VII). The documents in this book challenge us to discern not only the enduring features of the Puritan movement but also the special circumstances to which each writer was responding. Always, the colonists were aware of how vulnerable they were to hostile opinion in England. The defensiveness Weld and John Cotton expressed in writing English friends (chaps. 2, 22) helps explain the urgency of publicizing John Eliot's missionary ventures to the Native Americans (part VI). The documents in this book challenge us in other ways as well, for each implies or acknowledges the presence of other texts.

[8] Foster (1991) stresses the incorporation of the radicals. Hall (1972) notes the objections of conservatives.

[9] This doublespeak is explicated in Holifield (1974), and the uses of baptism in Brown and Hall (1997).

Other voices hover around these texts: the voices of historians in the nineteenth, twentieth, and now twenty-first centuries arguing among themselves about the nature of Puritanism. The extensive bibliographical references are a guide to these debates for those who want to know more about them. But let me call attention to four major questions that tax every historian of seventeenth-century Puritanism.

The most basic of these questions is whether Puritanism was ever a coherent, clearly organized movement, given all the different directions so-called Puritans would take in the seventeenth century and given, too, the porous boundary between Puritans and other contemporaries.[10] On the American side of the Atlantic, the temptation to apply the label Puritan to everything we find in early New England is irresistible: thus we have studies of the "Puritan" family when much of what is being described is consistent with family life in England among a certain social stratum.

A second question concerns authoritarianism: were Puritans distinctively authoritarian, prone to censoring others, to defending hierarchies of spiritual or social merit, and to denying freedom of conscience to those who disagreed with them? No easy answer is at hand. Compared with modern ways of thinking, all of English culture in the early seventeenth century was infused with authoritarianism, be it of parents, husbands, ministers, or civil rulers, an authority always held in check among Puritans, however, by the assumption that legitimacy flowed from observing the will of God and serving the ends of justice and equity. On the other hand, the people who lived in the villages and towns of seventeenth-century New England never marched in lockstep, as any swatch of court records will reveal. Parents had only limited control over their children, and towns often ignored (or creatively observed!) the statutes enacted by the central government. What was *said* about authority, and even what was written in law books, was not the same as what happened in everyday life. How to combine authority and diversity in telling the history of early New England is perhaps the greatest challenge of the present moment.

A third question has to do with how we understand religion as creed and practice. The ministers in early New England aspired to regulate the attitudes and practices of their congregations. Yet much slipped away or was ignored. A friend asked me recently if ministers did as their theology would seem to dictate: describe children who died early in life as sinners condemned to hell. Thomas Shepard (see chap. 3), who taught and believed in reprobation, referred to a dying child of his as "innocent," which certainly suggests otherwise, as does the poetry of

---

[10] A good point of entry to this debate is Collinson (1980).

Anne Bradstreet. It may be that every religious system makes do with contradictions. If this is so, Puritanism offers plenty of examples.

A fourth question involves the relative (and changing) importance of religion in people's lives. Did Puritanism (or religion) "decline"? Were the social norms of Puritan communalism overtaken by the values and practices of merchants and land speculators? Did religion matter only to a minority of the colonists, those who made their way into full church membership? No other assertions about Puritanism have been more tenaciously defended or, in recent years, more heatedly denied. Much depends on how religion itself is defined—whether narrowly, as only one kind of church membership (whereas the colonists themselves acknowledged the validity of more than one kind), or perhaps so tightly bounded that ambivalence or dissent betoken decline, with no space left open for negotiation. The spirit of this anthology coincides, however, with much recent scholarship suggesting that Puritanism should be defined broadly and that it was capable of renewal in response to social change.[11]

A generation or two ago, historians were debating whether Puritanism was an important source of our democratic tradition. Further back in time, during the early decades of the twentieth century, the great reaction against nineteenth-century Victorianism confused it with the seventeenth-century Puritans, both being condemned as hypocritical and prudish. The risk we run either in appropriating Puritanism for contemporary ends or in tarring it with so broad a brush is that we take the movement out of context. To learn that Increase Mather, a most learned man, thought that blood rained from the sky and that lightning signaled God's wrath (chap. 30) is to be reminded that the colonists were contemporaries of Shakespeare and Milton, as close to the Middle Ages as to us. Far from being modern, though in certain respects reacting strongly against feudalism and Scholasticism, the people whose world we enter through these texts must be approached on their own terms if we are to understand them.

EDITORIAL PRINCIPLES

Every text in this book has a context that is briefly indicated in a headnote; introductions to each part sketch a larger framework. Those introductions and headnotes also direct the reader to scholarship that is listed in a bibliographical note. To ease the task of reading these texts,

[11] The irrelevance of Puritanism is argued most forcefully in Rutman (1965); the failure of communitarian values is suggested in Bailyn (1955) and Martin (1991). Counterarguments appear in Foster (1971) and Peterson (1997). Hall (1989) argues for a broad understanding of religion.

capitalization, spelling, and the punctuation of possessives have been modernized, contractions have been written out, italics eliminated, errors silently corrected, and citations of Scripture standardized. Otherwise, the punctuation of the originals has been respected. Words or other matter in brackets are modern editorial additions. For two writers, Mary Rowlandson and Anne Bradstreet, the spelling remains unchanged. Quotations from Scripture have been identified as fully as possible without, however, indicating which English translation (Geneva or King James) was being used (the great majority are KJV) or, in every instance, correcting the verses. It was also impractical to annotate those passages in texts (e.g., in John Clarke's *Ill Newes*) which are pastiches of Scripture. Every abridgment is indicated by ellipses. Considering that printing practices in the seventeenth century allowed for great variety in how a text was punctuated (rarely did an author oversee this), readers are warned to regard the versions printed here as accurate reproductions of the source as cited but not as critical editions based on comparing every version. The two exceptions to this statement are Rowlandson's *Sovereignty* and *A Conference Held . . . at Boston*. The Western calendar changed in the eighteenth century from "old style" to "new style" (n.s.). The "old style" calendar of the colonists was peculiar in that the new year began in March, and numbers were used instead of the names of months or days. The dates reproduced in these texts are as in the source texts, that is, ten days behind the Gregorian calendar, but with this major exception: the new year begins January 1.

In preparing the texts, headnotes, and annotation I have benefited greatly from the assistance of Adrian Weimer, Peter Becker, and Eric Unverzagt. The anonymous readers' reports were quite useful to me also. I am grateful to the publishers and learned societies that have granted permission to include certain images and documents in this book: the American Antiquarian Society, the Colonial Society of Massachusetts, the Connecticut Historical Society, the Massachusetts Historical Society, Northeastern University Press, and the Worcester Art Museum.

I dedicate this book to my grandsons John Brewster and Samuel Drisko Hall and to their cousins Matthew Edward and Benjamin Hall Parker. May this be a legacy that reminds them of the Marvins, Russells, Greenwoods, Holbrooks, and those whose names they bear.

Permissions

The Colonial Society of Massachusetts gave permission to reprint the following from its *Publications*: "The Autobiography of Thomas Shepard," vol. 27 (1932): 343–400; "The Confessions of Thomas Shepard," ed. George Selement and Bruce Woolley, vol. 58 (1981): 33–34, 106–9, 111–13, 133–35; and *The Notebook of John Fiske*, ed. Robert G. Pope, vol. 47 (1974): 146–51.

The Connecticut Historical Society gave permission to reprint Ann Fitch's relation from 'The East Windsor Conversion Relations 1700–1725," ed. Kenneth J. Minkema, *Bulletin of the Connecticut Historical Society* 51 (1985): 32–34.

The Massachusetts Historical Society gave permission to reprint John Winthrop's "Modell of Christian Charity" from *Winthrop Papers*, vol. 2 (Boston, 1931): 282–295.

Northeastern University Press gave permission to reprint Samuel Willard's account of Elizabeth Knapp's possession from *Witch-Hunting in New England, 1638–1692: A Documentary History*, ed. David D. Hall (Boston, 1991).

PART I

From the Old World to the New

From the Old World to the New

Why did thousands of people known as "Puritans" risk a hazardous ocean voyage and emigrate to New England? The first to arrive were the "Pilgrims" who founded Plymouth in 1620, followed by the much larger migration to Massachusetts that began in 1628. For all of those who came during these years, the "wilderness" they entered was a strange, even ominous environment. Yet it was also a refuge from their enemies in England and, more grandly, a space that promised better things. Now that they were free to do as they wished, what kind of church and civil government did the colonists create, and what kind of rules did they seek to live by in everyday affairs? How did they relate to the Native Americans and, once their children came of age, what stories did the founders tell about old England and the meaning of their new land?

Answering these questions was immensely important to the colonists. Far more Puritans stayed in England in the 1630s than departed for the New World. Those who left faced complaints that they were deserting the cause in their native country at a time of need. It was said of them, too, that in their new homeland they were becoming dangerously radical.

The "Pilgrims" deserved a little of this reputation, for they were "Separatists" who in England had renounced the Church of England because it was "unlawful" or idolatrous. Already living in exile in the Netherlands, some of them sailed on the *Mayflower* and founded Plymouth. Their story was told by one of their leaders, William Bradford, in perhaps the greatest work of history writing in early New England, *Of Plymouth Plantation*. To the north of Plymouth, the Massachusetts Bay Company, which received a charter from the government of Charles I to colonize a large stretch of land, organized the founding of Salem in 1629 and, in 1630, a cluster of towns that included Boston and Charlestown. Other towns sprang up, including Roxbury and Dorchester on the southern edge of Boston's harbor. Beyond them lay Braintree and Dedham; on the coast to the north, Newbury and Ipswich. Inland, along the Charles, were Newtown (renamed Cambridge) and Watertown; further inland were Concord and Sudbury. Some of the emigrants moved as far away as Springfield on the Connecticut River and, downstream from Springfield, founded a cluster of towns — Windsor, Hartford, Wethersfield — that formed the nucleus of the colony of Connecticut, along with Saybrook at the river's mouth. New Haven (1638) was an independent political jurisdiction until 1665; Rhode Island was another independent jurisdiction, a cluster of towns loosely affiliated with each other and offering a place of refuge for persons expelled from the orthodox colonies.

Early on, the dangers were many — the sickness that led to so many deaths the first winter at Plymouth or the "starving time" of the first winter after the "Great Migration," when food ran short and cattle had no fodder. Some people became disheartened and returned to their old home, but others soon came in their stead. The leaders of the Massachusetts Bay Company had expected everyone to live in close proximity, but the colonists spread themselves across the landscape seeking access to the fur trade, much needed timber, and good land, especially meadow for their cattle. The Massachusetts Bay Company awarded each town a large grant of land that the towns distributed to each household or family free of charge. A farming economy came into being and, by the 1640s, the survival of the colonies was assured when local surpluses of cattle, butter, and grain found a market in the West Indies. Soon, artisans were constructing ships, a fishing industry sprang up, and an ironworks was smelting ore and casting bars for export.

Political and social stability was as hard-won as economic prosperity. The "Mayflower Compact" was devised to support the tenuous authority of the leaders of Plymouth; and in Massachusetts, Connecticut, and New Haven (see part IV), compromises were struck between different interest groups — the towns wanted as much autonomy as possible, together with a low-cost civil government, but leaders such as John Winthrop, the first governor of Massachusetts, knew that central authority was necessary to hold things together and defend the colony against its enemies. Cambridge (originally Newtown) became the site of a printing press and a college, named Harvard in honor of the well-to-do emigrant John Harvard, who donated much of his property to the new institution when he died in 1638. Together, press and college were means of ensuring the continuity of culture between Europe and the New World: looking ahead, and "dreading to leave an illiterate ministry in the dust," the founders of Harvard were determined to perpetuate the standards of training they themselves had received at English universities. Thanks to practices such as catechizing, the colonists passed on to their children the high level of literacy they had already acquired.

Thus were familiar patterns of culture reestablished. Familiar, but also different. In 1630, the year John Winthrop started his journal-history of New England while en route, William Bradford of Plymouth also began to write a history of the "Pilgrim" Separatists. Others were sending letters to friends in England detailing what life was like in their new home and explaining why they had decided to emigrate.[1] Thomas Weld, a minister who arrived in 1632, assured his English friends that, contrary to rumor, the colonists were healthy and well fed. But Weld especially wanted to celebrate the freedom he was experiencing in the New World, freedom *from* "the unclean conversation of the wicked" and from active enemies of the Puritans, always "knocking at our doors, disturbing our sweet peace, or threatening violence," as well as freedom *to* live and worship in a place where "all things [are] so righteously, so religiously and impartially carried [out]." Puritans in England had been an embattled, much criticized minority. Three thousand miles away from king and bishops, they were able in "the free aire of the new worlde" to implement their program of reform in matters small and large — eliminating, for instance, "pagan" names for the months and days of the week, enforcing strict observance of the Sabbath, and pro-hibiting popular festivals such as May Day and "health-drinkings."

But the greatest advantage of having the Atlantic between them and England was that the colonists could implement the Puritan understand-ing of the church. "Our people here desire to worship God in spirit, & in trueth," John Cotton reported from Massachusetts in 1634, noting also that a principal reason people gave for emigrating was "that we mighte enjoy the libertye, not of some ordinances of god, but of all, & all in Purity." Two years later he drew on the language of Christian primitivism in remarking that the colonists "doe in generall professe, the reason of their comming over to us was, that they might be freed from the bondage of such humane inventions and ordinances as their soules groaned under."[2]

These expectations flowered into a system of church order that broke decisively with the episcopal system of the Church of England. The "Congregational Way," as the new system was called, included some features, such as the reorganization of the ministry into a collective of equals (pastor, teacher, elder, and deacon, the latter two being lay of-fices), that had been advocated by radical Puritans in England since the 1570s, following the example of Reformed churches in Europe. Others were unusual. The six that made the "Congregational Way" distinctive were (1) that each local congregation was equal in authority to all other congregations, none being subordinate to a higher body; (2) that each

---

[1] Emerson (1976) is an excellent collection.
[2] Bush (2001), 183–84, 217.

local church was founded on a covenant among its members; (3) that the office of the ministry existed only in relation to such congregations, not as an independent order; (4) that the local church was "gathered" or selective in its membership, not inclusive; (5) that candidates for church membership had to offer a "confession" of the divine "work of grace" they had experienced; and (6) that the "power of the keys" (Matt. 18:17), or the authority to make decisions on every aspect of church government, rested with the entire membership (although only men could actually vote).

One theological principle that guided the organizers of this system was the assumption that Scripture was law, binding Christians to observe the commands of God as revealed in the Old and New Testaments. Only if these commands were observed would a church be "lawful": "whatsoever is not done by the Word of God is sin."[3] The practice of covenanting drew on another idea, the church as a distinctive kind of community devoted to "edification." This understanding flowed from passages in the New Testament that described the church as a "house" or "temple" permeated with the presence of Christ through the Holy Spirit (e.g., Eph. 2:19–22). Church members were "one body in Christ" (Rom. 12:5), committed by their covenant to an ethic of "mutual helpfulness" and "edification": keeping watch over one another's ethical behavior, living in peace, providing assistance when needed, addressing fellow congregants as "brother" or "sister." This high understanding of the church descended to the Puritans from John Calvin, who declared in *Institutes of the Christian Religion* that the church is "all [of] the elect" who have "been called not only into the same inheritance of eternal life but also to participate in one God and Christ."[4] Gathering together in covenant all who were "visible saints," the church was the means of carrying on God's saving work in the world, or the history of redemption.

When the townspeople of Dedham, Massachusetts, began in 1637 to organize a congregation, they proceeded cautiously, hoping to realize in practice this ecclesiology and especially the ideals of "love" and "edification." At the same time they were realistic about human nature: their church, like others in New England, would need the tools of "discipline" (admonition and excommunication) to deal with anyone who violated the bonds of covenant. On what basis, then, should they choose the saints from among themselves? The answer was to employ a novel criterion for membership that nearby congregations in Massachusetts had begun to practice by 1636: not only would candidates have

---

[3] Coolidge (1970), 25.

[4] John Calvin, *Institutes of the Christian Religion*, trans. Ford Lewis Battles, 2 vols., The Library of Christian Classics (Phladelphia, 1960), 1010–16; 1016, n. 10 (bk. IV, chap. 1–4).

to demonstrate soundness in doctrine and evidence of moral behavior, but they would also have to deliver a "confession" describing the "work of grace" they had experienced (confessions from other congregations are included in part III).

Did this practice raise the bar so high that many of the emigrants were left outside the church? In the 1640s Presbyterians in England and Scotland, all of them critics of Congregationalism, alleged that "many thousands of people, who in former time have been reputed . . . very good Christians," were excluded, some even suggesting that the proportion ran as high as three-fourths of the colonists.[5] The ministers in New England insisted, on the contrary, that "far more" heads of families were admitted than excluded. Arriving at an aggregate figure is not possible (a much cited figure of one out of five adults is incorrect, erring badly on the low end), for the percentage varied from one congregation to another. In Dedham, at least 70 percent of the adults became members, with women rapidly outnumbering men in most of the churches. Nonetheless, there was enough discontent to worry the ministers, one of whom wrote John Cotton in 1642 to report that "many [are] murmuring that we come to make Heathens rather then convert Heathens to Christianity."[6]

Church membership mattered in its own right, but it also gave a parent the right to have his or her children baptized. Addressing the needs of those children and, in turn, *their* children, became a major problem for the colonists after 1650 once it was discovered that some of the children of the emigrants, though baptized and therefore included in the church, were never going to offer a relation. Should these "adult children" still be regarded as church members, and should *their* children be entitled to the sacrament of baptism? Most of the ministers said yes (notably at a synod that met in Cambridge, Massachusetts, in 1662), but a few complained that opening up baptism in this manner violated the purity that had meant so much to the emigrants. A long-lasting controversy over who had access to baptism accounts for some of the anxiety expressed in Increase Mather's *Pray for the Rising Generation* (chap. 9) and in his sermon on declension (chap. 30).

Bradford's evocation of "wilderness" at the conclusion of his history of Plymouth Plantation, book 1, reminds us, again, of the dangers and uncertainties the colonists were facing. Bradford had the many biblical references to wilderness in mind when he wrote. Those references embraced a range of meanings from wilderness as place of trial to wilderness as refuge. Outside the biblical context, wilderness could also sig-

---

[5] As was suggested by Thomas Lechford, *Plain Dealing* (London, 1642), 73.
[6] Bush (2001), 372.

nify "barbarism," or the opposite of "civilization."[7] What kind of place would it be for the emigrants? Would they live in peace with the native peoples or (as the Pilgrims imagined beforehand) be at the mercy of cruel, bloodthirsty enemies bent on their destruction? Was the wilderness they were entering home of a people allied with Satan? A deep ambivalence about the Native Americans — needing their skills and food supplies, yet fearing their intentions — marks the early pages of Bradford's *Of Plymouth Plantation* and, in the longer run of New England history, was played out in destructive warfare as well as in missions to convert the Indians to Christianity (see below, Pt. VI).

Bibliography

Anderson (1991) and Allen (1981), debating the motives for emigrating; Cressy (1987) and Thompson (1994) on social aspects of the emigration. On Congregationalism: Walker (1893), the foundational history, with texts; Miller (1933), chap. 6; Morgan (1963) on the new requirement of a relation; Coolidge (1970) on "edification" and idolatry; Hall (1972), chaps. 6, 10; Caldwell (1983), revisiting Morgan's genealogy; Foster (1991), chap. 4, on the "sectarian" directions of the 1630s; Pope (1969), Brown and Hall (1997), Holifield (1974), and Peterson (1997) on the evolution of baptismal policy.

[7] These meanings are surveyed in Carroll (1969) and, especially, Canup (1990).

Chapter 1

William Bradford, the "Pilgrims," and the Founding of Plymouth Plantation

In November 1620 a small group of English men and women reached the coast of New England. Another month passed before their ship, the *Mayflower*, anchored in Plymouth Bay, to the north of Cape Cod, and the emigrants went ashore to begin a permanent settlement at Plymouth. William Bradford (1589–1657) told the story of the "Pilgrims," the name by which this group became known in the nineteenth century, in a manuscript headed "Of Plimmoth Plantation." In his youth he had joined a group of Separatists, radical Puritans who pleaded the right of "conscience" to free themselves from "unlawful and anti-christian" aspects of the Church of England. In 1606 this group organized an independent (and therefore illegal) congregation in the village of Scrooby, Nottinghamshire, under the leadership of two former ministers in the Church of England, Richard Clyfton and John Robinson. The congregation made its way to Amsterdam in 1607/8 but removed in 1609 to Leiden in order to escape the disarray within another Separatist community, the "Ancient Church," and the controversies surrounding John Smyth, a former minister and fellow Separatist who repudiated infant baptism and the doctrine of original sin.[1]

By 1617 the Leiden congregation was initiating steps to secure a "patent" to territory in North America that belonged to the Virginia Company of London. Among the reasons that the congregation had for leaving the Netherlands was the exiles' anxiety that living in a foreign land would cause their children to "lose our language and our name of English," a process of assimilation that eventually occurred among the families who remained there.[2] Half of the passengers who had arrived on the *Mayflower* died during the first winter in New England, but the tiny colony was able to celebrate in November 1621 (the exact date is

[1] It should be noted, however, that John Robinson and his congregation eventually moderated their Separatism, arriving at a position some contemporaries dubbed "semi-Separatism."

[2] Edward Winslow, quoted in Canup (1990), 58.

not specified in the records) a harvest feast that Americans look back to as the first "Thanksgiving."

Much of Bradford's history consists of letters and other texts that document the community's efforts to obtain a patent, pay off their creditors in England, control the unruly "strangers" who intruded on them, and negotiate a durable peace with the Native Americans. Bradford was at the center of all these efforts; elected governor in April 1621, he was annually reelected from 1627 to 1656. When he began to write *Of Plymouth Plantation* in 1630, completing the first ten chapters before putting the manuscript down, he was sharply aware of the newly founded colony of Massachusetts Bay, to the north. Wanting to defend the path of Separatism against its Puritan critics, he began by recalling the struggles of the Christian church against the Antichrist. Bradford located the Pilgrims within the framework of this struggle, conflating their persecution and survival with the "deliverance" of Christian martyrs as narrated by the fourth-century Christian historian Eusebius and retold by the English martyrologist John Foxe in his *Book of Martyrs* (1559, 1565). The overriding theme of Bradford's story was God's protecting providence. Yet Bradford's certainty about God's providence often gave way to uncertainty, for he "recognize[d] the faithful search for God's will as the major quest of the pilgrim's life."[3] When Bradford described the "wilderness" that the emigrants had entered in 1620, he was writing as a moralist who understood the Christian life as constantly beset by adversity.

After a long interruption, he resumed writing in 1644 or 1645, now organizing his narrative around each year's events, or "annals." His audience had become the "young men" or "children" who had no first-hand experience of the early years and who were moving away from the communal center to live on "farms," a process that eventually affected every seventeenth-century New England town. Bradford rejoiced in the triumph of the Puritans in England and the "downfall of the Bishops, with their courts, canons, and ceremonies . . . it is the Lord's doing, and ought to be marvelous in our eyes!"[4] But he also complained that the "sacred bond" uniting the Separatist community in the early years was "as it were insensibly by degrees [beginning] to dissolve, or in a great measure, to weaken." He wrote, therefore, to create a lasting "memorial" of the "constant faithfulness" and self-sacrificing practices of the "ancient members" of the community as counterweight to the "decay and want thereof" among the next generation.

[3] Levin (1972), 17.
[4] Bradford (1912), 1:14, a marginal note he added.

Bibliography

Howard (1971); Levin (1972); Rosenmeier (1972); Anderson (2003), contesting Axtell (1985) and others on the Pilgrims' policy toward Native Americans; Gallagher and Werge (1976). The related primary sources are reprinted in Arber (1897) and Young (1841). See also Bradford's "Dialogue Between young Men Born in New England and Sundry Ancient Men that Came Out of Holland and Old England," in Young (1841).

WILLIAM BRADFORD

 *Of Plymouth Plantation*

And first of the occasion and inducements thereunto; the which, that I may truly unfold, I must begin at the very root and rise of the same. The which I shall endeavor to manifest in a plain style, with singular regard unto the simple truth in all things; at least as near as my slender judgment can attain the same.

Chapter 1

It is well known unto the godly and judicious, how ever since the first breaking out of the light of the gospel in our honorable nation of England (which was the first of nations whom the Lord adorned therewith after the gross darkness of popery which had covered and overspread the Christian world),[5] what wars and oppositions ever since, Satan hath raised, maintained and continued against the saints, from time to time, in one sort or other. Sometimes by bloody death and cruel torments; other whiles imprisonments, banishments and other hard usages; as being loath his kingdom should go down, the truth prevail and the churches of God revert to their ancient purity and recover their primitive order, liberty and beauty.

But when he could not prevail by these means against the main truths of the gospel, but that they began to take rooting in many places, being watered with the blood of the martyrs and blessed from heaven with a gracious increase; he then began to take him to his ancient stratagems,

---

[5] England's priority in bringing about the Reformation, an assertion made by the mid-sixteenth-century historians John Bale and John Foxe, was keyed to the career of John Wycliff, the fourteenth-century church reformer and translator of the Bible into English.

used of old against the first Christians. That when by the bloody and barbarous persecutions of the heathen emperors he could not stop and subvert the course of the gospel, but that it speedily overspread, with a wonderful celerity, the then best known parts of the world; he then began to sow errors, heresies and wonderful dissensions amongst the professors[6] themselves, working upon their pride and ambition, with other corrupt passions incident to all mortal men, yea to the saints themselves in some measure, by which woeful effects followed. As not only bitter contentions and heartburnings, schisms, with other horrible confusions; but Satan took occasion and advantage thereby to foist in a number of vile ceremonies, with many unprofitable canons and decrees, which have since been as snares to many poor and peaceable souls even to this day.

So as in the ancient times, the persecutions by the heathen and their emperors was not greater than of the Christians one against other: — the Arians and other their complices against the orthodox and true Christians. As witnesseth Socrates in his second book.[7] His words are these: "The violence truly (saith he) was no less than that of old practiced towards the Christians when they were compelled and drawn to sacrifice to idols; for many endured sundry kinds of torment, often rackings and dismembering of their joints, confiscating of their goods; some bereaved of their native soil, others departed this life under the hands of the tormentor, and some died in banishment and never saw their country again, etc."

The like method Satan hath seemed to hold in these later times, since the truth began to spring and spread after the great defection made by Antichrist, that man of sin.[8]

For to let pass the infinite examples in sundry nations and several places of the world, and instance in our own, when as that old serpent could not prevail by those fiery flames and other his cruel tragedies, which he by his instruments put in use everywhere in the days of Queen Mary and before, he then began another kind of war and went more closely to work; not only to oppugn but even to ruinate and destroy the kingdom of Christ by more secret and subtle means, by kindling the flames of contention and sowing the seeds of discord and bitter enmity

[6] Professing Christians.

[7] Lib. 2, chap. 22 (correctly, 27) Bradford (1912). Socrates Scholasticus, fourth-century C.E. Greek historian, author of *History of the Church from 306 to 409 A.D.* Bradford was quoting the London 1577 edition. Arians (named after Arius, 250–336 C.E.) were a powerful fourth-century sect that denied the full divinity of Christ. The theological/political conflict between Arians and the (Trinitarian) followers of Athanasius escalated to the point of violence.

[8] 2 Thess. 2:3.

amongst the professors (and seeming reformed) themselves. For when he could not prevail by the former means against the principal doctrines of faith, he bent his force against the holy discipline and outward regiment of the kingdom of Christ, by which those holy doctrines should be conserved, and true piety maintained amongst the saints and people of God.

Mr. Fox recordeth how that besides those worthy martyrs and confessors which were burned in Queen Mary's days and otherwise tormented, "Many (both students and others) fled out of the land to the number of 800, and became several congregations, at Wesel, Frankfort, Basel, Emden, Markpurge, Strasbourg and Geneva, etc."[9] Amongst whom (but especially those at Frankfort) began that bitter war of contention and persecution about the ceremonies and service book, and other popish and anti-Christian stuff, the plague of England to this day, which are like the high places in Israel which the prophets cried out against, and were their ruin. Which the better part sought, according to the purity of the gospel, to root out and utterly to abandon. And the other part (under veiled pretences) for their own ends and advancements, sought as stiffly to continue, maintain and defend. As appeareth by the discourse thereof published in print, anno 1575; a book that deserves better to be known and considered.[10]

The one side labored to have the right worship of God and discipline of Christ established in the church, according to the simplicity of the gospel, without the mixture of men's inventions; and to have and to be ruled by the laws of God's Word, dispensed in those offices, and by those officers of pastors, teachers and elders, etc. according to the Scriptures.[11] The other party, though under many colors and pretences, endeavored to have the episcopal dignity (after the popish manner) with their large power and jurisdiction still retained; with all those courts, canons and ceremonies, together with all such livings,[12] revenues and subordinate officers, with other such means as formerly upheld their anti-Christian greatness and enabled them with lordly and tyrannous power to persecute the poor servants of God. This contention was so

---

[9] Foxe (1837), 6:430. In this paragraph and its sequel, Bradford summarizes the history of the "Marian exiles," Protestants who left England rather than accept the Catholicism reimposed by Mary Tudor (1553–1558), but returning after her halfsister, Elizabeth, a Protestant, succeeded to the throne.

[10] A brieff discours off the troubles begonne at Franckford (1575), narrating disputes among the Marian exiles, some of whom wanted to adopt the Reformed model of church government while others preferred an episcopal system, which Bradford himself opposed. Collinson (1967), 153.

[11] That is, no bishops as there are in an episcopal system.

[12] Livings: funded positions in the Church; Bradford is accusing the Church leaders of avarice.

great, as neither the honor of God, the common persecution, nor the mediation of Mr. Calvin and other worthies of the Lord in those places, could prevail with those thus episcopally minded; but they proceeded by all means to disturb the peace of this poor persecuted church, even so far as to charge (very unjustly and ungodily yet prelatelike) some of their chief opposers with rebellion and high treason against the emperor, and other such crimes.

And this contention died not with Queen Mary, nor was left beyond the seas. But at her death these people returning into England under gracious Queen Elizabeth, many of them being preferred to bishoprics and other promotions according to their aims and desires, that inveterate hatred against the holy discipline of Christ in his church hath continued to this day. Insomuch that for fear it should prevail, all plots and devices have been used to keep it out, incensing the queen and state against it as dangerous for the commonwealth; and that it was most needful that the fundamental points of religion should be preached in those ignorant and superstitious times. And to win the weak and ignorant they might retain divers harmless ceremonies; and though it were to be wished that divers things were reformed, yet this was not a season for it.[13] And many the like, to stop the mouths of the more godly, to bring them on to yield to one ceremony after another, and one corruption after another; by these wiles beguiling some and corrupting others till at length they began to persecute all the zealous professors in the land (though they knew little what this discipline meant) both by word and deed, if they would not submit to their ceremonies and become slaves to them and their popish trash, which have no ground in the Word of God, but are relics of that man of sin.[14] And the more the light of the gospel grew, the more they urged their subscriptions to these corruptions. So as (notwithstanding all their former pretences and fair colors) they whose eyes God had not justly blinded might easily see whereto these things tended.

And to cast contempt the more upon the sincere servants of God; they opprobriously and most injuriously gave unto and imposed upon them that name of Puritans, which is said the Novatians out of pride did assume and take unto themselves.[15] And lamentable it is to see the effects which have followed. Religion hath been disgraced, the godly grieved, afflicted, persecuted, and many exiled; sundry have lost their

---

[13] Rationales of the conservative leaders of the Church for not undertaking full reform.

[14] The "man of sin" (2 Thess. 2:3), synonym for the Antichrist.

[15] Eusebius, *Ecclesiastical History*, bk. 6, chap. 43, Bradford (1912). A mid-third-century sect marked by a refusal to reconcile with those who apostatized during persecution, the Novatians (after their founder, the bishop Novatus) called themselves the Katharoi, the "pure": hence "Puritans."

lives in prisons and other ways. On the other hand, sin hath been countenanced; ignorance, profaneness and atheism increased, and the papists encouraged to hope again for a day.

This made that holy man Mr. Perkins[16] cry out in his exhortation to repentance, upon Zephaniah 2: "Religion (saith he) hath been amongst us this thirty-five years; but the more it is published, the more it is contemned and reproached of many, etc. Thus not profaneness nor wickedness but religion itself is a byword, a mockingstock, and a matter of reproach; so that in England at this day the man or woman that begins to profess religion and to serve God, must resolve with himself to sustain mocks and injuries even as though he lived amongst the enemies of religion." And this, common experience hath confirmed and made too apparent.[17]

But that I may come more near my intendment.

When as by the travail and diligence of some godly and zealous preachers, and God's blessing on their labors, as in other places of the land, so in the north parts, many became enlightened by the Word of God and had their ignorance and sins discovered unto them, and began by his grace to reform their lives and make conscience of their ways; the work of God was no sooner manifest in them but presently they were both scoffed and scorned by the profane multitude; and the ministers urged with the yoke of subscription, or else must be silenced. And the poor people were so vexed with apparitors and pursuivants and the commissary courts, as truly their affliction was not small. Which, notwithstanding, they bore sundry years with much patience, till they were occasioned by the continuance and increase of these troubles, and other means which the Lord raised up in those days, to see further into things by the light of the Word of God. How not only these base and beggarly ceremonies were unlawful, but also that the lordly and tyrannous power of the prelates ought not to be submitted unto; which thus, contrary to the freedom of the gospel, would load and burden men's consciences and by their compulsive power make a profane mixture of persons and things in the worship of God. And that their offices and callings, courts and canons, etc. were unlawful and anti-Christian; being such as have no warrant in the Word of God, but the same that were used in popery and still retained. Of which a famous author[18] thus writeth in his Dutch

---

[16] William Perkins (1558–1602), noted teacher at Cambridge and moderate Puritan; the reference is to *A Godly and Learned Exposition of Christ's Sermon On the Mount* (1618), 421.

[17] Opposite this passage Bradford wrote, "A late observation, as it were by the way, worthy to be noted," dated 1646, remarking on the "downfall of the bishops" and giving 1630 as "about the year" he began to write his narrative. Bradford (1912), 1:14–16.

[18] Emmanuel van Meteren, *General History of the Netherlands* (1608), trans. Edward Grimstone (London, 1609), bk. 25, fol. 119, Bradford (1912).

commentaries, at the coming of King James into England: "The new king (saith he) found there established the reformed religion according to the reformed religion of King Edward VI, retaining or keeping still the spiritual state of the bishops, etc. after the old manner, much varying and differing from the Reformed churches in Scotland, France and the Netherlands, Emden, Geneva, etc., whose reformation is cut, or shapen much nearer the first Christian churches, as it was used in the apostles' times."

So many, therefore, of these professors as saw the evil of these things in these parts, and whose hearts the Lord had touched with heavenly zeal for his truth, they shook off this yoke of anti-Christian bondage, and as the Lord's free people joined themselves (by a covenant of the Lord) into a church estate, in the fellowship of the gospel, to walk in all his ways made known, or to be made known unto them, according to their best endeavors, whatsoever it should cost them, the Lord assisting them.[19] And that it cost them something this ensuing history will declare.

These people became two distinct bodies or churches, and in regard of distance of place did congregate severally; for they were of sundry towns and villages, some in Nottinghamshire, some of Lincolnshire, and some of Yorkshire where they border nearest together. In one of these churches (besides others of note) was Mr. John Smith, a man of able gifts and a good preacher, who afterwards was chosen their pastor. But these afterwards falling into some errors in the Low Countries, there (for the most part) buried themselves and their names.[20]

But in this other church (which must be the subject of our discourse) besides other worthy men, was Mr. Richard Clyfton, a grave and reverend preacher, who by his pains and diligence had done much good, and under God had been a means of the conversion of many. And also that famous and worthy man Mr. John Robinson, who afterwards was their pastor for many years, till the Lord took him away by death. Also Mr. William Brewster a reverend man, who afterwards was chosen an elder of the church and lived with them till old age.[21]

But after these things they could not long continue in any peaceable condition, but were hunted and persecuted on every side, so as their

[19] Almost certainly Bradford was quoting the covenant used by the Scrooby Separatists.

[20] John Smith or Smyth (d. 1612), former minister in the Church of England who participated in organizing a Separatist congregation in Gainsborough, Lincolnshire; this group emigrated to Amsterdam in 1608.

[21] John Robinson (c. 1576–1625), an ordained minister who became a Separatist; he remained in Leiden with the majority of the congregation rather than emigrate. William Brewster (d. 1644), postmaster in Scrooby, where the Separatist congregation met in his house.

former afflictions were but as fleabitings in comparison of these which now came upon them. For some were taken and clapped up in prison, others had their houses beset and watched night and day, and hardly escaped their hands; and the most were fain to flee and leave their houses and habitations, and the means of their livelihood.

Yet these and many other sharper things which afterward befell them, were no other than they looked for, and therefore were the better prepared to bear them by the assistance of God's grace and Spirit.

Yet seeing themselves thus molested, and that there was no hope of their continuance there, by a joint consent they resolved to go into the Low Countries, where they heard was freedom of religion for all men; as also how sundry from London and other parts of the land had been exiled and persecuted for the same cause, and were gone thither, and lived at Amsterdam and in other places of the land.[22] So after they had continued together about a year, and kept their meetings every Sabbath in one place or other, exercising the worship of God amongst themselves, notwithstanding all the diligence and malice of their adversaries, they seeing they could no longer continue in that condition, they resolved to get over into Holland as they could. Which was in the year 1607 and 1608; of which more at large in the next chapter.

[Chapters 2 and 3 cover the exodus from England to the Netherlands and the transfer of the congregation from Amsterdam to Leiden, where it began to prosper under the leadership of John Robinson.]

Chapter 4

Showing the Reasons, and Causes of Their Removal

After they had lived in this city [Leiden] about some eleven or twelve years (which is the more observable being the whole time of that famous truce between that state and the Spaniards)[23] and sundry of them were taken away by death and many others began to be well stricken in years (the grave mistress of experience having taught them many things), those prudent governors with sundry of the sagest members began both deeply to apprehend their present dangers and wisely to foresee the future and think of timely remedy. In the agitation of their thoughts, and much discourse of things hereabout, at length they began to incline to this conclusion: of removal to some other place. Not out of

[22] A handful of Separatists formed a congregation in Amsterdam as early as 1595; this became known as the "Ancient Church." Its troubles are narrated in Morgan (1963).

[23] War between the Netherlands and Spain had been interrupted by a truce in 1609 that ended in 1618, when the Thirty Years War began.

any newfangledness or other such like giddy humor by which men are oftentimes transported to their great hurt and danger, but for sundry weighty and solid reasons, some of the chief of which I will here briefly touch.

And first, they saw and found by experience the hardness of the place and country to be such as few in comparison would come to them, and fewer that would bide it out and continue with them. For many that came to them, and many more that desired to be with them, could not endure that great labor and hard fare, with other inconveniences which they underwent and were contented with. But though they loved their persons, approved their cause and honored their sufferings, yet they left them as it were weeping, as Orpah did her mother-in-law Naomi, or as those Romans did Cato in Utica who desired to be excused and borne with, though they could not all be Catos.[24] For many, though they desired to enjoy the ordinances of God in their purity and the liberty of the gospel with them, yet (alas) they admitted of bondage with danger of conscience, rather than to endure these hardships. Yea, some preferred and chose the prisons in England rather than this liberty in Holland with these afflictions. But it was thought that if a better and easier place of living could be had, it would draw many and take away these discouragements. Yea, their pastor would often say that many of those who both wrote and preached now against them, if they were in a place where they might have liberty and live comfortably, they would then practice as they did.[25]

Secondly. They saw that though the people generally bore all these difficulties very cheerfully and with a resolute courage, being in the best and strength of their years; yet old age began to steal on many of them; and their great and continual labors, with other crosses and sorrows, hastened it before the time. So as it was not only probably thought, but apparently seen, that within a few years more they would be in danger to scatter, by necessities pressing them, or sink under their burdens, or both. And therefore according to the divine proverb, that *a wise man seeth the plague when it cometh, and hideth himself*, Proverbs 22:3, so they like skillful and beaten soldiers were fearful either to be entrapped or surrounded by their enemies so as they should neither be able to fight nor fly. And therefore thought it better to dislodge betimes to some place of better advantage and less danger, if any such could be found.

Thirdly. As necessity was a taskmaster over them so they were forced to be such, not only to their servants but in a sort to their dearest

---

[24] Ruth 1:14; Marcus Porcius Cato (95 B.C.E. to 46 B.C.E.), also called Cato the Younger, held the gates of Utica long enough to evacuate his men by sea and then committed suicide.

[25] A commonsense response by Robinson to Puritan critics of Separatism.

children, the which as it did not a little wound the tender hearts of many a loving father and mother, so it produced likewise sundry sad and sorrowful effects. For many of their children that were of best dispositions and gracious inclinations, having learned to bear the yoke in their youth and willing to bear part of their parents' burden, were oftentimes so oppressed with their heavy labors that though their minds were free and willing, yet their bodies bowed under the weight of the same, and became decrepit in their early youth, the vigor of nature being consumed in the very bud as it were. But that which was more lamentable, and of all sorrows most heavy to be borne, was that many of their children, by these occasions and the great licentiousness of youth in that country, and the manifold temptations of the place, were drawn away by evil examples into extravagant and dangerous courses, getting the reins off their necks and departing from their parents. Some became soldiers, others took upon them far voyages by sea, and others some worse courses tending to dissoluteness and the danger of their souls, to the great grief of their parents and dishonor of God. So that they saw their posterity would be in danger to degenerate and be corrupted.

Lastly (and which was not least), a great hope and inward zeal they had of laying some good foundation, or at least to make some way thereunto, for the propagating and advancing the gospel of the kingdom of Christ in those remote parts of the world; yea, though they should be but even as stepping-stones unto others for the performing of so great a work.

These and some other like reasons moved them to undertake this resolution of their removal; the which they afterward prosecuted with so great difficulties, as by the sequel will appear.

The place they had thoughts on was some of those vast and unpeopled countries of America, which are fruitful and fit for habitation, being devoid of all civil inhabitants, where there are only savage and brutish men which range up and down, little otherwise than the wild beasts of the same. This proposition being made public and coming to the scanning of all, it raised many variable opinions amongst men and caused many fears and doubts amongst themselves. Some, from their reasons and hopes conceived, labored to stir up and encourage the rest to undertake and prosecute the same; others again, out of their fears, objected against it and sought to divert from it; alleging many things, and those neither unreasonable nor unprobable; as that it was a great design and subject to many unconceivable perils and dangers; as, besides the casualties of the sea (which none can be freed from), the length of the voyage was such as the weak bodies of women and other persons worn out with age and travail (as many of them were) could never be able to endure. And yet if they should, the miseries of the land which they should be exposed unto, would be too hard to be borne and likely, some or all of them together, to consume and utterly to ruinate them. For there they should be liable to famine and nakedness and the want, in a manner, of all things. The change of air, diet and drinking of water would infect their bodies with sore sicknesses and grievous diseases. And also those which should escape or overcome these difficulties should yet be in continual danger of the savage people, who are cruel, barbarous and most treacherous, being most furious in their rage and merciless where they overcome; not being content only to kill and take away life, but delight to torment men in the most bloody manner that may be; flaying some alive with the shells of fishes, cutting off the members and joints of others by piecemeal and broiling on the coals, eat the collops of their flesh in their sight whilst they live, with other cruelties horrible to be related.[26]

And surely it could not be thought but the very hearing of these things could not but move the very bowels of men to grate within them and make the weak to quake and tremble. It was further objected that it would require greater sums of money to furnish such a voyage and to fit them with necessaries, than their consumed estates would amount to; and yet they must as well look to be seconded with supplies as presently to be transported. Also many precedents of ill success and lamentable miseries befallen others in the like designs were easy to be found, and not forgotten to be alleged; besides their own experience, in their former troubles and hardships in their removal into Holland, and how hard a thing it was for them to live in that strange place, though it was a neighbor country and a civil and rich commonwealth.

It was answered, that all great and honorable actions are accompanied with great difficulties and must be both enterprised and overcome with answerable courages. It was granted the dangers were great, but not desperate. The difficulties were many, but not invincible. For though there were many of them likely, yet they were not certain. It might be sundry of the things feared might never befall; others by provident care and the use of good means might in a great measure be prevented; and all of them, through the help of God, by fortitude and patience, might either be borne or overcome. True it was that such attempts were not to be made and undertaken without good ground and reason, not rashly or lightly as many have done for curiosity or hope of gain, etc. But their condition was not ordinary, their ends were good and honorable, their calling lawful and urgent; and therefore they might

[26] The editors of the 1912 edition searched in vain for the source of this clearly derivative, secondhand account.

expect the blessing of God in their proceeding. Yea, though they should lose their lives in this action, yet might they have comfort in the same and their endeavors would be honorable. They lived here but as men in exile and in a poor condition, and as great miseries might possibly befall them in this place; for the twelve years of truce were now out and there was nothing but beating of drums and preparing for war, the events whereof are always uncertain. The Spaniard might prove as cruel as the savages of America, and the famine and pestilence as sore here as there, and their liberty less to look out for remedy.

After many other particular things answered and alleged on both sides, it was fully concluded by the major part to put this design in execution and to prosecute it by the best means they could.

[Chapter 5 summarizes the congregation's debate about the "particular place to pitch upon" and the conclusion, to "live as a distinct body . . . under the general government of Virginia." Negotiations with the Virginia Company and various London merchants are traced in the rest of chapters 5 and 6; chapters 7 and 8 describe the departure from Leiden in July 1620, the arrival at Southampton, and the first attempt to set out in two ships, one of which proved unseaworthy, leaving only the Mayflower *to make the voyage.]*

Chapter 9

Of Their Voyage, and How They Passed the Sea; and of Their Safe Arrival at Cape Cod

September 6 [1620]. These troubles being blown over, and now all being compact together in one ship, they put to sea again with a prosperous wind, which continued divers days together, which was some encouragement unto them; yet, according to the usual manner, many were afflicted with seasickness. And I may not omit here a special work of God's providence. There was a proud and very profane young man, one of the seamen, of a lusty, able body, which made him the more haughty; he would alway[s] be contemning the poor people in their sickness and cursing them daily with grievous execrations; and did not let to tell them, that he hoped to help to cast half of them overboard before they came to their journey's end, and to make merry with what they had; and if he were by any gently reproved, he would curse and swear most bitterly. But it pleased God before they came half seas over, to smite this young man with a grievous disease, of which he died in a desperate manner, and so was himself the first that was thrown overboard. Thus his curses light on his own head, and it was an astonishment to all his fellows for they noted it to be the just hand of God upon him. . . .

But to omit other things (that I may be brief) after long beating at sea they fell with that land which is called Cape Cod; the which being made and certainly known to be it, they were not a little joyful. After some deliberation had amongst themselves and with the master of the ship, they tacked about and resolved to stand for the southward (the wind and weather being fair) to find some place about Hudson's River for their habitation. But after they had sailed that course about half the day, they fell amongst dangerous shoals and roaring breakers, and they were so far entangled therewith as they conceived themselves in great danger; and the wind shrinking [shrieking] upon them withal, they resolved to bear up again for the Cape and thought themselves happy to get out of those dangers before night overtook them, as by God's good providence they did. And the next day they got into the Cape harbor where they rid in safety.

A word or two by the way of this cape. It was thus first named by Captain Gosnold and his company, anno 1602, and after by Captain Smith was called Cape James; but it retains the former name amongst seamen.[27] Also, that point which first showed those dangerous shoals unto them they called Point Care, and Tucker's Terror; but the French and Dutch to this day call it Malabar by reason of those perilous shoals and the losses they have suffered there.

Being thus arrived in a good harbor, and brought safe to land, they fell upon their knees and blessed the God of heaven who had brought them over the vast and furious ocean, and delivered them from all the perils and miseries thereof, again to set their feet on the firm and stable earth, their proper element. And no marvel if they were thus joyful, seeing wise Seneca was so affected with sailing a few miles on the coast of his own Italy, as he affirmed,[28] that he had rather remain twenty years on his way by land than pass by sea to any place in a short time, so tedious and dreadful was the same unto him.

But here I cannot but stay and make a pause, and stand half amazed at this poor people's present condition; and so I think will the reader, too, when he well considers the same. Being thus passed the vast ocean, and a sea of troubles before in their preparation (as may be remembered by that which went before), they had now no friends to welcome them nor inns to entertain or refresh their weatherbeaten bodies; no houses or much less towns to repair to, to seek for succor. It is recorded in

[27] Bartholomew Gosnold had explored the coast in 1602 and John Smith in 1614; it was Smith who named the region and provided an elementary map in *A Description of New England* (London, 1616).

[28] Epist. 53, Bradford (1912), a reference to the Epistles of Seneca.

Scripture[29] as a mercy to the Apostle and his shipwrecked company that the barbarians showed them no small kindness in refreshing them, but these savage barbarians, when they met with them (as after will appear) were readier to fill their sides full of arrows than otherwise. And for the season it was winter, and they that know the winters of that country know them to be sharp and violent, and subject to cruel and fierce storms, dangerous to travel to known places, much more to search an unknown coast. Besides, what could they see but a hideous and desolate wilderness, full of wild beasts and wild men and what multitudes there might be of them they knew not. Neither could they, as it were, go up to the top of Pisgah to view from this wilderness a more goodly country to feed their hopes; for which way soever they turned their eyes (save upward to the heavens) they could have little solace or content in respect of any outward objects. For summer being done, all things stand upon them with a weatherbeaten face, and the whole country, full of woods and thickets, represented a wild and savage hue. If they looked behind them, there was the mighty ocean which they had passed and was now as a main bar and gulf to separate them from all the civil parts of the world. If it be said they had a ship to succor them, it is true; but what heard they daily from the master and company? But that with speed they should look out a place (with their shallop) where they would be, at some near distance; for the season was such as he would not stir from thence till a safe harbor was discovered by them, where they would be, and he might go without danger; and that victuals consumed apace but he must and would keep sufficient for themselves and their return. Yea, it was muttered by some that if they got not a place in time, they would turn them and their goods ashore and leave them. Let it also be considered what weak hopes of supply and succor they left behind them, that might bear up their minds in this sad condition and trials they were under; and they could not but be very small. It is true, indeed, the affections and love of their brethren at Leiden was cordial and entire towards them, but they had little power to help them or themselves; and how the case stood between them and the merchants at their coming away hath already been declared.[30]

What could now sustain them but the Spirit of God and his grace? May not and ought not the children of these fathers rightly say: *Our fathers were Englishmen which came over this great ocean, and were*

[29] Acts 28, Bradford (1912).

[30] In chapters 6 and 7, Bradford described the negotiations between the "merchants and adventurers" (chief among them the merchant Thomas Weston and two agents of the congregation), the "great discontents" the emigrants felt about the conditions agreed to by those agents, and the final breakdown of negotiations just as the group was leaving for the New World.

ready to perish in this wilderness; but they cried unto the Lord, and he heard their voice and looked on their adversity, etc.[31] *Let them therefore praise the Lord, because he is good: and his mercies endure forever.*[32] *Yea, let them which have been redeemed of the Lord, shew how he hath delivered them from the hand of the oppressor. When they wandered in the desert wilderness out of the way, and found no city to dwell in, both hungry and thirsty, their soul was overwhelmed*[33] *in them. Let them confess before the Lord his lovingkindness and his wonderful works before the sons of men.*[34]

[Chapter 10 describes the search for a "place of habitation," the earliest encounters with Native Americans, and the decision to "pitch their dwelling" in Plymouth.]

The Second Book

The rest of this history (if God give me life, and opportunity) I shall, for brevity's sake, handle by way of annals, noting only the heads of principal things, and passages as they fell in order of time, and may seem to be profitable to know, or to make use of. And this may be as the Second Book.

THE REMAINDER OF ANNO 1620

I shall a little return back, and begin with a combination made by them before they came ashore; being the first foundation of their government in this place. Occasioned partly by the discontented and mutinous speeches that some of the strangers[35] amongst them had let fall from them in the ship: That when they came ashore they would use their own liberty, for none had power to command them, the patent they had being for Virginia and not for New England, which belonged to another government, with which the Virginia Company had nothing to do. And partly that such an act by them done, this their condition considered, might be as firm as any patent, and in some respects more sure.

[31] Deut. 26:5, 7, Bradford (1912).
[32] Ps. 107:1, 2, 4–5, 8, Bradford (1912).
[33] The editors of the 1912 edition note that the word "fainted" is used in both the King James and Geneva versions of this verse.
[34] Dan. 2:19.
[35] "Strangers": passengers who had not been members of the Leiden congregation. Approximately half of the 102 passengers on board the *Mayflower* joined the group from London, some of them hired as servants and others, such as the soldier Miles Standish and the cooper John Alden, hired because of their special skills. Forty-one men signed the compact; another 24, most of them sons, did not.

The form was as followeth:

In the name of God, Amen. We whose names are underwritten, the loyal subjects of our dread Sovereign Lord King James, by the grace of God of Great Britain, France, and Ireland King, Defender of the Faith, etc. Having undertaken, for the glory of God and advancement of the Christian faith and honor of our King and country, a voyage to plant the first colony in the northern parts of Virginia,[36] do by these presents solemnly and mutually in the presence of God and one of another, covenant and combine ourselves together into a civil body politic, for our better ordering and preservation and furtherance of the ends aforesaid; and by virtue hereof to enact, constitute and frame such just and equal laws, ordinances, acts, constitutions and offices, from time to time, as shall be thought most meet and convenient for the general good of the colony, unto which we promise all due submission and obedience. In witness whereof we have hereunder subscribed our names at Cape Cod, the 11th of November, in the year of the reign of our Sovereign Lord King James, of England, France and Ireland the eighteenth, and of Scotland the fifty-fourth. Anno Domini 1620.[37]

After this they chose, or rather confirmed, Mr. John Carver (a man godly and well approved amongst them) their governor for that year. And after they had provided a place for their goods, or common store (which were long in unlading for want of boats, foulness of the winter weather and sickness of divers) and begun some small cottages for their habitation; as time would admit, they met and consulted of laws and orders, both for their civil and military government as the necessity of their condition did require, still adding thereunto as urgent occasion in several times, and as cases did require.

In these hard and difficult beginnings they found some discontents and murmurings arise amongst some, and mutinous speeches and carriages in other; but they were soon quelled and overcome by the wisdom, patience, and just and equal carriage of things, by the governor and better part, which clave faithfully together in the main.

But that which was most sad and lamentable was, that in two or three months' time half of their company died, especially in January and February, being the depth of winter, and wanting houses and other comforts; being infected with the scurvy and other diseases which this long

---

[36] The grant of land by the English Crown to the Virginia Company, chartered in 1606, extended to the Hudson River. The accident of settling north of Cape Cod meant that the congregation's "patent" was invalid, as the restless "strangers" realized. The colony acquired a substitute patent in 1621.

[37] The "compact" was printed for the first time in *A Relation, or Journal* [*Mourt's Relation*] (1622); subsequent printings, and variations among them, are noted in Walker (1893), chap. 5.

voyage and their inaccommodate condition had brought upon them. So as there died some times two or three of a day in the foresaid time, that of 100 and odd persons, scarce fifty remained.[38] And of these, in the time of most distress, there was but six or seven sound persons who to their great commendations, be it spoken, spared no pains night nor day, but with abundance of toil and hazard of their own health, fetched them wood, made them fires, dressed them meat, made their beds, washed their loathsome clothes, clothed and unclothed them. In a word, did all the homely and necessary offices for them which dainty and queasy stomachs cannot endure to hear named; and all this willingly and cheerfully, without any grudging in the least, showing herein their true love unto their friends and brethren; a rare example and worthy to be remembered. Two of these seven were Mr. William Brewster, their reverend elder, and Myles Standish, their captain and military commander, unto whom myself and many others were much beholden in our low and sick condition. And yet the Lord so upheld these persons as in this general calamity they were not at all infected either with sickness or lameness. And what I have said of these I may say of many others who died in this general visitation, and others yet living; that whilst they had health, yea, or any strength continuing, they were not wanting to any that had need of them. And I doubt not but their recompense is with the Lord.

. . . All this while the Indians came skulking about them, and would sometimes show themselves aloof of[f], but when any approached near them, they would run away; and once they stole away their tools where they had been at work and were gone to dinner. But about the 16th of March, a certain Indian came boldly amongst them and spoke to them in broken English, which they could well understand but marveled at it. At length they understood by discourse with him, that he was not of these parts, but belonged to the eastern parts where some English ships came to fish, with whom he was acquainted and could name sundry of them by their names, amongst whom he had got his language. He became profitable to them in acquainting them with many things concerning the state of the country in the east parts where he lived, which was afterwards profitable unto them; as also of the people here, of their names, number and strength, of their situation and distance from this place, and who was chief amongst them. His name was Samoset.[39] He

---

[38] The exact figure of deaths was fifty-three, including eight of twelve wives.

[39] "For he [Samoset] had learned some broken English amongst the Englishmen that came to fish at Monchiggon [Monhegan Island]. . . . We questioned him of many things. He was the first savage we could meet withal. He said, he was not of these parts; but of Morattigon [actually, of Pemaquid, now Bristol, Maine], and one of the sagamores or lords thereof; and had been eight months in these parts." *A Relation*, repr. in Arber

told them also of another Indian whose name was Squanto, a native of this place, who had been in England and could speak better English than himself.

Being, after some time of entertainment and gifts dismissed, a while after he came again, and five more with him, and they brought again all the tools that were stolen away before, and made way for the coming of their great sachem, called Massasoit.[40] Who, about four or five days after, came with the chief of his friends and other attendance, with the aforesaid Squanto. With whom, after friendly entertainment and some gifts given him, they made a peace with him (which hath now continued this twenty four years) in these terms:

1. That neither he nor any of his should injure or do hurt to any of their people.
2. That if any of his did hurt to any of theirs, he should send the offender, that they might punish him.
3. That if anything were taken away from any of theirs, he should cause it to be restored; and they should do the like to his.
4. If any did unjustly war against him, they would aid him; if any did war against them, he should aid them.
5. He should send to his neighbors confederates to certify them of this, that they might not wrong them, but might be likewise comprised in the conditions of peace.
6. That when their men came to them, they should leave their bows and arrows behind them.[41]

After these things he returned to his place called Sowams, some forty miles from this place, but Squanto continued with them and was their interpreter and was a special instrument sent of God for their good beyond their expectation. He directed them how to set their corn, where to take fish, and to procure other commodities, and was also their pilot to bring them to unknown places for their profit, and never left them till he died. He was a native of this place, and scarce any left alive besides

---

(1897), 450–51. Earlier in the year, an English ship had carried him from Monhegan Island to Cape Cod.

[40] Died in 1662; see Bradford (1912), 1:200, n. 1

[41] "This treaty was renewed by Ousamequin [Massasoit] and his son, Mooanam [Wamsutta, or Alexander], in 1639, with certain additions to the terms, one of them being that 'he or they shall not give, sell, or convey away any of his or their lands, territories, or possessions whatsoever, to any person or persons whomsoever, without the priutie and consent of this government, other than to such as this government shall send and appoint.'" Bradford (1912), 1:202, n. 1. Recent historical work criticizes the colonists for their aggression toward the Native Americans; for a critique of this approach and an alternative reading, see Anderson (2003), chap. 2.

himself.[42] He was carried away with divers others by one Hunt,[43] a master of a ship, who thought to sell them for slaves in Spain. But he got away for England and was entertained by a merchant in London, and employed to Newfoundland and other parts, and lastly brought hither into these parts by one Mr. Dermer,[44] a gentleman employed by Sir Ferdinando Gorges and others for discovery and other designs in these parts. . . .

The spring now approaching, it pleased God the mortality began to cease among them, and the sick and lame recovered apace, which put as [it] were new life into them; though they had borne their sad affliction with much patience and contentedness, as I think any people could do. But it was the Lord which upheld them, and had beforehand prepared them; many having long borne the yoke, yea from their youth [Lam. 3:27]. Many other smaller matters I omit, sundry of them having been already published in a journal made by one of the company; and some other passages of journeys and relations already published, to which I refer those that are willing to know them more particularly.[45] And being now come to the 25 of March I shall begin the year 1621.

ANNO 1621

. . . Afterwards they (as many as were able) began to plant their corn, in which service Squanto stood them in great stead, showing them both the manner how to set it, and after how to dress and tend it. Also he told them, except they got fish and set with it (in these old grounds) it would come to nothing, and he showed them that in the middle of April they should have store enough come up the brook, by which they began to build, and taught them how to take it, and where to get other provisions necessary for them; all which they found true by trial and experience. . . . In this month of April whilst they were busy about their seed, their governor (Mr. John Carver) came out of the field very sick, it being a hot day, he complained greatly of his head, and lay down, and within a few hours his senses failed, so as he never spake more till he died. . . . Shortly after William Bradford was chosen governor in his stead. . . .

---

[42] The only surviving member of the Patuxet, an Algonquin group that was destroyed in a sickness about 1617, and "one of twenty captives" captured in 1614 by an English explorer and taken to England. *A Relation*, in Arber (1897), 456.

[43] Thomas Hunt, a shipmaster who participated in John Smith's 1614 voyage to the coast of New England. A fuller account of his aggression toward the Native Americans may be found in Bradford (1912), 1:204, n. 2.

[44] Thomas Dermer sailed for Newfoundland in 1615 with Captain John Smith (completing the voyage without him) and made several subsequent exploratory trips, the reports of which were widely read.

[45] These texts are reprinted in Arber (1897).

Having in some sort ordered their business at home, it was thought meet to send some abroad to see their new friend Massasoit, and to bestow upon him some gratuity to bind him the faster unto them; as also that hereby they might view the country and see in what manner he lived, what strength he had about him, and how the ways were to his place, if at any time they should have occasion. . . . They found his place to be forty miles from hence, the soil good and the people not many, being dead and abundantly wasted in the late great mortality, which fell in all these parts about three years before the coming of the English, wherein thousands of them died, they not being able to bury one another, their skulls and bones were found in many places lying still above ground where their houses and dwellings had been, a very sad spectacle to behold. . . .[46]

[November 1621] They began now to gather in the small harvest they had, and to fit up their houses and dwellings against winter, being all well recovered in health and strength and had all things in good plenty. For as some were thus employed in affairs abroad, others were exercised in fishing, about cod and bass and other fish, of which they took good store, of which every family had their portion. All the summer there was no want; and now began to come in store of fowl, as winter approached, of which this place did abound when they came first (but afterward decreased by degrees). And besides waterfowl there was a great store of wild turkeys, of which they took many, besides venison, etc. Besides they had about a peck a meal a week to a person, or now since the harvest, Indian corn to that proportion. Which made many afterwards write so largely of their plenty here to friends in England, which were not feigned but true reports.[47]

. . . [1632] Though the partners[48] were thus plunged into great en-

---

[46] Edward Winslow and Stephen Hopkins made this trip, which Winslow described in *A Relation*. The editors of the 1912 edition provide extensive information on the epidemics that devastated the Native American population: Bradford (1912), 1:221, n. 1.

[47] Edward Winslow described the festivities in a letter dated 11 December 1621, printed in *A Relation*: "Our corn did prove well, and, GOD be praised! we had a good increase of Indian corn; and our barley indifferent good: but our pease not worth the gathering; for we feared they were too late sown. . . . Our harvest being gotten in, our governor sent four men on fowling; that so we might, after a more special manner, rejoice together, after we had gathered the fruit of our labors. They four, in one day, killed as much fowl as, with a little help besides, served the Company almost a week. At which time, amongst other recreations, we exercised our arms; many of the Indians coming amongst us. And, amongst the rest, their greatest King, Massasoit, with some ninety men; whom, for three days, we entertained and feasted." *A Relation*, in Arber (1897), 488–89.

[48] The founding of Plymouth had been financed by a group of London merchants, the "adventurers." The efforts to repay these merchants included, in 1626, an agreement on the part of a small group of colonists (the "partners") to remit £200 a year for nine years.

gagements, and oppressed with unjust debts, yet the Lord prospered their trading, that they made yearly large returns, and had soon wound themselves out of all if yet they had otherwise been well dealt withall; as will more appear hereafter. Also the people of the Plantation began to grow in their outward estates, by reason of the flowing of many people into the country, especially into the Bay of the Massachusetts. By which means corn and cattle rose to a great price, by which many were much enriched and commodities grew plentiful. And yet in other regards this benefit turned to their hurt, and this accession of strength to their weakness. For now as their stocks increased and the increase vendible, there was no longer any holding them together, but now they must of necessity go to their great lots. They could not otherwise keep their cattle, and having oxen grown they must have land for plowing and tillage. And no man now thought he could live except he had cattle and a great deal of ground to keep them, all striving to increase their stocks. By which means they were scattered all over the Bay quickly and the town in which they lived compactly till now was left very thin and in a short time almost desolate. And if this had been all, it had been less, though too much; but the church must also be divided, and those that had lived so long together in Christian and comfortable fellowship must now part and suffer many divisions. First, those that lived on their lots on the other side of the Bay, called Duxbury,[49] they could not long bring their wives and children to the public worship and church meetings here, but with such burthen as, growing to some competent number, they sued to be dismissed and become a body of themselves. And so they were dismissed about this time though very unwillingly. But to touch this sad matter, and handle things together that fell out afterward; to prevent any further scattering from this place and weakening of the same, it was thought best to give out some good farms to special persons that would promise to live at Plymouth, and likely to be helpful to the church or commonwealth, and so tie the lands to Plymouth as farms for the same; and there they might keep their cattle and tillage by some servants and retain their dwellings here. And so some special lands were granted at a place general called Green's Harbor,[50] where no allotments had been in the former division, a place very well meadowed and fit to keep and rear cattle good store. But alas, this remedy proved worse than the disease; for within a few years those that had thus got footing there rent

---

As Bradford repeatedly noted, the debt seemed only to increase, because of unfair practices by the creditors.

[49] Duxbury became a separate town in 1637, although settlement occurred before this year.

[50] "It is not known when these lands were granted at Green's Harbor, which in 1640 became known as Rexhame, and before 1641 as Marshfield." Bradford (1912), 2:53, n. 1.

themselves away, partly by force and partly wearing the rest with importunity and pleas of necessity, so as they must either suffer them to go or live in continual opposition and contention. And others still, as they conceived themselves straitened or to want accommodation, broke away under one pretence or other, thinking their own conceived necessity and the example of others a warrant sufficient for them. And this I fear will be the ruin of New England, at least of the churches of God there, and will provoke the Lord's displeasure against them.

Source: Bradford (1912), corrected against Morison (1952).

Chapter 2

Thomas Weld

"WE DREAM NOT OF PERFECTION"

The excitement of arriving in New England after experiencing "persecution" in England is nowhere better expressed than in the letter that follows. Thomas Weld (1595–1661) graduated from Trinity College, Cambridge, in 1614 and was ordained a minister in the Church of England in 1618. Vicar of the parish of Terling, Essex, he pursued a vigorous program of reform in the village until he was dismissed in 1632. Weld passed through the Netherlands before emigrating to Massachusetts, where, almost immediately, he was elected to the office of pastor in Roxbury. Writing to his former congregation, he described the satisfaction of freeing himself from the "corruptions" of the state church and the "unclean conversation" of those everyday English people who rejected the Puritan-style "reformation of manners." Yet Weld was careful to insist that he was not a perfectionist. He knew that the colonists were facing a public relations problem at home, with their enemies characterizing them as Separatists. His optimism about the health of the colonists and their supply of food countered other letters and reports describing the "starving time" of 1630–1631 when food ran short. Weld wanted to encourage some of his former parishioners to join him, as several families soon did. His letter probably circulated widely in manuscript copies. He wrote it in late 1632.

THOMAS WELD

To His Former Parishioners at Terling

Most dear and well beloved in Terling, even all that love the Lord Jesus Christ's gospel, and myself, rich and poor, weak and strong, young and old, male and female I [write] unto you all in one letter wanting time to mention you all in particular, you being all dear unto me yea most dear to my heart in Jesus Christ, for whom I bow the knee to the Father of lights [James 1:17] longing to hear of your great welfare and spiritual growth in his dear Son: from your presence though I be placed and must see your faces no more yet I shall after a few weary days ended and all tears wiped away, and though happily never on earth yet in the New Jerusalem. And here though we cannot be suffered to live together yet there we shall enjoy together sweet society in all fullness of perfection to all eternity. O blessed forever blessed be his holy Name. And let the heaven and earth and sea and men, witness of his favor to us and ours and sound out his glorious praises, yea let all within us, without us, yea all that we can ring out the riches of his grace from sea to sea, from New England to old and from old to New, for all his abundant mercies temporal, spiritual and eternal past present and to come, bestowed continued and renewed and multiplied on us all, in particular, on me and mine, for he hath laden me and crowned me with mercies ever since our last embracing, drowned in tears for our sad departure, as Paul told his dear friend weeping because that they should see each other no more [Acts 20:37–38]. To Holland in Holland from Holland mercies, mercies; to New England in New England abundance of mercies, I have cause to stand and wonder had I but a heart so affected, that I and all are passed the deeps and are alive and well. Yea mercy mercy in the Lord inwardly outwardly, in spite of devils and storms as cheerful as ever, my wife all the voyage on the sea better than at land, and seasick but one day in eleven weeks, at sea my children never better in their lives. They went ill into the ship but well there and came forth well as ever. Myself had not one ounce of seasickness, nor one motion or inclination thereunto not all the way. *Stand still and behold the salvation of the Lord* [Exod. 14:13]. And not only I and all mine well and safe but all in the ship being near eighty passengers yea some very aged, twelve persons being all able to make well nigh one thousand years, some very young and hanging on the breast, some women big with child and one delivered of a lusty child within forty hours after she landed. She and the child well, and so continue to this day. Another woman in our ship of sixty years old who had labored of a consumption and strong cough of the lungs seven years is not only alive but came forth of the ship fully cured of the cough as fresh as [an] eagle that hath cast her bill and renewed her strength. I am the eyewitness of this and we hope God may add to her fifteen years to her life.

And not only all safe in our ship but all safe in the ships that came this spring out of England laden with passengers cattle and goods. Wherein not a man woman or child died by the way nor since that came to shore, nor any of them that came weakly to land but abide strong through God's mercy to this day. Our ships being all in this admirable manner arrived there was holden and that by authority a public solemn day of thanksgiving to God for his mercy[1] within seven days after landing, from which I am persuaded God smelt a savor of rest as in Noah's sacrifice when he came forth of the ark. Here we are come into as goodly a land as ever mine eyes beheld. Such groves, such trees such an air as I am fully contented withal and desire no better while I live, yea I see assuredly with industry and self-denial men may subsist as well here as in any place. The plantation is now set upon fishing for a staple commodity store of salt I see already for the fish and a ship to go to the salt islands for more where are mountains of salt for the fetching, and shallops made and tackling provided to catch it withal and to send it into other countries to fetch in all other commodities. Here is also rape oil, which is like to be a sta come [sic].[2] Here I find three great blessings peace plenty and health in a comfortable measure. The place well agreeth with our English bodies that they were never so healthy in their native country, generally all here, as never could be rid of the headache, toothache cough and the like are now better and freed here and those that were weak are now well long since and I can hear of but two weak in all the plantation. God's Name be praised and although there was wanting at the first, that provision at the first glut of people that came over two years since, but blessed be God here is plenty of corn that the poorest have enough. Corn is here at five shillings six [pence] a bushel, in truth you cannot imagine what comfortable diet the Indian corn do make and what pleasant and wholesome food it makes. Our cattle of all do thrive and feed exceedingly. I suppose that such as are to come need bring no more or little or no provision except malt (but no more of these things). I would have none aim at outward matters in such an attempt as this, lest the Lord meet him in the way as he met Balaam with a drawn sword [Num. 22:31] but at things of an higher nature and more spiritual nature.

O how hath my heart been made glad with the comforts of his house and the spiritual days in the same wherein all things are done in the form and pattern showed in the mount [Exod. 25:40] members provided church officers elected and ordained sacrament administered, scandals prevented censured. Fast days and holy feast days and all such things by authority commanded and performed according to the precise rule. Mine eyes blessed be God do see such administration of justice in civil government. All things so righteously so religiously and impartially

---

[1] This "day of thanksgiving" was ordered to acknowledge "the prosperous success" of Protestants in the Thirty Years War, "and for the safe arrival of the last ship and all the passengers etc." Winthrop (1996), 81.

[2] Possibly should be read as "staple." Here as in chapter 28, "staple" refers to a product or commodity that could be sold in Europe and therefore sustain the economy, as tobacco was doing for the Chesapeake settlements.

carried, I am already fully paid for my voyage who never had so much in the storms at sea as one repenting thought rested in my heart. Praised and thanked be God who moved my heart to come and made open the way to me. And I profess if I might have my wish in what part of the world to dwell, I know no other place on the whole globe of the earth where I would be rather than here. We say to our friends that doubt this Come and see and taste. Here the greater part are the better part, here Mordecai speaketh kindly to the hearts of his people. Here are none of the men of Gibea the sons of Belial knocking at our doors disturbing our sweet peace or threatening violence [Esther 10:3; Judg. 19:22]. Here, blessed be the Lord God forever, our ears are not beaten nor the air filled with oaths, swearers nor railers, nor our eyes and ears vexed with the unclean conversation of the wicked. Here it is counted an honor by the worst to lay hold on the skirt of a Jew [Zech. 8:23]. Here if any be, our sanballets [mockers; Neh. 4:1] would thrust in themselves yet could not. Here the rudest have a charge and dare not break it. I say the Lord continue and enlarge it still these sweet encouragements and make us walk worthy and it is enough. I desire no more till I come in heaven. Conceive us not as if we went about to justify ourselves or dream of perfection,[3] no God knows we think ourselves the poorest and unworthiest of all his servants justly else he might spew us out of his mouth [Rev. 3:16]. Only we desire to breathe after perfection and to know what is the rule and to walk in it. Nor as if we went about to condemn other places besides our own or other men besides ourselves. No no, I assure you we look at our dear native country as the place where the Lord showed us mercy and to his holy ordinances there is the holy means of our God (if ever we had it) we had it there, we pray for your congregations public and private, we fast and pray for you, we love you dearly you lie next to our hearts. Sorrow[full] we are when we hear any evil betide you: glad when any good. We desire to do this forever. And *let our tongue cleave to the roof of our mouth* if we forget [Ps. 137:6]. You my beloved have the like affection towards us as we have towards you in the Lord, yet we cannot but mourn for the spots and blemishes that are among your meetings which the Lord of his infinite mercy cleanse away. To return to my own particular at my first landing I was so far from wanting a place of receipt that I was so importuned in four several places that it was a trouble to know what friend to gratify. At last I rested with Mr. Masell at Charles Town where

[3] In *The Humble Request* (London, 1630), issued by John Winthrop and other leaders of the 1630 migration to dispel rumors of their disloyalty to Church and Crown, they wrote, "Wee are not of those that dreame of perfection in this world" and refer to "the Church of England, from whence wee rise, our dear Mother." *Winthrop Papers*, 7 vols. (Boston, 1929–   ), 2:232.

now I am with my family most kindly entertained till I know where God shall dispose of me. I am most earnestly entreated to be in four several congregations and all have sought by public and solemn fasting and prayer that God would move my heart thither if it be his will.

The blessing of God be with you all my dear hearts. I desire now to hear from you hoping that by this time the Lord hath provided some faithful pastor to teach and watch over you in the Lord. Once more farewell. The Lord comfort your hearts, bottle your tears, pardon your sins, supply your wants, work all your works for you, know your souls in adversity, and preserve you to his everlasting kingdom.

Source: *Publications of the Colonial Society of Massachusetts* 13 (1912): 130–31, compared with Emerson (1976), 94–98, with many differences of punctuation.

Chapter 3

Thomas Shepard on His Life
in Old and New England

Thomas Shepard's autobiography (a title supplied by modern editors) recounts the deteriorating situation of "forward" Puritans once the leadership of the Church of England began to crack down on nonconformity. The autobiography also records the vigor and resilience of the Puritan movement at the local level, and especially in counties such as Essex in southeastern England, where Shepard first began his ministry. After graduating from Emmanuel College, Cambridge, in 1624, Shepard (1605–1649) moved to Terling, where he witnessed the success of a coalition of gentry, townspeople, and university-trained ministers in bringing Puritan-style reforms from "the top down," as it were, to the community. In a county where "godly" ministers enjoyed broad support, a group of them arranged for Shepard to become a town lecturer, a position that spared him from participating in the liturgy and wearing clerical garments. A few years later, he and other ministers in the neighborhood were being "silenced" by anti-Puritan bishops, foremost among them William Laud, who personally chastised Shepard. Explaining his decision to emigrate even though he had wondered whether it were better to "stay and suffer for Christ," Shepard tells us that he became "convinced . . . of the evil of ceremonies" practiced within the Church of England. Though he stopped short of Separatism, he refused to have his newborn son baptized in the Church. The eight reasons he gave for emigrating, to which he added another six, suggest that the decision to do so did not come easily. The historian Stephen Foster has pointed out that the process of radicalization that Shepard and others, such as John Cotton, experienced in the early 1630s had significant consequences for the shaping of the "Congregational Way" in New England.[1] In February 1636 the townspeople of Newtown (soon to be renamed Cambridge) organized a church and elected him their pastor.

[1] Foster (1991), chap. 4. John Cotton's "Reasons" for emigrating are printed in Young (1841), 438–44; see also another list in [Increase Mather], *The Life and Death Of That Reverend Man of God, Mr. Richard Mather* (Cambridge, 1670), 12–15.

Another theme of the autobiography is the intertwining of family and religion. Shepard dedicated the autobiography to his son Thomas (the second of that name, the first having died as an infant), intending it as a record of God's providential care to those in covenant and a "legacy" that would strengthen the son's relationship with God. Such legacies (as Anne Bradstreet termed her "Meditations") were also a means by which "parents perpetuate their lives in their posterity" (see below, pt. III). The intertwining of religion and family encompassed, in Shepard's case, the sacrament of baptism. Although he and his wife refused to have their newborn son Thomas baptized until the family reached New England, this decision suggests the importance of the ordinance to them, as does the language Shepard used and the emotions he felt when he was finally able to administer the sacrament. The text that follows omits the story of the Shepards' first, unsuccessful attempt to emigrate and his conversion during his student years at Cambridge.

Bibliography

McGiffert (1972); Webster (1997).

THOMAS SHEPARD

🏵 *"To My Dear Son": An Autobiography* 🏵

To my dear son Thomas Shepard with whom I leave these records of God's great kindness to him, not knowing that I shall live to tell them myself with my own mouth, that so he may learn to know and love the great and most high God, the God of his father.

In the year of the Lord 1634, October 16, myself, wife, and family with my first son Thomas committed ourselves to the care of our God to keep us one and to carry us over the mighty seas from old England to New England. But we had not been two days on the sea, but that the wind arose and drove our ship almost upon the sands where the Lord did most apparently stretch forth his hands in saving of us from them when we were within a very little ready to be dashed in pieces upon them. . . . Now one cause of our going at this time of winter was because my wife was conceived of this second son Thomas, and because we were persecuted in old England for the truth of Christ which we profess here we durst not stay to make ourselves known, which would have been at the baptizing of the child. Hence we hastened for New England, and therefore though thou, my dear son, wast not born then, yet thou wert in the dangers of the sea in thy mother's womb then, and see how God hath miraculously preserved thee, that thou art still alive and thy mother's womb and the terrible seas have not been thy grave. Wonder at and love this God forever.

After that we came from the sea my first son fell sick in passing from the ship to the shore in the boat, of which sickness within a fortnight after he died at Yarmouth. . . . But the Lord preserved us and provided for me and my wife a hiding place from the knowledge of our enemies and from their malice, by the means of Mistress Corbet in Norfolk, in one of whose houses we stayed all that hard winter with our dear friend Mr. Roger Harlakenden[2] and enjoyed a sweet time together in a most retired manner. So the winter being spent and my wife's time of travail in childbed drawing nigh, we were much perplexed whither to go and where to stay that we might not be known, and keep the child so secretly as that it might not be baptized until it came to take of that ordinance in purity in old[3] England. And being thus doubtful what to do, the Lord by letters from London called us to come thither where my wife might have all help in the time of her extremity and my child kept secret. And this we concluded for to do, and therefore took our leave of this our winter house, and in our way to London we went to Mr. Burrows his house, a godly, able minister, where my wife, when she was big and great with child of thee, my son Thomas — she fell down from the top to the bottom of his stairs with her back so hurt that all of us did think and fear her child could not but be slain or hurt with this sore fall, but herself felt not much hurt and her child had none. Oh, remember, my son, to know and love this God that here did pity and spare thee in thy mother's womb a second time! From this place we went to London, my wife thus big with child very safe and well, and there the Lord provided for my wife and self and friends a very private house where our friends did us all the good they could and our enemies could do us no hurt, where my wife on the Sabbath day, being April 5, 1635, was delivered mercifully of this second son Thomas, which name I gave him because we thought the Lord gave me the first son I lost on sea in this again, and hence gave him his brother's name. And so the mother growing strong, the child began to grow weak, and I did verily think would have died of a sore mouth, which I taking to heart, the Lord awakened me in the night and stirred me up to pray for him, and that with very much fervency, as I thought, and many arguments to press the Lord for his life came in, as:

---

[2] The Harlakendens were the principal family in Earle's Colne, Essex; as Shepard subsequently noted, Roger joined in the emigration and settled with Shepard in Cambridge, where he died in 1638.

[3] Probably he meant to write New England.

(1) The glory the Lord should have by betrusting me with this child: he should be the Lord's forever.

(2) Because this kindness would be to me fruit in season, if in the time of my privacy, persecution, sorrow for the loss of my first child he would give me this and that other in this.

(3) Because though it was brought very low, yet then was the Lord's time to remember to help.

(4) Because I thought if the Lord should not hear me now, my soul would be discouraged from seeking to him because I sought for the first and could not prevail for his life, and this was sore if the Lord should not hear me for this.

(5) Because all healing virtue was in Christ Jesus' hands who was very tender to all that brought their sick unto him.

(6) Although my sins might hinder him from doing this, yet I told the Lord his mercy should be the more wonderful if in healing my child of his sickness he would withal heal me of my sins.

And thus after a sad heavy night the Lord shined upon me in the morning, for I found him suddenly and strangely amended of his sore mouth which I did expect would have been his death. Oh, the tenderness of our God! Remember, therefore, my son, this mercy of the Lord to thee. Thus the child with the mother having recovered their strength, we set a second time to sea, and when we went the child was so feeble that divers of our friends did conclude the child could [not] live until it came to New England in a close ship, but the care of God was so great that it was made much better by the sea and more lively and strong. . . . And thus after a[n] eleven weeks' sail from old England we came to New England shore where the mother fell sick of a consumption and thou, my child, wert put to nurse to one goodwife Hopkins who was very tender of thee. And after we had been here divers weeks, on the seventh of February or thereabout God gave thee the ordinance of baptism whereby God is become thy God and is beforehand with thee that whenever thou shalt return to God, he will undoubtedly receive thee — and this is a most high and happy privilege, and therefore bless God for it.[4] And now after that this had been done thy dear mother died in the Lord, departing out of this world to another, who did lose her life by being careful to preserve thine, for in the ship thou wert so feeble and froward both in the day and night that hereby she lost her strength and at last her life. She hath made also many a prayer and shed many a tear in secret for thee, and this hath been oft her request: that if the Lord did

---

[4] Not until the congregation in Cambridge had been formally organized at the beginning of February and Shepard ordained as minister could he baptize his son. He is possibly quoting language used in that service.

not intend to glorify himself by thee, that he would cut thee off by death rather than to live to dishonor him by sin. And therefore know it: if thou shalt turn rebel against God and forsake God and care not for the knowledge of him nor to believe in his Son, the Lord will make all these mercies woes and all thy mother's prayers, tears, and death to be a swift witness against thee at the great day . . . [blank page in MS].

T. {My Birth and Life} S:

In the year of Christ 1604[5] upon the fifth day of November, called the Powder Treason Day, and that very hour of the day wherein the Parliament should have been blown up by popish priests, I was then born, which occasioned my father to give me this name Thomas, because he said I would hardly believe that ever any such wickedness should be attempted by men against so religious and good [a] Parliament. My father's name was William Shepard, born in a little poor town in Northamptonshire called Fossecut near Towcester, and being a prentice to one Mr. Bland, a grocer, he married one of his daughters of whom he begat many children—three sons: John, William, and Thomas; and six daughters: An[na], Margaret, Mary, Elizabeth, Hester, Sarah—of all which only John, Thomas, Anna, and Margaret are still living in the town where I was born, viz., Towcester in Northamptonshire, six miles distant from the town of Northampton in old England. I do well remember my father and have some little remembrance of my mother. My father was a wise, prudent man, the peacemaker of the place, and toward his latter end much blessed of God in his estate and in his soul, for there being no good ministry in the town he was resolved to go and live at Banbury in Oxfordshire under a stirring ministry, having bought a house there for that end. My mother was a woman much afflicted in conscience, sometimes even unto distraction of mind, yet was sweetly recovered again before she died, and I being the youngest she did bear exceeding great love to me and made many prayers for me. But she died when I was about four years old, and my father lived and married a second wife not dwelling in the same town, of whom he begat two children, Samuel and Elizabeth, and died when I was about ten years of age. But while my father and mother lived, when I was about three year old, there was a great plague in the town of Towcester which swept away many in my father's family, both sisters and servants. I being the youngest and best beloved of my mother was sent away the day the plague brake out to live with my aged grandfather and grandmother in

---

[5] Actually, 1605, as the context shows. The reference is to a plot, now commemorated on Guy Fawkes Day, to blow up Parliament.

Fossecut, a most blind town and corner, and those I lived with also being very well to live yet very ignorant. And there was I put to keep geese and other such country work all that time, much neglected of them, and afterward sent from them unto Adthrop, a little blind town adjoining, to my uncle, where I had more content but did learn to sing and sport as children do in those parts and dance at their Whitsun Ales,[6] until the plague was removed and my dear mother dead who died not of the plague but of some other disease after it. . . . But my father at last was visited with sickness, having taken some cold upon some pills he took, and so had the hickets [hiccups] with his sickness a week together, in which time I do remember I did pray very strongly and heartily for the life of my father and made some covenant, if God would do it, to serve him the better as knowing I should be left alone if he was gone. Yet the Lord took him away by death, and so I was left fatherless and motherless when I was about ten years old, and I was committed to my stepmother to be educated who therefore had my portion which was £100 which my father left me. But she neglecting my education very much, my brother John, who was my only brother alive, desired to have me out of her hands and to have me with him, and he would bring me up for the use of my portion. And so at last it was granted, and so I lived with this my eldest brother who showed much love unto me and unto whom I owe much, for him God made to be both father and mother unto me. . . . And so the Lord blessed me in my studies and gave me some knowledge of the Latin and Greek tongues, but much ungrounded in both. But I was studious because I was ambitious of learning and being a scholar, and hence when I could not take notes of the sermon I remember I was troubled at it and prayed the Lord earnestly that he would help me to note sermons. And I see cause of wondering at the Lord's providence therein, for as soon as ever I had prayed (after my best fashion) then for it, I presently the next Sabbath was able to take notes who the precedent Sabbath could do nothing at all that way. So I continued till I was about fifteen years of age and then was conceived to be ripe for the university, and it pleased the Lord to put it into my brother's heart to provide and to seek to prepare a place for me there, which was done in this manner: one Mr. Cockerell, Fellow of Emmanuel College in Cambridge, being a Northamptonshire man, came down into the country to Northampton and so sent for me, who upon examination of me gave my brother encouragement to send me up to Cambridge. And so I came up, and though I was very raw and young, yet it pleased God to open the hearts of others to admit me into this

---

[6] Whitsun or Whitsunday, the occasion for games and drinking to which "the godly" objected.

college a pensioner,[7] and so Mr. Cockerell became my tutor. But I do here wonder and I hope I shall bless the Lord forever in heaven that the Lord did so graciously provide for me, for I have oft thought what a woeful estate I had been left in if the Lord had left me in the profane, ignorant town of Towcester where I was born, that the Lord should pluck me out of that sink and Sodom, who was the least in my father's house, forsaken of father and mother, yet that the Lord should fetch me out from thence by such a sweet hand. The first two years I spent in Cambridge was in studying and in much neglect of God and private prayer which I had sometime used, and I did not regard the Lord at all unless it were at some fits. The third year, wherein I was sophister, I began to be foolish and proud and to show myself in the public schools, and there to be a disputer about things which now I see I did not know then at all but only prated about them. And toward the end of this year when I was most vile (after I had been next unto the gates of death by the smallpox the year before), the Lord began to call me home to the fellowship of his grace. . . .[8]

And thus I continued till I was six years' standing, and then went half a year before I was master of arts to Mr. Weld's house at Terling in Essex where I enjoyed the blessing of his and Mr. Hooker's[9] ministry at Chelmsford. But before I came there I was very solicitous what would become of me when I was master of arts, for then my time and portion would be spent, but when I came thither and had been there some little season until I was ready to be master of arts, one Dr. Wilson had purposed to set up a lecture and give £30 per annum to the maintenance of it, and when I was among those worthies in Essex where we had monthly fasts they did propound it unto me to take the lecture and to set it up at a great town in Essex called Coggeshall, and so Mr. Weld especially pressed me unto it and wished me to seek God about it, and after fasting and prayer the ministers in those parts of Essex had a day of humiliation, and they did seek the Lord for direction where to place the lecture. And toward the evening of that day they began to consider whether I should go to Coggeshall or no; most of the ministers were for it because it was a great town, and they did not know any place did

---

[7] Pensioner and sophister (below): standard terms for a boarder and for someone who has completed two years of training.

[8] Shepard went on to relate his conversion.

[9] Shepard was participating in the social and political network among the godly in Essex, the "best country" in England for young radicals like himself. Thomas Hooker became lecturer in Chelmsford in 1626. He and Thomas Weld, vicar of Terling, were soon deprived of their positions and emigrated to Massachusetts. Samuel Stone, also a graduate of Emmanuel College, Cambridge, emigrated in 1633, shared with Thomas Hooker the ministry of Newtown, and went with him and the congregation to Hartford in 1636, selling their houses and lands to Shepard's friends. Hunt (1983), 196–97.

desire it but they. Mr. Hooker only did object against my going thither for being but young and unexperienced, and there being an old yet sly and malicious minister in the town who did seem to give way to it to have it there, did therefore say it was dangerous and uncomfortable for little birds to build under the nests of old ravens and kites. But while they were thus debating it, the town of Earle's Colne, being three mile off from Essex, hearing that there was such a lecture to be given freely and considering that the lecture might enrich that poor town, they did therefore just at this time of the day come to the place where the ministers met, viz., at Terling in Essex, and desired that it might be settled there for three years (for no longer was it to continue in any place because it was conceived if any good was done it would be within such a time, and then if it went away from them the people in a populous town would be glad to maintain the man themselves, or if no good was done it was pity they should have it any longer). And when they thus came for it the ministers with one joint consent advised me to accept of the people's call and to stay among them if I found upon my preaching a little season with them that they still continued in their desires for my continuance there. And thus I, who was so young and weak and unexperienced and unfit for so great a work, was called out by twelve or sixteen ministers of Christ to the work, which did much encourage my heart, and for the Lord's goodness herein I shall, I hope, never forget his love, for I might have been cast away upon a blind place without the help of any ministry about me. I might have been sent to some gentleman's house to have been corrupted with the sins in it. But this I have found: the Lord was not content to take me from one town to another, but from the worst town, I think, in the world to the best place for knowledge and learning, viz., to Cambridge, and there the Lord was not content to give me good means but the best means and ministry and help of private Christians, for Dr. Preston and Mr. Goodwin were the most able men for preaching Christ in this latter age.[10] And when I came from thence the Lord sent me to the best country in England, viz., to Essex, and set me in the midst of the best ministry in the country by whose monthly fasts and conferences I found much of God. And thus the Lord Jesus provided for me of all things of the best.

So being resolved to go unto Earle's Colne in Essex after my commencing master of arts and my sinful taking of orders about a fortnight after of the bishop of Peterborough, viz., Bishop Dove, I came to the town and boarded in Mr. Cosins his house, an aged but godly and

---

[10] John Preston (d. 1628), master of Shepard's college, whose preaching first "awakened" Shepard; Thomas Goodwin (d. 1680), who was also famous for his evangelical preaching.

cheerful Christian and schoolmaster in the town, and by whose society I was much refreshed, there being not one man else in all the town that had any godliness but him that I could understand. So having preached upon the Sabbath day out of 2 Corinthians 5:19, all the town gave me a call and set to their hands in writing, and so I saw God would have me to be there, but how to be there and continue there I could not tell. Yet I sinfully got a license to officiate the cure of the bishop of London's register before my name was known, and by virtue of that I had much help. But when I had been there awhile and the Lord had blessed my labors to divers in and out of the town, especially to the chief house in the town, the Priory, to Mr. Harlakenden's children where the Lord wrought mightily upon his eldest son, Mr. Richard (now dwelling there), and afterward on Mr. Roger, who came over with me to New England and died here, Satan then began to rage, and the commissaries, registers, and others began to pursue me and to threaten me, as thinking I was a nonconformable man (when for the most of that time I was not resolved either way, but was dark in those things). Yet the Lord, having work to do in this place, kept me, a poor, ignorant thing, against them all until such time as my work was done. By strange and wonderful means, notwithstanding all the malice of the ministers round about me, the Lord had one way or other to deliver me. The course I took in my preaching was (1) to show the people their misery; (2) the remedy, Christ Jesus; (3) how they should walk answerable to his mercy, being redeemed by Christ. And so I found the Lord putting forth his strength in my extreme weakness and not forsaking of me when I was so foolish as I have wondered since why the Lord hath done any good to me and by me. . . .

So when I had preached awhile at Earle's Colne about half a year the Lord saw me unfit and unworthy to continue me there any longer, and so the bishop of London, Mountain, being removed to York and Bishop Laud (now archbishop) coming in his place, a fierce enemy to all righteousness and a man fitted of God to be a scourge to his people,[11] he presently (having been not long in the place) but sent for me up to London and there, never asking me whether I would subscribe (as I remember) but what I had to do to preach in his diocese, chiding also Dr. Wilson for setting up this lecture in his diocese, after many railing speeches against me, forbade me to preach, and not only so, but if I

[11] George Mountain (Montaigne), supporter of the Laudian program who became bishop of York in 1628; William Laud (executed in 1645), favored by Charles I and made archbishop of Canterbury in 1633 but well before this the unofficial leader of an anti-Puritan campaign to enhance "catholic" aspects of the Church of England. Shepard wrote a fuller, more pungent description of his encounter with Laud, included in the 1932 printing of the "autobiography," 368n.

went to preach anywhere else his hand would reach me. And so God put me to silence there which did somewhat humble me, for I did think it was for my sins the Lord set him thus against me. Yet when I was thus silenced the Lord stirred me up friends. The house of the Har-lakendens were so many fathers and mothers to me, and they and the people would have me live there though I did nothing but stay in the place. But remaining about half a year after this silencing among them, the Lord let me see into the evil of the English ceremonies, cross, sur-plice, and kneeling, and the bishop of London, viz., Laud, coming down to visit, he cited me to appear before him at the court at Reldon where, I appearing, he asked me what I did in the place, and I told him I studied; he asked me what? I told him the [church] fathers; he replied I might thank him for that, yet charged me to depart the place. I asked him whither should I go. To the university, said he. I told him I had no means to subsist there, yet he charged me to depart the place. Now about this time I had great desire to change my estate by marriage, and I had been praying three year before that the Lord would carry me to such a place where I might have a meet yoke fellow. And I had a call at this time to go to Yorkshire to preach there in a gentleman's house, but I did not desire to stir till the bishop fired me out of this place. . . . And now I perceived I could not stay in Colne without danger, and hereupon receiving a letter from Mr. Ezekiel Rogers, then living at Rowley in Yorkshire,[12] to encourage me to come to the knight's house, called Sir Richard Darley, dwelling at a town called Buttercrambe, and the knight's two sons, viz, Mr. Henry and Mr. Richard Darley, promising me £20 a year for their part, and the knight promising me my table, and the let-ters sent to me crying with that voice of the man of Macedonia, *Come and help us* [Acts 16:9]. Hereupon I resolved to follow the Lord to so remote and strange a place, the rather because I might be far from the hearing of the malicious Bishop Laud who had threatened me if I preached anywhere. So when I was determined to go, the gentlemen sent a man to me to be my guide in my journey, who coming with me, with much grief of heart I forsook Essex and Earle's Colne and they me, going, as it were, now I knew not whither. . . .

Now as soon as I came into the house I found divers of them at dice and tables. Mr. Richard Darley, one of the brothers, being to return to London the Monday after and being desirous to hear me preach, sent me speedily to my lodging (the best in the house), and so I preached the day after once, and then he departed, the day after, having carefully desired my comfortable abode there. But I do remember I never was so

---

[12] Ezekiel Rogers (d. 1661), rector of a parish in Yorkshire; he emigrated in 1638, bring-ing some of his congregation with him, and founded the town of Rowley, Massachusetts.

low sunk in my spirit as about this time, for (1) I was now far from all friends; (2) I was, I saw, in a profane house, not any sincerely good; (3) I was in a vile wicked town and country; (4) I was unknown and exposed to all wrongs; (5) I was unsufficient to do any work, and my sins were upon me, etc. And hereupon I was very low and sunk deep, yet the Lord did not leave me comfortless. For though the lady was churlish, yet Sir Richard was ingenious, and I found in the house three servants, viz., Thomas Fugill, Mistress Margaret Touteville, the knight's kinswoman that was afterward my wife, and Ruth Bushell (now married to Edward Michelson),[13] very careful of me, which somewhat refreshed me. But it happened that when I had been there a little while there was a marriage of one Mr. Allured, a most profane young gentleman, to Sir Richard's daughter, and I was desired to preach at their marriage, at which sermon the Lord first touched the heart of Mistress Margaret with very great terrors for sin and her Christless estate, whereupon others began to look about them, especially the gentlewoman lately married, Mistress Allured, and the Lord brake both their hearts very kindly. Then others in the family, viz., Mr. Allured, he fell to fasting and prayer and great reformation. Others also were reformed and their hearts changed the whole family brought to external duties; but I remember none in the town or about it brought home. And thus the Lord was with me and gave me favor and friends and respect of all in the family, and the Lord taught me much of his goodness and sweetness. And when he had fitted a wife for me, he then gave me her who was a most sweet humble woman, full of Christ, and a very discerning Christian, a wife who was most incomparably loving to me and every way amiable and holy and endued with a very sweet spirit of prayer. And thus the Lord answered my desires: when my adversaries intended most hurt to me, the Lord was then best unto me and used me the more kindly in every place. For the Lord turned all the sons and Sir Richard and Mr. Allured so unto me that they not only gave her freely to be my wife but enlarged her portion also. And thus I did marry the best and fittest woman in the world unto me after I had preached in this place about a twelvemonth, for which mercy to me in my exiled condition in a strange place I did promise the Lord that this mercy should knit my heart the nearer to him and that his love should constrain me. But I have ill requited the Lord since that time and forgot myself and my promise also.

But now when we were married in the year 1632, she was unwilling to stay at Buttercrambe, and I saw no means or likelihood of abode there, for Bishop Neile coming up to York, no friends could procure my

---

[13] The Michelsons came to Massachusetts c. 1635 and settled with Shepard in Cambridge.

liberty of him without subscription.[14] And hereupon the Lord gave me a call to Northumberland, to a town called Heddon, five mile beyond Newcastle. . . . Now when I was here the Lord blessed my poor labors both to the saints and to sundry others about and in Newcastle, and I came here to read and know more of the ceremonies, church government and estate, and the unlawful standing of bishops than in any other place. I lived at Mistress Fenwick's house for a time, about a twelvemonth or half a year, and then we went and dwelt alone in a town near Heddon, called [blank], in a house which we found haunted with the devil, as we conceived, for when we came into it a known witch went out of it. And being troubled with noises four or five nights together, we sought God by prayer to remove so sore a trial, and the Lord heard and blessed us there and removed the trouble. But after we were settled the bishop put in a priest who would not suffer me to preach publicly anymore. Hereupon means was made to the bishop of Durham, Bishop Morton, and he professed he durst not give me liberty because Laud had taken notice of me. So I preached up and down in the country and at last privately in Mr. Fenwick's house, and there I stayed till Mr. Cotton, Mr. Hooker, Stone, Weld went to New England, and hereupon most of the godly in England were awakened and intended much to go to New England. And I having a call by divers friends in New England to come over and many in old England desiring me to go over and promising to go with me, I did thereupon resolve to go thither, especially considering the season. And thus the Lord blessed me in this dark country and gave me a son called Thomas, anno 1633, my poor wife being in sore extremities four days by reason she had an unskillful midwife. But as the affliction was very bitter, so the Lord did teach me much by it, and I had need of it, for I began to grow secretly proud and full of sensuality, delighting my soul in my dear wife more than in my God, whom I had promised better unto, and my spirit grew fierce in some things and secretly mindless of the souls of the people. But the Lord by this affliction of my wife learnt me to desire to fear him more and to keep his dread in my heart. And so, seeing I had been tossed from the south to the north of England and now could go no farther, I then began to listen to a call to New England. The reasons which swayed me to come to New England were many. (1) I saw no call to any other place in old England nor way of subsistence in peace and comfort to me and my family. (2) Divers people in old England of my dear friends desired me to go to New England, there to live together, and

---

[14] Richard Neile (d. 1640), a fervent supporter of the Laudian program, was made bishop of York in 1631. To "subscribe" was to submit to the regulations of the Church of England concerning worship, etc.

some went before and writ to me of providing a place for a company of us, one of which was John Bridge,[15] and I saw divers families of my Christian friends who were resolved thither to go with me. (3) I saw the Lord departing from England when Mr. Hooker and Mr. Cotton were gone, and I saw the hearts of most of the godly set and bent that way, and I did think I should feel many miseries if I stayed behind. (4) My judgment was then convinced not only of the evil of ceremonies but of mixed communion and joining with such in sacraments, though I ever judged it lawful to join with them in preaching. (5) I saw it my duty to desire the fruition of all God's ordinances which I could not enjoy in old England. (6) My dear wife did much long to see me settled there in peace and so put me on to it. (7) Although it was true I should stay and suffer for Christ, yet I saw no rule for it now the Lord had opened a door of escape. Otherwise I did incline much to stay and suffer, especially after our sea storms. (8) Though my ends were mixed and I looked much to my own quiet, yet the Lord let me see the glory of those liberties in New England and made me purpose, if ever I should come over, to live among God's people as one come out from the dead, to his praise, though since I have seen as the Lord's goodness, so my own exceeding weakness to be as good as I thought to have been. And although they did desire me to stay in the north and preach privately, yet (1) I saw that this time could not be long without trouble from King Charles; (2) I saw no reason to spend my time privately when I might possibly exercise my talent publicly in New England; (3) I did hope my going over might make them to follow me; (4) I considered how sad a thing it would be for me to leave my wife and child (if I should die) in that rude place of the north where was nothing but barbarous wickedness generally, and how sweet it would be to leave them among God's people, though poor; (5) my liberty in private was daily threatened, and I thought it wisdom to depart before the pursuivants came out, for so I might depart with more peace and less trouble and danger to me and my friends. And I knew not whether God would have me to hazard my person and comfort of me and all mine for a disorderly manner of preaching privately (as it was reputed) in those parts. So after I had preached my farewell sermon at Newcastle I departed from the north in a ship laden with coals for Ipswich, about the beginning of June, after I had been about a year in the north, the Lord having blessed some few sermons and notes to divers in Newcastle from whom I parted filled with their love. And so the Lord gave us a speedy voyage from thence to Ipswich in old England, whither I came in a disguised manner with my

---

[15] John Bridge, who arrived before Shepard, held important offices in both congregation and town.

wife and child and maid, and stayed a while at Mr. Russell's house, another while at Mr. Collins his house, and then went down to Essex to the town where I had preached, viz., Earle's Colne, to Mr. Richard Harlakenden's house where I lived privately but with much love from them all, as also from Mr. Joseph Cooke, and also with friends at London and Northamptonshire.[16] And truly I found this time of my life wherein I was so tossed up and down and had no place of settling, but kept secret in regard of the bishops, the most uncomfortable and fruitless time to my own soul especially that ever I had in my life. And therefore I did long to be in New England as soon as might be, and the rather because my wife, having weaned her first son Thomas, had conceived again and was breeding, and I knew no place in England where she could lie in without discovery of myself, danger to myself and all my friends that should receive me, and where we could not but give offense to many if I should have my child not baptized. And therefore, there being divers godly Christians resolved to go toward the latter end of the year if I would go, I did therefore resolve to go that year, the end of that summer I came from the north. . . . And so, when the Lord had recovered my wife [after she gave birth to another son, also named Thomas, in April 1635], we began to prepare for a removal once again to New England. And the Lord seemed to make our way plain (1) because I had no other call to any place in England; (2) many more of God's people resolved to go with me, as Mr. Roger Harlakenden and Mr. Champney, etc.; (3) the Lord saw our unfitness and the unfitness of our going the year before, and therefore giving us good friends to accompany us and good company in the ship, we set forward, about the tenth of August, 1635, with myself, wife, and my little son Thomas, and other precious friends, having tasted much of God's mercy in England and lamenting the loss of our native country when we took our last view of it. . . . And so the Lord after many sad storms and wearisome days and many longings to see the shore, the Lord brought us to the sight of it upon October 2, anno 1635, and upon October the third we arrived with my wife, child, brother Samuel, Mr. Harlakenden, Mr. Cooke, etc., at Boston with rejoicing in our God after a longsome voyage, my dear wife's great desire being now fulfilled, which was to leave me in safety from the hand of my enemies and among God's people, and also the child under God's precious ordinances.

Now when we came upon shore we were kindly saluted and enter-

---

[16] Two Cookes, Joseph and Edward, Edward Champney, John Russell, and Edward Collins all came from Essex to be with Shepard in Cambridge, where they played prominent roles in local and colony affairs; Champney and Collins were also lay officers of the church.

tained by many friends and were the first three days in the house of Mr. Coddington, being treasurer at that time, and that with much love.

When we had been here two days, upon the Monday, October 5, we came (being sent for by friends at Newtown) to them to my brother Mr. Stone's house. And that congregation being upon their removal to Hartford at Connecticut, myself and those that came with me found many houses empty and many persons willing to sell, and hence our company bought off their houses to dwell in until we should see another place fit to remove unto. But having been here some time, divers of our brethren did desire to sit still and not to remove further, partly because of the fellowship of the churches, partly because they thought their lives were short and removals to new plantations full of troubles, partly because they found sufficient for themselves and their company. Hereupon there was a purpose to enter into church fellowship, which we did the year after about the end of the winter, a fortnight after which my dear wife Margaret died, being first received into church fellowship which, as she much longed for, so the Lord did so sweeten it unto her that she was hereby exceedingly cheered and comforted with the sense of God's love, which continued until her last gasp.[17]

No sooner were we thus set down and entered into church fellowship but the Lord exercised us and the whole country with the opinions of Familists,[18] begun by Mistress Hutchinson, raised up to a great height by Mr. Vane[19] too suddenly chosen governor, and maintained too obscurely by Mr. Cotton, and propagated too boldly by the members of Boston and some in other churches, by means of which division by these opinions the ancient and received truth came to be darkened, God's name to be blasphemed, the churches' glory diminished, many godly grieved, many wretches hardened, deceiving and being deceived, growing worse and worse. The principal opinion and seed of all the rest was this, viz., that a Christian should not take any evidence of God's special grace and love toward him by the sight of any graces or conditional evangelical promises to faith or sanctification, in way of ratiocination (for this was evidence and so a way of works), but it must be without the sight of any grace, faith, holiness, or special change in himself, by immediate revelation in an absolute promise. And because that

---

[17] A contemporary description of her rapture when, on her deathbed, she was admitted to the newly organized church in Cambridge was published by Cotton Mather in *The Temple Openings* (Boston, 1709), 30–31.

[18] Familists: members of an obscure sect, the "Family of Love," but also an epithet for persons advocating the free movement of the Holy Spirit. Winship (2002).

[19] Henry Vane (1613–1662), member of an aristocratic family, arrived in Massachusetts in October 1635 and was elected governor the following May, only to be replaced in May 1637 by Winthrop; he played an important role in the controversy. See Winship (2002).

the whole scriptures do give such clear, plain, and notable evidences of favor to persons called and sanctified, hence they said that a second evidence might be taken from hence but no first evidence. But from hence it arose that, as all error is fruitful, so this opinion did gender above a hundred monstrous opinions in the country, which the elders perceiving, having used all private brotherly means with Mr. Cotton first and yet no healing hereupon, they publicly preached both against opinions publicly and privately maintained, and I account it no small mercy to myself that the Lord kept me from that contagion and gave me an heart or light to see through those devices of men's heads, although I found it a most uncomfortable time to live in contention. And the Lord was graciously pleased by giving witness against them to keep this poor church spotless and clear from them.

Source: *Publications of the Colonial Society of Massachusetts* 27 (Boston, 1932), 352–400, compared with McGiffert (1972).

Chapter 4

The Town of Dedham Organizes
a Gathered Church

The organizing of the Dedham, Massachusetts, congregation in 1637 and 1638, as narrated in the church records by John Allin (1596?–1671), a graduate of Cambridge and minister in the Church of England who emigrated to New England in 1637, reveals in extraordinary detail how the colonists conceived of the true church. After agreeing on a set of principles, the thirty families in the newly founded town entrusted the task of forming a congregation to Allin and Ralph Wheelock (1600–1684), another Cambridge graduate and former minister. The two identified eight other men who agreed to becoming "further acquainted with the tempers and gifts of one another."

What may astonish modern readers is the commitment of these people to an ethics of "edification" and "love." To them the church was no ordinary place but a manifestation of Christ's kingdom. The modern reader may also find amusing, as the founders most definitely did not, the rigorous scrutiny of one another and the irritation it aroused in Joseph Kingsbury. A troublesome issue of church-state relations intruded as the group moved toward the formal organizing of a church: was it consistent with the differentiation of church and state that the founders allow the civil government the right to authorize (or forbid) their doing so? Once past this hurdle, the eight founders began to admit other townspeople to the congregation. By the close of the 1640s, 70 percent of the adult men in Dedham were members, as were many of their wives; in some families the wives but not the husbands joined. As of this same decade, all but 20 percent of children born in the town were incorporated through the ordinance of baptism. These percentages declined sharply as the founders died away and the second generation came of age; even so, the congregation refused to accept the new policy on baptism advocated by a synod that met in 1662, the so-called "halfway covenant," until late in the century.

Bibliography
Morgan (1963); Lockridge (1970), 31–36; Bozeman (1988), chap. 4.

JOHN ALLIN

🌺 A Brief History of the Church of Christ 🌺 at Dedham

A brief history of the church of Christ (gathered) in his Name, at Dedham in New England the eighth day of the ninth month 1638 relating only such passages of providence and carriages of the affairs thereof both in and about the gathering of the church and the proceedings thereof as were thought most material and useful both for the present state of that church to review upon any occasion and also for future ages to make use of in any case that may occur wherein light may be fetched from any examples of things past, no way intending hereby to bind the conscience of any to walk by this pattern or to approve of the practice of the church further than it may appear to be according to the rule of the gospel.

The township of Dedham consisting of about thirty families residing there 1637 being come together by divine providence from several parts of England: few of them known to one another before, it was thought meet and agreed upon that all the inhabitants that affected church communion or pleased to come, should meet every fifth day of the week at several houses in order, lovingly to discourse and consult together such questions as might further tend to establish a peaceable and comfortable civil society, and prepare for spiritual communion in a church society, that we might be further acquainted with the (spiritual) tempers and gifts of one another, and partly that we might gain further light in the ways of Christ's kingdom and government of his church, which we thought might much conduce to this end.

The order of which meetings was this[:] the question being propounded and agreed upon the week before, the master of the family where the meeting was, began and concluded with prayer: and he first speaking as God assisted to the question others that pleased spake after him as they saw cause to add, enlarge or approve what was spoken by any or purposely to treat of the question: or else to propound any questions pertinent to the case or any objections or doubts remaining in any conscience about the same, so it were humbly and with a teachable heart not with any mind of caviling or contradicting. Which order was so well observed as generally all such reasonings were very peaceable, loving, and tender, much to edification. . . .

QUESTION 1: Whether such as in the judgment of charity look upon one another as Christians may assemble together, speak and hear the

Word, pray and fast, or confer together being out of church order as we were and many unknown to each other.

ANSWER. Affirmatively, that taking one another for Christians nothing yet appearing to the contrary; all Christians by virtue of their union with Christ and one with another have a common right to and use of all such privileges and spiritual helpers unto edification as naturally flows from that union as to justification adoption, etc., so to the Word prayer and fasting as a help thereto and to the gift one of another for mutual edification but for instituted privileges and ordinances they were to be enjoyed only in the order instituted by Christ.

QUESTION 2. Concerning the duties of Christian love, how far we stood bound thereto in our condition.

ANSWER: to all such Christian and spiritual duties of love as flows from that union with Christ and one another; as to exhort admonish privately comfort, to communicate and improve any gift received to mutual edification, to relieve the wants of each other, etc.

QUESTION 3. Whether having these privileges of Christian communion and being bound to such duties we may not rest in such a condition and look no further.

ANSWER: negatively, we may not, but [must] seek for a further union and communion even such as may interest us in and convey unto us all the ordinances of Christ's instituted worship both because it is the command of God that the whole Christ should be received and submitted unto and so in his kingly office and the outward administration of his kingdom, and also because the spiritual condition of every Christian is such as stand in need of all instituted ordinances for the repair of the saints and edification of the body of Christ. Eph. 4.

QUESTION 4. What is that further and nearer union and communion to be sought after for such ends[?]

ANSWER. Church communion of the fellowship of a certain number of visible saints or believers agreeing to live together in spiritual communion with Christ and one another in the use of all the holy instituted ordinances and worship of the gospel. And that this is an institution of Christ in the gospel that the saints of Christ should be distributed into particular visible congregations enjoying their distinct officers, etc. is clear; Matt. 18:[20] where two or three agree together, and 1 Cor. 1:1,16; Phil. 1:1; Rev. 1 the seven churches of Asia.

QUESTION 5. Concerning the matter of such a church the proper matter of such a church is visible believers or saints. . . .

6. That the band of this society that knit them together is a mutual consent or profession of the covenant of grace or an application of the covenant of the gospel to a number of saints whereby they professing

their faith do lay claim to all the grace [and] privileges of the gospel, and promise to the Lord and one unto another to live together in such communion with the Lord and one another according [to the] rule of the gospel in everything. The ground of which covenant was shewed from . . . the practice of the Lord who never took any people unto himself to worship him according to his ordinances as a church, but by covenant: as appears in the stories of Abraham and his family constituted a church by covenant Gen. 15 and 17 the people of Israel coming out of Egypt Exod. 20, etc. and when they broke that covenant this caused their divorce from the Lord, and when they were restored again in any way of solemn reformation it was by renewing this covenant as many examples shew. . . .[1]

7. Concerning the manner of gathering saints together into covenant it ought to be so ordered as the high and spiritual ends there may best be attained according to rules of Christian prudence so that the communion may be spiritual[ly] edifying and the persons knit firmly in the band of love, that also the ordinances may be kept in purity, and a sweet communion maintained in the churches, it is requisite that professors being strangers to one another before, meeting from many parts should be well acquainted with the hearts and states of one another — join by way of confession and profession of their faith and that this be publicly testified for the better union of the hearts of other Christians unto them. But the number and what persons should first join it is not much material so they be such as are living stones [Eph. 4:12]; and such as may have some measure of faithful care and deserving to keep the churches pure and also be of that innocency of life as may invite other saints more willingly to join to them. . . .

11. Concerning the discerning and receiving members into the church to partake with them in these ordinances. It was concluded that only visible saints or believers were to be received who ought to make their faith and holiness visible not only by their baptism for then papists, heretics and many visible atheists that are baptized must be received, not only by a civil restrained life and some religious duties performed: . . . but such as by a profession of an inward work of faith and grace declared by an holy life suitable thereto may persuade the church to embrace them with such a brotherly love as ought to be amongst saints in so near a covenant. Phil. 1:3–4.

12. For the duty of every member to the church [is, first] that every one in general ought to bear a reverent respect to the church and to obey in the Lord every ordinance dispensed by her officers or whole body in the name of Christ according to his rule and secondly to im-

---

[1] New Testament citations were also listed: Matt. 12; 2 Cor. 9:13, 1 Tim. 6:12.

prove faithfully whatsoever light knowledge or other gifts they have for the edification and peace of the whole church. And that especially in acts of discipline as in receiving and casting out members and electing officers, etc.

Lastly that every member owe unto one another all duties of brotherly love especially faithfulness to the souls of one another in watching over each other admonishing and exhorting one another, etc. in love wisdom and pity and for the better settling of a body newly gathered and continuance of spiritual and endeared affections of love to be free and frequent in communicating to one another the inward workings and dealings of the Lord with their souls.

. . . The society looked at John Allin (whom the whole town had invited to the town with thoughts of future employment in public work) to set upon the work with such as might be thought meet. Whereupon I at first [opened] the ca[u]se and work to Mr. Wheelock desiring his . . . assistance if the Lord upon opening of our spiritual conditions should so far close our hearts together intending after that, that we two should agree upon a third and so three agree upon a fourth, etc. till we might find a competent number[.] But upon the trial made of that way we found it a very slow way and also that we should [need] the help of many spirits to discern and judge of the fitness and unfitness of everyone: and so we agreed to gather to[gether] about eight persons more whom we had best hopes of for soundness of grace and meet gifts for such a work and then after solemn invocations and humiliation of ourselves before the Lord that search all hearts: everyone to open their conditions and declare the workings of God in their souls and so the whole company approve or leave out as the Lord should guide us to judge of every one's conditions or fitness for the work. And accordingly we invited into us first a third person and by mutual consent a fourth, etc. till we were ten. Then setting apart a day of solemn fasting and prayer among ourselves to humble and prepare our hearts to draw so nigh the Lord and to seek direction from him to walk by his rule in building such an house to himself we . . . all agreed on these conclusions. 1. That in looking out fit matter for the foundation of a church we should resp[ect] the soundness of grace above all things so far as we can discern the same[.] 2. Amongst such to respect things very desirable in the beginning viz: first a spirit of wisdom and discerning to keep the church pure in the adding of members unto it. Secondly such meekness, amiableness of spirit and innocency of life as might win the love and desires of all godly souls to come unto the church cheerfully. Secondly we concluded that everyone should go forth and leave themselves and their case to the scanning of the rest, who did mutually promise to be faithful and impartial in [giving] their judgment on everyone's case as they conceived and so inform the company of any sin or offences that any knew to be in any such person so to be tried. Thirdly that everyone laying aside all ambitious desires of being taken into the work, and overmuch bashfulness in refusing the same should willingly submit themselves to the judgment of the whole company to be taken, or left or ordered, by the rule of the gospel, as to the call and voice of God.

These things agreed upon everyone went out in their order and their cases being scanned were called in again[.] The issue was this that John Allin, Ralph Wheelock, John Luson, John Frary, Eleazer Lusher and Robert Hinsdell were by general consent agreed upon and called to proceed in preparing themselves and setting themselves apart for such a work. Mr. Edward Allin in regard to some offences which the company could not at present clear up was desired to wait till further consideration. Anthony Fisher by his rash carriage and speeches savoring of self confidence, etc. had given some offence and the company thought it meet to seek the humbling and trial of his spirit with some serious admonition from the Lord. Joseph Kingsbury . . . was [considered] too much addicted to the world and so [it was] thought meet to require his answer to the particulars and deal further in his case as it should require: in his answer he cleared some things to satisfaction [but] in some others the company could not see his innocency but partly to help him to see and prevent his danger of falling therein, and partly to try his spirit how it would submit to an ordinance they left a gentle exhortation with him to consider of. Thomas Morse was thought by the company to be so dark and unsatisfying in respect of the work of grace that though his life was innocent in respect of men yet they had not grounds to embrace him into this society except they should see further and so declared unto him.

After this we had many meetings all the ten persons combining together sometimes spending the time in fasting and prayer exercising the gifts of prayer in everyone at their seasons and trying out the cases of those four persons not formerly resolved upon, endeavoring by inquiry, observation, and hearing their further answers to discover the mind of God concerning them either by clearing up their cases to satisfaction, or by following home admonitions from the Lord and means of further conviction as their cases required that we might see how they would be humbled and moved further to seek the Lord. . . .

Anthony Fisher after some meetings was brought to see and acknowledge his failings in carriage of himself: but the pride and height of his spirit wherewith he was charged as the root of it which especially we endeavored to have him see and be humbled for; that he could not see nor be brought unto by many meetings and following home of the means of conviction upon him, but at last the Lord by some pertinent scriptures alleged which did impute such effects to pride as the cause of them did so convince him and in another meeting humbled him as that the company hoped well and took good satisfaction and with some exhortations to seek earnestly for the pardon and healing of those evils and to keep a diligent watch over his heart we approved him as one for the foundation of the church. Joseph Kingsbury remaining stiff and unhumbled and not clearing himself to satisfaction neither being zealous of his heart in respect of those evils we feared in him remained long under the admonition of the company but at last when we desired to bring of things to some conclusion and desired to know the mind of God about him the Lord left him, without any provocation thereto, unto such a distempered passionate flying out upon one of the company whom the Lord had used of to follow home things close upon him and that to charge him in a matter of injustice wherein we could generally clear him, that we then saw evidently such an unsubdued spirit to the Lord . . . that we concluded [to give] . . . him wholly over, and left him to the judgment of the church when it should be gathered. . . .[2]

Things being thus far cleared up in respect of the company being now eight persons we . . . about the beginning of October came to resolutions to cast ourselves upon the Lord and venture with such help as he should afford rather than to delay so great and needful a work any longer: whereupon we resolved again to seek the Lord in [a] solemn manner and to make a further scrutiny or trial of ourselves in the same manner we did formerly and if it appeared that we could with comfortable satisfaction find a convenient number that could close together with that persuasion of the integrity of all and with that brotherly love which was meet then presently to proceed unto solemn profession and covenant together: now upon the second trial of ourselves we joined unto us John Hunting who had been with us in some conferences before and given us some good taste of his spirit and gifts but desiring the rest of the company to make a new relation of the dealings of God with them and how they had found the Lord with them in the preparations of themselves to this work of the Lord hitherto, and also desiring to scan and seek satisfaction in any offences discovered by any since we were approved partly to give satisfaction to John Hunting newly come to us and partly for our more clear proceedings in this work. In this way of trial I say some new objections were made against Edward Allin which yet at last were satisfied and he still joined to the company. . . .

The rest of the company (some few scruples except which arose about one or two) were continued with the same approbation of all as before . . . : These eight persons John Allin, Ralph Wheelock, Edward Allin,

---

[2] He was admitted in 1641.

John Luson, John Frary, John Hunting, Eleazar Lusher and Robert Hinsdell were set apart by the Lord for this service who therefore endeavored now in a more special manner to prepare themselves to the Lord and to close with one another in brotherly love and unity of judgment and affection. . . .

The Lord thus far clearing up our way before us we agreed upon the eighth day of the ninth month 1638 to make our public profession and enter into solemn covenant with the Lord and one another giving notice to the magistrates and by letters unto the several churches of this our purpose that we might enjoy not only the countenance and encouragement of the magistrates therein but also the advice and counsel of the churches in so weighty a work that nothing might be done therein against the rule of the gospel so far as by any advice we could receive help: but in giving notice to the governor hereof we understood by some that the General Court had ordained that no churches should be gathered without the advice of other churches, which we conceived might be prejudicial to the liberty of God's people and some seeds of usurpation upon [the] liberties of the gospel:[3] wherefore we desired the governor[4] to inform us of that law and the true intent thereof: which he professed was only this that the Court or law enacted did no way intend to abridge such a liberty of gathering into church fellowship privately as if it were unlawful or as if such a church were not a true church rightly gathered. But that the scope was this that if any people of unsound judgment or erroneous way, etc. should privately set up churches amongst them the commonwealth would not so approve them as to communicate that freedom and other privileges unto them[5] which yet [it] did unto others or protect them in their government if they saw their way dangerous to the public peace. Which answer gave us satisfaction in that scruple. . . .

The day before mentioned we agreed generally should be spent in fasting and prayer in public and solemn manner and for the more solemn and orderly performance of the duties thereof we agreed in this manner that first Mr. Wheelock should begin with solemn prayer and confession of sin: After him Mr. John Allin to follow first with solemn

[3] On March 3, 1636, the General Court ordered that it would not "hereafter, approve of any . . . as shall henceforth join in any pretended way of church fellowship, without they shall first acquaint the magistrates, and the elders of the greater part of the churches in this jurisdiction, with their intentions, and have their approbation herein." Shurtleff (1853), 1:168. The preceding month, the organizers of the church in Cambridge had made a special point of seeking the "approbation" of the magistrates and of neighboring churches. Winthrop (1996), 168–69.

[4] John Haynes.

[5] The teeth in the statute of 1636 was that members of unauthorized churches would not be admitted to freemanship.

prayer also as the Lord should guide and assist. Secondly by way of exercise of his gifts to speak to the assembly which he did according to the occasion upon the last words of the twentieth verse of the first chapter of the Revelation:[6] Thirdly conclude again with prayer for a blessing on the word spoken and for assistance and guidance of the Spirit in the following work to be performed: Fourthly that he should begin to make profession both of the doctrine of faith and of the grace of faith or work thereof in himself: and then that the others in an order agreed upon should follow everyone testifying their consent to the doctrine of faith before professed and declaring the workings of God's grace in their hearts. Which was accordingly performed. . . .

Whereunto the brethren exhorting us did encourage us to proceed to our covenant. . . . We whose names are subscribed having found by woeful experience the unsteadfastness of our hearts with God, and proneness to go astray from his ways (for which we desire to abase and humble ourselves in his presence) and now desiring to be joined forever to the Lord, and to cleave together in spiritual love and communion according to his holy institution that we might enjoy in his Name such holy helps as the Lord Jesus in wisdom and compassion have ordained in his gospel for his people thereby to let out himself unto them, and to build them up in faith and holiness till he have prepared them for everlasting communion with himself. We do therefore in the Name and presence of God, and our Lord Jesus Christ, and before his people here assembled solemnly enter into covenant with the Lord our God professing and acknowledging the Lord Jesus Christ our blessed Redeemer to be the only priest, prophet, and king of his church and (through the help of his grace) his [the] only merit we rest upon for our pardon and peace with the faith his [the] only teaching and righteous government with all the blessed ordinances of his kingdom we do embrace and submit unto in all things as the only rule of our lives: renouncing all our own righteousness with all the doctrines, devices and commandments of men not agreeing with his holy Word. Especially all the superstitious and tyrannous commands of Antichrist and his adherents wherein we have in any kind been entangled. Professing and promising (through the help of his rich and free grace) henceforth not to live unto ourselves but unto the Lord Jesus who have bought us with his blood avoiding carefully all such things as be offensive to his majesty and dishonorable to our profession of his Name, with all such dangerous temptations as our

[6] "The mystery of the seven stars which thou sawest in my right hand, and the seven golden candlesticks. The seven stars are the angels of the seven churches: and the seven candlesticks are the seven churches." The 1636 law tested the "two kingdom" theory of church and state that protected the church from the intervention of the civil state in religious affairs. Hall (1972), chap. 6; and see below, chap. 15.

sinful hearts are wont to be drawn aside withal, in special the inordinate cares of, and entanglements in the affairs of this life. Promising and professing also through the help of the Lord to live together in this our holy fellowship according to the rule of love in all holy watchfulness over each other and faithful mutual helpfulness in the ways of God for the spiritual and temporal comfort and good of one another in the Lord. And all to the setting forth of the praise of his rich grace in Christ who have called us in his abundant mercy to this holy fellowship with his majesty and one with another.

This form of our covenant being publicly read it was demanded by Mr. John Allin whether they all consented thereto and that they would testify the same by lifting up of hands which accordingly was done by all the eight persons named before viz: John Allin, Ralph Wheelock, Edward Allin, John Luson, John Hunting, John Frary, Eleazer Lusher and Robert Hinsdall. . . .

The church being thus through the infinite mercy of the Lord set up as a spiritual house to the Lord Jesus, the next day we held a church meeting both to give thanks to the Lord for his mercy and to take care that according to the power of [the keys] Jesus committed unto us [Matt. 18:17], we might see all things . . . in which meetings Mr. John Allin was deputed by the church to exercise his gifts received every Lord's day to the edification of the church till officers might be chosen to teach by office: the grounds hereof were 1 Cor. 12:7, and 3:22.

Soon after divers of the neighbors expressed their desires to be joined to the church. Wherefore considering the Lord Jesus had committed unto us the keys of his kingdom in his Name and according to his rule to open and shut the doors of his house knowing the Lord is the king of saints Rev. 1, etc. and churches should be churches of saints 1 Cor. 1:1, Phil. 1:1, and knowing of what weight and consequence it was for the preservation of the purity of the church and ordinances of Christ with the spiritual communion we had joined ourselves in, and that brotherly love that was meet that we should be very watchful especially in the first beginnings of the church. Being also weak of judgment and of little or no experience in this work, and having yet no officers to commit this care unto, for these reasons the church agreed at present to meet once every week and besides other occasions to hear the professions of such as desired communion with us.

. . . The manner of our proceedings was this[:] after anyone had declared his desires to the church he was desired to declare the workings of God in his heart and what grounds he could declare of his right unto the ordinances at least so far as by the breathings of his soul after Christ the church might see somewhat in him that might persuade them to conceive some true workings of faith and repentance in his soul. After which profession of the party anyone that desired further satisfaction in any particular propounded his questions and took his answers. Which being done the party being dismissed everyone of the church beginning at the youngest and so upward declared whether the Lord persuaded his heart to take satisfaction or what his scruple was that remained: whereby all having spoken we collected things together and if anything in his profession remained doubtful, or any offence had been given by his life the church agreed to send their mind unto the party by such of the brethren: either to testify their approbation or to give notice what was yet doubtful to any which after repaired to them for further clearing of things, or to give them some loving instructions and admonitions, or exhortations in the Name of the Lord as the church saw every case required, and so to see how the same would be accepted and improved by every soul. In this way the church continued all the winter and beginning of spring till officers were set up by the Lord April 24 . . . the persons joined to the church before the choice of elders were:

Margaret Allin the wife of John Allin who gave a clear and plentiful testimony of the gracious dealings of the Lord with her.

2ly Henry Phillips who appeared to the church a tender and broken hearted Christian.

3ly the wife of John Luson who after long acquaintance of the church with her condition and temptations wherein she appeared to be much humbled and constant in her affections to the Lord Jesus the church took satisfaction in her and received her.

4ly the wife of John Frary who gave good satisfaction both in public and private.

5ly the wife of Joseph Kingsbury who appeared to the church a tender hearted soul full of fears and temptations, but truly breathing after Christ.

6ly John Dwight who after some scruples wherein the church waited a good while for satisfaction yet gave good, comfortable satisfaction to the church.

7ly Robert Kempe who seemed to the church a plain hearted Christian though some objections were moved about his carriage of things in his particular calling yet they being cleared he was received.

8ly Daniel Fisher who appeared to be a tender hearted and hopeful Christian young man: as also divers of the church that had long known him testified, and so was easily and gladly received.

9ly the wife of Eleazer Lusher who after some scruples in respect of some former passages: yet by the good use she made of her afflictions with the poor, and of the public ministry with the private dealings of the church with her, etc. appeared to the church much humbled and to have much perfected and thriven in the ways of God with a great change in the whole frame of her spirit and carriage, to the great satisfaction of the church.

10thly the wife of John Hunting who notwithstanding some scruples a while sticking in some of the church yet at length gave good satisfaction and was received.

Source: *The Records of Baptisms, Marriages and Deaths, and Admissions to the Church . . . in the Town of Dedham, Massachusetts*, ed. Don Gleason Hill (Dedham, Mass., 1888 [Dedham Records 2]), 1–15.

PART II

Theology in New England

THE PLIGHT OF SINNERS AND THE
STAGES OF REDEMPTION

Theology in New England

THE PLIGHT OF SINNERS AND THE
STAGES OF REDEMPTION

Theological language appears in virtually every selection in this book. This language may seem esoteric (or seriously mistaken) to modern readers, but it was well understood among the colonists. Doing theology and defending orthodoxy were professional tasks undertaken by the clergy, who in doing so relied on methods and information they learned at Cambridge and Oxford or, later on, at Harvard College. First and foremost among these methods was mastering the ancient or classical languages (Hebrew, Greek, and Latin) in order to better understand the Bible. The tools of logic and rhetoric were crucial means of analyzing and arranging theological and philosophical arguments.[1] The ministers were also familiar with the history of the Christian church and, especially, with theological debates provoked by the Protestant Reformation. Roman Catholicism remained a powerful foe, and other enemies lurked within the Reformed (Calvinist) tradition. A theological controversy in the Netherlands between the followers of Jacobus Arminius (the "Arminians") and their critics reached a climax at the Synod of Dort in 1618–1619, which concluded with the anti-Arminians affirming five points that reemphasized the unconditioned primacy of God in the history of redemption: the total depravity of humans; their unconditional election to salvation; the limited scope of the Atonement (Christ's death is efficacious for some but not for all); irresistible grace; and the perseverance of the saints (once elected to salvation, always elected).[2]

[1] These skills or subjects are described in the chapters on the Harvard College curriculum in Morison (1936).

[2] The full text of the "canons" is in Jaroslav Pelikan and Valerie Hotchkiss, eds., *Creeds and Confessions of Faith in the Christian Tradition*, 4 vols. (New Haven, Conn., 2003), 2:569–600; the same volume contains the Westminster Confession.

Throughout the seventeenth century the colonists accepted these propositions as true, using as their benchmark certain catechisms, creeds, and confessions, but especially the Westminster Confession of 1647, which a synod in New England acknowledged in 1648 and again in 1680.

Taking orthodoxy for granted, ministers in New England focused their attention on the "practical divinity," a form of preaching that was fashioned in late-sixteenth- and early-seventeenth-century England by theologians and pastors such as William Perkins, Richard Sibbes, John and Richard Rogers, Arthur Dent, Richard Greenham, and Arthur Hildersham. At the core of the practical divinity were two assumptions, that the gospel promise of redemption was implemented "experimentally," through actual experience, in the lives of those who would become saints, and that this experience unfolded in a sequence of stages. The practical divinity was like a road map or chart that laid out these stages: "effectual call" or "vocation," followed by "justification," followed by "sanctification" (see Thomas Shepard's catechism, chap. 5). But the practical divinity also included a much more evocative language, at once scriptural and deeply psychological, of being wounded in the "heart" and laid low because of sin, of anxiety intermixed with joy, of seeing the living, suffering, forgiving Christ and sensing his love for sinners, of temptation and pilgrimage. A passage from John Cotton's catechism captures the essentials of this language: "Q. How doth the ministry of the gospel help you in this cursed estate? A. By humbling me yet more and then raising me up out of this estate. Q. How doth the ministry of the gospel humble you more? A. By revealing the grace of the Lord Jesus in dying to save sinners and yet convincing me of my sin in not believing on him and of mine utter insufficiency to come to him, and so I feel myself utterly lost."[3]

As in this passage, so in general the ministers reaffirmed the core message of the Protestant Reformation, that salvation was God's free gift to humans. To this message they added an emphasis (found also in the Reformers) on "new obedience," or observing the moral rules God has proclaimed. As defined by Cotton, "new obedience" was "a grace of the Spirit whereby I forsake any former lusts and vain company, and walk before the Lord in the light of his Word and in the communion of his saints."[4] The practical divinity thus held out two goals, not only a transformation of the "heart" or inner self but also a transformation of the outward or public self from willful lawlessness to the disciplined performance of "duties." In principle the first was the motor that drove the second, a point the ministers reiterated in counseling people who frequently wondered if they were "hypocrites," that is, only going

---

[3] Quoted in Emerson (1965), 128–129.
[4] Ibid., 129.

Mr, Richard Mather,

Figure 1. The Reverend Richard Mather (d. 1670), holding an open Bible. Woodcut by John Foster, c. 1670. Courtesy of the American Antiquarian Society

through the motions of "duties" without having truly experienced the work of grace (see chap. 11). Truth be told, the ministers counseled everyone, church member or no, that God expected them to observe his moral laws.

Puritan sermons were evangelical in proposing that Christ came to save everyone who responded in faith, affective in defining true religion as a matter of the "heart" and its responses, rational in declaring that the entire process depended on an intellectual knowledge of truth, and moralistic in emphasizing the importance of observing God's laws. In keeping with the humanism and Scholasticism the ministers learned at college, they described humans as "rational animals" who acted voluntarily. God had chosen to respect this voluntarism in how he constituted the ministry. Their role was to act as intermediary or "means of grace" between God (or Christ) and humans, limited in doing so to persuasion through speech and writing and hoping for the presence of the Holy Spirit to make their message effective. It was God's self-limiting that enabled the ministers to describe the covenant of grace as both "absolute" and "conditional" — entirely his doing, yet also obligating humans to respond to the ministers. This dialectic — a delicate dialectic, at best — is what Thomas Hooker describes in his sermon below (chap. 6).

The themes that interested the ministers changed over time; orthodoxy was never static or its boundaries absolutely certain. A dramatic moment of debate was the "Antinomian controversy" of 1636–1638, excerpted in a document that follows, a selection from the ministers' debates with one another (chap. 8). By the 1670s and 1680s second-generation ministers in New England were preaching a "new baptismal piety" tied to the growing importance of baptism as a door to church membership. Broader changes in the intellectual climate were making their way from Europe to the colonies. New approaches to logic in place of Scholasticism, a new attention to "reason," and the rise of Pietism gradually entered the curriculum at Harvard and newly founded Yale. The lay narratives that appear in parts III and IV of this collection can also be usefully compared for shifts of emphasis, especially the growing attention to children or young people.

Some historians of the practical divinity have argued that it introduced a greater measure of human responsiveness than was permitted within sixteenth-century Reformed orthodoxy. Others have proposed that it created a treadmill of "legalism," binding would-be Christians to a routinized striving for God's favor without ever gaining assurance of salvation. Such interpretations remain controversial.

Bibliography

Miller (1956 [originally 1935]), now much challenged, as is Miller (1943); Miller (1939), needing correction but useful on detailing wider intellectual allegiances (chaps. 3–4); Haller (1938); Fiering (1972) on the faculty psychology; Wallace (1982); Lake (1982) on "experimental predestination"; Stoever (1978), summarizing Scholastic orthodoxy; Cohen (1986), questioning the "legalism" interpretation; von Rohr (1986) on "covenant theology" and its doubleness as absolute/conditional; Knight (1994); Winship (2001, 2002). On trends in late-seventeenth-century New England: Miller (1953); Middlekauff (1971), correcting some of Miller's account; Holifield (1974); Fiering (1981). On the Reformed tradition and English developments: Muller (1986); Dever (2000), with useful footnotes reviewing historians' interpretations.

Chapter 5

Thomas Shepard's Catechism

ON THE FALL AND REDEMPTION OF HUMANKIND

Catechisms summarize Christian doctrine and describe the obligations of God's law. The Protestant reformers of the sixteenth century depended on catechisms to instruct ordinary people in the principles of their faith. Most catechisms were arranged so that instruction unfolded by way of question and answer. Learning a catechism mixed recitation with reading, the oral with the written or printed. For many children, learning a catechism was thus a step toward becoming literate in the sense of knowing how to read. (Primers, a common name for books that introduced children to reading, usually contained a catechism.) For the Native Americans, learning a catechism was an important doorway to mastering the basic elements of Christian doctrine, as the "confessions" in part VI indicate. So important was catechizing that thirteen different ministers produced versions for their own congregations; two others were written for the use of the Native Americans. Of these local texts, only John Cotton's *Spiritual Milk for Boston Babes* (1656) gained a wider audience. Eventually, most congregations came to rely on the *Shorter Catechism* (1648) produced by the Westminster Assembly of Divines.

Thomas Shepard (1605–1649) wrote *The First Principles of the Oracles of God* (1655) for his congregation in Cambridge, Massachusetts; it circulated in manuscript before being published. Working within the framework of Reformed Protestant orthodoxy, his goals were clarity and simplicity, not originality. In the portions that follow, the catechism describes Adam's fall and the intercession of Christ, the stages by which saving grace is applied to sinners, and the obligations of Christians under the "law"—this last a standard feature of catechisms in the Reformed tradition, which invariably included the Ten Commandments, as did Shepard's (omitted here). Shepard was reiterating a humanist or Scholastic commonplace when he defined "man" as "rational" and having "free will." Such ideas must not be read as anti-Calvinist.

Bibliography

Torrance (1959), containing the major Reformed catechisms, with commentary; Green (1996) on English catechisms up to 1740.

THOMAS SHEPARD

❧ *First Principles of the Oracles of God* ❧

Question. What is the best and last end of man?

Answer. To live to God (Rom. 6:10–11, Gal. 3:19, 2. Cor. 5:3, 15).

Q. How is man to live unto God?

A. Two ways. First, by faith in God (Ps. 37:3). Secondly, by observance of God (Eccles. 12:13). . . .

Q. When did God create man?

A. The sixth day (Gen. 1:27).

Q. How did God create man?

A. He made him a reasonable creature, consisting of body and an immortal soul, in the image of God (Gen. 2:7, 1:28).

Q. What is the image of God, wherein he was made?

A. That hability of man to resemble God, and wherein he was like unto God, in wisdom, holiness, righteousness, both in his nature, and in his government of himself and all creatures (Col. 3:10, Eph. 4:24, Gen. 1:26).

Q. What became of man, being thus made?

A. He was placed in the garden of Eden, as in his princely court, to live unto God, together with the woman which God gave him (Gen. 2:15). Thus much of God's creation.

Q. What is his providence?

A. Whereby he provideth for his creatures, being made, even to the least circumstance (Ps. 145:16, Prov. 16:33).

Q. How is God's providence distinguished?

A. It is either, first, ordinary and mediate, whereby he provideth for his creatures by ordinary and usual means (Hos. 2:22). Secondly, extraordinary and immediate, whereby he provideth for his creatures by miracles, or immediately by himself (Ps. 6:4, Dan. 3:17). . . .

Q. Doth God govern all creatures alike?

A. No, but some he governs by a common providence, and others by a special providence, to wit, angels and men, to an eternal estate of happiness in pleasing him, or of misery in displeasing him (Deut. 30:15–16).

Q. What of God's providence appears in his special government of man?

A. Two things. 1. Man's apostasy, or fall. 2. His recovery, or rising again.

Q. Concerning man's fall, what are you to observe therein?

A. Two things. 1. His transgression, in eating the forbidden fruit (Gen. 2:17). 2. The propagation of this unto all Adam's posterity.

Q. Was this so great a sin, to eat of the forbidden fruit?

A. Yes, exceedingly great, this tree being a sacrament of the covenant; also he had a special charge not to eat of it: and in it the whole man did strike against the whole law, even when God had so highly advanced him.

Q. What are the causes of this transgression?

A. The blameless cause was the law of God (Rom. 5:13). And hence, as the law did it, so God did it, holily, justly, and blamelessly (Rom. 7:10–12).

Q. What are the blameable causes?

A. Two, principally. 1. The devil abusing the serpent to deceive the woman (Gen. 3:1). 2. Man himself, in abusing his own free will, in receiving the temptations which he might have resisted (Eph. 7:29). . . .

Q. What are the particular punishments inflicted on the causes of this sin?

A. Besides the fearful punishment of the devils, mentioned Jude 6, and that of the serpent and the woman (Gen. 3:14, 16), the punishment of man was, first, sin original and actual. Secondly, death (Gen. 5:5).

Q. What is sin?

A. The transgression of God's law (John 3:4).

Q. What is original and actual sin?

A. First, original sin is the contrariety of the whole nature of man to the law of God, whereby it, being averse from all good, is inclined to all evil (Eccles. 8:11, Gen. 6:5, Rom. 6:20). Secondly, actual sin is the continual jarring of the actions of man from the law of God, by reason of original sin, and so man hath no free will to any spiritual good (Isa. 65:2–3, James 1:14–15, Isa. 1:11). . . .

Q. Is this sin, and the punishment of it derived to all men's posterity?

A. Yes (John 3:3, Eph. 2:3).

Q. How is it propagated?

A. By the imputation of Adam's sin unto us, and so the punishment must needs follow upon it (Rom. 5:13).

Q. Why should Adam's sin be imputed to all his posterity?

A. Because we were in him as the members in the head, as children in his loins, as debtors in their surety, as branches in their roots, it being just, that as if he standing, all had stood, by imputation of his righteousness, so he falling, all should fall, by the imputation of his sin.

Q. Thus have you seen man's apostasy from God. What is his recovery?

A. It is the return of man to the favor of God again, merely out of favor, and the exceeding riches of his free grace (Eph. 2:12–13, Rom. 5:8).

Q. How are we brought into favor, and what are the parts of this recovery?

A. Two ways. First, by redemption (2 Cor. 5:19–20). Secondly, by application hereof (Titus 3:6).

Q. What is redemption?

A. The satisfaction made, or the price paid, to the justice of God for the life and deliverance of man out of the captivity of sin, Satan, and death, by a Redeemer, according to the covenant made between him and the Father (1 Cor. 6:20, Luke 1:74, Isa. 55:10–11). . . .

Q. Thus much of redemption, the first part of his recovery. What is application?

A. Whereby the Spirit, by the Word and ministry thereof, makes all that which Christ as mediator hath done for the church, efficacious to the church as her own (John 16:14, Titus 3:5–7, John 10:16, Rom. 10:14, 17, Eph. 5:25–26).

Q. What is the church?

A. The number of God's elect (Heb. 12:23, John 17:9–11, 10:16, Eph. 1:22–23).

Q. How doth the Spirit make application to the church?

A. 1. By union of the soul to Christ (Phil. 3:9–10). 2. By communion of the benefits of Christ to the soul.

Q. What is this union?

A. Whereby the Lord, joining the soul to Christ, makes it one spirit with Christ, and so gives it possession of Christ, and right unto all the benefits and blessings of Christ (1 Cor. 6:17, John 17:21, Rom. 8:32, 1 John 5:12).

Q. How doth the Spirit make this union?

A. Two ways. 1. By cutting off the soul from the old Adam, or the wild olive tree, in the work of preparation (Rom. 11:23–24). 2. By putting or ingrafting the soul into the second Adam, Christ Jesus, by the work of vocation (Acts 26:18).

Q. What are the parts of the preparation of the soul to Christ?

A. They are two. 1. Contrition, whereby the Spirit immediately cuts off the soul from its security in sin, by making it to mourn for it, and separating the soul from it, as the greatest evil (Isa. 61:1,3, Jer. 4:3–4, Matt. 11:20, 28). 2. Humiliation, whereby the Spirit cuts the soul off from self-confidence in any good it hath or doth; especially by making it to feel its want and unworthiness of Christ, and hence submitteth to be disposed of as God pleaseth (Phil. 3:7–8, Luke 16:9, 15:17–19).

Q. What are the parts of vocation of the soul to Christ?

A. 1. The Lord's call and invitation of the soul to come to Christ, in the revelation and offer of Christ and his rich grace (2 Cor. 5:10). 2. The receiving of Christ, or the coming of the whole soul out of itself unto Christ, for Christ, by virtue of the irresistible power of the Spirit in the call, and this is faith (Jer. 3:32, John 6:44–45, 10:16, Isa. 55:5).

Q. Thus much of our union. What is the communion of Christ's benefits unto the soul?

A. Whereby the soul possessed with Christ, and right unto him, hath by the same Spirit fruition of him, and all his benefits (John 4:10, 14).

Q. What is the first of those benefits we do enjoy from Christ?

A. Justification, which is the gracious sentence of God the Father, whereby for the satisfaction of Christ apprehended by faith, and imputed to the faithful, he absolves them from the guilt and condemnation of all sins, and accepts them as perfectly righteous to eternal life (Rom. 3:24–25, 4:6–8, 8:33–34).

Q. What difference is there between justification and sanctification?

A. Justification is by Christ's righteousness inherent in Christ only; sanctification is by a righteousness from Christ inherent in ourselves (2 Cor. 5:21, Phil. 3:9). 2. Justification is perfected at once, and admits of no degrees, because it is by Christ his perfect righteousness. Sanctification is imperfect, being begun in this life (Rev. 12:1, Phil. 3:11).

Q. What is the second benefit next in order to justification, which the faithful receive from Christ?

A. Reconciliation, whereby a Christian justified is actually reconciled, and at peace with God (Rom. 5:1, John 2:12). And hence follows his peace with all creatures.

Q. What is the third benefit next unto reconciliation?

A. Adoption, whereby the Lord accounts the faithful his sons, crowns them with privileges of sons, and gives them the spirit of adoption — the same spirit which is in his only-begotten Son (1 John 3:2, Rom. 8:11, 14–17).

Q. What is the fourth benefit next to adoption?

A. Sanctification, whereby the sons of God are renewed in the whole man, unto the image of their heavenly Father in Christ Jesus, by mortification, or their daily dying to sin by virtue of Christ's death: and by vivification, their daily rising to newness of life, by Christ's resurrection (1 Thess. 5:23, Eph. 4:24, Jer. 31:32, Rom. 6:7–8).

Q. What follows from this mortification and vivification?

A. A continual war and combat between the renewed part, assisted by Father, Son, and Holy Ghost, and the unrenewed part, assisted by Satan and this evil world (Rom. 7:21–23).

Source: Thomas Shepard, *The First Principles of the Oracles of God* (London, 1655), omitting some citations of Scripture.

Chapter 6

Thomas Hooker on Vocation,
or the Gospel Promise

Thomas Hooker's contemporaries regarded him as a remarkably effective preacher of the "practical divinity." One measure of their respect is the extent to which his sermons were published in England, beginning with *The Poor Doubting Christian Drawne unto Christ* (1629) and extending well past his death in New England in 1647. Which of these books contain sermons he gave in England and which those he preached in New England is not easy to resolve,[1] but in both places he lingered on "the application of redemption," a master theme of the practical divinity. He liked to compare his sermons to a mirror in suggesting their effect on sinners: "here you have a clear looking glass, wherein you may be able to judge of the faces of the state and temper of your souls. I beseech you consider it well . . . either you have Christ in you, or you have him not in you."[2] As this quotation (from his ministry in Hartford, Connecticut) indicates, he insisted on the desolate condition of sinners and the imperative upon them to "prepare" for grace by humbling themselves and becoming sorrowful for sin. That in doing so they might fall into despair, overcome with "horror" at their own corruptions, was an everpresent possibility. Yet as he does in the text in this chapter, Hooker offered the antidote of the mercy that God offers sinners through Jesus Christ, urging those who are troubled in conscience to take comfort from the gospel promise of free grace. Christ is "able to do that for the poor sinner which all the means and things in the world could not do," he affirms in the sermon that follows.

Yet there is much the sinner must do. Faith, for Hooker, is "an energetic movement," a deeply affective response to the promise. Because faith is both passive and active, receiving and responding, it has a key place in the reciprocal relationship between divine power and human

---

[1] See Sargent Bush, Jr., "Establishing the Hooker Canon," in Williams et al. (1975), 378–89. The sermon that follows is part of a longer series Hooker preached on the stages of redemption.

[2] Quoted in Denholm (1961), 203.

activity.[3] But the anchor of this reciprocity is a God who is moved by "love and kindness" to "persuade" sinners to accept the promise. Hooker's preaching thus belies the assertion that Puritan theology was deterministic. Nor does it conform to an alternative interpretation, that preachers in New England were softening the rigors of Calvinism.

Another theme of his preaching is the difference between receiving the message of faith and repentance outwardly and receiving it in "the soul" or "the heart." This distinction brings us close to the center of Puritan preaching, with its ever reiterated emphasis on faith that is "real" or "sincere" and a corresponding critique of "formalism" or "hypocrisy." Only the first kind has any lasting significance; only when and if the Word (and Spirit) penetrated to the very core of the self would the new birth or conversion occur. Despite the importance of the distinction, Hooker, Shepard, and second-generation ministers such as Increase Mather (chap. 9) insisted on the validity and significance of the "outward" or "external" covenant as a means of grace. Doing so enabled them to defend the practice of infant baptism against the Baptists (see chap. 22), who made faith a condition of receiving the sacrament.

Bibliography

Denholm (1961); Williams et al. (1975); Bush (1980), chap. 10; Gallagher and Werge (1976).

THOMAS HOOKER

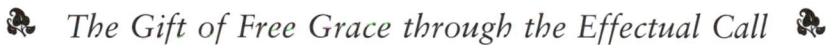

The Gift of Free Grace through the Effectual Call

*Every man therefore that hath heard and hath learned
of the Father cometh unto me.*
—John 6:45

The ingrafting of the humble and broken-hearted sinner into Christ, as we have heard, consists of two particular passages: the first was being put into the stock; secondly, the ingrafting into the same [Rom. 11:16–21]. As in ingrafting naturally, so of implanting spiritually of the soul into Christ. When the soul is brought unto this, then a sinner comes to be partaker of all the spiritual benefits: all shall be communicated to us. Now the point at this present to be handled is called by the stream of divines [theologians] vocation, and I term it the putting in of the soul when the soul is brought out of the world of sin to lie upon and to close

---

[3] Bush (1980), 205.

with the Lord Jesus Christ. And this hath two particular passages in it: partly the call on God's part, partly the answer on ours. The call on God's part is this: when the Lord by the call of his gospel doth so clearly reveal the fullness of mercy and certifies to the soul by the work of his Spirit that the soul humbled returns answer to God's call.

In the first, observe two passages: first, the means whereby God will call the sinner unto him. The sinner is afraid to appear before God whom he hath offended, and [who] may therefore proceed in justice against him for those sins which have been committed by him. Now besides the law which discovers a man's sin unto him, he now prepares another means, the voice of his gospel. He lets in many sweet inklings into the soul, of his love and kindness, to allure him, to call him and draw him to himself.

Secondly, the Lord doth not only appoint the means, namely, the ministry of his gospel, whereby the soul may be brought unto him and receive communion with him; but by the work of his Spirit he doth bring all the riches of his grace into the soul truly humbled, so that the heart cannot but receive the same and give answer thereto and give an echo of the subjection of itself to be governed thereby. That we have finished already. There must be hearing before coming, not of the law, to terrify a man,[4] but of the gospel, to persuade and allure a man to come unto the Lord and receive mercy and kindness from him. The gospel is the means ordained by God to call home the soul unto him. But this will not do the deed. There must be something else or the sinner will be at a stand and cannot come on cheerfully and receive the grace offered him. Therefore besides the means, we have the special cause expressed, which is the Lord. For when a man hath heard, that is one thing; but that is not all, for the principal cause is the Lord. God the Father alone can buckle the heart to receive the grace appointed and the mercy offered to the soul; and without the principal cause, all other means, I mean the ministers of the gospel, although it be *a savor of life unto life*, yet it may be *a savor of death unto death* [2 Cor. 2:16], unless the Spirit of the Lord goes with it. For when the gospel is only revealed to the understanding,[5] and that only conceives of the letter thereof, and it soaks not and sinks not into the heart: this we call an outward call-

---

[4] To preach "the law" was, quite commonly, linked with preaching "terror": that is, preaching that under the law all humans stood condemned, without hope of eternal life. See Hall (1972), 163–64.

[5] "God made man an understanding creature, indued with rational faculties, the understanding to be the leading faculty, and the will to be the appetite of the soul, according to reason." John Davenport, *The Saints Anchor-Hold, In All Storms and Tempests* (London, 1661), 66. This succinct description of the "faculty psychology" on which the ministers depended is amplified in Miller (1939), chaps. 9–10; Fiering (1972).

ing; that is the phrase of divines. When some light flash is imparted and communicated unto the soul and is not set on sufficiently, that is an outward calling. But when God the Father doth accompany the dispensation of the gospel with the powerful operation of the Spirit, and it puts its hand to the key of the gospel and unlocks a blind mind and a hard heart, there the soul learns thoroughly and effectually the way of salvation.

. . . I will discourse four questions unto you, which will be useful for the clear explication of the text: first, what the lesson is that a man must learn before he come; secondly, why the Father is said to teach, and not the Son, nor the Holy Ghost; thirdly, what is the manner how the Father doth teach the soul when he will call it home to himself; fourthly, what is the frame and disposition of the soul, how doth the heart behave itself when it hath in truth learned the lesson. When the Lord will propound unto and learn the souls of his that belong to him, you must not think the truth tedious, because they will give us light into all the truth that shall be hereafter discussed out of the Word.

He that hath heard and learned of the Father, what is the lesson that he must learn before he can come? . . . For answer hereunto, the lesson that the soul must learn is this, namely, the fullness of the mercy and grace and salvation that God the Father hath provided and also offered to the poor humbled sinner in and through the Lord Jesus Christ, which indeed is able to do that for a poor sinner which all the means and things in the world could not do and yet notwithstanding he needs. I have heretofore discussed the poor miserable plight which a sinner hath brought himself into by his manifold rebellions. There is no help, no hope of himself in what he hath or doth to relieve and succor himself, and therefore he falls flat at the footstool of the Almighty and is content to be at his disposing. Now the lesson that the soul must learn is the fullness, greatness, and freeness of the perfect salvation which is brought unto us through the Lord Jesus Christ. And that we may not learn this lesson by halves but fully and perfectly, and that your minds may conceive of the same, give me leave to lay it out fully, because it will be profitable for our ensuing discourse; and this lesson discovers itself in three things, as in three lines, as I may so term it.

The first is this, that the soul may learn there is enough sufficiency in the mercy of God to fill up all the empty chinks of the soul and supply all the wants that a sinner hath and relieve him in all those necessities that either do or can befall him. This is the condition of every son of man since the fall of Adam, that there is not only a great deal of weakness in the soul, but there is a great deal of wants and emptiness in the soul.

Now this is the fullness of the mercy of God, that whatsoever our weaknesses, wants, or necessities be, there is full sufficiency enough in that mass to fill up all and to give the soul full content in every particular. . . . Be your miseries what they can be, here is relief seasonable and suitable to all your wants, miseries, and necessities. Nay, this is not only for the present necessity. Mercy is not only able to relieve your present necessity but your future also. It is not with mercy as with the widow of Sarepta, who thought when the meal in the barrel, and the oil in the cruse was spent, she should then surely perish [1 Kings 17:12]. No, it is not so in the fullness and sufficiency of this mercy; it hath not only enough to do you good for the present and to succor you in all present wants; but what miseries soever shall befall thee, or what troubles shall betide thee for future times, the fullness of God's mercy lays in provision against such necessities and times of miseries and vexations. For a poor sinner may be driven to a stand after this manner: It is true, saith the sinner, I have heretofore committed many sins. God hath sealed up the pardon of them unto me, and those sins which have heretofore pleased me, God hath given me a sight of them in some power and measure against them. But what if more sins, if more temptations, if more corruptions, if more guilt, if more horror seize upon my heart, how then shall I succor myself? But now this is the fullness and sufficiency of mercy: it doth not only ease a man in regard of present necessity, but lays provision for all future wants and calamities that can befall the soul (Ps. 130:7). . . . Therefore he is called the Father of mercy, as who should say, he begets mercy, even a generation of mercies, from day to day; and it is a large generation of new mercies framed and made to encourage poor souls. Therefore it is said, *With the Lord there is a fountain of life* [Ps. 36:9]. Look, as it is with a fountain, there is not only water in it for the present, but it feeds several cocks and conduits and, though it runs out daily, it enlargeth itself daily: so with the Lord there is a fountain of life. If there be a fountain of death in thy soul, in regard of thy sins to kill thee; so a fountain in God to quicken thee. Hence it comes to pass that the Lord, speaking of his mercy, calls it *the exceeding riches of his mercy* (Eph. 2:7). I say, the Lord hath not only fullness of mercy, but he is rich in all his fullness. Nay, he exceeds in all the riches of the fullness of his mercy. . . .

Then [let me] wind up the point: thou seest, thou findest, thou feelest many sorrows now assailing thee; thou expectest more trouble to befall thee, and thou dost conceive more than thou dost fear. Thy sorrows outbid thy heart, thy fears outbid thy sorrows, and thy thoughts go beyond thy fears; and yet here is the comfort of a poor soul: in all his misery and wretchedness, the mercy of the Lord outbids all these, whatsoever may, can, or shall befall thee. Gather, then, up briefly and shut up this first passage. Many are the sorrows of the righteous, guilt of sin perplexing the sinner, and filthiness of sins tyrannizing and domineering over the soul; nay, many fears and cares for future times. For a sinner saith, Sometimes my condition is marvelous poor, my estate marvelous miserable. What if small temptations, what if small corruptions, what if such a fall should betide me, what then shall become of my soul? Nay, a man's imagination exceeds all fears. The soul thinks with itself, Should the Lord deal in justice, and should my sins get the victory over me, which I hope will never be, for what shall I then do for succor? Yet this is the comfort of a poor soul; let it read this lesson: the Lord is able, and mercy can do excessive, exceeding abundantly above all. Thy sorrows are abundant; thy fears are very abundant; thy imaginations are excessive, exceeding abundant, exceeding above all present sorrows, above all future fear, and above the course of all imaginations. This discourse shall serve for the first passage.

We will now add the second. The soul is not yet fully satisfied, but replies, It is true, there is bread enough in my Father's house; that I yield, and that I confess. There is abundance of mercy in God, a world of mercy that pardoned Manasses and saved Saul. . . . This is the tenor of mercy: God requires of a man that he should believe; now mercy doth help to perform the duty commanded. The Lord, as he requires the condition of thee, so he worketh the condition in thee. He makes thee believe that thou shalt be saved as there is fullness of grace in himself to do thee good if thou dost receive the same. This is the difference between the two covenants, the covenant of works and the covenant of grace.[6] The first covenant runs, Adam shall do and live. Now it stood upon the use and abuse of his free will, either to do the will of God, and be blessed; or to break the law, and be cursed. It was in his power to receive the life, and thus either by breach or not doing the condition required, Adam must perform. But it is not so here. The Lord indeed requires a condition: No man can be saved but he must believe; but here is the privilege: that the Lord as he makes this condition with the soul, so also he keepeth us in performing the condition, for the Lord he requires that the soul should rest upon him, and he makes him also to do it; he requires the soul to cleave unto him. There is the tenor of this covenant: *A new heart will I give you, and a new spirit I will put within you, and I will take away your stony heart and give you a heart of flesh, and I will put my spirit within you and cause you to walk in my statutes* (Ezek. 36:26–27). Or if they will walk in my ways, out of thine own power, then I will vouchsafe this mercy and favor. Now the Lord re-

---

[6] A key term in the Antinomian controversy, the "covenant of works" refers to the relationship between God and Adam that was broken with Adam's disobedience and, more largely, to the uselessness of obedience to the law ("works") under the gospel dispensation of grace.

quires this condition and works it also in his children; he requires this of them, and he works this in them, for their everlasting good. The Lord saith, *This is the covenant I will make with the house of Israel; I write my laws in their hearts, and they shall not need to be taught* (Heb. 8:9). Men must know God and believe in the Lord. Now as the Lord requires this as the condition of the covenant, so the Lord will work this in them, as he requires this of them. John 1:12 the text saith, *To them that believe, he gave them power to be the sons of God.* Now if a man will believe, he shall be saved. Now then he makes a man believe that he may be a son. This is the second passage whereby the soul of a sinner comes to be cheered: for that there is not only abundance of sufficiency in the Lord Jesus Christ, but that mercy, as it is able to do him good, so it will make him partaker of the good.

The third particular is this: that as mercy hath all good and will make us partakers of what it hath, so also it will dispose of us and of that it bestoweth upon us. Mercy will not only have a sinner, but it will rule and order that grace it hath bestowed upon the soul. For if mercy purchase a soul at so high a rate as the blood of the Lord Jesus, it is right that the soul purchased by grace and supplied with grace, that mercy should dispose it for the honor of God. *You are not your own*, saith the Apostle, *but bought with a price* [1 Cor. 6:19–20]. Therefore you must glorify the Lord in body and soul. Nay, it is not only right that mercy should do it, but reason, and beneficial to the soul that mercy should do thus. Nay, I say, unless that mercy should rule a man, he had not been able to give full content to the soul. If the Lord should leave any poor soul to the destiny of his own heart and the malice of Satan, he would run to ruin presently. He is not able to supply his own wants and to dispose of his own spirit and employ aright his own soul. For if Adam in his innocency had a stock in his own hands, fell and perished; then if mercy should put a man into the same estate that Adam was, a man should bring himself into the same misery that Adam was brought into. But there is that fullness of that mercy that is in Christ, that it will bestow all good needful for me; so also, it will dispose of that good in me so that Satan shall never prevail, the world shall never overcome, nor my corruptions bear sway in me; but the Lord shall rule me forever. And this is the fullness of God's mercy. Gather up the point, then, that we may see what we must learn. There is sufficiency in mercy to supply all wants. Nay, there is ability in mercy to communicate that it hath and we stand in need of. Nay, mercy will preserve us; and that it giveth to us against all oppositions that can befall thee. This is the lesson that the soul must learn that it may be able in some measure to see the way and learn the path that leadeth to everlasting happiness. This is the first lesson that the soul must learn of God the Father.

For the use of this. Is this the lesson the soul must learn? Then look wisely upon it, and when this comes upon thee, and sorrow assails thee heavily, do not look into the black book of conscience and think there to find supply. Neither look into the book of the privileges and performances and think to find power out of thy own sufficiency. Look not on thy sins to pore upon them, whereby thou shalt be discouraged; neither look into thy own sufficiency, thinking thereby to procure anything to thyself. These are but lessons of the lower form. It is true, thou must see thy sins and sorrow for them; but this is for the lower form, and thou must get this lesson beforehand. And when thou hast gotten this lesson of contrition and humiliation, look only to God's mercy, and the riches of his grace; and be sure as you take out this lesson, take it not out by halves, for then you wrong mercy, and yourselves too, if you think that bare works will serve, and that is all. No, no, mercy will rule you. Therefore take all the lesson out, and then the heart will be cheered, and thy soul in some measure enabled to come on to the Lord and will see some glimpses of consolation from the Spirit. . . .

The third question is this: after what manner doth the Lord teach the soul? Christ speaks now of the work of the Spirit; and that you may not be mistaken, know this, that the work of the Spirit doth always go with and is communicated by the Word. Therefore if the question be, after what manner doth God teach the soul to spell out this lecture of mercy and pardon?

I answer briefly: the Lord teacheth the soul by his Spirit. I told you that before that not only the Father, but the Son and Holy Ghost also teacheth, the Father from himself, the Son from the Father, and the Holy Ghost from both. Therefore understand what I say. The Spirit of the Lord doth not only in the general make known God's mercy, but doth in particular, with strength of evidence, present to the broken-hearted sinner the right of the freeness of God's grace to the soul. Nay, it holds those special considerations to the heart and presenteth the heart with them. Not only so, but in the second place, the Spirit doth forcibly soak in the relish of that grace into the heart, and by the over-piercing work doth leave some dint of supernatural and spiritual virtue on the heart. The Spirit doth not only with truth bring home the evidence to the heart, but it is still whispering, and calling, and making known the same, and forcibly soaketh in the relish of the freeness of God's grace, and leaveth a dint of supernatural virtue upon the soul. We will express the points because it is somewhat difficult and is the scope of that place (2 Tim. 1:7), *The Lord hath not given you the spirit of fear, but of a sound mind.* The spirit of fear is the spirit of bondage, in humiliation and contrition. When the Spirit showeth a man his sins and showeth him that he is in bondage and in fetters, lets him get out how he can: this is the spirit of fear and of bondage. In the second place, there is the spirit of power. But what is this spirit of power? You must imagine this spirit of power doth not intimate any particular grace, but [is] as it were the sinews and strength of the work of the Spirit, conveying itself through the frame of the heart. And this I term to be the effectual work of the Spirit of God. When the soul is humbled, the Lord sweetly communicates into the soul a supernatural and spiritual virtue. Lastly, as it is in nature: take a knife, if it be rubbed on a lodestone, it will draw iron unto it. Now it cannot do that because it is a knife, but because it is rubbed on a stone and receives virtue therefrom. So it is with a heart humbled: it is a fit subject for the grace of God to work upon. The love of God is like the lodestone, and if the heart be rubbed thereupon and affected with the sweetness thereof, it will be able to close with that mercy and come to that mercy and go to God from whence that mercy comes.

What is the behavior of the soul, when it hath learned this lesson from the Lord?

I answer, when these two things meet together in the soul, then it hath learned two lessons. The first is this: when the soul, having heard of that plentiful redemption that is in Christ, as also having apprehended the revelation thereof, it cometh to close with the work of the Spirit, revealing, presenting, and offering grace to the heart. Nay, it comes to give entertainment to the riches of that mercy revealed to the soul. There is in the mercy of God, and in the blessed truth of the promises, a great excellency. Now when this is so plentifully brought home to the heart that it breaks through all oppositions which may hinder the work of the Spirit upon the soul, when it is brought home by the Spirit of God, and the heart gives way and closes with it, so that there is nothing between that and the soul; this I take to be the first frame of the soul that begins to learn this lesson. It begins to close to the truth, to give way to the sweetness that is in it, and bids adieu to all delight [in] sins and whatsoever may be a hindrance unto it from receiving of this grace into the soul. This is the first passage.

The second, with which I will conclude, is this, that as the soul closeth with that mercy and welcometh it, and the heart is content to take up mercy upon those terms, so in the second place there is an impression and disposition left upon the soul that it is framed and disposed. There is a kind of print which the soul hath with it, so that as the mercy of God is revealed to the soul and communicated to the soul, so there is a kind of impression, frame, and print, which the heart retaineth and hath wrought upon it by this grace and free favor of God made known. Therefore that phrase Romans 6:17 is a marvelous pattern to our purpose. The text saith, *They were delivered to this form of doctrine.* Look as it is with a seal: if the seal be set to the wax and leave an impression, just so many letters upon the wax as in the seal, then it is wholly sealed. So the Spirit of God through Christ in the promises doth reveal all the freeness and grace of mercy in Christ. Now when the Spirit doth leave an impression on the soul, that man is delivered into the truth. I conclude all in Acts 26:18. When Saul was sent to preach to the Gentiles, the text saith, he was but *to bring them out of darkness into light.* Mark, when the Lord doth come to work effectually upon the soul, he brings men from under the power of darkness. Whereas the understanding was dark and blinded, when the Spirit comes, it turns it from the darkness and power of sin, unto the power of light and grace.

Lastly, the power of the heart doth these two things: for not only some of the heart must be brought to God, but the whole heart, therefore in the precious promises of grace and salvation there is fullness of all good to draw all the faculties of the soul unto the Lord. And therefore the faithfulness and the truth of God is mainly revealed in the promises. Now that fits the understanding and makes it look to God for pardon, for power, and mercy.

Source: Thomas Hooker, "The Soules effectuall Calling to Christ," in *The Soules Vocation* (London, 1638), 33–48.

Chapter 7

Thomas Shepard on Sin

Thomas Shepard (1605–1649), who first appears in this book describing his ministry in England (chap. 3), was famous in his day for insisting on the "saving work" of humiliation for sin and for warning of the dangers of hypocrisy. Jonathan Mitchell, who attended services in the Cambridge church where Shepard preached, noted in his diary that "a terrible and excellent sermon of Mr. Shepard's awakened me. He taught, that there are some seem to be found and saved by Christ, and yet afterwards they perish."[1]

Shepard's practical divinity had several dimensions, only one of which is indicated in the passage on sin that follows. Here, his purpose is to lead people to experience the reality of their condition as sinners. In Shepard's model of the order of salvation, the first step or stage after being "effectually called" is an intellectual "conviction" of sin, followed by "compunction," the stage he is describing in this passage. Shepard directed this advice alike at saints, hypocrites, the indifferent, and the hostile, for he knew from his own spiritual history that the saints invariably became careless about sin and that the visible church contained hypocrites who excused themselves from doing what was necessary. In passages not repeated here, Shepard speaks at length of Christ's compassion for sinners and the offer of free grace.

Bibliography
Cohen (1986), chaps. 6–7, describing the relationship between Shepard's preaching and the confessions made in Cambridge; Hall (1989), chap. 3; Winship (2002); Gallagher and Werge (1976).

THOMAS SHEPARD

 *The Sound Believer*

. . . A sinner will never part with his sin; a bare conviction of sin doth but light the candle to see sin; compunction burns his fingers, and that

---

[1] Cotton Mather, *Magnalia Christi Americana* (1702; repr., 2 vols., 1853), 2:84–85; and for other contemporary estimations, John A. Albro, *Life of Thomas Shepard* (1847); repr., *Works of Thomas Shepard*, 3 vols. (Boston, 1853), 1: cxxii.

only makes him dread the fire. *Cleanse your hands, ye sinners, and purify your hearts, ye double-minded men*, saith the Apostle James (4:8). But how should this be done? He answers (v. 9), *Be afflicted, and mourn, and weep; turn your laughter into mourning*. So Joel 2:12. The prophet calls upon his hearers to turn from their sin unto the Lord; but how? *Rend your hearts, and not your garments* [Joel 2:13]. Not that they were able to do this, but by what sorrow he requires of all in general he thereby effectually works in the hearts of all the elect in particular; for every man naturally takes pleasure, nay, all his delight and pleasure is in nothing else but sin. . . . And therefore it undeniably follows, that the Lord must first put gall and wormwood to those dugs, before the soul will cease sucking, or be weaned from them; the Lord must first make sin bitter, before it will part with it; load it with sin, before it will sit down and desire ease. And look, as the pleasure in sin is exceeding sweet to a sinner, so the sorrow for it must be exceeding bitter, before the soul will part from it.

It is true, I confess, a man sometime may part with sin without sorrow; the unclean spirit may go out for a time, before he is taken, bound, and slain by the power of Christ. But such a kind of parting is but the washing of the cup; it is unsafe and unsound, and the end of such a Christian will be miserable: for a man to hear of his sin, and then to say, I will do no more so, without any sense of sorrow for it, would not have been approved by Paul. . . . No, the Lord abhors such whorish wiping the lips. . . .

But you will say, what is this compunction, and wherein doth it consist? . . . In general it is whereby the soul is affected with sin, and made sensible of sin; but more particularly, compunction is nothing else but the pricking of the heart, or the wounding of the soul with such fear and sorrow for sin and misery as severs the soul from sin. . . .

I say the Lord Christ, in this work of compunction, lets into the heart of a secure sinner a marvelous fear and terror of the direful displeasure of God, of death, and hell, the punishment of sin. Oh beloved, look upon most men at this day; this is the great misery lying upon them, they do not fear the wrath to come, they fear not death nor damning, even then when they hear and know it is their portion. . . .

The Lord Christ therefore lets in this fear . . . before Christ come, the soul may see its misery, but it apprehends it far off, and hoping to escape it, and hence doth not fear it; but when the Lord Jesus comes, he presents a man's danger, death, wrath, and eternity near unto him, and hence hath no hope to escape it, as now he is, and therefore doth fear; and seeing the misery exceeding great, he hath an exceeding great (though ofttimes deep) fear of it; as men near death, and apprehending it so, begin then to be troubled, and cry out when it is too late. . . .

Hence it follows that they are strong fears, because the almighty hand of the Spirit sets them on, and shakes the soul; they are not weak fears, which a man can shake off, or cure by weak hopes, sleep, or business, etc., like some winds that shake the tree, but never blow it down; but these fears cast down the tallest cedar, and appall the heart, and cool the courage and boldness of the most impenitent and audacious sinner. . . . And hence you shall observe, if the soul, after sad fears, grows bold and careless again, the Spirit pursues it with more cause of fear; and now the soul cries out, Did the Lord ever elect thee? Christ shed his blood to save his people *from* their sins; thou livest yet *in* thy sins. Did he ever shed his blood for thee? Thou hast sinned against conscience after thou hast been enlightened, and fallen back again. Hast not thou therefore committed the impardonable sin? . . . Is not the day of grace therefore now past? . . . Thus the Spirit pursues with strong fears till [the] proud man falls down to the dust before God.

Source: Thomas Shepard, *The Sound Believer* (London, 1645), 57–58, 64–67, 69–71.

Chapter 8

The Antinomian Controversy
John Cotton Debates the Other Ministers

Much to everyone's surprise, the ministers who had arrived in New England by the mid-1630s discovered that they had different ways of preaching the "practical divinity." Tensions emerged around a handful of questions that owed their importance to circumstances of the 1630s, like the policy of requiring candidates for church membership to describe the "work of grace" and the complaints of "deadness" that were a sign of the colonists' high hopes for deeper, more fervent experiences of grace and holiness now that they were liberated from the "corruptions" of the Church of England.[1] Another reason the ministers began to distrust each other was the influence of Anne Hutchinson (1591– 1643), who was telling lay men and women that most of the ministers were false teachers who had not received the "seal of the Spirit." She asserted as well that people could not trust the "signs" or "work" of "sanctification" as evidence that they were saved. Terming such evidence "legal," she urged people to rely on the "witness of the Spirit," advice that John Cotton reiterated in his sermons.[2]

By mid-1636 the ministers were beginning to worry about the divisive consequences of Mrs. Hutchinson's message and to wonder whether Cotton was responsible for it, as Hutchinson seems to have implied. After a face-to-face meeting in October 1636 with Cotton, Mrs. Hutchinson, and another minister sympathetic to her position (John Wheelwright), the ministers in December drew up a list of "points, wherein they suspected Mr. Cotton did differ from them, and . . . propounded them to him, and pressed him to a direct answer, affirmative or negative, to every one." Cotton answered these questions, the ministers reviewed in writing his responses, and Cotton responded at much

---

[1] The "confessions" of candidates for membership in Cambridge frequently refer to deadness under "the means of grace."

[2] Hall (1968), 412; for Cotton's warnings to this effect, see *A Sermon Preached . . . At Salem* (Boston, 1713), and the sermon series *The New Covenant; or, A Treatise unfolding the order and maner of the giving and receiving of the Covenant of Grace to the Elect* (London, 1654).

greater length.[3] Debate continued, with Cotton responding (probably during the summer) to the "only three things of weight [that] are left controversial." The text of his response, which incorporates "objections" by the other ministers, follows. In September a special synod of the ministers produced a list of eighty-two "errours," each accompanied by a "confutation." Some of these can be traced to Cotton or Hutchinson or possibly Henry Vane, who defended a Spirit-centered path of salvation in his later years in England, but it is also likely that the list was based on opinions the ministers had encountered in England or found in books.

The debates between the ministers turned into a rhetorical morass, for each side painted the other as doctrinally suspect.[4] Rhetorical excess aside, certain differences were real. How were earnest Christians to gain assurance of salvation? What outward signs could be relied upon as evidence of the interior, invisible workings of grace? For Shepard and his allies, Christians could count on reliable "marks and signs" of the work of grace, reliable because hypocrites could not sustain a life of righteousness. Human activities such as repentance and "holiness," properly evaluated, were such signs. These ministers also argued that the Holy Spirit worked through a regularly instituted "means of grace," the ministries of preaching and sacraments. The Holy Spirit and the human will always collaborated, with faith being understood as an active response to the "effectual call," or gospel promise of salvation. Summing up this theory, one historian has remarked that the "spiritual rebirth" of humans "is accomplished through created means, including [their] own distinctively human faculties." From this angle of vision the gospel promise was conditional in the sense of requiring a human response, although the ministers were quick to add, as Hooker said in *The Soules Vocation*, that the promise was also utterly without conditions, or "absolute."[5]

John Cotton declared that the true saint waited, without acting, on the motions of the Holy Spirit. Faith for him was "passive," and the only certain basis of assurance was the "witness of the Spirit." Sanctification was, at best, a secondary "sign," not a "first evidence." He defended himself by citing a roster of sixteenth- and early-seventeenth-century Reformers, especially Calvin: "Let Calvin answer for me," he remarks in the text that follows.[6] Eventually, in his final set of answers

---

[3] These exchanges were published for the first time in Hall (1968).

[4] See Shepard's autobiography (chap. 3 above); Shepard, *The Parable of the Ten Virgins Opened & Applyed* (London, 1660); repr. in *The Works of Thomas Shepard*, ed. John Albro, 3 vols. (Boston, 1853), 2:241; chap. 14.

[5] Stoever (1978), 63; Hall (1968), 229 n. 25.

[6] The annotations and index in Hall (1968) indicate Cotton's sources.

to questions, he conceded that sanctification could be "a firm and strong argument" for justification and that the Holy Spirit "doth evidence our justification both ways, sometime in an absolute promise, sometime in a conditional."[7]

Bibliography

This sketch of the debate between the ministers relies on Stoever (1978), Cohen (1986), Dever (2000), and the sources. Hall (1968, 1991); Miller (1943); Knight (1994); Winship (2002); Gallagher and Werge (1976).

JOHN COTTON

A Conference . . . Held at Boston

A conference that Mr. John Cotton had with the elders of the congregations in New-England, touching three questions that are here discussed on:

Upon revisal of all that hath been written by our brethren, only three things of weight are left controversial, if my hopes fail me not.

1. Touching gracious conditions, or qualifications, wrought in the soul before faith.
2. Touching the gathering of our first evident assurance of our faith from sanctification.
3. Touching the active power of faith, and other spiritual gifts of grace in a Christian conversation. . . .

QUESTION 1. Whether there be any gracious conditions, or qualifications, in the soul before faith, of dependence unto which, such promises are made?

You grant it. We deny it, for these reasons. Reason 1. If there be any gracious conditions, or qualifications, wrought in us before faith of dependence; then, before we receive union with Christ: the reason is, for by faith of dependence it is, that we first received union with Jesus Christ, John 1:12. But there be no gracious conditions wrought in us before we received union with Jesus Christ; therefore there be no gracious conditions, or qualifications, wrought in us before faith of dependence. Minor [reason]. If we cannot bring forth good fruit, till we be good trees; nor become good trees, until we be grafted or united unto Jesus Christ; then there can be no gracious conditions, or qualifications,

---

[7] Ibid., 195, 401, 405, quoting *The Way of Congregational Churches Cleared* (1648), where he printed answers to five questions that overlap his responses of midsummer.

wrought in us, before we receive union with Christ. But we cannot bring forth good fruit, till we become good trees; nor become trees of righteousness, until we be grafted into Jesus Christ. . . . A second proof of the minor. If there be any gracious conditions, or qualifications wrought in us before union with Christ, then we may be in a state of grace and salvation, before we be in Christ: But that cannot be: Acts 4:12, *Neither is there salvation in any other; for there is none other name under heaven given amongst men, whereby we may be saved.* Reason 2. If there be any gracious condition or qualification in us before faith, then there may be something in us pleasing unto God before faith: But there is nothing in us pleasing unto God before faith; for without faith (and therefore before faith) it is impossible to please God. . . .

Objection. But there must be some saving preparatives wrought in the soul, to make way for faith, and our union with Christ. For we must be cut off from the old Adam, before we can be grafted into the new: We must be dead to the first husband, before we can be married unto another.

Answer. 1. To works of creation there needeth no preparation; the almighty power of God calleth them to be his people, that were not his people, 1 Pet. 2:10. And by calling them to be so, he maketh them to be so, Rom. 9:25–26: *As he saith in Hosea, I will call them, my people, which were not my people; and her, beloved, which was not beloved. V. 26, And it shall come to pass that in the place where it is said unto them, Ye are not my people, there shall they be called, the children of the living God.* . . .

We are dead to our first husband, the law by the body of Christ, Rom. 7:4, and therefore it is by the virtue of Christ's death we have fellowship with Christ; and that giveth the deadly stroke unto our first husband.

Question 2. Whether a man may evidence his justification by his sanctification?

The state of the question is thus unfolded. It is granted of all hands.

First, to take a man's sanctification, for an evident cause or ground of his justification, is flat popery. Secondly, to take a man's sanctification, for an evident cause or ground of that faith whereby he is justified, is utterly unsafe; for faith is built upon Jesus, the Christ, the head cornerstone, Eph. 2:20, Matt. 16:16, and not upon works: A good work floweth from faith not faith from them.

Thirdly, to take common sanctification, that is, such a reformation and a change of life as floweth only from a spirit of bondage, restraining from sin, and constraining unto duty, and sometimes accompanied with enlargement and comforts in duty; yet without the sense and feeling of the need of Christ, and before union with him, to take such a sanctification for an evident sign of justification, is to build upon a false and sandy foundation.

Fourthly, that when a man hath first attained assurance of faith, of his justification, by the witness of the Spirit of Christ, in a free promise of grace, made to him in the blood of Christ, Acts 13:38–39, so he may discern, and take his sanctification as a secondary witness, for an evident sign and effect of his justification.

Thus far we consent. There remaineth controverted this question. Whether a man may gather his first evidence . . . of his justification from his sanctification?

You hold the affirmative. We hold in the negative part.

The first argument. As Abraham came to the first assurance of his justification, so we, and all that believe, as Abraham did; for he is made a pattern to us in point of justification. . . . But Abraham came to his first assurance of justification not from his sanctification, not from any promise made thereunto, but from a free promise of grace; Rom. 4:18, *Who against hope, believed in hope, that he might become the father of many nations: according to that which was spoken, So shall thy seed be.* V. 19, *And being not weak in faith, he considered not his own body, now dead, when he was above an hundred years old, neither the deadness of Sarah's womb.* V. 20, *He staggered not at the promise of God through unbelief, but was strong in faith, giving glory to God.* V. 21, *And being fully persuaded that what he had promised he was able to perform.* V. 22, *And therefore it was imputed unto him for righteousness.*

The promise was absolute, and free, so shall thy seed be as the stars of heaven: this he believed with full assurance of faith, resting only on the faithfulness and grace, and power of him that promised, Rom. 4:21. Therefore we, and all the children of Abraham, come to our first assurance of our justification, not from our sanctification, or from any promise made thereunto; but from the free promise of grace. . . .

The proof of the proposition. It will not stand with the righteousness of God to declare and pronounce a man just, upon the sight of such an imperfect righteousness, as our best sanctification is: And therefore when God declareth, and pronounceth us righteous; he doth it not upon any sight of any sanctification, or righteousness of ours: but only upon the sight of the perfect righteousness of Christ imputed unto us. . . .

The third argument. If the promise be made sure of God unto faith out of grace, then it is not first made sure to faith out of works. But the promise is made sure of God to faith out of grace, Rom. 4:5, *To him that worketh not, but believeth on him*, that justifieth the ungodly, his faith is accounted for righteousness. Therefore the promise is not first made sure to faith out of works.

Proof of the major. From the opposition of grace, and works, Rom. 11:6, *And if by grace then it is no more of works; otherwise grace is no more grace.*

Objection [1]. The opposition standeth not only between grace and works, but between grace and the merit of works; now no man ascribeth assurance of faith in the promise to the merits of works.

ANSWER. The opposition standeth not only between grace and the merit of works: but also between grace and the debt due to works; for so the Apostle Paul expresseth it, Rom. 4:4, *Now to him that worketh is the reward not reckoned of grace, but of debt.*

If the assurance of faith of our justification do spring from sight of sanctification, it is by right of some promise made unto such a work, and the right which a man hath by promise to a work, maketh the assurance of the promise, but due debt unto him: and then the promise is not sure to him out of grace. . . .

Objection 2. In 2 Pet. 1 from v. 5–10 the Apostle exhorteth us, by adding one gift of sanctification to another, to *make our calling and election sure*.

ANSWER. Let Calvin answer for me: This assurance (saith he) whereof Peter speaketh, by adding grace to grace, is not in my judgment to be referred unto conscience, as if the faithful did thereby before God come to know themselves called, and chosen; but if any man will understand it by making it sure before men, there will be no absurdity in this sense: Nevertheless it might be extended further, that everyone may be confirmed in their calling, by their godly and holy life. But that is a proof, not from the cause; but from a sign, and effect.[8]

Objection 3. There be many conditional promises in the gospel, which are made to the gifts and duties of sanctification; which are all in vain, if poor drooping souls, finding such gifts, and duties of sanctification in themselves, may not take comfort from them, according to the promise.

ANSWER 1. The conditional promises are made to poor drooping souls, not in respect of such conditions, or as they are qualified with such gifts and duties of sanctification; but in respect of their union with Christ. . . . Whereupon, we look for the blessing, not in our gifts and duties: but in going still unto Christ, for a clearer and fuller manifesta-

---

[8] John Calvin, *Commentarius in Petri Apostoli Epistolam Posteriorem*; repr. in *Opera . . . Omnia* (1896), 55, cols. 447–50. Cotton referred to Calvin several other times in the *Conference*; see Hall (1968) for specifics.

tion of him to us, and of comfort in him. As for example, a thirsty soul, to whom promise is made that he shall be satisfied; he looketh not presently to be satisfied from his thirsting, nor from any right his thirsting might give him in the promise; but he looketh to be satisfied by going unto Christ, in drinking more abundantly of him by his Spirit, as Christ himself directeth such drooping souls to do. . . .

ANSWER 3. Such conditional promises are not in vain, though poor drooping souls have found no comfort by them, and though they cannot suck present comfort from them, and from their good conditions according to them. Reason 1. Because these promises being dispensed in a covenant of free grace made in Christ, by them do work (if they were not wrought before) or at least confirm such conditions in the soul. . . . Reason 2. The promises are not in vain to such souls, in whom such good conditions are wrought; because they direct them where they may find comfort, and satisfying to their hearts' desire: to wit, not by clearing their good conditions in themselves; but by coming unto Christ, and drinking a more full draught of his Spirit; as Christ directeth thirsty souls to do, in the place even now alleged John 7:37, *If any man thirst, let him come to me, and drink.* . . .

I come now to the third and last controversy, if indeed it be a controversy, and not some mistake, as I would gladly hope it is.

If our brethren do conceive that gifts of sanctification though they be living and active, yet they are not active of themselves to any spiritual holy duty acceptable to God but as faith is active in them: and if they conceive that faith though it be living, yet is not active to go out of itself to Christ, but as it is stirred up and helped of Christ by his Spirit then there is no controversy left in this case. . . . Only because in this part concerning the activeness of faith, this controversy remaineth. . . . Whether faith concur as an active instrumental cause to our justification?

. . . Now in this we all consent; that in receiving the gift of faith we are merely passive. But yet a double question here ariseth.

QUESTION 1. Whether in receiving of Christ (or the Spirit, who cometh into our hearts in his Name) we be merely passive?

QUESTION 2. Whether our faith be active to lay hold upon the righteousness of Christ, before the Lord do first impute the righteousness of Christ unto us. . . .

[To this second question] we conceive no. For these reasons. Reason 1. If the sin of Adam were imputed unto us for our condemnation, as soon as we were alive by natural life before we had done any act of life, good or evil: then the righteousness of Jesus Christ is imputed unto us to our justification, as soon as we be alive unto God by faith, before we have done any act of faith . But the former is plain. . . . Therefore the latter also. Reason 2. If our faith be first active, to lay hold upon Christ for his righteousness, before God imputeth it unto us; then we take Christ's righteousness to ourselves, before it be given unto us. But that we cannot do, for in the order of nature,[9] giving is the cause of taking; unless we take a thing by stealth. . . .

Objection 1. To believe on the name of Christ is an act of faith; to believe on the name of Christ, is to receive Christ, John 1:12. Therefore the receiving of Christ is by an act of faith.

Source: *A Conference Mr. John Cotton Held at Boston With the Elders of New-England* (London, 1646), modified on the authority of two manuscript versions. Hall (1968), 175–94.

---

[9] A Scholastic term, paired with "order of time," indicating a double perspective on the sequencing of stages.

Chapter 9

Increase Mather on the New Baptismal Piety

How to defend the sacrament of infant baptism against the Baptists and, in the same breath, how to tell church members admitted on the basis of their baptism that, despite being within the covenant, they still had far to go before they were fully members of the body of Christ — these were questions the second-generation minister Increase Mather addressed in *Pray for the Rising Generation* (1678). Mather wanted to sustain the founders' emphasis on conversion or the inward work of grace, a topic on which he preached and published frequently throughout his long tenure as minister of Second Church, Boston. At the Cambridge synod of 1662, Mather had sided with the minority in opposing a decision to extend the privilege of baptism to the children of "adult children" of the church (i.e., parents who owed their own membership to having been baptized themselves). But by the 1670s Mather changed his mind and attempted, unsuccessfully, to persuade his congregation to adopt the synod's key recommendation, later to be nicknamed the "halfway covenant." In sermons like the one that follows, he insisted on the significance of the "external" covenant established by Genesis 17:7 and the continuity of grace within families, asserting, in a sentence that modern historians have frequently quoted, that "the vein of election doth run through the loins of godly parents for the most part." In this same sermon he stressed the importance of mothers in the spiritual economy of the household, an expectation that can also be found in the personal writings of Anne Bradstreet and Sarah Goodhue (pt. III). A careful reading of this sermon indicates, however, that he took back much of what he offered: baptism and family nurture were meaningless without the infusion of saving grace through the Holy Spirit, and if persons who were baptized did not profit from their being in the covenant to experience conversion, they would be worse off, not better.

Bibliography
Middlekauff (1971), chaps. 5, 7; Holifield (1974), chap. 6.

INCREASE MATHER

🦋 *Pray for the Rising Generation* 🦋

*1 Chron. 28:9, If thou seek him,
he will be found of thee.*

God in his providence doth many times so order, as that the last words of his eminent servants shall be of most weighty consideration. The Scripture sets a special emphasis and remark upon the last words of David, 2 Sam. 23:1, *Now these are the last words of David* — the sweet singer of Israel; not that he never spake any words after those, but they were expressed by him, toward the close of his days, not very long before he left the world. The same is to be said concerning the words now before us; they are amongst the last, yea, the dying speeches of that holy man of God; who perceiving that the time of his departure was at hand, layeth a most solemn charge upon his son Solomon, that he should endeavor to approve himself a faithful servant of his father's God. . . . wherefore the doctrine which may at present be insisted on from the words, is,

Doctrine. That the children of godly parents are under peculiar advantages and encouragements to seek the Lord. For the clearing of this doctrine, two things may be attended. 1. To inquire what is implied in this seeking the Lord which the text speaketh of. 2. How it doth appear that the children of godly parents are under peculiar advantages and encouragement so to do?

QUESTION 1. What is implied in this seeking the Lord?

[ANSWER] 1. It doth imply that men by nature are such as have lost God. The sinner hath lost himself, Luke 15:32, *Thy brother was lost, and is found*, yea, and he hath lost God too. He is wandered from his father's house. Hence the Apostle said to the Ephesians, they were without God in the world. Yea, it is true concerning children of godly parents as well as others, Eph. 2:3, we (saith the holy Apostle) *were by nature the children of wrath even as others*. We that are Jews and descended of holy ancestors, we that are now converted, and made apostles of Christ, by nature were subjects of the wrath and righteous displeasure of God. Not but that some of the children of godly men, have grace wrought in them whilst in a state of infancy, as John Baptist was filled with the Holy Ghost from his mother's womb; but they do not derive that grace from their parents, and therefore it is not natural but supernatural, when any of the children of sinful men are made gracious.

[ANSWER] 2. Seeking the Lord doth imply a sense of this lost condition. Sense of want puts men upon seeking. The prodigal was hunger-bitten before he would seek to be reconciled to his father. When he saw that he was fain to live upon husks, and that there was no way but he must perish with hunger, except he sought unto his father for a supply, he would do so. If a man hath lost a thing, except he know that he hath lost it, he will not seek after it. Hence in the parable concerning the lost piece of silver, it is said, *what woman if she lose a piece of silver, doth not light a candle, and sweep the house, and seek diligently till she find it*, Luke 15:8. So that there must be sense of loss before there will be seeking or finding. Nor will men seek the Lord, except they be by his Spirit made sensible, that they have lost his favor, and are through sin and the fall become miserable.

[ANSWER] 3. This seeking doth imply earnest desire to find God. That which a man seeketh after he would be glad to find. . . . As it was with David himself, Ps. 63:1, *O God thou art my God, early will I seek thee: my soul thirsteth for thee, my flesh longeth for thee, in a dry and thirsty land where no water is*. How are the desires and affections of a thirsty man carried out after water, in a thirsty land where no water is? When the desires of the soul are in like manner carried out after God, that is seeking him.

[ANSWER] 4. Seeking the Lord doth imply diligence in the use of means in order to obtaining favor of God. The end implies the means which is necessary in order to obtaining that end, now the favor of God is the end of this seeking. . . .

[ANSWER] 5. Seeking the Lord doth imply the worship and service of God. . . . And we read in the sacred history of David, that when he had subdued his enemies, he burnt their images and idols, in an holy indignation at the sin of idolatry. Now he doth exhort his son Solomon, to follow his father's steps in being loyal to God in the matters of his worship. All these particulars may be intended here. If thou seek the Lord, i.e., if thou art sensible of thy lost estate by nature, so as to desire reconciliation with God in the first place, and dost therefore repent of sin, and believe in Christ, and continuest to worship and serve God, according to his own will, then be assured that thou shalt enjoy his favor, and be everlastingly blessed.

QUESTION 2. We come now to the second thing propounded, viz. to shew how it doth appear that the children of godly parents are under peculiar advantages and encouragement to seek the Lord.

ANSWER 1. In that the vein of election doth run through the loins of godly parents for the most part. Though it be not wholly, and only so, that elect parents have none but elect children, or that elect children are always born to elect parents yet God hath seen meet to cast the line of election so, as that generally elect children are cast upon elect parents, John directs one of his epistles [2 John 1], to the elect lady and her children, whom he also found walking in the truth. Not only the mother, but the children did belong to God. As usually so it is, that if the mother be elect, at leastwise some of the children are so too. There are many scriptures which do intimate this truth. . . . Moreover, experience and observation doth confirm this truth, that de facto it hath been so. For the elect are not found in all places alike, but in some nations more than in others, and that for many generations successively. And in some families more than in others. There are some families in the world, that God hath designed to shew peculiar mercy to them, from generation to generation. And if an account should be taken concerning all the godly men that are now alive in the world, doubtless it would be found, that the greatest part of them are sprung from godly parents. Though there may be many converted ones in the world, whose parents did not fear God, yet for the generality of true believers they are such as have descended from believing parents.

[ANSWER] 2. The Lord hath established his covenant not only with parents, but with children also. Gen. 17:7, *I will establish my covenant between me and thee, and thy seed after thee, in their generations, for an everlasting covenant, to be a God to thee and to thy seed after thee.* The saints in all ages are concerned in Abraham's covenant, under which children are comprehended. To say that the covenant was extended to children under the Old Testament, but not under the New,[1] is to lessen the grace of God in these days of the gospel. Yea then the Jews would have been great losers by believing on Christ. If they could have said, in former times our children were interested in the gracious covenant of God, but if we embrace the gospel, they shall have no part in the Lord, this would have been such an objection against believing as could never have been answered. Wherefore, we shall find that those scriptures which relate to gospel times, expressly declare, that not only believers themselves, but their children also, are subjects of the Lord's gracious covenant with his people. . . . Now this consideration is a great encouragement to seek the Lord. So it was to them, Jer. 3:22, *We come unto thee, for thou art the Lord our God.* We are thy covenant people, and that doth encourage us to come unto thee. And this did encourage David to seek and hope for the Lord's salvation. Ps. 86:16, *Save the son of thine handmaid.* And the Apostle did encourage the Jews to repent and return unto the Lord, from this argument, viz. in that they were the children of the covenant. Acts. 3:19, 25. From thence it is evident, that the children of godly parents stand in a peculiar relation unto God, and that therefore he will not cast them off, except there

---

[1] Baptists insisted that the church as described in the New Testament was not continuous with the "nation" or "temple" of the Old.

be great cause for it. Not surely as long as they seek him, and desire to return to him and serve him.

[ANSWER] 3. There are special promises belonging to such children. Not only the covenant in general, which is, as it were, a constellation of glorious promises, but there are peculiar promises made concerning them. There is a promise that they shall be blessed above other children. . . . The same thing is promised, Isa. 44:3, *I will pour my Spirit upon thy seed, and my blessing upon thine offspring.* And the Lord hath made a blessed promise of salvation to such children, Isa. 49:25, *I will save thy children.* . . . Now albeit these promises do not absolutely respect all the children of every godly man, only the elect amongst them, yet they are generally and indefinitely propounded; and that is encouragement as to parents to pray for their children, yea for all of them. . . . The child of a godly man may come before the Lord, and say, Lord thou hast promised to bestow grace, and give eternal blessings unto those that are children of such as fear thy name, my father, my mother thou knowest did fear thy name, why then may not that promise belong to me?

[ANSWER] 4. The children of godly parents are the subjects of much faithful prayer. . . . Now it is matter of great encouragement, that prayer is going: especially the prayers of godly parents will do much in order to obtaining mercy for their children. For they have a great natural affection toward their children, which when it is sanctified, maketh them to be the more earnest with the Lord for them. If a child were to ask prayers for his life, let him desire the prayers of his father, if his father be indeed one that hath an interest in heaven. It is said in the Fifth Commandment, *Honor thy father, and thy mother, that thy days may be long upon the land which the Lord thy God giveth thee,* Exod. 20:12, because as for dutiful children, their parents are engaged to pray much for them, and by that means do lengthen out their days. In the Hebrew it is, they shall prolong thy days, i.e. thy father and thy mother shall do so. How should they do it? even by praying for their posterity, and blessing them in the name of the Lord, and by that means prolonging their days not only upon the earth, but to eternity in heaven, of which that land of Canaan was a type. The prayers of godly parents have a great influence and interest in obtaining blessings temporal, spiritual, and eternal for their children. . . . Now this is a great encouragement to children, that prayer and faith hath been acting for them. Yea, that a stock of prayers hath been laid up for them. Is it not a great encouragement unto a child, when he can say, my gracious father hath carried my name before God in secret many a thousand time, even every day and night since I was born into the world? Certainly these prayers shall not fall to the ground. . . .

Use 4. Of Exhortation,

1. Let godly parents that are here before the Lord this day, suffer the word of exhortation. Do you endeavor to the utmost of your power, that your children may become seekers and servants of the only true God in Jesus Christ. And indeed when you present them to the Lord in baptism, you promise to do your utmost, that they may become faithful servants of that God who is Father, Son, and Spirit; take heed that you do not become guilty of violating that engagement. . . . It is a solemn thing, which it may be you have not duly considered, that the great God hath entrusted you with those that are his children, that so you may nurse them up for him: O then bring them up in the nurture and admonition of the Lord. It is not enough for parents to serve the Lord themselves, but they must use utmost endeavors that after they are dead, their children may walk in the ways of God. And if they be duly careful in that matter, they have reason to expect, that God will remember and establish his covenant with their children. For it is noted concerning Abraham, that his care was that his family after him (viz., after he should cease to be in the world) might keep the way of the Lord, and so did the Lord bring upon him the thing which he had spoken, and graciously promised with respect to Abraham's posterity. And in special you that are mothers have a great advantage put into your hands, to be instilling good principles into your children's souls betimes; Solomon's mother taught him: we do not read that Absalom's and Adonijah's mother taught them, as Bathsheba did her son Solomon. And it is not for nothing, that when children have proved thus or so, particular notice is taken in Scripture, that such or such were their mothers: Rehoboam did not prove well, and it is noted that his mother was an Ammonitess. On the other hand, Hezekiah, Jehoshaphat, Josiah were eminent servants of God, and the Scripture doth mention who were their mothers. O then you that are mothers should endeavor that your children (as Luther speaketh) may suck in religion from their mother's breasts.

And let all godly parents earnestly seek unto the Lord for their poor children: You ought to do so daily and particularly, and by name before the Lord and thus should you do every day: as we read concerning Job, that he offered burnt offerings for his children, according to the number of them all, thus did Job continually. Job 1:5. Remember that you are under peculiar encouragement so to do: if the children of godly parents have special encouragement to seek the Lord, then the same things must needs be true concerning such parents themselves, with respect to their children. And it is eminently true with respect to the children of New England inasmuch as they are the posterity of such as have been sufferers on the account of the name and truth of the Lord Jesus. Are not such parents pronounced blessed twice over? Matt. 5:11–12, even blessed in themselves, and in their posterity? Who knoweth but God may remember the kindness of the fathers in these churches (who followed him into this wilderness whilst it was a land not sown) unto their children after them?

... [Addressing "children"] Consider, 3. The evil that is in your not seeking the Lord. What a grief of mind will this be to children of godly parents? The father of a fool hath no joy. Alas! there is many a poor parent may say to their children, as Jephtah upon another account spake to his daughter, Judg. 11:35, *He rent his clothes, and said, Alas my daughter, thou hast brought me very low, thou art one of them that trouble me.* Why should you bring your parents down with sorrow to their graves? ... Remember that this will aggravate your sin, and condemnation, that you were born of godly parents, and did not walk in their steps, Jer. 50:7, *They sinned against the hope of their fathers*; it is mentioned as the great aggravation of their sin. Such children roll reproach upon the covenant of God; they cause men to say, there is nothing in being in covenant with God, nor is it any mercy to be born of parents that fear the Lord; and will not the Lord judge you for causing such a vile reproach to be cast upon his holy covenant? You will be most inexcusable before the Lord another day. ... All the instructions, exhortations, admonitions, prayers, examples of thy godly parents, will be brought in as so many witnesses for thy condemnation at the last day; yea, the tears of thy blessed parents will be as oil to make the everlasting flames of hell burn the more vehemently upon thy soul, throughout the days of eternity; *the Lord will cast thee off forever*; thy father that begat thee, thy mother that bare thee, will not pity thee when thou shalt be sentenced to eternal death at the last day. Remember Dives; *in hell he lift up his eyes being in torments*, and cried, *Father Abraham! Have mercy on me*; but all the mercy his Father Abraham would shew to him, was, he said, *Son, remember that in thy life-time thou hadst thy good things* [Luke 16: 23–25]; as if he had said, nay, thou art justly dealt with. So will thy parents say to thee, Remember that in thy life-time we instructed thee, and thou hadst good counsel give to thee many a time, but thou wouldest not regard it. Oh consider of it! Yea know, that if thou diest in thy sins, thy godly parents will stand forth, and testify against thee, before the Lord Jesus, at the last day; as that blessed man Mr. Bolton, would sometimes solemnly profess to his children, Children, let any of you meet me at the day of judgment, in an unregenerate Christless estate if you dare, I will then testify against you before the Lord. Yea, thy gracious parents will join with the Lord Jesus, in passing a sentence of eternal condemnation upon thee. ...

Be thankful to the Lord in that he hath given you to be born of godly parents: in that you have been (as David speaketh) cast upon the Lord from the womb. And he hath been your God from your mother's belly. Ps. 22:10. You might have been born of such parents as would have nursed you up in ignorance, profaneness or idolatry, and so your souls have been under a necessity of perishing forever, but the Lord hath given you to be of parents that have designed you for God, and for his glory. Yea it was for your sakes especially that your fathers ventured their lives upon the rude waves of the vast ocean. Was it not with respect unto posterity, that our fathers came into this wilderness? That they might train up a generation for Christ: Bless God that ever you had such fathers.

. . . Plead the Lord's gracious covenant with him, he is very willing that you should do so: *Ask me concerning my sons and concerning the work of my hands command ye me.* Isa. 45:11. You say you cannot give grace to your own souls. True: But hath not the Lord in the covenant of grace said, *I will give you a new heart*, Ezek. 36:26. Plead that promise, you especially that have had the covenant sealed to you; why should you let your baptism lie by you, as if it were of no use? Go to God in secret, and say, Lord thou hast promised to give a new heart to the children of thy servants, and thy covenant hath been sealed to me in my baptism; oh give me a new heart.

. . . Do not rest in anything that is external: Not in your relation to godly parents, and visible relation to God on that account; it is not your parents seeking unto God will save you, except you seek him yourselves also. . . . I have known some that have been so foolish as to think they should be saved, only because they were the children of godly parents, though they lived in the neglect of God, and of their own souls. Beware of so perverting the truth delivered unto you. And rest not in being outwardly civil and blameless; was not Paul so before his conversion, Phil. 3:6. And they that have been advantaged with a religious education, oftentimes are so, though never truly converted. Beware also of taking up a form of godliness without the power of it. O you that are the children of godly parents, if you outwardly observe the Sabbath day, and pray in secret, and read the Scriptures (all which things I charge you in the Name of the Lord, that you attend unto them whilst you live), you will be apt to rest here, without an interest in the glorious righteousness of the Son of God, but for the love of your immortal souls, I beseech you, deceive not yourselves; build not upon a false foundation, look to it, in the fear of God, that your hearts be perfect before him.

Source: Increase Mather, *Pray for the Rising Generation* (Boston, 1678).

PART III

Patterns of Piety and Devotion

The doctrines taught in sermons and catechisms provided the basic framework for a "practical divinity" directed at making sinners into sincere Christians, a transformation of the self based on biblical passages such as John 3:3, "Except a man be born again, he cannot see the kingdom of God," and 2 Cor. 5:17, "Therefore if any man be in Christ, he is a new creature: old things are passed away; behold, all things are become new." The texts in this section, all of them by or about lay men and women, record the quest for this transformation, the struggle to achieve assurance of salvation, the challenge of resisting the temptations of "the world," and the possibility of veering off into despair.

We have already encountered some of the men and women in Dedham describing the work of grace (as candidates for church membership), though we lack the full texts of what they said. A large number of such confessions survive from Cambridge during the years of Thomas Shepard's ministry, as do others from Chelmsford, Massachusetts, and East Windsor, Connecticut. But the colonists also described the workings of grace and the practice of devotion in autobiographies, diaries, and poetry, in narratives written for private use, in responses to extraordinary "afflictions," and (through third persons) in accounts of extreme distress or "diabolical possession." These texts bring us remarkably close to understanding the work of grace as it was experienced among these people and to grasp the significance, for them, of the Bible and the "means of grace" on which they relied: prayer, listening to sermons, meditation, the sacraments of baptism and the Lord's Supper.

The way to Christ was never "easy." It demanded that people change how they behaved in the world, giving up their lawlessness and becoming disciplined servants of God. Beginning with the Ten Commandments, the God of the Puritans prescribed moral rules for the faithful to observe. Other rules flowed from Puritan objections to traditional calendar customs and popular or court culture, practices such as playing sports on Sundays, Maypole celebrations, "mixed" dancing, and attending the theater. Thomas Shepard's story of how he transformed a wedding celebration (chap. 3) is an example of Puritan moralism in action, as is John Trumbull's hard-won determination (see below, chap. 11) to observe the Sabbath. The shorthand name in New England for these moral rules was "duties." As John Winthrop noted of himself (chap. 10), the true Christian was constant in performing certain duties, which for him included regular participation in the "means," that is, hearing sermons (which he did almost to excess) and practicing other aspects of devotion or worship such as prayer and meditation. Always, the good Puritan endeavored to distance him- or herself from the alternative moral order of "the world."

But as Winthrop also remarked, the real challenge was to transform the inner self, the unredeemed and rebellious "heart" that, because of its sinful cast, rebelled against God. Redemption depended on acknowledging the fundamental corruption of the self (original sin) and the ongoing will to do wrong. "I was told that I should labor still for a deeper sense of my sin and misery," Esther Bissell declared before the congregation in East Windsor, "and that I should take heed of drawing back, and that I should beg of God to give me a sight of the corruption of my own nature, and the wickedness of my own heart."[1] Subduing the inner self, though a human activity, was ultimately the doing of the Holy Spirit as embodied in the Word, the only power strong enough to shatter the defenses of pride and bring the sinner to recognize her or his utter unworthiness. Thus it happened that, step by halting step, laypeople began to move through the stages of redemption that the ministers laid out in their sermons: "conviction" (or "compunction"; see Thomas Shepard in chap. 7) and "humiliation" or "repentance," a process people had to repeat again and again before they could truly acknowledge their dependence on God's mercy.

The narratives in part III are saturated in Scripture and rarely refer to formal points of doctrine or employ the Scholastic terminology on which the ministers depended. Nonetheless, the shadow of doctrinal controversy falls across John Winthrop's "Christian Experience" (chap. 10) and the confessions made in Cambridge and Chelmsford. When Winthrop acknowledged that he had become careless about the doctrine of justification, he was referring to the "Antinomian controversy" of 1636–1637, when ministers and laypeople engaged in a sharp debate about the proper basis of assurance of salvation: could people of "weak faith" rely on the evidence of "duties" or did doing so threaten the Protestant doctrine of justification by faith alone? (See Anne Hutchin-

---

[1] Kenneth P. Minkema, "The East Windsor Conversion Relations 1700–1725," *Connecticut Historical Society Bulletin* 51 (1986), 24.

son's "examination," chap. 21). No matter how this question was answered, achieving assurance of salvation was, for many persons, a process that posed the risk of slipping into "security." Here, indeed, the "practical divinity" created a tension from which there was no easy exit, insisting on the one hand that the saints would have "certain" knowledge of their "union" with Christ and, on the other, emphasizing the "hypocrisy" that deceived many into thinking they were saved. Self-scrutiny could result in something close to spiritual ecstasy, but it could also produce deep uncertainty or confusion and, at an extreme, spiritual despair, as laypeople struggled for assurance of salvation, worrying all the while that they were actually hypocrites. The confessions in Cambridge, Chelmsford, and East Windsor are remarkably frank about the ups and downs of a spiritual journey that seemed to have few clear benchmarks.

These contradictory possibilities may have created a mood of excessive scrupulosity among some of the colonists, an unwillingness to declare themselves saved that manifested itself in the widespread reluctance (especially after 1650) to participate in the Lord's Supper, the reason being that anyone participating in this sacrament was asked to heed a particular passage of Scripture, 1 Cor. 11:27–30, which warns (v. 29) that "he that eateth and drinketh unworthily, eateth and drinketh damnation to himself, not discerning the Lord's body." The ministers responded in several ways to these tensions. One strategy is clearly evident in the confessions made in Chelmsford, a listing of signs or marks by which a person may differentiate hypocrisy from being in a state of grace. Another was to urge constant self-examination and resort to the "means," a remedy Mary Rowlandson (chap. 26) practiced with a fresh intensity once she was redeemed from her captivity. In the wilderness she learned anew the lesson of vanity: that the "world" was worthless and that the saint must sustain the guise of pilgrim, "in but not of the world." Late in life Anne Bradstreet wrote a poem on the same theme, "As weary pilgrim"; in another poem (not included in this collection) she dramatized the conflict between "the flesh and the spirit." Similar verse was written by colonists such as Michael Wigglesworth. As covenanted pilgrims, Bradstreet and Rowlandson believed that God watched over them. But their confidence in God's loving care was tested by misfortunes that were deeply painful, like the death of Mary Rowlandson's young daughter or her own captivity. Yet the pilgrims were expected to regard these misfortunes ("afflictions," to use seventeenth-century terminology) as God's way of prompting them to renew the process of self-examination. "Thinking on death" was another means of remaining spiritually alert. The gravestone art that emerged after 1660, with its inscriptions of "memento mori" and "tempus fugit," reminded the living that preparation for death was ever ongoing, not a task that could be postponed to the last minutes of existence. Death itself was a charged moment, for the time to repent was slipping away.

Broadly speaking, healing was how the colonists understood the spiritual life, the healing necessary to overcome the sinner's estrangement from God and the perils of the pilgrim's road. Healing flowed from the persistent, routinized practice of devotion. The colonists relied on several different rituals or practices. First and foremost among these was prayer, which several different ministers applied to Elizabeth Knapp (chap. 13). Another important ritual was the fast day, a third the devotional reading that John Trumbull and Mary Rowlandson pursued. Participating in church services was no less crucial. Only within the walls of the meetinghouse were the sacraments of baptism and the Lord's Supper available.

Bibliography

Miller (1939), chaps. 1–2; Wakefield (1957); McGiffert (1972); McGee (1976); Tipson (1978); Hambrick-Stowe (1982), a pathbreaking study of devotional practices; Cohen (1986); Hambrick-Stowe (1988); Ludwig (1966) on gravestone art; Geddes (1981) on death. The "scrupulosity" thesis is advanced in Morgan (1961) and reiterated in Hall (1989), chaps. 3–5; Brown and Hall (1997).

Chapter 10

John Winthrop on Becoming a Christian

John Winthrop wrote his "Christian Experience" in January 1637, "in the forty-ninth year of my age just complete[d]," as he noted at the end. He was prompted to do so by "some differences in our church" (the Boston congregation of which he was a member) about assurance of salvation and the difference between grace and works. He had been listening to John Cotton, who shared the ministry with John Wilson, complaining that too many of the colonists were relying on "works" or a "righteousness of [their] own," a critique strongly seconded by another member of the congregation, Anne Hutchinson (see chap. 21). Already at odds with Mrs. Hutchinson and some of her allies, Winthrop played a major role in the censoring of the "Antinomians" that unfolded later in the year. But in January he was also realizing that he had become careless about justification by faith and its implications for assurance of salvation. The story he told in the "Experience" begins with his childhood in England, moving forward to his marriage and the sermons he heard preached by Ezekiel Culverwell. Like others among the godly, Winthrop developed "an unsatiable thirst after the Word of God and could not misse a good sermon." He also began to read in the "practical divinity," in which Puritan ministers outlined the way of grace and provided guidance on how to tell the difference between true faith and hypocrisy. Winthrop struggled to absorb the lesson that he must surrender all self-confidence, trust entirely in the mercy of God, and learn to "love him though he should cast me off." A spell of sickness when he was about thirty brought him to his lowest point of recognizing he was "worthy of nothing." At some moment thereafter, he felt "the good sprit of the Lord breathe upon my soul" and was "ravished with love." Yet the ups and downs resumed as ecstasy waned and he struggled anew with "continual conflicts between the flesh and the spirit."

Bibliography

Cohen (1986).

JOHN WINTHROP

 *"Christian Experience"*

[December 1636]. Upon some differences in our church about the way of the Spirit of God in the work of justification, myself dissenting from the rest of the brethren, I had occasion to examine mine own estate, wherein the Lord wrought marvelously upon my heart, reviving my former peace and consolation with much increase and better assurance than formerly. And in the midst of it (for it continued many days) he did one time dart a beam of wrath into my soul, which struck me to the heart, but then the Lord Jesus showed himself and stood between that wrath and my soul. Oh how sweet was Christ then to my soul. I thought I never prized him before, I am sure never more, nor ever felt more need of him. Then I kept him close to my heart and could not part with him. Oh how my heart opened to let him in. Oh how was I ravished with his love! my prayers could breathe nothing but Christ and love and mercy, which continued with melting and tears night and day.

In my youth I was very lewdly disposed, inclining unto and attempting (so far as my years enabled me) all kind of wickedness, except swearing and scorning religion, which I had no temptation unto in regard of my education. About ten years of age, I had some notions of God, for in some great frighting or danger, I have prayed unto God, and found manifest answer; the remembrance whereof many years after, made me think that God did love me, but it made me no whit the better.

After I was twelve years old, I began to have some more savor of religion, and I thought I had more understanding in divinity than many of my years; for in reading of some good books I conceived, that I did know divers of those points before, though I knew not how I should come by such knowledge (but since I perceived it was out of some logical principles, whereby out of some things I could conclude others), yet I was still very wild, and dissolute, and as years came on, my lusts grew stronger, but yet under some restraint of my natural reason; whereby I had the command of myself, that I could turn into any form. I would, as occasion required, write letters, etc. of mere vanity; and if occasion were, I could write others of savory and godly counsel.

About fourteen years of age, being in Cambridge,[1] I fell into a lingering fever, which took away the comfort of my life. For being there neglected and despised, I went up and down mourning with myself; and being deprived of my youthful joys, I betook myself to God, whom I did

[1] Cambridge University, as a student.

believe to be very good and merciful, and would welcome any that would come to him, especially such a young soul, and so well qualified as I took myself to be; so as I took pleasure in drawing near to him. But how my heart was affected with my sins, or what thoughts I had of Christ, I remember not. But I was willing to love God, and therefore I thought he loved me. But so soon as I recovered my perfect health, and met with somewhat else to take pleasure in, I forgot my former acquaintance with God, and fell to former lusts, and grew worse than before. Yet some good moods I had now and then, and sad checks of my natural conscience, by which the Lord preserved me from some foul sins, which otherwise I had fallen into. But my lusts were so masterly as no good could fasten upon me, otherwise than to hold me to some task of ordinary duties, for I cared for nothing but how to satisfy my voluptuous heart.

About eighteen years of age (being a man in stature, and understanding as my parents conceived me) I married into a family under Mr. Culverwell[2] his ministry in Essex; and living there sometimes I first found the ministry of the Word to come home to my heart with power (for in all before I found only light), and after that I found the like in the ministry of many others. So as there began to be some change which I perceived in myself, and others took notice of. Now I began to come under strong exercises of conscience (yet by fits only). I could no longer dally with religion. God put my soul to sad tasks sometimes, which yet the flesh would shake off, and outwear still. I had withal many sweet invitations, which I would willingly have entertained, but the flesh would not give up her interest. The merciful Lord would not thus be answered, but notwithstanding all my stubbornness and unkind rejections of mercy, he left me not till he had overcome my heart to give up itself to him, and to bid farewell to all the world, and until my heart could answer, Lord what wilt thou have me to do?

Now came I to some peace and comfort in God and in his ways, my chief delight was therein. I loved a Christian, and the very ground he went upon. I honored a faithful minister in my heart and could have kissed his feet: Now I grew full of zeal (which outran my knowledge and carried me sometimes beyond my calling), and very liberal to any good work. I had an unsatiable thirst after the Word of God and could not miss a good sermon, though many miles off, especially of such as did search deep into the conscience. I had also a great striving in my heart to draw others to God. It pitied my heart to see men so little to

[2] In 1605, aged seventeen, Winthrop married Mary Forth, whose family lived in Great Stanbridge, where the well-known Puritan preacher Ezekiel Culverwell (d. 1631) was the rector. She died in 1615.

regard their souls, and to despise that happiness which I knew to be better than all the world besides, which stirred me up to take any opportunity to draw men to God, and by success in my endeavors I took much encouragement hereunto. But these affections were not constant, but very unsettled. By these occasions I grew to be of some note for religion (which did not a little puff me up), and divers would come to me for advice in cases of conscience; and if I heard of any that were in trouble of mind I usually went to comfort them; so that upon the bent of my spirit this way and the success I found of my endeavors, I gave up myself to the study of divinity, and intended to enter into the ministry, if my friends had not diverted me.

But as I grew into employment and credit thereby, so I grew also in pride of my gifts, and under temptations which set me on work to look to my evidence more narrowly than I had done before (for the great change which God had wrought in me, and the general approbation of good ministers and other Christians, kept me from making any great question of my good estate), though my secret corruptions, and some tremblings of heart (which was greatest when I was among the most godly persons) put me to some plunges; but especially when I perceived a great decay in my zeal and love, etc. And hearing sometimes of better assurance by the seal of the Spirit, which I also knew by the Word of God, but could not nor durst say that ever I had it;[3] and finding by reading of Mr. Perkins and other books that a reprobate might (in appearance) attain to as much as I had done[4]; finding withal much hollowness and vainglory in my heart, I began to grow very sad, and knew not what to do: I was ashamed to open my case to any minister that knew me; I feared it would shame myself and religion also, that such an eminent professor as I was accounted, should discover such corruptions as I found in myself, and had in all this time attained no better evidence of salvation; and [if] I should prove a hypocrite it was too late to begin anew: I should never repent in truth, having repented so oft as I had done. It was like hell to me to think of that in Heb. 6.[5] Yet I should sometimes propound questions afar off to such of the most godly ministers as I met, which gave me ease for the present, but my heart could not find where to rest; but I grew very sad and melancholy; and now to

---

[3] John Cotton insisted on the priority of the "seal of the Spirit" in gaining assurance of salvation, a point expanded on by Anne Hutchinson. See Hall (1968), questions 1–5 and 7 of the "sixteen questions" debated by the clergy.

[4] William Perkins (1558–1602), a moderate Puritan who wrote extensively about the spiritual life; Winthrop may have been reading *A Treatise Tending unto a Declaration Whether a Man be in the Estate of Damnation, or in the Estate of Grace* (1588).

[5] Heb 6:4, For it is impossible for those who were once enlightened . . . 6, If they shall fall away, to renew them again with repentance.

hear others applaud me, was a dart through my liver; for still I feared I was not sound at the root, and sometimes I had thoughts of breaking from my profession, and proclaim myself an hypocrite. But those troubles came not all at once but by fits, for sometimes I should find refreshing in prayer, and sometimes in the love that I had had to the saints: which though it were but poor comfort (for I durst not say before the Lord that I did love them in truth), yet the Lord upheld me, and many times outward occasions put these fears out of my thoughts. And though I had known long before the doctrine of free justification by Christ, and had often urged it upon my own soul and others, yet I could not close with Christ to my satisfaction. I have many times striven to lay hold upon Christ in some promise, and have brought forth all the arguments that I had for my part in it. But instead of finding it to be mine, I have lost sometimes the faith of the very general truth of the promise, sometimes after much striving by prayer for faith in Christ, I have thought I had received some power to apply Christ unto my soul: but it was so doubtful as I could have little comfort in it, and it soon vanished.

Upon these and the like troubles, when I could by no means attain sure and settled peace; and that which I did get was still broken off upon every infirmity; I concluded there was no way to help it, but by walking more close with God and more strict observation of all duties; and hereby though I put myself to many a needless task, and deprived myself of many lawful comforts, yet my peace would fail upon every small occasion, and I was held long under great bondage to the law (sin, and humble myself; and sin, and to humiliation again; and so day after day) yet neither got strength to my sanctification, nor bettered my evidence, but was brought to such bondage, as I durst not use any recreation, nor meddle with any worldly business, etc. for fear of breaking my peace (which even such as it was, was very precious to me) but this would not hold neither, for then I grew very melancholy and mine own thoughts wearied me, and wasted my spirits.

While I wandered up and down in this sad and doubtful estate (wherein yet I had many intermissions, for the flesh would often shake of[f] this yoke of the law, but was still forced to come under it again) wherein my greatest troubles were not the sense of God's wrath or fear of damnation, but want of assurance of salvation, and want of strength against my corruptions; I knew that my greatest want was faith in Christ, and fain would I have been united to Christ, but I thought I was not holy enough; I had many times comfortable thoughts about him in the Word, prayer, and meditation, but they gave me no satisfaction, but brought me lower in mine own eyes, and held me still to a constant use of all means, in hope of better things to come. Sometimes I was very confident that he had given me a hungering and thirsting soul after Christ, and therefore would surely satisfy me in his good time. Sometimes again I was ready to entertain secret murmurings, that all my pains and prayers, etc., should prevail no more; but such thoughts were soon rebuked: I found my heart still willing to justify God. Yea, I was persuaded I should love him though he should cast me off.

Being in this condition it pleased the Lord in my family exercise to manifest unto me the difference between the covenant of grace, and the covenant of works (but I took the foundation of that of works to have been with man in innocency, and only held forth in the law of Moses to drive us to Christ). This covenant of grace began to take great impression in me, and I thought I had now enough: To have Christ freely, and to be justified freely was very sweet to me; and upon sound warrant (as I conceived) but I would not say with any confidence, it had been sealed to me, but I rather took occasion to be more remiss in my spiritual watch, and so more loose in my conversation.

I was now about thirty years of age, and now was the time come that the Lord would reveal Christ unto me, whom I had long desired, but not so earnestly as since I came to see more clearly into the covenant of free grace. First therefore he laid a sore affliction upon me wherein he laid me lower in mine own eyes than at any time before, and showed me the emptiness of all my gifts and parts, left me neither power nor will, so as I became as a weaned child. I could now no more look at what I had been or what I had done, nor be discontented for want of strength or assurance, mine eyes were only upon his free mercy in Jesus Christ. I knew I was worthy of nothing, for I knew I could do nothing for him or for myself. I could only mourn, and weep to think of free mercy to such a vile wretch as I was. Though I had no power to apply it yet I felt comfort in it. I did not long continue in this estate, but the good Spirit of the Lord breathed upon my soul, and said I should live. Then every promise I thought upon held forth Christ unto me, saying, I am thy salvation. Now could my soul close with Christ, and rest there with sweet content, so ravished with his love, as I desired nothing nor feared anything, but was filled with joy unspeakable and glorious, and with a spirit of adoption. Not that I could pray with more fervency or more enlargement of heart than sometimes before, but I could now cry My Father with more confidence. Methought this condition and that frame of heart which I had after, was in respect of the former like the reign of Solomon; free, peaceable, prosperous, and glorious, the other more like that of Ahaz, full of troubles, fears and abasements [2 Chron. 28]. And the more I grew thus acquainted with the Spirit of God, the more were my corruptions mortified and the new man quickened. The world, the flesh, and Satan, were for a time silent, I heard not of them: but they would not leave me so. This estate lasted a good time (divers months), but not always alike, but if my comfort and joy slackened awhile, yet my peace continued, and it would return with advantage. I was now grown familiar with the Lord Jesus Christ, he would oft tell me he loved me. I did not doubt to believe him. If I went abroad he went with me, when I returned he came home with me. I talked with him upon the way, he lay down with me, and usually I did awake with him. Now I could go into any company and not lose him: and so sweet was his love to me, as I desired nothing but him in heaven or earth.

This estate would not hold, neither did it decline suddenly, but by degrees. And though I found much spiritual strength in it, yet I could not discern but my hunger after the Word of God, and my love to the saints had been as great (if not more) in former times. One reason might be this, I found that the many blemishes and much hollow-heartedness which I discerned in many professors, had weakened the esteem of a Christian in my heart. And for my comfort in Christ, as worldly employments, and the love of temporal things did steal away my heart from him, so would his sweet countenance be withdrawn from me. But in such a condition he would not long leave me, but would still recall me by some word or affliction, or in prayer or meditation, and I should then be as a man awakened out of a dream, or as if I had been another man. And then my care was (not so much to get pardon, for that was sometimes sealed to me, while I was purposing to go seek it, and yet sometimes I could not obtain it without seeking and waiting also but) to mourn for my ingratitude towards my God, and his free and rich mercy. The consideration whereof would break my heart more, and wring more tears from mine eyes, than ever the fear of damnation or any affliction had done; so as many times, and to this very day, a thought of Christ Jesus, and free grace bestowed on me melts my heart that I cannot refrain.

Since this time I have gone under continual conflicts between the flesh and the spirit, and sometimes with Satan himself (which I have more discerned of late than I did formerly); many falls I have had, and have laid long under some, yet never quite forsaken of the Lord. But still when I have been put to it by any sudden danger or fearful temptation, the good Spirit of the Lord hath not failed to bear witness to me, giving me comfort and courage in the very pinch, when of myself I have been very fearful, and dismayed. My usual falls have been through deadheartedness and presumptuousness, by which Satan hath taken advantage to wind me into other sins. When the flesh prevails the Spirit withdraws, and is sometimes so grieved as he seems not to acknowledge his own work. Yet in my worst times he hath been pleased to stir, when he would not speak, and would yet support me that my faith hath not failed utterly.

The doctrine of free justification lately taught here took me in as drowsy a condition as I had been in (to my remembrance) these twenty years, and brought me as low (in my own apprehension) as if the whole work had been to begin anew. But when the voice of peace came, I knew it to be the same that I had been acquainted with before, though it did not speak so loud nor in that measure of joy that I had felt sometimes. Only this I found, that I had defiled the white garments of the Lord Jesus. That of justification in undervaluing the riches of the Lord Jesus Christ and his free grace, and setting up idols in mine own heart, some of them made of his silver, and of his gold; and that other garment of sanctification by many foul spots which God's people might take notice of, and yet the inward spots were fouler than those.

The Lord Jesus who (of his own free grace) hath washed my soul in the blood of the everlasting covenant, wash away all those spots also in his good time. Amen, even so do Lord Jesus.

John Winthrop   The twelfth of the eleventh month 1636[/37] in the forty-ninth year of my age just complete[.]

Source: Robert C. Winthrop, *Life and Letters of John Winthrop*, 2 vols. (Boston, 1864–1867), 165–73, compared with the version (based on a different manuscript) printed in *Winthrop Papers* 3:338–44. The title was almost certainly provided by someone other than Winthrop himself.

Chapter 11

Laypeople Describe the Work of Grace

The narratives of spiritual experience by lay men and women that follow were, for the most part, unknown until recently. Offered by candidates for church membership, one set of these texts was recorded in Cambridge between circa 1637 and 1648. Others appear in the Chelmsford, Massachusetts, church records and still others, dating from 1700 and later, survive from the East Windsor, Connecticut, congregation of Timothy Edwards. These testimonies mirror the preaching of the ministers about the "steps" or "way" to salvation. Although God's will in choosing some to be saved was mysterious, the preachers taught that "election" was an event or process the saints would actually experience. No confession or "relation" reports a single, concentrated moment of transformation. Instead, the narratives describe a multistage process beginning with an emphasis on recognizing one's absolute unworthiness as a sinner. "Humiliation" or repentance followed, as did the experience of hearing the joyful "promise" of salvation offered freely to sinners through and by Christ Jesus. Hope gives way to fear, and fear to a sense of peace, in a thaumaturgy that frequently involves the figure of the devil. The narratives assume that the seat or site of this process is the "heart." Otherwise, religion is mere "formality" and the would-be saint a hypocrite. As in Winthrop's "Experience," a recurrent theme is resisting the temptation of resting on "duties," as though performing them were satisfactory evidence of being united with Christ. Especially in the Cambridge narratives, the uneasiness about "duties" may reflect the contemporary "Antinomian" critique of sanctification as a basis for assurance of salvation. The relations from East Windsor echo a theme of sermons of the late seventeenth century, the urgency of acting while there is still time to do so.

Much can be learned from confessions such as John Trumbull's about the social experience of being a Puritan in England—for example, the slights heaped upon the "godly," the tensions that emerged within the workplace, and their rejection of traditional English customs. Conversely, these texts also note the great pleasure of encountering the "love" of the saints. These lay Puritans had a remarkable memory of sermons and an equally remarkable knowledge of the Bible, which they treated as illuminating their quest. In their narratives, some acknowledge the importance of "godly" parents in setting them on the right road; others refer to sickness as prompting them to deeper self-examination. The relaters in Cambridge included lay women and men of every social level — servants and college students, artisans and farmers, magistrates and housewives. The Cambridge and Chelmsford relations were written down by the ministers or perhaps someone else, a process that accounts for the incomplete sentences or phrases that appear in them.[1] It was common for ministers and church members to question candidates; occasionally these questions are reported in the texts.

Bibliography

Morgan (1963); Caldwell (1983), which, with Cohen (1986), provides the closest reading of the Cambridge texts. Those from East Windsor remain unstudied.

 CONFESSIONS FROM THE CAMBRIDGE CONGREGATION

Edward Hall

This is the first of the narratives recorded by Thomas Shepard. Edward Hall was a freeman in 1638, minor officeholder, and modest property holder. He may have been about twenty-nine when he was admitted.

The first means of his good was Mr. Glover's ministry whereby he saw his misery from Jeremiah 7 *the temple of the Lord* and that he was without Christ. But he went from thence to another place under the sense of an undone condition. But in that place he was deprived of the ordinances of God and hence the scripture came oft to mind *what if a man win the world and lose his soul* [Mark 8:36]? Hence he desired to come to that place again but the minister was gone. But Mr. Jenner came and by him he saw more evil in himself. But Mr. S[hepard] came and then the Lord did more clearly manifest himself to him from John 3 concerning the new birth. And here he saw more of his misery and that he had followed examples and duties and made them his Christ and lived without Christ. Hereby the Lord let him see he was Christless and built upon false foundations and by this text he saw himself no new creature but only a mended man. Now when the Lord did humble him under this, he saw the want of Christ and that without him he must

---

[1] McCarl (1991) has the most careful analysis of how these texts came into being.

perish. And afterward John 5:40 was opened — *you will not come to me to have life*. And here he saw how freely Christ was offered and hereby the Lord did stay and comfort his spirit and so was stirred up with more vehemency to seek Christ. And then that promise was opened — *the son of man came to seek that which was lost* [Luke 19:10]. And he did not know but the Lord might seek him. And out of that text 1 Peter 2:[6–7a] that *unto you that believe he is precious*, and here he saw his unbelief in cleaving to Christ by fits and starts. And since the Lord brought him to this place, he found his worldliness and this bred many fears whether ever any work of Christ in him was in truth, and that he was one that might fall short of Christ and that he was humbled. But his heart was not deep enough and hence he was put to more search whether ever he was humbled. Yet the Lord made it more clear from Ephraim's condition, Jer. 31:18, that the Lord had made him loathe himself and this made him loathe him. And here he hath found more enmity of his heart against the Lord than ever before. But hearing the Lord was willing to take away his enmity, he by Rev. 22:17 was brought nearer to the Lord.

John Trumbull

A mariner, John Trumbull arrived in the mid-1630s
and became a freeman of the colony in 1640.

I lived in sin without contradiction in a town without means, not only abusing God but his people, [I] used to take God's Name to grieve the spirits of the people of God, though I knew them not, regarding nothing but back and belly and fulfilling my own lusts. In riper times by a schoolmaster I saw swearing a grievous sin, but fell from swearing by God [to] by the creature. Afterward coming to the sea by some men checking me there for them I left those sins. And having by sea lost all time I thought I would learn to read it again. And reading *Poor Man's Pathway*,[2] they told me the more I read the more I would delight in it but I read in it only to learn to read. And at last I heard he that read that book over and it should be a witness against him [Deut. 31:26]. And though [I] thought it a serious book, then reading [a] book of repentance, learning some sins yet I lived in, so saw my misery. Yet this broke me that I saw wrath and sin and was yet alive. After this I was moved to seek after some other means. And so resorting to a place where the means were twice, my spirit being oppressed for God's wrath

[2] Thomas Turvell, *The Poore Mans Path-way to Heaven. Wherein, each one may clearely see, whether he be in the state of salvation or damnation* (London, 1616).

and sin, the Lord preached by one of his servants: *How much are you better than they* [Matt. 6:26]? And so showed the Lord had more respect to one sinful than unto many others beside. And the Lord rejoiced more in one lost creature than in many others [Luke 15:4–7]. And hence I thought yet there might be mercy. And handling another text— *Thy glory is above the heavens* [Ps. 113:4]—hearing [of the] excellency of God's attributes, I saw the Lord's excellency. And so I saw the evil of sin, that it should separate [me] from his glory as the creature could not desire God again. So I resolved no more to sin, but then many friends set themselves against me that I would go mad as other ministers with study. And others would disgrace me in streets and threaten me, but I thought hath not Christ suffered more and long enough by thy sins? So I was carried on with desires to know Christ and the Lord supported me many ways. And the Lord opening that of Peter—no redemption but by blood of Christ and no price but in Christ's blood [1 Pet. 4:18–19]—hence saw the price of blood. Hence desired it that it might purge me from sin and sickliness. And hence hearing— *Thy name is a precious ointment poured out* [Song of Sol. 1:3]—hence I found a heart to desire Christ but could not believe hearing of election in world should be found out. Hence waited upon God in means.[3] Yet wanting company of saints and means I went not much forward hearing many reproaches on saints. And after this I came to acquaint [myself] with saints and had many temptations to lay down all again. Yet hearing shall I begin in spirit and end in the flesh [Gal. 3:3], so I went to prayer after much means for Christ. Hearing one out of Isaiah 11—Christ would bring leopards and lions, men of subtle and bloody dispositions by his scepter and righteousness [Isa. 11:4, 6]. And pondering these things how this could be it made my spirit to be swallowed up how Christ could be this miserable. I thought he that had subdued death and hell, he could subdue the pride of my heart. And it made me wonder that men should scramble for world and wonder that I should sin. Nay ready to leave off works of my calling yet I remembered six days I might labor [Exod. 20:9–10] and desired to the Lord to help me against works. And being in a stand and being fair weather, I was loath to go to prayer where others were at. But walking on the deck took a book *To Live Well and to Die Well*[4] which affected me. But in the evening there being a sore storm and our mast lost, thinking what would become of me if peace [not] made with God and desiring the Lord to clear up my condition, Satan told me: thou hast no interest in Christ because I had broken the Sab-

---

[3] The "means of grace": the means (or "ordinances") God established to serve as the regular instruments of conversion. See Stoever (1978).

[4] William Perkins, "How to live well, and to die well," pt. 7 of *A treatise tending unto a declaration* (London, 1591).

bath and that I must die in misery. But then I thought no duties can save
[my] soul, but only Christ. But how should I know how Christ was
mine? Hence I considered what Lord had done, but could find nothing
but that he that sins hath an advocate, Jesus Christ [1 John 2:1]. But
how know you he is an advocate? Then seeing keeping his commands
was an evidence, then I remembered though I was vile yet I did love
Sabbaths and saints and so prayed. And the Lord, we looking for death,
at last brought us safe. So when we came to London I heard Mr. Sedg-
wick showing four signs of repentance: (1) universal respect to all commands which a hypocrite had respect to some of them; (2) there was a
retiredness in saints. Saints went most in private between God and their
souls, and there I saw somewhat which did help me; (3) durableness in
service, a hypocrite went on till his ends were accomplished; (4) growth
in grace and there I thought I had falsely applied all because I had more
love to saints' zeal against sin than ever. And hence thought rather than
hear my condemnation read to go out. And then staying, the objections
were answered as Peter, though had no such affections at last as when
he denied his [Matt. 26:34–35; 69–75]. Another time, hearing that *the
last shall be first* [Matt. 20:16] and how a hypocrite might outstrip a
saint and hearing of the different actions. And hearing a new creature
opened [2 Cor. 5:17] there was a concept of itself, and hearing out of 12
Proverbs right way how far a hypocrite might go.[5] He never see sin [as
the] greatest evil and wrath of God the greatest curse and then I could
not tell whether I had seen sin or no.

William Andrews

*A freeman and therefore a church member by 1634,
William Andrews was also an occasional officeholder
in Cambridge, and a man of means.*

I was brought up of godly parents with whom I remained till seventeen
years of age, instructed in the principles of religion. After that bound
prentice in Ipswich in a religious family and had not much knowledge
living out. But I came into godly men's company so that I grew to some
knowledge and thought my estate very good and had some comfort in
it, performing duties. Yet by sermons of worthy men as Mr. Carter of
Bramford, *If righteous scarcely be saved, where shall the ungodly appear* [l Pet. 4:18][?] Upon the burial of a very godly man, where he
showed the difficulty of being saved and so how that good men came to
heaven, one could come at no time to him but reading or praying or

---

[5] Proverbs 12 contrasts the way of a righteous man with that of the wicked and foolish.

hearing or living in his calling. And if such a man hardly to heaven as if an eel should go through a hole and leave her skin behind her. Now this did mightily strike me, although before I thought my estate good and old Mr. Rogers preaching on 5 Deuteronomy how they promised yet they broke all.[6] So out of 22 of Genesis of Abra[ha]m gave up Isaac his only son, of a promise,[7] and hence showed a man ought to slay his dearest sins though as dear as his only son. Now I knew I was guilty of some sins and hence it did lay hold on me. So Matthew 5[:20] — *except your righteousness exceed* [the] *righteousness of scribes and Pharisees* — and if such so strict not saved, what would become of others whose hearts were vile and lives too? Hence cast down by this, I was laid up under great torment of conscience. And a long time going to sea, yet being persuaded that those promises [in] Matthew 5 did belong to me — *blessed be them that mourn and thirst.*[8] And indeed I had oft temptation to kill myself hence durst not carry a knife about me nor go near water. And after some comfort, fell from it again as out of 57 of Isaiah preached by Mr. Phillips [v.] 15: I dwell with contrite spirit. This stayed my heart and made me resolve against every known sin. Yet I lay long under trouble and loath to eat much as unworthy of them. And at sea I got books, searching between a true believer and a temporary, as Dike and Rogers's *Seven Treatises.*[9] And I sought to God to give peace and searched after promises that he would take away stony heart. And lying long thus and bring some promise to light to give me comfort. And at last the Lord sent me thus such a measure of comfort that I could not contain, which did cast me down more than any other things that the Lord should manifest such mercy to me. And it did much astonish me that the Lord should look upon me at that time. Afterward I doubted whether these comforts were right because men might taste of heavenly gift [Heb. 6:4–6] and hence afraid of unpardonable sin [Matt. 12:31]. And by another book I saw difference between comfort of hypocrites and others. The one did cast them down which stayed me. And after this in Spain I fell very sick and sought the Lord but could find no comfort. And some of my men read Psalms 16[:5–6] — *my lines are fallen in a pleasant place* — which gave me much joy and so I desired my men to carry me and cast me into sea if I died because I thought papists

---

[6] "Old Mr. Rogers" was probably Richard; see Winship (2002).

[7] "[O]f a promise" refers to the events in Genesis 17 and 18 when God tells Abraham that Sarah, Isaac's mother, will bear a son in her old age.

[8] Matt. 5:4, 6, Blessed are they that mourn: for they shall be comforted. . . . Blessed are they which do hunger and thirst after righteousness: for they shall be filled.

[9] Richard Rogers, *Seven Treatises* (London, 1603); the second reference is possibly to Daniel Dyke's *The Mystery of Self-Deceiving; or, A Discourse of the Deceitfulness of Man's Heart* (London, 1615).

would dig me up or no. And so I bless God for what I have found here. Temptation—I built a new ship and my mind much upon it even upon the Sabbath. And I desired to deliver me from this whatever he did with me. But that ship was split and all drowned but a few, four of my men myself naked upon the main topsail in very cold weather and on a morning some on the shore came with a boat. And glad I was that I lost my ship and so lost my sin. After that I heard of New England. I came hither, God making way, and when I saw the people my heart was knit to them much and thought I should be happy if I should be joined and united to them. And when I came, God made way both in removing the minister and also in selling off all that I had. And sat down at Charlestown where I was received. Afterward my wife in my absence came hither, which I bless God for.

Brother Moore's Wife

The narrator is probably Joan, wife of Golden Moore,
a woman in her twenties.

I thought my condition was good though I lived in a profane place from my father. And my father asking me if I would come to New England I refused, which the Lord hath made sad to me since. And hearing Romans 8:7—*carnal heart is enmity against God*—and there I saw I was carnal and not subject to the will of God. And so hearing out of Lynn,[10] Romans 6[:23], *that wages of sin is death* showing a wicked man wrought for devil as one for his wages. And hearing lest sin deserve death much more I that had committed so many. And I saw I could not satisfy wrath of God and the Lord discovered sin of nature enough forever to condemn me. And hearing Christ came to save sinners [l Tim. 1:15], my heart was somewhat quickened. And so I saw my own emptiness and poverty of spirit and hearing out of Matthew 5, poor in spirit were blessed which supported my heart somewhat. And Mr. Whiting preaching out of Mark 13:35—*watch*—and out of Matthew 5—*hungry blessed*—I doubted whether that promise belonged to me. But I desired to wait upon God in means till he should reveal himself more sufficiently to me. And hearing out of Isaiah 30:18—*blessed are those that wait for him*—he showed it was good for some to wait all their days to humble them. And out of Isaiah 55—*come and buy wine*

---

[10] Lynn, Massachusetts, where Samuel Whiting (to whom she subsequently refers) was minister.

and milk[11] — I could not but wonder at the freeness of God's grace which did much break my heart. And out of that place — *with everlasting kindness I'll embrace thee* [Isa. 54:81] — which did much affect me and so I resolved to turn from my sin to the Lord. And so hearing — *let unrighteous forsake his ways and turn and I'll have mercy* [Isa. 55:7]. And when I came hither out of John 13:19 and of doubtings and differences between and hearing of that it stayed my heart. So when Mr. Burr taught out of Isaiah and hearing of spiritual pride and I felt I could not mourn and feared Lord had given me up to hardness of heart. And speaking to my husband how knew it viz. if not affected with hardness of heart. Being fearful of being humbled enough — *out of [the] depths I have cried to the Lord* [Ps. 130:1] — that it was a mercy to be free from depths. And from 30 of Exodus when the Lord had laid foundation, nothing between Christ and the soul.[12] And so when the Lord filled the temple I found Lord had filled my soul with glorious apprehensions of himself.

Source: *Thomas Shepard's Confessions*, ed. George Selement and Bruce Woolley, Publications of the Colonial Society of Massachusetts 58 (Boston, 1981), 33–34, 106–9, 111–13, 133–35. More Cambridge relations are printed in McCarl (1991), and *The Diary of Michael Wigglesworth, 1653–1657*, ed. Edmund S. Morgan (New York, 1965). Selement and Woolley, though occasionally inaccurate, identify the ministers named in these texts.

 CONFESSIONS FROM THE CHELMSFORD CHURCH

Thomas Hincksman

Respecting Thomas Hincksman's relation that the Lord seized for convictions soon after his coming to Concord, he being about fourteen years old, such as with putting him upon the exercise of private prayers, but now the . . . of the adversary and prompting attending it but in a formal way, oft reminding him there was time enough before him and he was yet young, etc. Till it pleased God by the ministry of Mr. Bulkeley[13] on Psalms 62:8–9, *Trust in the Lord, pour forth the heart before him, surely men of low degree are vanity*, etc. to awaken him. This

---

[11] Isa. 55:1, Ho, every one that thirsteth, come ye to the waters, and he that hath no money; come ye, buy, and eat; yea, come, buy wine and milk without money and without price.

[12] Exodus 30 describes the specifications for building and maintaining the altar.

[13] Peter Bulkeley (1583–1659), one of the founders of Concord, where he served as pastor.

moved him to consider how vain, unprofitable (for so he explained vanity), and sinful he was in his life, ways, actions, etc. This caused trouble in his spirit and sadness so as the honored Mr. Flint, his master,[14] taking notice of it at length had him go to Mr. Bulkeley and so he made known his condition to him. He applied himself in many speeches to him and in special in these scriptures John 6:37, *Him that cometh to me I will in no wise cast out*, and Matt. 11:28, *Come unto me all ye that are weary*, etc., which was for present quieting to his spirit and put him upon seeking to God afresh, etc.

Yet afterward the adversary prevailed so far as to force him to break off from the duty, Satan tempting him and telling him that 'twas not his right to seek after God, etc. In such tossings of spirit he was till he went to his pastor and advised with him. He encouraged him to pray and not to give over. And to that he objected touching his sin and that he never repented as he should. The Lord by him set home these scriptures: Ezek. 36:26, *A new heart also will I give you and a new spirit*, etc.; Isa. 55:7, *Let the wicked forsake his way*, etc. *and turn to the Lord and he will have mercy upon him and to our God and he will abundantly pardon us* [Isa. 55:8], *for my thoughts are not as your thoughts*, etc. Whence he had some sweet encouragement to go on in seeking of God, etc.

Yet again (that there was nothing in him, nor could he do anything, etc. being considered by him) it was wrought in him some perplexedness of mind but that the Lord was gracious and directed those scriptures to him: Isa. 54:7 (the words he mentioned not they were these, *For a small moment I have forsaken ye, but with great mercies will I gather ye with everlasting kindness will I have mercy on ye*); Isa. 43:25 (he named not the scripture, but the words), *I even am he that blotteth out thy transgressions for mine own sake and will not remember thy sin*; and, Isa. 55:1, *Ho, every one that thirsteth come ye to the waters, come buy wine and milk without money*, etc. These set him a work to go afresh to God and to desire that he would . . . to do these for him, etc. Afterward that scripture was objected to him: *He that believeth not is condemned* [John 3:18] which set sadly on him till what time Mr. Bulkeley in his catechizing handled that question, how may one know whether he hath faith or no? And among other things he answered if the soul['s] satisfaction be placed above on Christ and placed on that scripture Hab. 2:4, *His soul which is lifted up is not upright in him but the just shall live by his faith*. Hereupon his soul was drawn to take to Christ and riches of God's grace in him alone [Eph. 2:7].

Afterward the Lord did further strengthen and encourage him in this way, from the preaching of Mr. Bulkeley on Psalms 71:5, *Thou art my*

---

[14] Thomas Flint, a wealthy settler and church member.

hope, O Lord God: God, you art my trust from my youth. Whereon he showed 'twas a blessed thing where the beginning of our days are given up to God and divers reasons he had. Amongst others these in regard of God: first 'twas God that blesses youth with many blessings and blessed helps; second, God required this of youth; third, God does take it kindly at their hands who do give their youth to God. The consideration of which, seeing he served God, had enkindled in him a desire to give up himself in his youth unto God did greatly refresh his soul and from thence forward the Lord hath helped him to care to attend upon the ministry and ordinances and by them in some measure he trust to profit. This being that his desire, even that he may receive the benefit of them, etc.

Mrs. Hincksman

Thomas Hincksman's wife, her relation. She was first convinced of her estate by nature by means of her godly parent oft instructing of her and telling her what her condition by nature was and how to get out of the same. Thereupon she was stirred up to seek unto God by prayer, but 'twas in too formal a way and God taking away her father she went on in such a dead formal way for a season till God met her soul by Mr. Bulkeley's ministry on 2 Cor. 6:2, *Behold now is the accepted time, now is the day of salvation.* The day is the time of the gospel with whom it is given to a particular soul when the soul have lived under the light of the gospel and hath rejected it and the heart do grow more hard and dead, etc. She went along with it, as looking at it, as her condition. Yet after, he adding some cautions, showed that if yet the soul be awakened to seek to improve their day better, there is yet hope and it hath the day still, which afforded some encouragement to her. The day, in respect of her, was not yet at an end, yet by reason of her sin and corruptions she feared her condition, etc. Then to Col. 1:14, *In whom we have redemption through his blood,* here the question, how know that you have a part in the blood of Christ? He answered: first, consider how the heart is carried in love to Christ to do or suffer aught for Christ; second, how the blood of Christ hath softened the heart; and third, whether then best content with Christ alone, etc. Which things upon examination seemed to her refreshing.

But afterward, being in doubt touching her condition, fearing that the work was not in truth, she repaired to Mr. Bulkeley and asked how a soul might know that there were any beginnings of grace in truth. Answered, if sensible of misery, loathing of sin, seeking after the righteousness of Christ, attending in all the ways that God hath appointed to seek Christ in. Which brought her some comfort considering God had wrought her heart to such a frame. Yet after she met with some further trouble again about her condition and some fears because she could not find growth but rather declining. But from Mr. Bulkeley on Eph. 2:8, [For] *by grace ye are saved*, clearing a state of grace and salvation by these particulars amongst others: 1. the esteeming the working out our salvation as the greatest work; 2. the soul not satisfied with beginnings but striving after more grace. This gave her some refreshing again. Yet after she was troubled in spirit in cause of her spiritual deadness, unprofitableness, etc. though then this she found, viz. a desire of her soul not to forsake the Lord but to follow hard after him.

Then from Psalms 72:7, in his days shall the righteous flourish and abundance of peace, Mr. Bulkeley showed us the kingdom of Solomon, so of Christ, is a kingdom of peace. . . . Objection, many are dear to God but want that peace. Answered, there are degrees of peace. The want of peace there arises from want of subjection to Christ's kingdom. Saying of the least degrees where true: 1. a soul will not part with the beginnings of peace for the world; 2. the soul is in a quiet waiting upon God for a return when 'tis interrupted, etc. This gave some present stay, but after the temptations returned again. And she was tempted that she was a hypocrite and all her professions in vain. Then going to Mr. Bulkeley he [urged?] her not to let her hold go [Prov. 4:13], but to commit her soul in sincerity unto God in the use of all his means and he would never leave her. This encouraged her.

Afterward she being exercised with some untoward afflictions and withal with inward griefs of spirit, God yet stirred up her heart to seek more diligently after him and that God would manifest himself to her soul. And pondering upon her condition she hoped that she had given up herself to God and so waiting the Lord answered to her salvation next Sabbath by Mr. Bulkeley on Psalms 81:8–10, *Hear O my people*, etc. *I am the Lord your God*, etc., where he observed that to those that desire and seek that God be their God, he is willing to be. The Lord setting in with it she became in some measure persuaded that God was her God. After from Psalms 92[:10], *with horn shall you exalt*, etc., whence he observed that these that truly believe in God love, fear, and obey him whatever promise God hath made such a soul ought to apply. Objected, how do you know this? Answer: if a care of keeping first with God, etc. From this she found further stay and refreshment.

After upon her move hither her fears revived and lest she should fall again into a fearful frame and her desire being to find God in his ordinances, from Song of Sol. 1:2, *Let him kiss*, etc. Objection, that the lively, etc. powerful application of the Word to the soul by the Spirit is esteemed as [the] greatest token of Christ's love and sought after by a

gracious heart in the perfection of which she found God appeared to
some reviving to her. And then by Mr. Bulkeley again on John 14, if I go
away I will send the comforter, where he gave signs. How we may know
the Spirit to be a comforting spirit to us? 1. By some measure of true
sorrow for sin agoing before. 2. The carrying the soul in love to Christ.
3. The putting on the soul to purge itself. 4. The . . . the soul in God's
cause and in suffering affliction for Christ. And this further tending to
clear her condition from that Psalms 21, ye . . . expecting the liberty
of, etc., also the true child of God the subject of this glorious liberty
[Rom. 8:21]. Here how know that God is our father? Answer: that a
childlike love to God as a father and to go to him in our wants; fear to
offend him; and, obedience to him in all things. Which God applied to
her to . . . comfort and refreshing her soul.

After the Lord suffered her to be exercised with some strong temptations of Satan yet he helped her by these scriptures: 1 Cor. 10[:13],
There is no temptation happened to ye but that which is common,
etc. . . . whom God loveth he loveth forever even with an everlasting
love [Jer. 31:1]. Thus from time to time she professed she found God in
his Word and even the public ministry as from that Acts 2[:37], *When
they heard this they were pricked,* etc. Objection: God will sooner or
later break a sinner's heart whom he intends to save. Some [words illeg-
ible] sight of sin causing some restlessness in the soul; from a fear of
falling into former sins; and, from a hatred of sin and this from a delight to have sin discovered and a mourning for sin, etc. Which things
did show that she had had that rule of God upon her to true conviction.

After going to Mr. Bulkeley in his sickness the fear of his death
wrought some discouragement in her till the end help her to consider,
though the stream be cut off yet the fountain remains. There hearing
Mr. Edward Bulkeley[15] on that Balaam *desired to die the death of the
righteous* [Num. 23:10], he answered that how one should know
whether his desires be right and sincere? He answered that then they are
laborious, grieving, waiting, and submissive desires. The perusing of
which was some cheering to her and so from Rom. 8:28, *with all things
shall work together for good,* etc. Objected: how know that I such [are]
truly of Lord God? Answered: when the Word of God being made
known to us, we submit to it without gainsaying; when we prefer the
honor of God before our own; and, when we show a sincere love to
those that are truly beloved of God. These she found to lead to some
spiritual quickening in her. Her burden she professes it is, that she is . . .
to fear to lose again that she hath gained and to grow deadening. Yet

---

[15] Edward Bulkeley (1614–1699) was ordained in 1642 and succeeded his father in the
ministry of Concord.

she still finds God merciful to her in supplying fresh encouragement and receiving as for that Rom. 8:30, *Whom he predestines them also he called in.* In discovery of effectual calling, how is it known? First, consider whether ye hath chosen the Lord for thy only portion; second, whether thy heart doth subject to the call of God in his Word; third, whether there be true love to those that are called of God. By which her heart is further drawn to attend the Lord in his own ordinances. And 'tis the earnest desire of her soul he would more and more manifest himself unto her and so she does beg our prayers to that end.

Source: *The Notebook of the Reverend John Fiske, 1644–1675*, ed. Robert G. Pope, Publications of the Colonial Society of Massachusetts 47 (Boston, 1974), 146–51. Ellipses indicate illegible words or cryptic passages.

A CONFESSION FROM EAST WINDSOR, CONNECTICUT

Ann the Wife of Joseph Fitch her Relation Taken February 26, 1700/01

I have had convictions ever since I was a child. When I was about seven years old I had such fears of death, that I sometimes had little or no appetite or disposition to my daily food so that for at times wholly forbore it. And I asked my parents what I should do to be saved and they told me that I should pray to God to pardon my sins, and accept me in Jesus Christ. And I did then pray to God and continued therein for about a twelve month while I lived on this side [of] the river.[16] And a little after my father removed from hence I went to Mr. Mather[17] for counsel, and went on in the use of means for a while, but quickly grew very inconstant and negligent and very sinfully resisted God's Spirit when he moved and stirred me up to prayer and the use of means for my soul's good, till I was about fourteen years of age. And from that time I have been constant at least in secret prayer, etc. And I had whilst on the other side of the river many convictions wrought by the hearing of the Word preached, so that I thought whatever else in the world I neglected, I would seek after the making of my peace with God, and make that to be my chief care or main business. And being once reproved in private for slothfulness and told of the slothful servant spoken of in the scripture, etc. [Matt. 25:26], I thought it was a hard saying though I knew it belonged to me so that I had temptations to have gone

[16] Divided by the Connecticut River, the townspeople of Windsor on the east side organized their own congregation and hired Timothy Edwards in 1694 to preach to them.
[17] Samuel Mather (1651–1728) became minister in Windsor in 1685.

no more for counsel, but that so wrought upon me that notwithstanding my surest purposes of staying away I went sooner again than before. And then I saw more of my ignorance of God and of a self-righteous spirit in me and what a dreadful thing it was for me to pray to a God that I did not know. And so I went on [in] the use of means and was met with from time to time, and awakened by the Word, and ever since I came to live on this side my sense of my sad condition hath rather increased than otherwise. And many a time since the Word came so home to me that I thought it was on purpose for me and could not be more suitable for me than it was. And the counsels which I had from my parents stirred me up to be the more earnest for mercy, and I thought sometimes that I had so wickedly resisted the Spirit of God that he had quite given me up and would strive with me no longer. I thought the time of God's striving with me was just at an end. And going from time to time for private advice I endeavored to take the counsels and direction that were given me, but I found and felt such dreadful hardness of heart, that I thought I grew worse and worse. And in particular I have seen that I have had a very vile wicked heart in that I could no better take the dying counsels and warnings of my father, who said much to his children and to me among the rest upon his deathbed. And I have thought often that his death was because God was angry with me for my sins. I thought that my resisting God's Spirit was the cause of my so long seeking in vain, and greatly feared this last summer, that God would quickly leave me either to despair or security; and the Word preached here on the day of fasting and prayer kept on purpose to seek to God for the pouring out of his Spirit in this place, came with power upon my heart, and was more quickening to me than usually it had been before. And I was stirred up by it to more seriousness, diligence, and earnestness in the use of means that so I might be converted and in particular in praying for God's Spirit. And the first time I was sick my trouble increased, and I was more afraid of hell than before, and after I grew better I thought that sickness was sent as a warning to me to prepare for death, and that if I did not improve it, another severe sickness of which I should not recover would come and that in a little time. And though I was stirred up thereby to do more for my soul than I had done before, yet I did not as I thought I would when I was sick. And about three weeks after I was taken sick again, and the very first hour I was taken, I was much struck with a great and trembling fear of death and hell, and then my sins soon appeared to me both for number and nature after another manner than ever they did before, though before they had lain heavy upon me yet nothing to what they did then. And as my sickness increased my sense of sin both of heart and life increased, and then my actual sins in particular, as my resisting the Spirit, standing out against Christ so long and in improvement of time. And many other things were so set in order before my eyes, that I thought I was the greatest sinner that ever was in the world, and wondered that God would suffer me to live a minute, and also saw I had a very wicked heart, so full of hardness and unbelief that I could no more believe nor repent than I could make a world, and that I was quite dead in sin and had no good in me so that I could not think so much as one good thought. And I thought it was a dreadful thing that I had such a nature in me as that I hated God, and then I also saw that I had greatly provoked God by trusting in my own righteousness. And then for several days I expected every hour that I should die and go to hell, and then my sins and God's wrath were so amazing to me that I can't express it, so that though my bodily pain was very great, yet such was the anguish of my spirit that I thought it ten times greater, and so great that no affliction that ever I felt in my life was in any measure like it. And I was amazed to think that I should be so slighty as I had been in the use of means, in the time of health though then I used to think I did what I could; and I had such a sight of God's greatness and majesty that I dare hardly speak for fear I should offend him, and wondered that he did not strike sinners dead in a moment when they sinned against him and that he had not so dealt with me. And then I saw that my own righteousness was as filthy rags [Isa. 64:6] and I thought it was worse than nothing a thousand times, and I thought I dare not bring it with me before God in any duty for never so much. And though I had trembling dread daily and hourly of God's dreadful and eternal wrath yet I saw myself such a sinner, and so vile that I could surely justify him, if he should then have taken away my life and cast me into hell. And [I] had such a sight of the evil that is in sin that I was fully convinced that sin deserved nothing but wrath and many things of that nature I then saw and too many now to relate. And then I thought, if I could but have the least hope or glimpse of God's face it would be enough. And after this that place came to mind, *Jesus Christ came into the world to save sinners* [1 Tim. 1:15], and it so affected me that I thought it a wonderful thing that Christ should die for sinners, and never thought that he did die for sinners before as I did then, and I hoped that God would be merciful to me for his sake, so that the thoughts of it were refreshing and comfortable to me, and that also he is able to save to the very uttermost. I thought he was able to save and he was willing and God delighted in mercy and I must hope in his mercy and I could do no other. And that upon the encouragement he had given me in his Word and that place also, *He retaineth not his anger forever because he delighteth in mercy* [Mic. 7:18], and some text much in those words, begins, freely man than any of the rest, as much at least encouraged me to venture my soul upon God's grace in Christ, for I thought though I was unworthy and deserved nothing yet God gave freely that if I was saved it must be from free grace alone. I have also found as I hope a grant to love God and the Lord Jesus Christ above all, and a desire to live a holy life, and have been enabled to mourn for sin as against God and Christ. And though I have had fears about my state lest it should not be safe, yet however it be with me I have been enabled to praise God for what he hath done for my soul, since I have experienced these things, and desire the prayers of [the] people of God with whom I desire to join in fellowship in this church, that he would discover Jesus Christ more and more to me, and keep me from doing anything that is displeasing to him, and that as he hath given me a new life so that he would by his grace enable me to live a new life.

Source: "The East Windsor Conversion Relations, 1700–1725," ed. Kenneth P. Minkema, *Connecticut Historical Society Bulletin* 51 (1985): 32–34.

Chapter 12

Anne Bradstreet on Vanity
and the Practice of Meditation

Anne Bradstreet (1612?–1672), who arrived in New England in 1630, was a meditative writer within a literary tradition that includes the English poets John Donne and George Herbert and her only equal as a meditative poet in New England, Edward Taylor.[1] Meditation was a disciplined exercise of reflection, a means of becoming closer to God and of experiencing more richly his sheltering love. Long practiced within the Christian tradition, it became a significant feature of Puritan spirituality. According to the literary historian Barbara Lewalski, seventeenth-century meditative writers engaged in both "occasional" and "deliberate" forms of meditation, the first consisting of reflections prompted by "daily events and circumstances," the second of reflections prompted by routine or recurrent events, like the Lord's Supper.[2] Bradstreet's prose meditations, written over a period of time and dedicated to her children as a "legacy" to ensure their well-being, exemplify the "occasional" mode, for each begins with some circumstance of motherhood, housekeeping, or the external world and transposes it into a spiritual lesson. (Edward Taylor's "Preparatory Meditations" on the Lord's Supper exemplify the other mode.)[3] Bradstreet also composed meditations in poetry, including the untitled poem that begins, "As weary pilgrim, now at rest." She was sixty when she wrote about the pilgrim's journey, an experience another Puritan writer near the beginning of the century described as being "in all places strangers . . . travelers and sojourners. . . . Our dwelling is but a wandering, and our abiding but as a fleeting, and in a word our home is nowhere but in the heavens — to that house not made with hands, whose maker and builder is God."[4] The pilgrim had her heart set on reaching heaven, always preferring the things that were truly valuable to those that were merely temptations (vanities) of the moment. "As weary pilgrim" embodies the

---

[1] See Donald E. Stanford, *The Poems of Edward Taylor* (New Haven, Conn., 1960).
[2] Lewalski (1979), 150–51, quoted in Hambrick-Stowe (1988), 19.
[3] Edward Taylor, "Preparatory Meditations," in Stanford, *Poems.*
[4] Quoted in Hambrick-Stowe (1982), 13, 16.

vanitas tradition that the English Puritan John Bunyan drew on for *Of Pilgrims Progress* (1678), which begins, "As I walk'd through the wilderness of this world." The same tradition lies behind Thomas Smith's self-portrait. The poem engraved on the paper below the skull, itself an emblem of human mortality and the transience of earthly pleasures, reads,

> Why why should I the world be minding
> therein a World of Evils finding
> Then farewell World: Farewell thy Jarres
> thy Joies thy Toiles thy Wiles thy Warres.
> Truth sounds Retreat: I am not Sorye.

In Bradstreet's poem, the asceticism of the pilgrim prepares her for a joyous encounter with Christ that Bradstreet likened to a wedding with Christ as her suitor/husband. Her prose meditations owe some of their tension to the possibility that the saints will know seasons of spiritual dryness or affliction, when God seems to desert them.

Bibliography

Lewalski (1979); Hambrick-Stowe (1982); Rowe (1986) on Edward Taylor; Hambrick-Stowe (1988), containing other meditative verse by Bradstreet and Taylor.

ANNE BRADSTREET

❧ *For my dear son Simon Bradstreet* ❧

Parents perpetuate their lives in their posterity, and their manners in their imitation. Children do naturally rather follow the failings than the virtues of their predecessors, but I am persuaded better things of you. You once desired me to leave something for you in writing that you might look upon when you should see me no more. I could think of nothing more fit for you, nor of more ease to my self, than these short meditations following. Such as they are I bequeath to you: small legacies are accepted by true friends, much more by dutiful children. I have avoided encroaching upon others' conceptions, because I would leave you nothing but mine own, though in value they fall short of all in this kind, yet I presume they will be better prized by you for the author's sake. The Lord bless you with grace here, and crown you with glory hereafter, that I may meet you with rejoicing at that great day of appearing, which is the continual prayer, of your affectionate mother, A.B. March 20, 1664.

    1. There is no object that we see; no action that we do; no good that

we may enjoy; no evil that we may feel, or fear, but we may make some spiritu[a]l advantage of all: and he that makes such improvement is wise, as well as pious.

6. The finest bread hath the least bran; the purest honey, the least wax; and the sincerest Christian, the least self love.

8. Downey beds make drowsy persons, but hard lodging keeps the eyes open. A prosperous state makes a secure Christian, but adversity makes him consider.

16. That house which is not often swept, makes the cleanly inhabitant soon loathe it, and that heart which is not continually purifying itself, is no fit temple for the Spirit of God to dwell in.

19. Corn, till it have passed through the mill and been ground to powder, is not fit for bread. God so deals with his servants: he grinds them with grief and pain till they turn to dust, and then are they fine manchet[5] for his mansion.

38. Some children are hardly weaned, although the teat be rubbed with wormwood or mustard, they will either wipe it off, or else suck down sweet and bitter together; so is it with some Christians, let God embitter all the sweets of this life, that so they might feed upon more substantial food, yet they are so childishly sottish that they are still hugging and sucking these empty breasts, that God is forced to hedge up their way with thorns, or lay affliction on their loins, that so they might shake hands with the world before it bid them farewell.

39. A prudent mother will not clothe her little child with a long and cumbersome garment; she easily foresees what events it is like to produce, at the best but falls and bruises, or perhaps somewhat worse, much more will the allwise God proportion his dispensations according to the stature and strength of the person he bestows them on. Large endowments of honor, wealth, or a healthful body would quite overthrow some weak Christians, therefore God cuts their garments short, to keep them in such a trim that they might run the ways of his commandment.

50. Sometimes the sun is only shadowed by a cloud that we cannot see his luster, although we may walk by his light, but when he is set we are in darkness till he arise again; so God doth sometime veil his face but for a moment, that we cannot behold the light of his countenance as at some other time, yet he affords so much light as may direct our way, that we may go forwards to the city of habitation, but when he seems to set and be quite gone out of sight, then must we needs walk in darkness and see no light, yet then must we trust in the Lord, and stay upon our God, and when the morning (which is the appointed time) is come, the sun of righteousness will arise with healing in his wings.

[5] The finest white rolls. Ellis (1867).

52. Had not the wisest of men taught us this lesson, that all is vanity and vexation of spirit, yet our own experience would soon have spelled it out; for what do we obtain of all these things, but it is with labor and vexation? When we enjoy them it is with vanity and vexation; and, if we lose them, then they are less than vanity and more than vexation: so that we have good cause often to repeat that sentence [Eccles. 1:2], *Vanity of vanities, vanity of vanities, all is vanity.*

53. He that is to sail into a far country, although the ship, cabin, and provision, be all convenient and comfortable for him, yet he hath no desire to make that his place of residence, but longs to put in at that port where his business lies: a Christian is sailing through this world unto his heavenly country, and here he hath many conveniences and comforts; but he must beware of desiring to make this the place of his abode, lest he meet with such tossings that may cause him to long for shore before he sees land. We must, therefore, be here as strangers and pilgrims, that we may plainly declare that we seek a city above, and wait all the days of our appointed time till our change shall come.

67. All the works and doings of God are wonderful, but none more awful than his great work of election and reprobation; when we consider how many good parents have had bad children, and again how many bad parents have had pious children, it should make us adore the sovereignty of God, who will not be tied to time nor place, nor yet to persons, but takes and chooses when and where and whom he pleases: it should also teach the children of godly parents to walk with fear and trembling, lest they, through unbelief, fall short of a promise: it may also be a support to such as have or had wicked parents, that, if they abide not in unbelief, God is able to graft them in: the upshot of all should make us, with the Apostle, to admire the justice and mercy of God, and say, how unsearchable are his ways, and his footsteps past finding out [Rom. 11:33].

  AS WEARY PILGRIM

As weary pilgrim, now at rest
Hugs with delight his silent nest
His wasted limbs, now lie full soft
That myrie[6] steps, have trodden oft
Blesses himself, to think upon
his dangers past, and travails done
The burning sun no more shall heat
Nor stormy rains, on him shall beat

---

[6] OED, sense 1: Of the nature of mire or marshy ground, swampy; hence, bogged down.

The briars and thorns no more shall scrat[ch]
nor hungry wolves at him shall catch
He erring paths no more shall tread
Nor wild fruits eat, in stead of bread
for waters cold he doth not long
for thirst no more shall parch his tongue
No rugged stones his feet shall gaul
nor stumps nor rocks cause him to fall
All cares and fears, he bids farewell
and means in safety now to dwell.
A pilgrim I, on earth, perplext
With sins with cares and sorrows vext
By age and pains brought to decay
and my clay house mouldring away
Oh how I long to be at rest
And soar on high among the blest.
This body shall in silence sleep,
Mine eyes no more shall ever weep
No fainting fits shall me assail
nor grinding pains, my body frail.
With cares and fears ne'r cumbred be
Nor losses know, nor sorrows see.
What tho' my flesh shall there consume
it is the bed Christ did perfume
And when a few years shall be gone
this mortal shall be cloth'd upon
A corrupt carcass down it lies
a glorious body it shall rise
In weakness and dishonor sown
in power 'tis rais'd by Christ alone
Then soul and body shall unite
and of their maker have the sight
Such lasting joys, shall there behold
as ear ne'er heard nor tongue ere told
Lord make me ready for that day
then Come dear bridegroom Come away[7]

August 31 1669

Source: Ellis (1867), 47–64, 42–44, compared with McElrath and Robb (1981),
where the punctuation follows the manuscript.

[7] Echoing Song of Sol. 2:10. Capitalizing the final "Come" makes the concluding words
the speech of Christ. Hambrick-Stowe (1982), 19 n. 11.

Chapter 13

A Story of Spiritual Confusion

ELIZABETH KNAPP'S "DIABOLICAL POSSESSION"

Hearing again and again the terrifying message that God would cast sinners off unless they experienced the work of grace, some people who felt they had not done so understandably imagined that their time was up: God's patience was exhausted, or else they were so unworthy he would never offer them mercy. Could it also be that they were victims of the devil's malice, either directly or through his agents? Witch-hunting in seventeenth-century New England fed on tensions such as these, though it also sprang from social conflict and efforts to explain misfortune. The means of healing those beset by the devil included rituals such as confession, prayer, and fasting as well as intervention by the civil state to put on trial anyone identified as a witch. Trials for witch-hunting in Connecticut and Massachusetts date from the 1640s. It should be noted, however, that civil hearings or informal investigations like the one reported in the narrative that follows often resulted in accusations being dismissed.

Elizabeth Knapp was the only child of James and Elizabeth (Warren) Knapp. James, a farmer, moved with his family to the newly founded town of Groton, Massachusetts, in 1662. For three months in 1671–1672 (October to January), Elizabeth, now sixteen and working as a servant in the household of the town minister, Samuel Willard (1640–1707), experienced what her contemporaries referred to as "diabolical possession." Possession may be defined as "the inhabiting of a human body by the devil, who then controlled his victim's verbal and physical actions."[1] Such experiences, almost all of them affecting single women in their teens and early twenties, were not uncommon in seventeenth-century New England if we include those afflicted by "specters" of local people.[2] The possessed were sometimes allowed to play the role of witch-finders, as Elizabeth Knapp attempted to do.

Once a medical diagnosis and cure of Elizabeth had been tried, Willard explored the possibility that her extraordinary fits were the outward

[1] Godbeer (1992), 106.
[2] Karlsen (1987), 223–24.

signs of sinful urges. Believing that Elizabeth had yielded to these temptations and signed a "compact" with the devil, he urged her to confess and repent as a means of resolving the conflict. Her story, as told by Willard in a letter to another minister, reveals a craving for "money" and her frustration with household chores (the devil offered to help her with some of these) and also with the expectations she faced as a pious young woman. Reiterating a theme of sermons addressed to a "declining" second and third generation, Elizabeth said of herself (although attributing the statement to the devil) that "her time [for accepting the gospel promise] was past and there was no hopes" for her, adding, when another person "advised her also to bethink herself of making her peace," that "it is too late for me." Being possessed allowed her to perform culturally illicit actions, such as mocking Willard. Much of what she reported about the devil was a mixture of popular and learned folklore (the devil promises her riches and asks her to sign a book in blood). The letter also details the methods of spiritual healing that local ministers attempted with the aid of the entire community. Elizabeth recovered from her fits, married, and became the mother of six children.

Bibliography

Demos (1982), chap. 4; Karlsen (1987), chap. 7, linking Knapp's fits with the constraints placed on women; Hall (1989), chaps. 3–4; Godbeer (1992), chap. 3 and Reis (1997) on the theological issues; Hall (1991, rev. ed. 1999), documenting the longer history of witch-hunting and possession.

SAMUEL WILLARD

A Brief Account of a Strange and Unusual Providence of God Befallen to Elizabeth Knapp of Groton

This poor and miserable object about a fortnight before she was taken, we observed to carry herself in a strange and unwonted manner. Sometimes she would give sudden shrieks, and if we inquired a reason, would always put it off with some excuse, and then would burst forth into immoderate and extravagant laughter, in such wise, as sometimes she fell onto the ground with it: I myself observed oftentimes a strange change in her countenance, but could not suspect the true reason, but conceived she might be ill, and therefore divers times inquired how she did, and she always answered well; which made me wonder: but the tragedy began to unfold itself upon Monday, October 30, 1671, after this manner (as I received by credible information, being that day my-self gone from home). In the evening, a little before she went to bed, sitting by the fire, she cried out, oh my legs! and clapped her hands on them, immediately, oh my breast! and removed her hands thither; and forthwith, oh I am strangled, and put her hands on her throat: those that observed her could not see what to make of it; whether she was in earnest or dissembled, and in this manner they left her (excepting the person that lay with her) complaining of her breath being stopped[.]

The next day she was in a strange frame (as was observed by divers), sometimes weeping, sometimes laughing, and [making] many foolish and apish gestures. In the evening, going into the cellar, she shrieked suddenly, and being inquired of the cause, she answered, that she saw two persons in the cellar; whereupon some went down with her to search, but found none; she also looking with them; at last she turned her head, and looking one way steadfastly, used the expression, what cheer old man? which, they that were with her took for a fancy, and so ceased; afterwards (the same evening), the rest of the family being in bed, she was (as one lying in the room saw, and she herself also after-wards related) suddenly thrown down into the midst of the floor with violence, and taken with a violent fit, whereupon the whole family was raised, and with much ado was she kept out of the fire from destroying herself[.] After which time she was followed with fits from thence till the Sabbath day; in which she was violent in bodily motions, leapings, strainings and strange agitations, scarce to be held in bounds by the strength of three or four: violent also in roarings and screamings, repre-senting a dark resemblance of hellish torments, and frequently using in these fits, divers words, sometimes crying out money, money, sometimes sin and misery with other words. On Wednesday [November 1], being in the time of intermission questioned about the case she was in, with reference to the cause or occasion of it, she seemed to impeach one of the neighbors, a person (I doubt not) of sincere uprightness before God, as though either she, or the devil in her likeness and habit, particularly her riding hood, had come down the chimney, stricken her that night she was first taken violently, which was the occasion of her being cast into the floor; whereupon those about her sent to request the person to come to her, who coming unwittingly, was at the first assaulted by her strangely, for though her eyes were (as it were) sealed up (as they were always, or for the most part, in those fits, and so continue in them all to this day), she yet knew her very touch from any other, though no voice were uttered, and discovered it evidently by her gestures, so powerful were Satan's suggestions in her[.] Yet afterward God was pleased to vindicate the case and justify the innocent, even to remove jealousies from the spirits of the party concerned, and [to the] satisfaction of the bystanders[.] For after she had gone to prayer with her she confessed that she believed Satan had deluded her, and hath never since complained of any such apparition or disturbance from the person.

These fits continuing (though with intermission), divers (when they had opportunity) pressed upon her to declare what might be the true and real occasion of these amazing fits. She used many tergiversations and excuses, pretending she would [declare it] to this and that young person, who coming, she put it off to another, till at the last, on Thursday night [November 2], she broke forth into a large confession in the presence of many, the substance whereof amounted to thus much: That the devil had oftentimes appeared to her, presenting the treaty of a covenant and proffering largely to her: viz. such things as suited her youthful fancy, money, silks, fine clothes, ease from labor to show her the whole world, etc.: that it had been then three years since his first appearance, occasioned by her discontent: that at first his apparitions had been more rare, but lately more frequent; yea, those few weeks that she had dwelt with us almost constant[ly], that she seldom went out of one room into another, but he appeared to her urging of her: and that he had presented her a book written with blood of covenants made by others with him, and told her such and such (of some whereof we hope better things) had a name there; that he urged upon her constant temptations to murder her parents, her neighbors, our children, especially the youngest, tempting her to throw it into the fire, on the hearth, into the oven; and that once he put a bill-hook into her hand, to murder myself, persuading her I was asleep, but coming about it, she met me on the stairs at which she was affrighted[.] The time I remember well, and observed a strange frame in her countenance and saw she endeavored to hide something, but I knew not what, neither did I at all suspect any such matter; and that often he persuaded her to make away with herself and once she was going to drown herself in the well, for, looking into it, she saw such sights as allured her, and was gotten within the curb, and was by God's providence prevented[.]

Many other like things she related, too tedious to recollect: but being pressed to declare whether she had not consented to a covenant with the devil, she with solemn assertions denied it, yea asserted that she had never so much as consented to discourse with him, nor had ever but once before that night used the expression, what cheer, old man? and this argument she used, that the providence of God had ordered it so, that all his apparitions had been frightful to her; yet this she acknowledged (which seemed contradictory, viz.:), that when she came to our house to school, before such time as she dwelt with us, she delayed her going home in the evening, till it was dark (which we observed), upon his persuasion to have his company home, and that she could not, when he appeared, but to go to him[.]

One evident testimony whereof we can say something to, viz.: the night before the thanksgiving, October 19,[3] she was with another maid that boarded in the house, where both of them saw the appearance of a man's head and shoulders, with a great white neckcloth, looking in at the window, at which they came up affrighted both into the chamber, where the rest of us were[.] They declaring the case, one of us went down to see who it might be; but she ran immediately out of the door before him, which she hath since confessed, was the devil coming to her; she also acknowledged the reason of her former sudden shriekings, was from a sudden apparition, and that the devil put these excuses into her mouth, and bid her so to say, and hurried her into those violent (but she saith feigned and forced) laughters: she then also complained against herself of many sins, disobedience to parents, neglect of attendance upon ordinances, attempts to murder herself and others; but this particular of a covenant she utterly disclaimed: which relation seemed fair, especially in that it was attended with bitter tears, self-condemnations, good counsels given to all about her, especially the youth then present, and an earnest desire of prayers: she sent to Lancaster for Mr. Rowlandson,[4] who came and prayed with her, and gave her serious counsels; but she was still followed, all this notwithstanding, with these fits: and in this state (coming home on Friday) I found her; but could get nothing from her, whenever I came in [her] presence she fell into those fits, concerning which fits, I find this noteworthy, she knew and understood what was spoken to her, but could not answer, nor use any other words but the forementioned, money, etc.: as long as the fit continued, for when she came out of it, she could give a relation of all that had been spoken to her: she was demanded a reason why she used those words in her fits, and signified that the devil presented her with such things, to tempt her, and with sin and misery to terrify her; she also declared that she had seen the devils in their hellish shapes, and more devils than anyone there ever saw men in the world. Many of these things I heard her declare on Saturday at night: On the Sabbath [November 5] the physician came, who judged a main part of her distemper to be natural, arising from the foulness of her stomach and corruptness of her blood, occasioning fumes in her brain, and strange fantasies; whereupon (in order to further trial and administration) she was removed home, and

[3] A day of special religious observance, giving thanks for favorable providences; not a fixed holiday.

[4] Joseph Rowlandson, husband of Mary and minister in nearby Lancaster.

the succeeding week she took physic, and was not in such violence handled in her fits as before; but enjoyed an intermission, and gave some hopes of recovery; in which intermission she was altogether senseless (as to our discovery) of her state, held under security and hardness of heart, professing she had no trouble upon her spirits, she cried Satan had left her. A solemn day[5] was kept with her, yet it had then (as I apprehend) little efficacy upon her; she that day again expressed hopes that the devil had left her, but there was little ground to think so, because she remained under such extreme senselessness of her own estate.

And thus she continued, being exercised with some moderate fits, in which she used none of the former expressions, but sometimes fainted away, sometimes used some strugglings, yet not with extremity, till the Wednesday following [November 15], which day was spent in prayer with her, when her fits something more increased, and her tongue was for many hours together drawn into a semicircle up to the roof of her mouth, and not to be removed, for some tried with the fingers to do it: From thence till the Sabbath seven night following: she continued alike, only she added to former confessions of her twice consenting to travel with the devil in her company between Groton and Lancaster, who accompanied her in [the] form of a black dog[6] with eyes in his back, sometimes stopping her horse, sometimes leaping up behind, and keeping her (when she came home with company) forty rod at least behind, leading her out of the way into a swamp, etc.: but still no conference would she own, but urged that the devil's quarrel with her was because she would not seal a covenant with him, and that this was the ground of her first being taken.

Besides this nothing observable came from her, only one morning she said God is a father, the next morning God is my father, which words (it is to be feared) were words of presumption, put into her mouth by the adversary. I suspecting the truth of her former story, pressed whether she never verbally promised to covenant with him, which she stoutly denied; only acknowledged that she had had some thoughts so to do: but on the forenamed November 26 she was again with violence and extremity seized by her fits in such wise that six persons could hardly hold her, but she leaped and skipped about the house perforce roaring and yelling extremely, and fetching deadly sighs, as if her heartstrings would have broken, and looking with a frightful aspect, to the amazement and astonishment of all the beholders, of which I was an eyewitness: the physician being then again with her, consented that the distemper was diabolical, refused further to administer, [and] advised to

---

[5] A fast day.
[6] See Hall (1989) on the folklore of black dogs.

extraordinary fasting; whereupon some of God's ministers were sent for: she meanwhile continued extremely tormented night and day, till Tuesday about noon; having this added on Monday and Tuesday morning that she barked like a dog, and bleated like a calf, in which her organs were visibly made use of: yea (as was carefully observed) on Monday night and Tuesday morning, whenever any came near the house, though they within heard nothing at all, yet would she bark till they were come into the house.

On Tuesday [November 28], about twelve of the clock, she came out of the fit, which had held her from Sabbath day about the same time, at least forty-eight hours, with little or no intermission, and then her speech was restored to her, and she expressed a great seeming sense of her state: many bitter tears, sighings, sobbings, complainings she uttered, bewailing of many sins forementioned, begging prayers, and in the hour of prayer expressing much affection: I then pressed if there were anything behind in reference to the dealings between her and Satan, when she again professed that she had related all. And declared that in those fits the devil had assaulted her many ways, that he came down the chimney, and she essayed to escape him, but was seized upon by him, that he sat upon her breast, and used many arguments with her, and that he urged her at one time with persuasions and promises of ease and great matters, told her that she had done enough in what she had already confessed, [that] she might henceforth serve him more securely; anon told her her time was past and there was no hopes unless she would serve him; and it was observed in the time of her extremity, once when a little moment's respite was granted her of speech, she advised us to make our peace with God and use our time better than she had done[.] The party advised her also to bethink herself of making her peace, [and] she replied, it is too late for me.

The next day was solemnized, when we had the presence of Mr. Buckley, Mr. Rowlandson, and Mr. Estabrook,[7] whither coming, we found her returned to a sottish and stupid kind of frame, much was pressed upon her, but no affection at all discovered: though she was little or nothing exercised with any fits, and her speech also continued: though a day or two after she was melancholy and being inquired of a reason, she complained that she was grieved that so much pains were taken with her, and did her no good, but this held her not long: and thus she remained till Monday [December 4], when to some neighbors there present she related something more of her converse with the devil, viz. that it had been five years or thereabouts, since she first saw him,

[7] Edward Buckley and Joseph Estabrook were the ministers in Concord.

and declared methodically the sundry apparitions from time to time, till she was thus dreadfully assaulted, in which the principal [matter] was, that after many assaults she had resolved to seal a covenant with Satan, thinking she had better do it than be thus followed by him, [she also declared] that once, when she lived at Lancaster, he presented himself and desired of her blood, and she would have done it, but wanted a knife[.] In the parley she was prevented by the providence of God interposing my father; a second time in the house he met her, and presented her a knife, and as she was going about it my father stepped in again and prevented [it], [so] that when she sought and inquired for the knife it was not to be found, and that afterward she saw it sticking in the top of the barn, and some other like passages[.]

She again owned an observable passage which she also had confessed in her first declaration, but is not there inserted, viz. that the devil had often proferred her his service, but she accepted not; and once in particular [he offered] to bring her in chips for the fire, [and] she refused, but when she came in she saw them lie by the fireside, and was afraid, and this I remark; I sitting by the fire spake to her to lay them on, and she turned away in an unwonted manner: She then also declared against herself her unprofitable life she had led, and how justly God had thus permitted Satan to handle her, telling them, they little knew what a sad case she was in. I after[ward] asked her concerning these passages, and she owned the truth of them, and declared that now she hoped the devil had left her, but being pressed, whether there were not a covenant, she earnestly professed, that by God's goodness she had been prevented from doing that, which she of herself had been ready enough to assent to; and she thanked God there was no such thing.

The same day she was again taken with a new kind of unwonted fit in which after she had been awhile exercised with violence, she got her a stick, and went up and down, thrusting and pushing here and there, and anon looking out a window, and cried out of a witch appearing in a strange manner in [the] form of a dog downward, with a woman's head, and [she] declared the person, other whiles that she appeared in her whole likeness, and described her shape and habit, [and] signified that she went up the chimney and went her way: What impression we read in the clay of the chimney, in [the] similitude of a dog's paw, by the operation of Satan, and in the form of a dog's going in the same place she told of, I shall not conclude; though something there was, as I myself saw, in the chimney in the same place where she declared the foot was set to go up. In this manner was she handled that night and the two next days, using strange gestures, complaining by signs when she could not speak, explaining that he was sometimes in the chamber, sometimes in the chimney; and anon assaults her, sometimes scratching her breast, beating her sides, strangling her throat, and she did oftentimes seem to our apprehension as if she would forthwith be strangled.

She declared that if the party were apprehended she should forthwith be well, but never till then; whereupon her father went and procured the coming of the woman impeached by her, who came down to her on Thursday night [December 7], where (being desired to be present) I observed that she was violently handled, and lamentably tormented by the adversary, and uttered unusual shrieks at the instant of the person's coming in, though her eyes were fast closed: but having experience of such former actings, we made nothing of it but waited the issue. God therefore was sought to, to signify something whereby the innocent might be acquitted or the guilty discovered; and he answered our prayers, for by two evident and clear mistakes she was cleared, and then all prejudices ceased, and she never more to this day hath impeached her of any apparition: in the aforementioned allegation of the person she also signified that sometimes the devil also, in the likeness of a little boy, appeared together with the person.

Friday was a sad day with her, for she was sorely handled with fits, which some perceiving pressed that there was something yet behind not discovered by her; and she after a violent fit, holding her between two and three hours did first to one, and afterwards to many acknowledge that she had given of her blood to the devil, and made a covenant with him; whereupon I was sent for to her; and understanding how things had passed, I found that there was no room for privacy[.] In another, already made by her so public, I therefore examined her concerning the matter; and found her not so forward to confess, as she had been to others, yet thus much I gathered from her confession: That after she came to dwell with us, one day as she was alone in a lower room, all the rest of us being in the chamber, she looked out at the window, and saw the devil in the habit of an old man, coming over a great meadow lying near the house, and suspecting his design, she had thoughts to have gone away, yet at length resolved to tarry it out, and hear what he had to say to her; when he came he demanded of her some of her blood, which she forthwith consented to, and with a knife cut her finger, he caught the blood in his hand, and then told her she must write her name in his book, she answered [that] she could not write, but he told her he would direct her hand, and then took a little sharpened stick, and dipped in the blood and put it into her hand, and guided it, and she wrote her name with his help.

What was the matter she set her hand to I could not learn from her; but thus much she confessed, that the term of time agreed upon with him was for seven years; one year she was to be faithful in his service, and then the other six he would serve her and make her a witch. She also related, that the ground of contest between her and the devil which was the occasion of this sad providence, was this, that after her covenant [was] made the devil showed her hell and the damned, and told her if she were not faithful to him, she should go thither and be tormented there; she desired of him to show her heaven, but he told her that heaven was an ugly place, and that none went thither but a company of base rogues whom he hated; but if she would obey him, it should be well with her: but afterward she considered with herself, that the term of her covenant was but short, and would soon be at an end, and she doubted (for all the devil's promises) she must at last come to the place he had shown her, and withal feared, if she were a witch, she should be discovered and brought to a shameful end; which was many times a trouble on her spirits; this the devil perceiving, [he] urged upon her to give him more of her blood, and set her hand again to his book, which she refused to do, but partly through promises, partly by threatenings, he brought her at last to a promise that she would sometime do it; after which he left not incessantly to urge her to the performance of it, once he met her on the stairs, and often elsewhere, pressing her with vehemence, but she still put it off; till the first night she was taken, when the devil came to her, and told her he would not tarry any longer: she told him she would not do it[;] he answered she had done it already, and what further damage would it be to do it again, for she was his sure enough. She rejoined she had done it already, and if she were his sure enough, what need [had] he to desire any more of her; whereupon he struck her the first night, again more violently the second, as is above expressed.

This is the sum of the relation I then had from her; which at that time seemed to be methodical. These things she uttered with great affection, overflowing of tears, and seeming bitterness: I asked of the reason of her weeping and bitterness, she complained of her sins, and some in particular, profanation of the Sabbath, etc.: but nothing of this sin of renouncing the government of God and giving herself up to the devil: I therefore (as God helped) applied it to her and asked her whether she desired not prayers with and for her; she assented with earnestness, and in prayer seemed to bewail the sin as God helped, then in the aggravation of it, and afterward declared a desire to rely on the power and mercy of God in Christ: she then also declared, that the devil had deceived her concerning those persons impeached by her, that he had in their likeness or resemblance tormented her, persuading her that it was they, that they bore her a spleen, but he loved her, and would free her from them, and pressed on her to endeavor to bring them forth to the censure of the law.

In this case I left her; but (not being satisfied in some things) I promised to visit her again the next day which accordingly I did, but coming to her, I found her (though her speech still remained) in a case sad enough, her tears dried up and senses stupefied, and (as was observed) when I could get nothing from her, and therefore applied myself in counsel to her, she regarded it not, but fixed her eye steadfastly upon a place, as she was wont when the devil presented himself to her, which was a grief to her parents, and brought me to a stand; in this condition I left her.

The next day [December 10], being the Sabbath, whether upon any hint given her, or any advantage Satan took by it upon her, she sent for me in haste at noon[.] Coming to her, she immediately with tears told me that she had belied the devil, in saying she had given him of her blood, etc.: professed that the most of the apparitions she had spoken of were but fancies, as images represented in a dream, earnestly entreated me to believe her, called God to witness to her assertion[.] I told her I would willingly hope the best, and believe what I had any good grounds to apprehend; if therefore she would tell a more methodical relation than the former, it would be well, but if otherwise, she must be content that everyone should censure according to their apprehension[.] She promised so to do, and expressed a desire that all that would might hear her; that as they had heard so many lies and untruths, they might now hear the truth, and engaged that in the evening she would do it[.] I then repaired to her, and divers more then went. She then declared thus much, that the occasion of it was her discontent, that the devil had sometimes appeared to her; that her condition displeased her; her labor was burdensome to her, she was neither content to be at home nor abroad; and had oftentimes strong persuasions to practice in witchcraft, had often wished the devil would come to her at such and such times, and resolved that if he would, she would give herself up to him soul and body: but (though he had oft times appeared to her, yet) at such times he had not discovered himself, and therefore she had been preserved from such a thing[.] I declared a suspicion of the truth of the relation, and gave her some reasons; but by reason of the company did not say much, neither could anything further be gotten from her.

But the next day I went to her, and opened my mind to her alone, and left it with her, declared (among other things) that she had used preposterous courses, and therefore it was no marvel that she had been led into such contradictions, and tendered her all the help I could, if she would make use of me, and more privately relate any weighty and serious case of conscience to me[.] She promised me she would if she knew anything; but said that then she knew nothing at all: but stood to the story she had told the foregoing evening: and indeed what to make of these things I at present know not, but am waiting till God (if he see meet) wind up the story, and make a more clear discovery. It was not many days before she was hurried again into violent fits after a different manner, being taken again speechless, and using all endeavors to make away with herself, and do mischief unto others; striking those that held her, spitting in their faces; and if at any time she had done any harm or frightened them she would laugh immediately; which fits held her sometimes longer, sometimes shorter[.] Few occasions she had of speech; but when she could speak, she complained of a hard heart, counselled some to beware of sin, for that had brought her to this, bewailed that so many prayers had been put up for her, and she still so hard-hearted and no more good wrought upon her; but being asked whether she were willing to repent, shaked her head, and said nothing.

Thus she continued till the next Sabbath [December 17] in the afternoon; on which day in the morning, being something better than at other times, she had but little company tarried with her in the afternoon, when the devil began to make more full discovery of himself: It had been a question before, whether she might properly be called a demoniac, or person possessed of the devil, but it was then put out of question[.] He began (as the persons with her testify) by drawing her tongue out of her mouth most frightfully to an extraordinary length and greatness, and [making] many amazing postures of her body; and then by speaking, vocally in her, whereupon her father and another neighbor were called from the meeting, on whom (as soon as they came in), he railed, calling them rogues, charging them for folly in going to hear a black rogue, who told them nothing but a parcel of lies, and deceived them, and many like expressions.

After exercise I was called, but understood not the occasion till I came and heard the same voice, a grum, low, yet audible voice it was. The first salutation I had was, oh! you are a great rogue. I was at first something daunted and amazed, and many reluctances I had upon my spirits, which brought me to a silence and amazement in my spirits, till at last God heard my groans and gave me both refreshment in Christ and courage: I then called for a light to see whether it might not appear a counterfeit, and observed not any of her organs to move, the voice was hollow, as if it issued out of her throat. He then again called me a great black rogue. I challenged him to make it appear [so]; but all the answer was, you tell the people a company of lies. I reflected on myself, and could not but magnify the goodness of God not to suffer Satan to bespatter the names of his people with those sins which he himself hath pardoned in the blood of Christ. I answered, Satan, thou art a liar and a deceiver, and God will vindicate his own truth one day: he answered nothing directly, but said, I am not Satan, I am a pretty black boy, this is my pretty girl; I have been here a great while[.] I sat still and answered nothing to these expressions; but when he directed himself to me again, oh! you black rogue, I do not love you: I replied through God's grace I hate thee; he rejoined, but you had better love me. These manner of expressions filled some of the company there present with great consternation, others put on boldness to speak to him, at which I was displeased, and advised them to see their call clear, fearing lest by his policy and [the] many apish expressions he used, he might insinuate himself, and raise in them a fearlessness of spirit of him. I no sooner turned my back to go to the fire, but he called out again, where is that black rogue gone?

I seeing little good to be done by discourse, and questioning many things in my mind concerning it, I desired the company to join in prayer unto God; when we went about that duty and were kneeled down, with a voice louder than before something he cried out, hold your tongue, hold your tongue, get you gone you black rogue, what are you going to do, you have nothing to do with me, etc.: but through God's goodness was silenced, and she lay quiet during the time of prayer, but as soon as it was ended, began afresh, using the former expressions, at which some ventured to speak to him: Though I think imprudently, one told him God had him in chains:[8] he replied, for all my chain, I can knock thee on the head when I please: he said he would carry her away that night. Another answered, but God is stronger than thou. He presently rejoined, that's a lie, I am stronger than God; at which blasphemy I again advised them to be wary of speaking, counselled them to get serious persons to watch with her, and left her, commending her to God.

On Tuesday [December 19] following she confessed that the devil entered into her the second night after her first taking, that when she was going to bed, he entered in (as she conceived) at her mouth, and had been in her ever since, and professed that if there were ever a devil in the world there was one in her, but in what manner he spoke in her she could not tell. On Wednesday night, she must forthwith be carried down to the Bay in all haste, she should never be well, till an assembly of ministers was met together to pray with and for her, and in particular Mr. Cobbett:[9] her friends advised with me about it; I signified to them, that I apprehended Satan never made any good motion, but it was out of season, and that it was not a thing now feasible, the season being then extremely cold, and the snow deep, that if she had been taken in the woods with her fits she must needs perish. On Friday [December 22]

---

[8] Orthodox doctrine held that the devil was subordinate to God, who allowed him only a limited freedom to act.

[9] Thomas Cobbett, minister in Ipswich and author of a book on prayer.

in the evening she was taken again violently, and then the former voice (for the sound) was heard in her again, not speaking, but imitating the crowing of a cock, accompanied with many other gestures, some violent, some ridiculous, which occasioned my going to her, where by signs she signified that the devil threatened to carry her away that night. God was again then sought for her, and when, in prayer, that expression was used, that God had proved Satan a liar, in preserving her once when he had threatened to carry her away that night, and was entreated so to do again, the same voice, which had ceased two days before, was again heard by the bystanders five times distinctly to cry out, oh, you are a rogue, and then ceased: but the whole time of prayer, sometimes by violence of fits sometimes by noises she made, she drowned her own hearing from receiving our petition, as she afterwards confessed.

Since that time she hath continued for the most part speechless, her fits coming upon her sometimes often, sometimes with greater intermission, and with great varieties in the manner of them, sometimes by violence, sometimes by making her sick, but (through God's goodness) so abated in violence that now one person can as well rule her, as formerly four or five. She is observed always to fall into her fits when any strangers go to visit her, and the more go the more violent are her fits: As to the frame of her spirits she hath been more averse lately to good counsel than heretofore, yet sometimes she signifies a desire of the company of ministers. On Thursday last [January 11, 1671/72], in the evening, she came [in] a season to her speech, and (as I received from them with her) again disowned a covenant with the devil, disowned that relation about the knife forementioned, declared the occasion of her fits to be discontent, owned the temptations to murder; declared that though the devil had power of her body, she hoped he should not of her soul, that she had rather continue so speechless than have her speech, and make no better use of it than formerly she had, expressed that she was sometimes disposed to do mischief, and [it] was as if some had laid hold of her to enforce her to it, and had double strength to her own, that she knew not whether the devil were in her or no if he were she knew not when or how he entered[.] That when she was taken speechless, she feared as if a string was tied about the roots of her tongue and reached down into her vitals, and pulled her tongue down, and then most when she strove to speak: On Friday [January 12], in the evening, she was taken with a passion of weeping and sighing, which held her till late in the night, at length she sent for me, but the unseasonableness of the weather and my own bodily indisposition prevented: I went the next morning, when she strove to speak something but could not, but was taken with her fits, which held her as long as I tarried, which was more than an hour, and I left her in them: and thus she continues speechless to this instant, January 15, and followed with fits: concerning which state of hers I shall suspend my own judgment, and willingly leave it to the censure of those that are more learned, aged, and judicious: only I shall leave my thoughts in respect of two or three questions which have risen about her: viz.

1. Whether her distemper be real or counterfeit: I shall say no more to that but this, the great strength appearing in them, and great weakness after them, will disclaim the contrary opinion; for though a person may counterfeit much, yet such a strength is beyond the force of dissimulation.

2. Whether her distemper be natural or diabolical, I suppose the premises will strongly enough conclude the latter, yet I will add these two further arguments: 1. the actings of convulsion, which these [fits] come nearest to, are (as persons acquainted with them observe) in many, yea the most essential parts of them quite contrary to these actings. 2. she hath no ways wasted in body, or strength by all these fits, though so dreadful; but [she hath] gathered flesh exceedingly, and hath her natural strength when her fits are off, for the most part.

3. Whether the devil did really speak in her. To that point, which some have much doubted of, thus much I will say to countermand this apprehension: 1. The manner of expression I diligently observed, and could not perceive any organ, any instrument of speech (which the philosopher makes mention of) to have any motion at all. Yea her mouth was sometimes shut without opening sometimes open without shutting or moving, and then both I and others saw her tongue (as it used to be when she was in some fits, when speechless) turned up circularly to the roof of her mouth. 2. The labial letters, divers of which were used by her, viz. B. M. P. which cannot be naturally expressed without motion of the lips, which must needs come within our ken, if observed, were uttered without any such motion, if she had used only linguals, gutturals, etc., the matter might have been more suspicious. 3. The reviling terms then used, were such as she never used before nor since in all this time of her being thus taken: yea, hath been always observed to speak respectfully concerning me. 4. They were expressions which the devil (by her confession) aspersed me, and others withal, in the hour of temptation, particularly she had freely acknowledged that the devil was wont to appear to her in the house of God and divert her mind, and charge her she should not give ear to what that black-coated rogue spoke. 5. We observed when the voice spake, her throat was swelled formidably, as big at least as one's fist. These arguments I shall leave to the censure of the judicious.

4. Whether she have covenanted with the devil or no: I think this is a case unanswerable, her declarations have been so contradictory, one to

another, that we know not what to make of them, and her condition is such as administers many doubts; charity would hope the best, love would fear the worst, but thus much is clear she is an object of pity, and I desire that all that hear of her would compassionate her forlorn state. She is (I question not) a subject of hope, and therefore all means ought to be used for her recovery. She is a monument of divine severity; and the Lord grant that all that see or hear, may fear and tremble.

Amen. Samuel Willard.

Source: Mather Papers, Boston Public Library, as printed in Hall (1991), 198–212. The dates in brackets are Samuel Willard's.

PART IV

The Good Society

The Good Society

Immediately after arriving in New England, the leaders of the Massachusetts Bay Company had to devise a structure of civil government for the new colony. The founders of Plymouth had already done so, and by the late 1630s the colonists who created two independent jurisdictions in Connecticut, one based in New Haven, the second in the river towns of Hartford, Windsor, and Wethersfield, had also put in place their frameworks of government.[1] As soon as these civil governments were up and running, they enacted social policies that were features of the Puritan movement — mandating literacy (the ability to read), requiring strict observance of the Sabbath, prohibiting card playing. As all English communities conventionally did, these governments also wanted to regulate the consumption of alcohol and prevent illicit (premarital or adulterous) relations between the sexes. Creating a viable economy once the influx of immigrants ceased by 1640 was another goal.

Responding to the first of these challenges, John Winthrop, the governor of the Massachusetts Bay Company, relied on the royal charter the company had received in March 1629 for the basic structure of the government: the governor and deputy governor, together with a small group of "Assistants," were joined in a "General Court" by "freemen" who were members of the company (that is, stockholders). This structure rapidly evolved into a system of representative government. Towns became the basic political unit, with the freemen in each town electing "deputies" (representatives) to a General Court or Assembly. Once a year, the freemen also elected the governor, deputy governor, and magistrates (or assistants). More unusual was the decision Winthrop and the other assistants made in October 1630 to redefine the meaning of freeman from stockholders to citizens of a civil state, a step that greatly enlarged the number of adult men who could participate in elections. The follow-

[1] See Andrews (1934 and 1935).

ing May, the General Court ruled that freemen must be church members. New Haven adopted the same rule; Connecticut did not.

Did this rule or other circumstances enable the church to dominate the civil government? The answer is no, because the colonists had a strong sense of how church and state were separate entities. Moreover, they were angered by the English system of church and state, which empowered the Church of England to intrude on civil affairs (ecclesiastical courts could inflict civil punishments and bishops were members of the House of Lords). Puritans complained, too, that the monarchy and Parliament had too much power over the churches. To safeguard against these intrusions, John Cotton and his fellow ministers agreed that clergy should never hold civil office and that any disciplinary actions taken by their congregations should not have civil consequences. Cotton spelled out these principles in lectures he preached in Boston in 1639–1640 (chap. 15). The clergy also insisted that the churches had "liberties" the civil state could not infringe. The law that limited the franchise to church members must be placed in the context of these practices and decisions. Its purpose, as Cotton made clear in writing to Lord Say and Sele, was to ensure that the civil government was sympathetic to the novel system of church government the colonists were establishing; harmony, not control, was the goal.

But did the Bible furnish rules for how to organize and regulate civil society? Surprisingly, the colonists were not of one mind on this matter, as became clear when the Massachusetts government decided that a code of laws was needed. In 1636 John Cotton declared that he was "apt to believe . . . that the word, and scriptures of God doe conteyne a short *supoluposis* [model or pattern], or platforme, not onely of theology, but also of other sacred sciences . . . [including] ethicks, eoconomicks, politicks, church-government, prophecy, academy." After he was asked to draft a law code, he relied heavily on Scripture in writing "Moses His Judicials"(1636). Scripture continued to weigh on Cotton and a few others in their speculations about the ideal form of civil government and the possibility of having "saints" as rulers of the commonwealth. Yet the "Body of Liberties" (1641), the first code of laws in the colony, relied mainly on the English common law, adjusting it to suit the Puritan bias against monopolies and primogeniture. Only in the listing of capital crimes did the "Body of Liberties" rely on the Bible, a step that had the effect of greatly reducing their number from those crimes as defined in English practice. Some of the provisions may strike us as extreme, but in practice few of these laws were fully enforced.[2]

___

[2] Bush (2001), 244; Haskins (1960); Murrin (1984), noting infrequent enforcement of the death penalty for adultery. For a fuller imagining of civil society, see [Anon.], *A Discourse about Civil Government in a New Plantation Whose Design is Religion* (Cam-

The colonists were typically Elizabethan in assuming that social hier-archy was both good and necessary. But could hierarchy be sustained in their new society? One way in which this question was addressed was in efforts to define the godly magistrate and to specify the nature of his authority. During a political crisis of the mid-1640s when his own ac-tions were under attack, John Winthrop wrote a strong defense of au-thority, his "little speech on liberty" (chap. 16). Cotton and his fellow ministers shared his concern, that the colonists not permit government by everyone. On the other hand, the leaders of the new colony refused to acknowledge the hereditary authority of the English aristocracy, a point Cotton made in writing to a Puritan aristocrat who had made ten "demands" as a condition of emigrating to Massachusetts.

Another aspect of political ideology was the assumption that govern-ment owed its authority to "the people" and their informed "consent." Cotton declared that government rested on the people, and Thomas Hooker, preaching the first election sermon in Connecticut in 1638, said so even more emphatically.[3] Puritans were not egalitarian or, in our modern sense of the term, democratic, yet they wanted safeguards against "tyranny" and "arbitrary" uses of power. These expectations had strong English precedents, but they also rested on a theological realism about power and how easily it was abused, a realism Cotton voiced in his lectures of 1639–1640. Other crucial goals or values were "peace" and the common good. As Winthrop famously argued in the "Model of Christian Charity," the people of a godly commonwealth were joined to each other in a social or civil covenant. As in church covenants, which evoked a fellowship grounded in "love," so in a civil covenant every person was responsible for the welfare of the whole. The "Model" and other texts of the time, like election sermons, sketch a strongly communitarian way of life in which self-interest gives way to "charity" (in the sense of love).

A cornerstone of economic and social policy was the generous distri-bution of land, a means of encouraging "competency" or a "comfort-able independence" for each family or household. The colonists also wanted the marketplace to function according to the norm of "justice" or fairness. With the "Weber thesis" (the German social theorist Max Weber's proposal that a work-oriented asceticism, or "Protestant ethic," evolved into a "spirit of capitalism") always in the background, his-torians disagree on how to interpret economic attitudes and practices among the colonists, some arguing that irreparable tensions arose be-tween the "market," on the one hand, and community on the other.

bridge, Mass., 1663), a text attributed to both John Cotton and John Davenport; and John Eliot, *A Christian Commonwealth* (London, 1660).

[3] Hooker's election sermon of 1638 is printed in *Collections of the Connecticut Histori-cal Society* 1 (1862): 19–20.

That the colonists endorsed "material opportunity" and the workings of the market is certain. But as the texts in part 7 indicate, they also worried about prosperity and its implications for religious fervor.

Where the presence of the Bible and theology may be felt is less in the specifics of civil government or economic policy than in the assumption that covenanted societies, having pledged to observe the will of God (this was Winthrop's point in the "Model"), were obliged to repent if they faltered in their obedience. Sin was a disease that infected the moral and social health of a community. Its symptoms included any outbreak of dissension or the waning of family "government." As early as the 1630s, and increasingly thereafter, the colonies employed certain ritual moments, such as fast days, to take stock of how well or badly they were doing in their covenantal obligations. In 1679, on the heels of King Philip's War and mounting disagreements, the ministers in Massachusetts met in synod to identify the moral failings of their day — collectively these added up to "declension" — and to recommend various remedies, including one that was relatively new, renewal of covenant. The "Result" of the synod specified what was wrong, expecting as it did so that a process of healing and renewal would follow thereafter.

Taking for granted that the family was the basic social unit, the colonists knew that Puritan ways of living would take root and flourish in the new world only if "well-ordered" families were able to transmit the parents' values to the next generation. That so many colonists prepared "legacies" addressed to their children bespeaks the felt anxiety about continuity and change — from the Old World to the New, from parent to child. The relationship between parents and children was framed not only by this burden but also by basic assumptions stemming from Elizabethan culture and Protestant theology. As is the case with so many other phases of Puritanism, historians have often assumed that theology, and especially the doctrine of election, dominated how the family was understood and how parents treated their children. The argument runs this way: an authoritarian, repressive theology, together with the anxiety that arose around the doctrine of election, made it impossible for parents to love their children and treat them kindly. Some interpreters have also suggested that the colonists "treated their offspring as miniature adults," expecting them to learn to read at a very early age and denying them that in-between stage we name "adolescence." But is it really so that "Puritan child-rearing ideas and practices had devastating effects on the development of healthy personalities," as some historians have argued?[4]

<hr />

[4] Beales (1985); Susan M. Juster and Maris A. Vinovskis, "Changing Perspectives on the American Family in the Past," *American Review of Sociology* 13 (1987): 201.

Certainly the colonists expected children to obey their parents, an attitude consistent with a broader emphasis on hierarchy and authority. An early-eighteenth-century schoolbook, the *New England Primer*, mirrored these expectations in specifying "the dutiful child's promises," among them "I will honour my Father & Mother," and "I will Obey my Superiours. I will Submit to my Elders." Yet these were commonplaces of the age, not unique to the Puritans. New England parents worried when their children became ill and mourned when death took them away (see Mary Rowlandson's "captivity" narrative, in chap. 26). As for husbands and wives, the relationship between them was patriarchal in that wives were to defer to their husbands. Wives could inherit property from their husbands or parents but were excluded from participating in civil and church government. When Anne Hutchinson tested these boundaries (see her "examination," chap. 21), the magistrates were enraged. But the fervent expressions of love for their husbands in Sarah Goodhue's and Bradstreet's prose and verse indicate the strength of an affectionate ideal of marriage among the colonists, who also recognized that women had distinctive spiritual capacities.

Bibliography

On political developments, Andrews (1934 and 1935); Morgan (1958); Breen (1970). On social history and social values, Rutman (1965), emphasizing the rapid breakdown of communalism; Lockridge (1970), arguing for a "peasant" society; Foster (1974), challenging Bailyn (1955); Crowley (1974); Innes (1995), reintroducing Weber; Valeri (1997); Newall (1998); Martin (1991) on entrepreneurs and communalism; Anderson (1991), chap. 4, and Vickers (1988) on "competency" and economic attitudes; Allen (1981) on English patterns transferred to New England. On families, Morgan (1944, rev. ed., 1966); Laslett (1965); Demos (1970); Greven (1970); Moran and Vinovskis (1982); Thompson (1986); for women, Koehler (1980); Moran (1980); Ulrich (1982); Porterfield (1992); and Norton (1996); for children, Slater (1977) and Beales (1985), an excellent review of interpretations.

Chapter 14

John Winthrop on the Social Ethics
of a Godly Commonwealth

Shortly before leaving England for New England in April 1630, John Winthrop wrote a discourse on Christian charity, using charity in the sense of "love" (1 Cor. 13:13). According to the traditional story, he delivered the "Model of Christian Charity" as a sermon on board the *Arbella* while crossing the Atlantic. But a close reading reveals allusions to the contemporary situation in England, and the text may already have been circulating in handwritten copies before the *Arbella* set sail. Notwithstanding its English roots, the discourse sermon is immensely important for the light it throws on Winthrop's thinking at a critical moment in his personal history, a moment no less critical for the colonizing venture he was leading. He knew that other such ventures, but especially the Virginia Company of London's efforts in the Chesapeake, had foundered on conflicts among the colonists and a disastrous erosion of common goals. The entirety of the "Model" is framed by the assumption that a people in covenant with God will enjoy his favor, but only by remaining faithful to the terms of that covenant. Hence the central purpose of the "Model": to specify those terms in advance and to enact, as it were, a collective pledge to observe them.

"Covenant" is therefore a key concept in the discourse, as are the terms charity, saint, and "body." The resonances of "body" stem from passages in Ephesians that guided the founders of the church in Dedham (chap. 4), and the same verses account for the phrasing of "knit together." Winthrop argued that the subordination of self-interest to the good of the whole was possible only within a community where most of the people were "saints" or "new creatures." Although he insisted on the importance of the secular principle of hierarchy, the "Model" is essentially about the close relationship between the good society and the gospel message of new birth. The closing passage, the much-cited evocation of the new settlement as a "city upon a hill," has generally been misread as suggesting a protomillennial way of thinking.

Bibliography

Foster (1971); Bozeman (1988), chap. 3, correcting the "millennial" interpretation; Bremer (1992); Innes (1995), chaps. 2–3; Bremer (1997), noting parallel themes in other English sermons; Dawson (1998), rejecting a secular/legal reading of the discourse and noting biblical and other sources; Dawson (1991) on its origins; Rutman (1965), arguing its irrelevance to the actual social history of New England.

JOHN WINTHROP

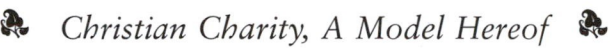 *Christian Charity, A Model Hereof*

God Almighty in his most holy and wise providence hath so disposed of the condition of mankind, as in all times some must be rich some poor, some high and eminent in power and dignity; others mean and in subjection.

The reason hereof.

1. Reason: first, to hold conformity with the rest of his works, being delighted to shew forth the glory of his wisdom in the variety and difference of the creatures and the glory of his power, in ordering all these differences for the preservation and good of the whole, and the glory of his greatness that as it is the glory of princes to have many officers, so this great King will have many stewards counting himself more honored in dispensing his gifts to man by man, than if he did it by his own immediate hand.

2. Reason: secondly, that he might have the more occasion to manifest the work of his Spirit: first, upon the wicked in moderating and restraining them: so that the rich and mighty should not eat up the poor, nor the poor, and despised rise up against their superiors, and shake off their yoke; 2ly in the regenerate in exercising his graces in them, as in the great ones, their love mercy, gentleness, temperance, etc., in the poor and inferior sort, their faith patience, obedience, etc.

3. Reason: thirdly, that every man might have need of other, and from hence they might be all knit more nearly together in the bond of brotherly affection: from hence it appears plainly that no man is made more honorable than another or more wealthy, etc., out of any particular and singular respect to himself but for the glory of his Creator and the common good of the creature, man; therefore God still reserves the property of these gifts to himself as Ezek. 16:17, he there calls wealth his gold and his silver, etc., Prov. 3:9, he claims their service as his due *honor the*

Lord with thy riches, etc. All men being thus (by divine providence) ranked into two sorts, rich and poor; under the first, are comprehended all such as are able to live comfortably by their own means duly improved; and all others are poor according to the former distribution. There are two rules whereby we are to walk one towards another: JUSTICE and MERCY. These are always distinguished in their act and in their object, yet may they both concur in the same subject in each respect; as sometimes there may be an occasion of shewing mercy to a rich man, in some sudden danger of distress, and also doing of mere justice to a poor man in regard of some particular contract, etc. There is likewise a double law by which we are regulated in our conversation one towards another: in both the former respects, the law of nature and the law of grace, or the moral law or the law of the gospel, to omit the rule of justice as not properly belonging to this purpose otherwise than it may fall into consideration in some particular cases: By the first of these laws man as he was enabled so withal [is] commanded [Matt. 19:19] to love his neighbor as himself[:] upon this ground stands all the precepts of the moral law, which concerns our dealings with men. To apply this to the works of mercy this law requires two things[:] first that every man afford his help to another in every want or distress[.] Secondly, that he perform this out of the same affection, which makes him careful of his own good according to that of our Savior Matt. [7:12], *Whatsoever ye would that men should do to you*. This was practiced by Abraham and Lot in entertaining the angels and the old man of Gibea [Gen. 18–19].

The law of grace or the gospel hath some difference from the former as in these respects first the law of nature was given to man in the estate of innocency; this of the gospel in the estate of regeneracy: 2ly, the former propounds one man to another, as the same flesh and image of God, this as a brother in Christ also, and in the communion of the same spirit and so teacheth us to put a difference between Christians and others. *Do good to all especially to the household of faith* [Gal. 6:10]. . . .

This law of the gospel propounds likewise a difference of seasons and occasions there is a time when a Christian must sell all and give to the poor as they did in the apostles' times. There is a time also when a Christian (though they give not all yet) must give beyond their ability, as they of Macedonia [2] Cor. [8:2] likewise community of perils calls for extraordinary liberality and so doth community in some special service for the church.[1] Lastly, when there is no other means whereby our Christian brother may be relieved in this distress, we must help him

---

[1] 2 Cor. 8:2, How that in a great trial of affliction the abundance of their joy and their deep poverty abounded unto the riches of their liberality.

beyond our ability, rather than tempt God, in putting him upon help by miraculous or extraordinary means. . . .[2]

The definition which the Scripture gives us of love is this love is *the bond of perfection* [Col. 3:14]. First, it is a bond, or ligament, 2ly, it makes the work perfect. There is no body but consists of parts and that which knits these parts together gives the body its perfection, because it makes each part so contiguous to other as thereby they do mutually participate with each other, both in strength and infirmity in pleasure and pain, to instance in the most perfect of bodies, Christ and his church make one body: the several parts of this body considered apart before they were united were as disproportionate and as much disordering as so many contrary qualities or elements but when Christ comes and by his Spirit and love knits all these parts to himself and each to other, it is become the most perfect and best proportioned body in the world Eph. 4:16. . . .

The next consideration is how this love comes to be wrought; Adam in his first estate was a perfect model of mankind in all their generations, and in him this love was perfected in regard of the habit, but Adam rent in himself from his Creator, rent all his posterity also one from another, whence it comes that every man is born with this principle in him, to love and seek himself only and thus a man continueth till Christ comes and takes possession of the soul, and infuseth another principle love to God and our brother. And this latter having continual supply from Christ, as the head and root by which he is united get the predominancy in the soul, so by little and little expels the former 1 John 4:7, *Love cometh of God and every one that loveth is born of God*, so that this love is the fruit of the new birth, and none can have it but the new creature [2 Cor. 5:17], now when this quality is thus formed in the souls of men it works like the Spirit upon the dry bones Ezek. 37:[7], bone came to bone, it gathers together the scattered bones or perfect old man Adam and knits them into one body again in Christ whereby a man is become again a living soul. . . .

From the former considerations ariseth these conclusions.

1. First, this love among Christians is a real thing not imaginary.
2ly. This love is as absolutely necessary to the being of the body of Christ, as the sinews and other ligaments of a natural body are to the being of that body.
3ly. This love is a divine spiritual nature free, active strong courageous permanent undervaluing all things beneath its proper object, and of all

---

[2] Winthrop then asked what rule should be observed in situations of giving, lending, and forgiving, answering his own question by insisting on "liberality" and urging forgiveness of debts among a godly people.

the graces this makes us nearer to resemble the virtues of our heavenly Father. . . .

It rests now to make some application of this discourse by the present design which gave the occasion of writing it. Herein are four things to be propounded: first, the persons, 2ly, the work, 3ly, the end, 4ly the means.

1. For the persons, we are a company professing ourselves fellow members of Christ, in which respect only though we were absent from each other many miles, and had our employments as far distant, yet we ought to account ourselves knit together by this bond of love, and live in the exercise of it, if we would have comfort of our being in Christ, this was notorious in the practice of the Christians in former times. . . .

2ly. For the work we have in hand, it is by a mutual consent through a special overruling providence, and a more than an ordinary approbation of the churches of Christ to seek out a place of cohabitation and consortship under a due form of government both civil and ecclesiastical. In such cases as this the care of the public must oversway all private respects, by which not only conscience, but mere civil policy doth bind us; for it is a true rule that particular estates cannot subsist in the ruin of the public.

31y. The end is to improve our lives to do more service to the Lord the comfort and increase of the body of Christ whereof we are members that ourselves and posterity may be the better preserved from the common corruptions of this evil world to serve the Lord and work out our salvation under the power and purity of his holy ordinances.

4ly. For the means whereby this must be effected, they are twofold, a conformity with the work and end we aim at, these we see are extraordinary, therefore we must not content ourselves with usual ordinary means whatsoever we did or ought to have done when we lived in England, the same must we do and more also where we go: That which the most in their churches maintain as a truth in profession only, we must bring into familiar and constant practice, as in this duty of love we must love brotherly without dissimulation [Rom. 12:9–10], we must love one another with a pure heart fervently [1 Pet. 1:22] we must *bear one another's burdens* [Gal. 6:2], we must not look only on our own things, but also on the things of our brethren, neither must we think that the Lord will bear with such failings at our hands as he doth from those among whom we have lived, and that for three reasons. . . .

[Reasons 1 and 2 are omitted.]

3ly. When God gives a special commission he looks to have it strictly observed in every article, when he gave Saul a commission to destroy Amaleck he indented with him upon certain articles and because he failed in one of the least, and that upon a fair pretence, it lost him the kingdom, which should have been his reward, if he had observed his commission [1 Sam. 15; 28:16–18]: Thus stands the cause between God and us, we are entered into covenant with him for this work, we have taken out a commission, the Lord hath given us leave to draw our own articles we have professed to enterprise these actions upon these and these ends, we have hereupon besought him of favor and blessing: Now if the Lord shall please to hear us, and bring us in peace to the place we desire, then hath he ratified this covenant and sealed our commission, [and] will expect a strict performance of the articles contained in it, but if we shall neglect the observation of these articles which are the ends we have propounded, and dissembling with our God, shall fall to embrace this present world and prosecute our carnal intentions, seeking great things for ourselves and our posterity, the Lord will surely break out in wrath against us be revenged of such a perjured people and make us know the price of the breach of such a covenant.

Now the only way to avoid this shipwreck and to provide for our posterity is to follow the counsel of Micah [6:8], *to do justly, to love mercy, to walk humbly with our God*, for this end, we must be knit together in this work as one man, we must entertain each other in brotherly affection, we must be willing to abridge ourselves of our superfluities, for the supply of others' necessities, we must uphold a familiar commerce together in all meekness, gentleness, patience and liberality, we must delight in each other, make others' conditions our own rejoice together, mourn together, labor, and suffer together, always having before our eyes our commission and community in the work, our community as members of the same body, so shall we *keep the unity of the spirit in the bond of peace* [Eph. 4:3], the Lord will be our God and delight to dwell among us, as his own people and will command a blessing upon us in all our ways, so that we shall see much more of his wisdom power goodness and truth than formerly we have been acquainted with, we shall find that the God of Israel is among us, when ten of us shall be able to resist a thousand of our enemies, when he shall make us a praise and glory, that men shall say of succeeding plantations: the Lord make it like that of New England: for we must consider that we shall be as a city upon a hill [Matt. 5:14], the eyes of all people are upon us; so that if we shall deal falsely with our God in this work we have undertaken and so cause him to withdraw his present help from us, we shall be made a story and a by-word through the world, we shall open the mouths of enemies to speak evil of the ways of God and all professors for God's sake; we shall shame the faces of many of God's worthy servants, and cause their prayers to be turned into curses upon us till we be consumed out of the good land whither we are going: And to shut up this discourse with that exhortation of Moses that faithful servant of the Lord in his last farewell to Israel Deut. 30:[15], Beloved *there is now set before us life, and good, death and evil in that we are commanded this day to love the Lord our God, and to love one another to walk in his ways and to keep his commandments and his ordinance, and his laws,* and the articles of our covenant with him that we may live and be multiplied, and that the Lord our God may bless us in the land whither we go to possess it: But if our hearts shall turn away so that we will not obey, but shall be seduced and worship other gods our pleasures, and profits, and serve them; it is propounded unto us this day, we shall surely perish out of the good land whither we pass over this vast sea to possess it; therefore let us choose life, that we, and our seed, may live; by obeying his voice, and cleaving to him, for he is our life, and our prosperity.

Source: *Winthrop Papers* 2:282–95.

Chapter 15

John Cotton On Democracy, Power, and Theocracy

How could the structure of civil government encompass both "authority" and "liberty"? Did the solution lie in having a "mixt" government, one part "aristocracy," the other part "democracy"? Could the interests of the churches and the civil state be protected so that neither trespassed on the other?

The colonists wrestled with these questions throughout the 1630s and early 1640s, often disagreeing on how to answer them. John Cotton took his turn at providing answers in a letter of 1636 to William Fiennes, Lord Say and Sele, a titled Puritan aristocrat who had befriended the founders of Massachusetts. Together with Robert Greville, Lord Brook, he was interested in emigrating himself, but only if ten "demands" were met. Basically, the two aristocrats wanted assurances that their social rank would secure them special rights and privileges within civil government. They disliked having the franchise tied to church membership, a practice they regarded as placing too much power in the hands of the churches.

In behalf of the Massachusetts government, Cotton commented on the ten demands and also wrote the letter that follows. Although he acknowledged "hereditary honor" as scriptural, he insisted that church membership, not "pre-eminence," was the necessary condition of being admitted to the rank of "magistracy" and the privileges of freemanship. "None are to be trusted with public permanent authority but godly men," his commentary concludes.[1] What he said in the letter is easy to misinterpret unless we keep in mind that "aristocracy" and "democracy" refer, not to social rank, but to structures of government. Far from employing "aristocracy" to deny participation by the people, Cotton outlined a "mixt" form of government that allowed leadership by the few and participation by all who were freemen. He refused to acknowledge social rank and hereditary privilege, and he defended the law of May 1631 that tied voting rights to church membership. Three years later, in the midst of a series of sermons on Revelation 13, Cotton

---

[1] Thomas Hutchinson, *The History of the Colony and Province of Massachusetts-Bay*, ed. L. S. Mayo, 3 vols. (Cambridge, Mass., 1936), 1:410–13.

returned to the question of church-state relations. Here, again, we may easily misinterpret "theocracy" to mean that the church dominated civil society. On the contrary, his intention was to keep them apart while insisting that both cooperated to ensure the rule of God's law. More pointedly, and with the unfavorable example of the Church of England in mind, he warned against allowing ministers to hold any political office or permitting church censures, such as excommunication, to have any civil consequences, as they had in the English system. Moreover, he warmly defended the rights of the people and warned against usurpations of power. He was speaking ostensibly of Roman Catholicism and the papacy, but these sermons also reflected the political context of the late 1630s.

Bibliography
Brown (1954); Morgan (1958); Breen (1970); Kupperman (1989).

JOHN COTTON

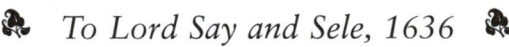 *To Lord Say and Sele, 1636*

Right honorable,

. . . God's institutions (such as the government of church and of commonwealth be) may be close and compact, and coordinate one to another, and yet not confounded. God hath so framed the state of church government and ordinances, that they may be compatible to any commonwealth, though never so much disordered in his frame. But yet when a commonwealth hath liberty to mould his own frame (*scripturae plenitudinem adoro*) I conceive the Scripture hath given full direction for the right ordering of the same, and that, in such sort as may best maintain the *euexia*[2] of the church. Mr. Hooker doth often quote a saying out of Mr. Cartwright (though I have not read it in him) that no man fashioneth his house to his hangings, but his hangings to his house.[3] It is better that the commonwealth be fashioned to the setting forth of God's house, which is his church: than to accommodate the church frame to the civil state. Democracy, I do not conceive that ever God did ordain as a fit government either for church or commonwealth. If the people be governors, who shall be governed? As for monarchy, and aristocracy, they are both of them clearly approved, and directed in Scrip-

---

[2] Health, well-being.
[3] Thomas Hooker (1586–1647); Thomas Cartwright (1535–1603), a major figure in the radical wing of the Elizabethan Puritan movement.

ture, yet so as referreth the sovereignty to himself, and setteth up theocracy in both, as the best form of government in the commonwealth, as well as in the church.

The law, which your Lordship instanceth in [that none shall be chosen to magistracy among us but a church member][4] was made and enacted before I came into the country; but I have hitherto wanted sufficient light to plead against it. 1st. The rule that directeth the choice of supreme governors, is of like equity and weight in all magistrates, that one of their brethren (not a stranger) should be set over them, Deut. 17:15 and Jethro's counsel to Moses was approved of God, that the judges, and officers to be set over the people, should be men fearing God, Exod. 18:21 and Solomon maketh it the joy of a commonwealth, when the righteous are in authority, and their mourning when the wicked rule, Prov. 29:21, Job 34:30. Your Lordship's fear, that this will bring in papal excommunication, is just, and pious: but let your Lordship be pleased again to consider whether the consequence be necessary. *Turpius ejicitur quam non admittitur*: non-membership may be a just cause of non-admission to the place of magistracy, but yet, ejection out of his membership will not be a just cause of ejecting him out of his magistracy. A godly woman, being to make choice of an husband, may justly refuse a man that is either cast out of church fellowship, or is not yet received into it, but yet, when she is once given to him, she may not reject him then, for such defect. Mr. Humfrey was chosen for an assistant (as I hear) before the colony came over hither: and, though he be not as yet joined into church fellowship (by reason of the unsettledness of the congregation where he liveth) yet the commonwealth do still continue his magistracy to him, as knowing he waiteth for opportunity of enjoying church fellowship shortly.[5]

When your Lordship doubteth, that this course will draw all things under the determination of the church, *in ordine ad spiritualia* (seeing the church is to determine who shall be members, and none but a member may have to do in the government of a commonwealth) be pleased (I pray you) to conceive, that magistrates are neither chosen to office in the church, nor do govern by directions from the church, but by civil laws, and those enacted in general courts, and executed in courts of justice, by the governors and assistants. In all which, the church (as the church) hath nothing to do: only, it prepareth fit instruments both to rule, and to choose rulers, which is no ambition in the church, nor dishonor to the commonwealth, the Apostle, on the contrary, thought it

[4] These brackets are Cotton's or Hutchinson's; they do not indicate additional material appearing for the first time in the present edition.

[5] John Humfry (1593–1653?), a founder of the Massachusetts Bay Company, was elected an assistant under the original charter and again in May 1632, before he actually arrived in Massachusetts in 1634.

a great dishonor and reproach to the church of Christ, if it were not able to yield able judges to hear and determine all causes amongst their bethren, 1 Cor. 6:1 to 5, which place alone seemeth to me fully to decide this question: for it plainly holdeth forth this argument: [if] it is a shame to the church to want able judges of civil matters (as v. 5) and an audacious act in any church member voluntarily to go for judgment, otherwhere than before the saints (as v. 1) then it will be no arrogance nor folly in church members, nor prejudice to the commonwealth, if voluntarily they never choose any civil judges, but from amongst the saints, such as church members are called to be. But the former is clear: and how then can the latter be avoided. If this therefore be (as your Lordship rightly conceiveth one of the main objections if not the only one) which hindereth this commonwealth from the entertainment of the propositions of those worthy gentlemen, we entreat them, in the name of the Lord Jesus, to consider, in meekness of wisdom, it is not any conceit or will of ours, but the holy counsel and will of the Lord Jesus (whom they seek to serve as well as we) that overruleth us in this case: and we trust will overrule them also, that the Lord only may be exalted amongst all his servants. What pity and grief were it, that the observance of the will of Christ should hinder good things from us!

But your Lordship doubteth, that if such a rule were necessary, then the church estate and the best ordered commonwealth in the world were not compatible. But let not our Lordship so conceive. For, the church submitteth itself to all the laws and ordinances of men, in what commonwealth soever they come to dwell. But it is one thing, to submit unto what they have no calling to reform: another thing, voluntarily to ordain a form of government, which to the best discerning of many of us (for I speak not of myself) is expressly contrary to rule. Nor need your Lordship fear (which yet I speak with submission to your Lordship's better judgment) that this course will lay such a foundation, as nothing but a mere democracy can be built upon it. Bodin confesseth, that though it be *status popularis*, where a people choose their own governors; yet the government is not a democracy, if it be administered, not by the people, but by the governors, whether one (for then it is a monarchy, though elective) or by many, for then (as you know) it is aristocracy.[6] In which respect it is, that church government is justly denied (even by Mr. Robinson) to be democratical, though the people choose their own officers and rulers.[7]

Nor need we fear, that this course will, in time, cast the commonwealth into distractions, and popular confusions. For (under correction)

[6] Jean Bodin, celebrated French political theorist; according to Bush (2001) Cotton was drawing on Bodin's *Six Bookes of a Commonwealth* (London, 1606).

[7] John Robinson, the Separatist pastor of the "Pilgrims" in England and Leiden, was notably sympathetic to "democratic" church government.

these three things do not undermine, but do mutually and strongly maintain one another (even those three which we principally aim at) authority in magistrates, liberty in people, purity in the church. Purity, preserved in the church, will preserve well-ordered liberty in the people, and both of them establish well-balanced authority in the magistrates. God is the author of all these three, and neither is himself the God of confusion, nor are his ways the ways of confusion, but of peace. . . .

Now the Lord Jesus Christ (the Prince of Peace) keep and bless your Lordship, and dispose of all your times and talents to his best advantage: and let the covenant of his grace and peace rest upon your honorable family and posterity throughout all generations.

Thus, humbly craving pardon for my boldness and length, I take leave and rest,
  Your Honors to serve in Christ Jesus, John Cotton

Source: Thomas Hutchinson, *The History of the Colony and Province of Massachusetts-Bay*, ed. L. S. Mayo, 3 vols. (Cambridge, Mass., 1936), 1:414–17; and, fully annotated, in Bush (2002), 242–49.

JOHN COTTON

🐉 *An Exposition upon the Thirteenth Chapter* 🐉
of the Revelation

. . . Let it be a seasonable advertisement to . . . all magistrates, how to make use of their authority to be as protectors of the church, and in respect of their spiritual estate, as children of the church, but not to give the horns to the church . . . you see it makes the church a monster, and it is to make a beast of the church: and so if you should make church officers justices of peace, or counselors, or prostitute your own government to them, that if the church condemn any, then you must do so too (as heretofore if a man were condemned by the church, and by them delivered to the secular power, they burn him presently), this puts your horns upon the churches' head, unto monstrous deformity: and therefore it is necessary for magistrates to keep their power in their own hands, and not to take things ipso facto, from the church. . . . It is a comfortable thing for churches to be strengthened and protected by civil magistrates: but if they captivate their power to the church, that what church rulers call for not according to the Word, but their lusts, that the civil magistrate must confirm, that makes the church a beast. . . . This may serve to teach us the danger of allowing to any mortal man an inordinate measure of power to speak great things, to allow to any man uncontrollableness of speech, you see the desperate danger of it: Let all the world learn to give mortal men no greater power than they are content they shall use, for use it they will: and unless they be better taught of God, they will use it ever and anon. . . .

This is one of the strains of nature, it affects boundless liberty, and to run to the utmost extent: whatever power he hath received, he hath a corrupt nature that will improve it in one thing or other; if he have liberty, he will think why may he not use it. Set up a pope as lord paramount over kings and princes, and they shall know that he hath power over them, he will take liberty to depose one, and set up another. Give him power to make laws, and he will approve, and disprove as he list. . . . It is therefore most wholesome for magistrates and officers in church and commonwealth, never to affect more liberty and authority than will do them good, and the people good; for whatever transcendent power is given, will certainly overrun those that give it, and those that receive it: There is a strain in a man's heart that will sometime or other run out to excess, unless the Lord restrain it. . . . It is necessary[,] therefore, that all power that is on earth be limited, church-power or other: If there be power given to speak great things, then look for great blasphemies, look for a licentious abuse of it. It is counted a matter of danger to the state to limit prerogatives; but it is a further danger, not to have them limited: They will be like a tempest, if they be not limited. . . . It is therefore fit for every man to be studious of the bounds which the Lord hath set: and for the people, in whom fundamentally all power lies, to give as much power as God in his Word gives to men: And it is meet that the magistrates in the commonwealth, and so officers in the churches should desire to know the utmost bounds of their power. . . .

Source: John Cotton, *An Exposition Upon The Thirteenth Chapter of the Revelation* (London, 1655), 17–18, 71–72.

Chapter 16

John Winthrop Defends His Understanding
of Authority

During the May 1645 session of the Massachusetts General Court, or "Court of Elections," eighty-one residents of Hingham, Massachusetts, petitioned the deputies complaining that several of the magistrates had intervened inappropriately to deny the townsmen's choice of a militia captain. The petition did not specify John Winthrop by name, but when questioned by the Court two of the town leaders named him as the person responsible for the magistrates' intervention. The petition touched a live nerve, for the deputies were perennially dissatisfied with what they took to be the high-handedness of the magistrates, who in turn were divided over how to behave toward the "lesser gentry" of the towns. The outcome of these tensions was a public trial in early June, with Winthrop, who was not reelected deputy governor, accused of acting illegally. After he defended himself, the two houses of the General Court agreed to compromise: Winthrop was exonerated, and some of the petitioners were fined.

Winthrop then asked for permission to deliver his "Little Speech on Liberty." Famously, he differentiated "natural" from "civil" liberty, declaring that the latter was appropriate in a covenanted society because it obligated everyone to subordinate individual self-interest to "authority." He insisted, as well, on the divine origins of magistracy, the implication being that no magistrate could be removed from office unless he "fail in faithfulness." As he pointed out, the relationship between magistrate and citizen was analogous to the relationship between Christ and those who are Christian. In each case, it is good and necessary that Christians subject themselves to an authority that embodies or enforces the "moral law." It has been suggested that the speech "did not contain a single new idea."[1] But it fills out what he meant by the opening sentence of the "Model of Christian Charity."

---

[1] Foster (1971), 88.

Bibliography
Brown (1954); Breen (1970); Foster (1971); Wall (1972); Bremer (2003).

JOHN WINTHROP

🐦 *A Little Speech on Liberty* 🐦

I suppose something may be expected from me, upon this charge that is befallen me, which moves me to speak now to you; yet I intend not to intermeddle in the proceedings of the Court, or with any of the persons concerned therein. Only I bless God, that I see an issue of this troublesome business. I also acknowledge the justice of the Court, and, for mine own part, I am well satisfied, I was publicly charged, and I am publicly and legally acquitted, which is all I did expect or desire. And though this be sufficient for my justification before men, yet not so before the Lord, who hath seen so much amiss in my dispensations (and even in this affair) as calls me to be humbled. For to be publicly and criminally charged in this Court, is matter of humiliation (and I desire to make a right use of it), notwithstanding I be thus acquitted. If her father had spit in her face (saith the Lord concerning Miriam), should she not have been ashamed seven days? Shame had lain upon her, whatever the occasion had been. I am unwilling to stay you from your urgent affairs, yet give me leave (upon this special occasion) to speak a little more to this Assembly. It may be of some good use, to inform and rectify the judgments of some of the people, and may prevent such distempers as have arisen amongst us. The great questions that have troubled the country, are about the authority of the magistrates and the liberty of the people. It is yourselves who have called us to this office, and being called by you, we have our authority from God, in way of an ordinance, such as hath the image of God eminently stamped upon it, the contempt and violation whereof hath been vindicated with examples of divine vengeance. I entreat you to consider, that when you choose magistrates, you take them from among yourselves, men subject to like passions as you are. Therefore when you see infirmities in us, you should reflect upon your own, and that would make you bear the more with us, and not be severe censurers of the failings of your magistrates, when you have continual experience of the like infirmities in yourselves and others. We account him a good servant, who breaks not his covenant. The covenant between you and us is the oath you have taken of us, which is to this purpose, that we shall govern you and judge your causes by the rules of God's laws and our own, according to our best skill. When you agree with a workman to build you a ship or house, etc., he undertakes as well for his skill as for his faithfulness, for it is his profession, and you pay him for both. But when you call one to be a magistrate, he doth not profess nor undertake to have sufficient skill for that office, nor can you furnish him with gifts, etc., therefore you must run the hazard of his skill and ability. But if he fail in faithfulness, which by his oath he is bound unto, that he must answer for. If it fall out that the case be clear to common apprehension, and the rule clear also, if he transgress here, the error is not in the skill, but in the evil of the will: it must be required of him. But if the case be doubtful, or the rule doubtful, to men of such understanding and parts as your magistrates are, if your magistrates should err here, yourselves must bear it.

For the other point concerning liberty, I observe a great mistake in the country about that. There is a twofold liberty, natural (I mean as our nature is now corrupt) and civil or federal. The first is common to man with beasts and other creatures. By this, man, as he stands in relation to man simply, hath liberty to do what he list; it is a liberty to evil as well as to good. This liberty is incompatible and inconsistent with authority, and cannot endure the least restraint of the most just authority. The exercise and maintaining of this liberty makes men grow more evil, and in time to be worse than brute beasts: *omnes sumus licentia deteriores.*[2] This is that great enemy of truth and peace, that wild beast, which all the ordinances of God are bent against, to restrain and subdue it. The other kind of liberty I call civil or federal, it may also be termed moral, in reference to the covenant between God and man, in the moral law, and the politic covenants and constitutions, amongst men themselves. This liberty is the proper end and object of authority, and cannot subsist without it; and it is a liberty to that only which is good, just, and honest. This liberty you are to stand for, with the hazard (not only of your goods, but) of your lives, if need be. Whatsoever crosseth this, is not authority, but a distemper thereof. This liberty is maintained and exercised in a way of subjection to authority; it is of the same kind of liberty wherewith Christ hath made us free. The woman's own choice makes such a man her husband; yet being so chosen he is her lord, and she is to be subject to him, yet in a way of liberty, not of bondage; and a true wife accounts her subjection her honor and freedom, and would not think her condition safe and free, but in her subjection to her husband's authority. Such is the liberty of the church under the authority of Christ, her king and husband; his yoke is so easy and sweet to her as a bride's

[2] "We all degenerate in the absence of control." Winthrop (1996), 587 n. 2, identifying the source as the Roman writer Terence.

ornaments; and if through frowardness or wantonness, etc., she shake it off, at any time, she is at no rest in her spirit, until she take it up again; and whether her lord smiles upon her, and embraceth her in his arms, or whether he frowns, or rebukes, or smites her, she apprehends the sweetness of his love in all, and is refreshed, supported, and instructed by every such dispensation of his authority over her. On the other side, you know who they are that complain of this yoke and say, let us break their bands, etc., we will not have this man to rule over us. Even so, brethren, it will be between you and your magistrates. If you stand for your natural corrupt liberties, and will do what is good in your own eyes, you will not endure the least weight of authority, but will murmur, and oppose, and be always striving to shake off that yoke; but if you will be satisfied to enjoy such civil and lawful liberties, such as Christ allows you, then will you quietly and cheerfully submit unto that authority which is set over you, in all the administrations of it, for your good. Wherein, if we fail at any time, we hope we shall be willing (by God's assistance) to hearken to good advice from any of you, or in any other way of God; so shall your liberties be preserved, in upholding the honor and power of authority amongst you.

Source: Winthrop (1908), 2:237–39, compared with Winthrop (1996), 584–89, which has many differences of punctuation, and annotates the references to Scripture.

Chapter 17

Sarah Goodhue on Family as a
Spiritual Community

The powerful presence of the family in everyday religion is captured in a "Valedictory and Monitory Writing" written circa 1681 by Sarah Whipple Goodhue (1641–1681), who spent her entire life in Ipswich, Massachusetts, where her father was a deacon, then elder, of the town church. In July 1661 she married Joseph Goodhue, son of another deacon, and the two began what seems to have been a remarkably satisfying marriage. Sarah gave birth on average every two years; she and Joseph were eventually to have ten children. The names she and her husband gave their children associate them with figures in the Bible, a common practice among the colonists. Late in her ninth pregnancy, moved by a "strong persuasion" of her death in or soon after childbirth, she wrote a letter of encouragement and exhortation to the people she valued most. Here she spoke of her interactions with parents, siblings, the "private society" (a devotional group that met for prayer and the reading over of sermons), children, husband, and "the Lord Jesus Christ." Regarding her baptized children as "in the bond of the covenant," she stressed, as ministers such as Increase Mather were also emphasizing (see chap. 9), the obligation to "improve" their advantages. Related to her emphasis on the baptismal covenant is her attentiveness to "portion," or inheritance, which for her as for Shepard and Bradstreet was as much spiritual as material. As the historian Laurel Ulrich has noted, Goodhue sought to balance "maternal love" with "paternal government." Confined as she often was to the household, she pursued in that setting a routine of devotional practices that were in keeping with the "devotional renaissance" of the late seventeenth century. Sarah Goodhue's premonition was accurate; she died suddenly three days after bearing healthy twins.

Bibliography
Ulrich (1982), chap. 8; Hambrick-Stowe (1982) on the devotional renaissance.

SARAH GOODHUE

🪶 *A Valedictory and Monitory Writing* 🪶

Dear and loving husband, if it should please the Lord to make a sudden change in thy family, the which I know not how soon it may be, and I am fearful of it:

Therefore in a few words I would declare something of my mind, lest I should afterwards have no opportunity: I cannot but sympathize and pity thy condition, seeing that thou hast a great family of children, and some of them small, and if it should please the Lord to add to thy number one more or two, be not discouraged, although it should please the Lord to deprive thee of thy weak help which is so near and dear unto thee. Trust in the living God, who will be an help to the helpless, and a father to the motherless: My desire is that if thou art so contented, to dispose of two or three of my children: If it please the Lord that I should be delivered of a living child, son or daughter, my desire is, that my father and mother should have it, if they please, I freely bequeath and give it to them. And also my desire is, that my cousin *Symond Stacy* should have *John* if he please, I freely bequeath and give him to him for his own if thou art willing. And also my desire is, that my cousin *Catharine Whipple* should have *Susanna,* which is an hearty girl, and will quickly be helpful to her, and she may be helpful to the child, to bring her up: These or either of these I durst trust their care under God, for the faithful discharge of that which may be for my children's good and comfort, and I hope to thy satisfaction: Therefore if they be willing to take them, and to deal well with them, answer my desire I pray thee, thou hast been willing to answer my request formerly, and I hope now thou wilt, this being the last so far as I know.

Honored and most loving father and mother I cannot tell how to express your fatherly and motherly love towards me and mine: It hath been so great, and in several kinds; for the which in a poor requital, I give you hearty and humble thanks, yet trusting in God that he will enable you to be a father and mother to the motherless: Be not troubled for the loss of an unworthy daughter; but rejoice in the free grace of God, that there is hope of rejoicing together hereafter in the place of everlasting joy and blessedness.

Brothers and sisters all, hearken and hear the voice of the Lord, that by his sudden providence doth call aloud on you, to prepare yourselves for that swift and sudden messenger of death: that no one of you may be found without a wedding garment [Matt. 22:11–12]; a part and portion in Jesus Christ: the assurance of the love of God, which will enable you to leave this world, and all your relations, though never so near and dear, for the everlasting enjoyment of the great and glorious God, if you do fear him in truth.

The private society, to which while here I did belong; if God by his providence come amongst you, and begin by death to break you; be not discouraged, but be strong in repenting, faith and prayers with the lively repeatal of God's counsels declared unto you by his faithful messengers: O pray each for another and with one another; that so in these threatening times of storms and troubles, you may be found more precious than gold tried in the fire. Think not a few hours time in your approaches to God misspent; but consider seriously with yourselves, to what end God lent to you any time at all: This surely I can through grace now say; that of the time that there I spent, through the blessing of God, I have no cause to repent, no not in the least.

O my children all, which in pains and care have cost me dear; unto you I call to come and take what portion your dying mother will bestow upon you: many times by experience it hath been found, that the dying words of parents have left a living impression upon the hearts of children; O my children be sure to set the fear of God before your eyes; consider what you are by nature, miserable sinners, utterly lost and undone; and that there is no way and means whereby you can come out of this miserable estate; but by the mediation of the Lord Jesus Christ: He died a reproachful death, that every poor humble and true repenting sinner by faith on God through him, might have everlasting life: O my children, the best counsel that a poor dying mother can give you is, to get a part and portion in the Lord Jesus Christ, that will hold, when all these things will fail; O let the Lord Jesus Christ be precious in your sight.

O children, neighbors and friends, I hope I can by experience truly say, that Christ is the best, most precious, most durable portion, that all or any of you can set your hearts' delight upon: I forever desire to bless and praise the Lord, that he hath opened mine eyes to see the emptiness of these things, and mine own; and to behold the fullness and riches of grace that is in the Lord Jesus Christ: To that end my children, I do not only counsel you, but in the fear of the Lord I charge you all, to read God's Word, and pray unto the Lord that he would be pleased to give you hearts and wisdom to improve the great and many privileges that the Lord is at present pleased to afford unto you, improve your youthful days unto God's service, your health and strength whilst it lasteth, for you know not how soon your health may be turned into sickness, your strength into weakness, and your lives into death; as death cuts the tree of your life down, so it will lie; as death leaveth you, so judgment will find you out: Therefore be persuaded to agree with your adversary quickly, whilst you are in the way of these precious opportunities: be sure to improve the lively dispensations of the gospel; give good attention unto sermons preached in public, and to sermons repeated in private. Endeavor to learn to write your father's hand, that you may read over those precious sermons, that he hath taken pains to write and keep from the mouths of God 's lively messengers, and in them there are lively messages: I can through the blessing of God along with them, say, that they have been lively unto me: And if you improve them aright, why not to all of you? God upbraideth none of the seed of Jacob, that seek his face in truth: My children be encouraged in this work, you are in the bond of the covenant, although you may be breakers of covenant, yet God is a merciful keeper of covenant. Endeavor as you grow up, to own and renew your covenant, and rest not if God give you life, but so labor to improve all the advantages that God is pleased to afford you, that you may be fit to enjoy the Lord Jesus Christ in all his ordinances. What hath the Lord Jesus Christ given himself for you? if you will lay hold upon him by true faith and repentance: And what will you be backward to accept of his gracious and free offers, and not keep in remembrance his death and sufferings, and to strengthen your weak faith; I thank the Lord, in some measure, I have found that ordinance, a life-making ordinance unto my soul.

Oh the smiles and loving embraces of the Lord Jesus Christ, that they miss of, that hold off, and will not be in such near relation unto their Head and Savior. The Lord grant that Christ may be your portions all.

My children, one or two words I have to say to you more, in the first place, be sure to carry well to your father, obey him, love him, follow his instructions and example, be ruled by him, take his advice, and have a care of grieving him: For I must testify the truth unto you, and I may call some of you to testify against yourselves; that your father hath been loving, kind, tender-hearted towards you all; and laborious for you all, both for your temporal and spiritual good: You that are grown up, cannot but see how careful your father is when he cometh home from his work, to take the young ones up into his wearied arms, by his loving carriage and care towards those, you may behold as in a glass, his tender care and love to you everyone as you grow up: I can safely say, that his love was so to you all, that I cannot say which is the child that he doth love best; but further I may testify unto you, that this is not all your father hath been doing for you, and that some of you may bear me witness, that he hath given you many instructions, which hath been to the end your souls might enjoy happiness, he hath reproved you often for your evils, laying before you the ill event that would happen unto you, if you did not walk in God's ways, and give your minds to do his will, to keep holy his sabbaths, to attend unto reading God's Word, hearing it preached with a desire to profit by it, and declaring unto you this way that he had experienced to get good by it; that was to pray unto the Lord for his blessing with it and upon it, that it might soak into the heart and find entertainment there: and that you should meditate upon it, and he hath told you, meditation was as the key to open the door, to let you in, or that into your heart, that you might find the sweetness of God's Word.

Furthermore, my children, be encouraged in this work, your father hath put up many prayers with ardent desires and tears to God on behalf of you all: which if you walk with God, I hope you will find gracious answers and showers of blessing from those bottled tears for you. O carry it well to your father, that he may yet be encouraged to be doing and pleading for your welfare: Consider that the Scripture holdeth forth many blessings to such children that obey their parents in the Lord, but there are curses threatened to the disobedient.

My children, in your life and conversation, live godly, walk soberly, modestly, and innocently: be diligent, and be not hasty to follow new fashions, and the pride of life, that now too much abounds. Let not pride betray the good of your immortal souls.

And if it please the Lord that you live to match yourselves, and to make your choice: Be sure you choose such as first do seek the kingdom of heaven.

My first, as thy name is *Joseph*, labor so in knowledge to increase,
As to be freed from the guilt of thy sins, and enjoy eternal peace.

Mary, labor so to be arrayed with the hidden man of the heart,
That with Mary thou mayest find, thou hast chosen the better part.

William, thou hadst that name for thy grandfather's sake,
Labor so to tread in his steps, as over sin conquest thou mayest make.

Sarah, Sarah's daughter thou shalt be, if thou continuest in doing well,
Labor so in holiness among the daughters to walk, as that thou mayest excel.

So my children all, if I must be gone, I with tears bid you all *Farewell*. The Lord bless you all.

Now dear husband, I can do no less than turn unto thee,
And if I could, I would naturally mourn with thee.

And in a poor requital of all thy kindness, if I could, I would speak some things of comfort to thee, whilst thou dost mourn for me.

A tender-hearted, affectionate and entire loving husband thou hast been to me several ways. If I should but speak of what I have found as to these outward things; I being but weakly natured: In all my burthens thou hast willingly with me sympathized, and cheerfully thou hast helped me bear them: which although I was but weak natured; and so the more unabled to go through those troubles in my way: Yet thou hast by thy cheerful love to me, helped me forward in a cheerful frame of spirit. But when I come to speak or consider in thy place, thy great pains and care for the good of my soul.

This twenty years experience of thy love to me in this kind, hath so instamped it upon my mind, that I do think that there never was man more truly kind to a woman: I desire forever to bless and praise the Lord, that in mercy to my soul, he by his providence ordered that I should live with thee in such a relation, therefore dear husband be comforted in this (although God by his providence break that relation between us, that he gave being to at first), that in thy place thou hast been a man of knowledge to discharge to God and my soul, that Scripture commanded duty, which by the effects in me wrought, through the grace of God, thou mayest behold with comfort our prayers not hindered; but a gracious answer from the Lord, which is of great price and reward. Although my being gone be thy loss, yet I trust in and through Jesus Christ, it will be my gain.

Was it not to this end that the Lord was pleased to enable thee and give thee in heart to take (as an instrument) so much pains for his glory and my eternal good, and that it might be thy comfort: As all thy reading of scriptures and writing of sermons, and repeating of them over to me, that although I was necessarily often absent from the public worship of God, yet by thy pains and care to the good of my soul, it was brought home unto me: And blessed be the Lord who hath set home by the operation of his Spirit, so many repeatals of precious sermons and prayers and tears for me and with me, for my eternal good: And now let it be thy comfort under all, go on and persevere in believing in God, and praying fervently unto God: Let not thy affectionate heart become hard, and thy tears dried away: And certainly the Lord will render a double portion of blessing upon thee and thine.

If thou couldest ask me a reason why I thus declare myself? I can answer no other but this; that I have had of late a strong persuasion upon my mind, that by sudden death I should be surprised, either at my travail, or soon after it, the Lord fit me for himself: although I could be very willing to enjoy thy company, and my children longer, yet if it be the will of the Lord that I must not, I hope I can say cheerfully, the will of the Lord be done, this hath been often my desire and thy prayer.

Further, if thou couldest ask me why I did not discover some of these particulars of my mind to thee before, my answer is because I knew that thou wert tender hearted towards me, and therefore I would not create thee needless trouble.

O dear husband of all my dearest bosom friends, if by sudden death I must part from thee, let not thy trouble and cares that are on thee make thee to turn aside from the right way.

> O dear heart, if I must leave thee and thine here behind,
> Of my natural affection here is my heart and hand.

Be courageous, and on the living God bear up thy heart in so great a breach as this.

Sarah Goodhue. Dear husband, if by sudden death I am taken away from thee, there is infolded among thy papers something that I have to say to thee and others. July 14, 1681.

Source: *The Copy of a Valedictory and Monitory Writing Left by Sarah Goodhue* (Portland, Me., 1805); no copy survives of a presumed 1681 printing.

Chapter 18

Anne Bradstreet: Verses Addressed to
Her Husband and Family

Anne Bradstreet, the only woman in seventeenth-century New England to publish a book of poetry, wrote expressively of her love for members of her family. Bradstreet felt responsible for the spiritual well-being of her children, likening the physical process of giving birth to the "new birth" of being reborn in Christ she wanted her children to experience, with her aid. The formal message of some of these poems is that love of God is of greater weight than love of husband or children. But the emotional tone gives equal if not greater weight to the bonds of marriage and parenting.

After a few years in Newtown (Cambridge), the Bradstreets lived in Ipswich, Massachusetts, for a decade before removing to Andover, where Anne spent the rest of her life. Anne had the first of her eight children in 1632 or 1633. Well read in Scripture, and familiar with the Greek and Roman classics as well as contemporary history and poetry, she was indebted to the tradition of "Protestant poetics" and the connections it established between meditation and poetry. A brother-in-law carried a collection of her poems to London, where they were published in 1650 under the title *The Tenth Muse Lately sprung up in America*. A second, enlarged edition, published in Boston in 1678, *Several Poems Compiled with great variety of Wit and Learning, full of Delight,* contained the "occasional" poems that follow.

Bibliography

Ellis (1867); Lewalski (1979); Hambrick-Stowe (1988); Schweitzer (1991); Daly (1978), correcting the argument that Bradstreet rebelled against Puritanism.

ANNE BRADSTREET

 To my Dear and loving Husband[1]

If ever two were one, then surely we.
If ever man were lov'd by wife, then thee;

Complemented by a series of poems lamenting her husband's absence: "A Letter to her

If ever wife was happy in a man,
Compare with me ye women if you can.
I prize thy love more than whole mines of gold,
Or all the riches that the East doth hold.
My love is such that rivers cannot quench,
Nor ought but love from thee, give recompense.
Thy love is such I can no way repay,
The heavens reward thee manifold I pray.
Then while we live, in love lets so persevere,
That when we live no more, we may live ever. /2

IN REFERENCE TO HER CHILDREN, 23 JUNE 1659[2]

I had eight birds hatcht in one nest,
Four cocks there were, and hens the rest,
I nurst them up with pain and care,
Nor cost, nor labor did I spare,
Till at the last they felt their wing.
Mounted the trees, and learn'd to sing;
Chief of the brood then took his flight,
To regions far, and left me quite:
My mournful chirps I after send,
Till he return, or I do end,
Leave not thy nest, thy dam and sire,
Fly back and sing amidst this quire.
My second bird did take her flight,
And with her mate flew out of sight;
Southward they both their course did bend,
And seasons twain they there did spend:
Till after blown by southern gales,
They norward steered with filled sails.
A prettier bird was no where seen,
Along the beach among the treen.
I have a third of color white,
On whom I plac'd no small delight;

Husband, absent upon Publick employment," "Another," "Upon my dear and loving husband his going into England, Jan. 16, 1661," "In my Solitary houres in my dear husband his Absence," "In thankfull acknowledgment for the letters I received from my husband out of England," "In thankfull Remembrance for my dear husbands safe Arrivall Sept. 3, 1661," and a poem on an illness he suffered, "For the restoration of my dear Husband from a burning Ague, June, 1661," all in Ellis (1867).

[2] Ellis (1867) transcribed the year as 1656, noting that it must be a misprint; McElrath and Robb (1981) read it as 1659, the date used here.

Coupled with mate loving and true,
Hath also bid her dam adieu:
And where Aurora first appears,
She now hath percht, to spend her years;
One to the academy flew
To chat among that learned crew:
Ambition moves still in his breast
That he might chant above the rest,
Striving for more than to do well,
That nightingales he might excel.
My fifth, whose down is yet scarce gone
Is 'mongst the shrubs and bushes flown,
And as his wings increase in strength,
On higher boughs he'll perch at length.
My other three, still with me nest,
Until they'r grown, then as the rest,
Or here or there, they'll take their flight,
As is ordained, so shall they light.
If birds could weep, then would my tears
Let others know what are my fears
Lest this my brood some harm should catch,
And be surpris'd for want of watch,
Whilst pecking corn, and void of care
They fall un'wares in fowlers snare:
Or whilst on trees they sit and sing,
Some untoward boy at them do fling.
Or whilst allur'd with bell and glass,
The net be spread, and caught, alas,
Or least by lime-twigs they be foil'd,
Or by some greedy hawks be spoil'd.
O would my young, ye saw my breast,
And knew what thoughts there sadly rest,
Great was my pain when I you bred,
Great was my care, when I you fed,
Long did I keep you soft and warm,
And with my wings kept off all harm,
My cares are more, and fears than ever,
My throbs such now, as 'fore were never:
Alas my birds, you wisdom want,
Of perils you are ignorant,
Oft times in grass, on trees, in flight,
Sore accidents on you may light.

O to your safety have an eye,
So happy may you live and die:
Mean while my days in tunes I'll spend,
Till my weak lays with me shall end,
In shady woods I'll sit and sing,
And things that past, to mind I'll bring.
Once young and pleasant, as are you,
But former toys (no joys) adieu.
My age I will not once lament,
But sing, my time so near is spent.
And from the top bough take my flight,
Into a country beyond sight,
Where old ones, instantly grow young,
And there with seraphims set song:
No seasons cold, nor storms they see;
But spring lasts to eternity,
When each of you shall in your nest
Among your young ones take your rest,
In chirping languages, oft them tell,
You had a dam that lov'd you well,
That did what could be done for young,
And nurst you up till you were strong,
And 'fore she once would let you fly,
She shew'd you joy and misery;
Taught what was good, and what was ill,
What would save life, and what would kill.
Thus gone, amongst you I may live,
And dead, yet speak, and counsel give:
Farewell my birds, farewell adieu,
I happy am, if well with you.

IN MEMORY OF MY DEAR GRANDCHILD ELIZABETH BRADSTREET, WHO DECEASED AUGUST, 1665 BEING A YEAR AND HALF OLD

Farewell dear babe, my heart's too much content,
Farewell sweet babe, the pleasure of mine eye,
Farewell fair flower that for a space was lent,
Then ta'en away unto eternity.
Blest babe why should I once bewail thy fate,
Or sigh thy days so soon were terminate;
Sith thou art settled in an everlasting state.

2.

By nature trees do rot when they are grown.
And plumbs and apples throughly ripe do fall,
And corn and grass are in their season mown,
And time brings down what is both strong and tall.
But plants new set to be eradicate,
And buds new blown, to have so short a date,
Is by his hand alone that guides nature and fate.

ON MY DEAR GRANDCHILD SIMON BRADSTREET, WHO DIED ON 16 NOVEMBER 1669 BEING BUT A MONTH, AND ONE DAY OLD

No sooner come, but gone, and fal'n asleep,
Acquaintance short, yet parting caus'd us weep,
Three flowers, two scarcely blown, the last i'th' bud,
Cropt by th' Almighty's hand; yet is he good,
With dreadful awe before him let's be mute,
Such was his will, but why, let's not dispute,
With humble hearts and mouths put in the dust,
Let's say he's merciful, as well as just,
He will return, and make up all our losses,
And smile again, after our bitter crosses.
Go pretty babe, go rest with sisters twain
Among the blest in endless joys remain.

Source: Ellis (1867), compared with McElrath and Robb (1981).

Chapter 19

The Ministers Complain of Public and Private Sins, and Offer a Remedy for Them

Leaders of New England communities repeatedly complained that the colonists were falling into sin. The purpose of these complaints was to orchestrate a process of renewal, a ritual cleansing of sin that would restore both the moral and social health of the community, the two being understood as interdependent. Another premise of these complaints was that a community that violated its covenant with God would suffer avenging judgments, as manifested in droughts, dissension, and war.

In November 1675, fearing that the outbreak of war with the Native Americans (King Philip's War; see below, pt. VI) meant that the colonists had "departed with a great backsliding" from God, the Massachusetts General Court enacted a dozen laws regulating such matters as cursing, the length of men's hair, the wearing of wigs, and illicit drinking. Realizing that these laws had not arrested "declension," and upset by the emergence of Baptists and Quakers, the ministers of Massachusetts asked the Court in 1679 to summon a synod to consider "what . . . may appear necessary for the preventing [of] schisms, heresies, profaneness, and [for] the establishment of the churches in one faith and order of the gospel." The Court agreed to do so, posing two questions for the synod that met in Boston in September: "What are the evills that have provoked the Lord to bring his judgments on New England?" and "What is to be donn that so these evills may be reformed." In October a delegation of ministers presented its report to the Court, which ordered the "Result," titled *The Necessity of Reformation With the Expedients subservient thereunto, asserted* (Boston, 1679), to be printed.[1]

The culminating act of the synod was to recommend a particular means of reform, "renewal of covenant."[2] As imagined by Increase Mather (1639–1723), minister of Second Church, Boston, chief promo-

---

[1] Shurtleff (1853–1854), 5:59–63, 215–16.

[2] Two contemporary sermons throw light on this ritual: Increase Mather, *Renewal of Covenant the Great Duty Incumbent on Decaying or Distressed Churches* (1677); and James Fitch, *An Explanation of the Solemn Advice* (Boston, 1679).

ter of the synod and author of *The Necessity of Reformation*, the ritual had two purposes: to strengthen the colonists' obedience to certain moral rules by leading congregations and towns through a ceremony of repentance and renewal, and to overcome the factionalism that was weakening the authority of the clergy and the churches. Like so many texts from the late seventeenth century, the recommendations of the synod must be read in two ways: as reflecting widely shared assumptions about covenant, sin, and God's providence; and as keyed to contemporary events and the politics of declension.[3] In the opening pages of *The Necessity of Reformation*, Mather plays on the theme of "our Fathers," rehearsing the image of the founders and the original "errand" he and others of his generation had constructed (see below, pt. VII).

Bibliography

Walker (1893), chap. 13; Miller (1953); Hall (1972), chap. 11; Foster (1991), chap. 5.

 INCREASE MATHER, THE NECESSITY OF REFORMATION

QUESTION 1. What are the evils that have provoked the Lord to bring his judgments on New England?

ANSWER. That sometimes God hath had, and pleaded a controversy with his people, is clear from the Scripture, Hos. 4:1 and 12:2, Mic. 6:1–2. Where God doth plainly and fully propose, state and plead his controversy, in all the parts and causes of it, wherein he doth justify himself, by the declaration of his own infinite mercy, grace, goodness, justice, righteousness, truth and faithfulness in all his proceedings with them; and judge his people, charging them with all those provoking evils which had been the causes of that controversy, and that with the most high, and heavy aggravation of their sins, and exaggeration of the guilt and punishment, whence he should have been most just, in pleading out his controversy with them, unto the utmost extremity of justice and judgment.

That God hath a controversy with his New-England people is undeniable, the Lord having written his displeasure in dismal characters against us. Though personal afflictions do oftentimes come only or chiefly for probation, yet as to public judgments it is not wont to be so; especially when by a continued series of providence[s], the Lord doth appear and plead against his people. 2 Sam. 21:1. As with us it hath been from year to year. Would the Lord have whetted his glittering

---

[3] For a cogent interpretation of this politics, see Foster (1991), chap. 5.

sword, and his hand have taken hold on judgment? Would he have sent such a mortal contagion like a besom of destruction in the midst of us? Would he have said, Sword! go through the land, and cut off man and beast? Or would he have kindled such devouring fires, and made such fearful desolations in the earth, if he had not been angry? It is not for nothing that the merciful God, who doth not willingly afflict nor grieve the children of men, hath done all these things unto us; yea and sometimes with a cloud hath covered himself, that our prayer should not pass through. And although 'tis possible that the Lord may contend with us partly on account of secret unobserved sins . . . nevertheless, it is sadly evident that there are visible, manifest evils, which without doubt the Lord is provoked by. For,

I. There is a great and visible decay of the power of godliness amongst many professors in these churches. It may be feared, that there is in too many spiritual and heart apostasy from God, whence communion with him in the ways of his worship, especially in secret, is much neglected, and whereby men cease to know and fear, and love and trust in him; but take up their contentment and satisfaction in something else. . . .

II. The pride that doth abound in New England testifies against us. Hos. 5:5, Ezek. 7:10. Both spiritual pride, Zeph. 3:11. Whence two great evils and provocations have proceeded and prevailed amongst us.

1. A refusing to be subject to order according to divine appointment, Num. 16:3, 1 Pet. 5:5.

2. Contention. Prov. 13:10. An evil that is most eminently against the solemn charge of the Lord Jesus, John 13:34–35. And that for which God hath by severe judgments punished his people, both in former and latter ages. This malady hath been very general in the country: we have therefore cause to fear that the wolves which God in his holy providence hath let loose upon us, have been sent to chastise his sheep for their dividings and strayings one from another; and that the wars and fightings, which have proceeded from the lust of pride in special, have been punished with the sword, James 4:1, Job 19:29.

Yea, and pride in respect to apparel hath greatly abounded. Servants, and the poorer sort of people are notoriously guilty in the matter, who (too generally) go above their estates and degrees, thereby transgressing the laws both of God and man, Matt. 11:8. Yea, it is a sin that even the light of nature, and laws of civil nations have condemned. 1 Cor. 11:14. Also, many, not of the meaner sort, have offended God by strange apparel, not becoming serious Christians, especially in these days of affliction and misery, wherein the Lord calls upon men to put off their ornaments, Exod. 33:5, Jer. 4:30. . . .

III. Inasmuch as it was in a more peculiar manner with respect to the Second Commandment, that our fathers did follow the Lord into this wilderness, whilst it was a land not sown, we may fear that the breaches of that commandment are some part of the Lord's controversy with New England. Church fellowship, and other divine institutions are greatly neglected. Many of the rising generation are not mindful of that which their baptism doth engage them unto, viz. to use utmost endeavors that they may be fit for, and so partake in, all the holy ordinances of the Lord Jesus. Matt. 28:20. There are too many that with profane Esau slight spiritual privileges. Nor is there so much of discipline, extended towards the children of the covenant, as we are generally agreed ought to be done.[4] On the other hand, humane inventions, and will-worship have been set up even in Jerusalem. Men have set up their thresholds by God's threshold, and their posts by his post. Quakers are false worshippers: and such Anabaptists as have risen up amongst us, in opposition to the churches of the Lord Jesus, receiving into their society those that have been for scandal delivered unto Satan,[5] yea, and improving those as administrators of holy things, who have been (as doth appear) justly under church censures, do no better than set up an altar against the Lord's altar. Wherefore it must needs be provoking to God, if these things be not duly and fully testified against, by everyone in their several capacities respectively. . . .

IV. The holy and glorious Name of God hath been polluted and profaned amongst us, more especially.

1. By oaths, and imprecations in ordinary discourse; yea, and it is too common a thing for men in a more solemn way to swear unnecessary oaths; whenas it is a breach of the Third Commandment, so to use the blessed Name of God. And many (if not the most) of those that swear, consider not the rule of an oath. Jer. 4:2. So that we may justly fear that because of swearing the land mourns, Jer. 23:10.

2. There is great profaneness, in respect of irreverent behavior in the solemn worship of God. It is a frequent thing for men (though not necessitated thereunto by any infirmity) to sit in prayer time, and some with their heads almost covered, and to give way to their own sloth and sleepiness, when they should be serving God with attention and intention, under the solemn dispensation of his ordinances. We read but of one man in the Scripture that slept at a sermon, and that sin hath like to have cost him his life, Acts 20:9.

V. There is much Sabbath-breaking; since there are multitudes that do profanely absent themselves or theirs from the public worship of God, on his holy day, especially in the most populous places [of] the land;

---

[4] Discipline, a coded plea to include baptized adults and their children within the covenantal watch of the church; the "Result" argues that churches should adopt the 1662 synod's entire program.

[5] That is, persons censored by their previous congregations, a charge previously made against the Baptist Obadiah Holmes (see pt. V).

and many under pretence of differing apprehensions about the beginning of the Sabbath,[6] do not keep a seventh part of time holy unto the Lord, as the Fourth Commandment requireth, walking abroad, and traveling (not merely on the account of worshipping God in the solemn assemblies of his people, or to attend works of necessity or mercy) being a common practice on the Sabbath day, which is contrary unto that rest enjoined by the commandment. Yea, some that attend their particular servile callings and employments after the Sabbath is begun, or before it is ended. Worldly, unsuitable discourses are very common upon the Lord's day, contrary to the scripture which requireth that men should not on holy times find their own pleasure, nor speak their own words, Isa. 58:13. Many that do not take care so to dispatch their worldly businesses, that they may be free and fit for the duties of the Sabbath, and that do (if not wholly neglect) after a careless, heartless manner perform the duties that concern the sanctification of the Sabbath. This brings wrath, fires and other judgments upon a professing people, Neh. 3:17–18, Jer. 17:27.

VI. As to what concerns families and the government thereof, there is much amiss. There are many families that do not pray to God constantly morning and evening, and many more wherein the Scriptures are not daily read, that so the Word of Christ might dwell richly with them. Some (and too many) houses that are full of ignorance and profaneness, and these not duly inspected;[7] for which cause wrath may come upon others round about them, as well as upon themselves. Josh. 22:20, Jer. 5:7 and 10:25. And many householders who profess religion, do not cause all that are within their gates to become subject unto good order as ought to be. Exod. 20:10. Nay, children and servants that are not kept in due subjection; their masters, and parents especially, being sinfully indulgent towards them. This is a sin which brings great judgments, as we see in Eli's and David's family. In this respect, Christians in this land, have become too like unto the Indians, and then we need not wonder if the Lord hath afflicted us by them. Sometimes a sin is discerned by the instrument that providence doth punish with. Most of the evils that abound amongst us, proceed from defects as to family government.

VII. Inordinate passions. Sinful heats and hatreds, and that amongst church members themselves, who abound with evil surmisings, uncharitable and unrighteous censures, back-bitings, hearing and telling tales, few that remember and duly observe the rule, with an angry counte-

---

[6] See Solberg (1977).

[7] In 1679 the General Court ordered such inspections. Shurtleff (1853–1854), 5: 240–41.

nance to drive away the talebearer: Reproachful and reviling expressions, sometimes to or of one another. Hence lawsuits are frequent, brother going to law with brother, and provoking and abusing one another in public courts of judicature, to the scandal of their holy profession, Isa. 58:4, 1 Cor. 6:6–7. . . .

VIII. There is much intemperance. The heathenish and idolatrous practice of health-drinking is too frequent. That shameful iniquity of sinful drinking is become too general a provocation. Days of training,[8] and other public solemnities, have been abused in this respect: And not only English but Indians have been debauched, by those that call themselves Christians, who have put their bottles to them, and made them drunk also. This is a crying sin, and the more aggravated in that the first planters of this colony did (as is in the patent expressed) come into this land with a design to convert the heathen unto Christ, but if instead of that, they be taught wickedness, which before they were never guilty of, the Lord may well punish us by them. Moreover, the sword, sickness, poverty, and almost all the judgments which have been upon New England, are mentioned in the Scripture as the woeful fruit of that sin. . . . It is a common practice for town-dwellers, yea and church members, to frequent public houses, and there to misspend precious time, unto the dishonor of the gospel, and the scandalizing of others, who are by such examples induced to sin against God. In which respect, for church members to be unnecessarily in such houses, is sinful, scandalous, and provoking to God. . . .

And there are other heinous breaches of the Seventh Commandment. Temptations thereunto are become too common, viz. such as immodest apparel, Prov. 7:10. Laying out of hair, borders, naked necks and arms, or, which is more abominable, naked breasts, and mixed dancings, light behavior and expressions, sinful company-keeping with light and vain persons, unlawful gaming, an abundance of idleness, which brought ruinating judgment upon Sodom, and much more upon Jerusalem (Ezek. 16:49) and doth sorely threaten New England, unless effectual remedies be thoroughly . . . applied. . . .

X. Inordinate affection to the world. Idolatry is a God-provoking, judgment-procuring sin. And covetousness is idolatry. Eph. 5:5. There hath been in many professors an insatiable desire after land, and worldly accommodations, yea, so as to forsake churches and ordinances, and to live like heathen, only that so they might have elbow room enough in the world. Farms and merchandising have been pre-

---

[8] Days when local militias met for training, occasions notable for the amount of drinking being done. See David W. Conroy, *In Public Houses: Drink and the Revolution of Authority in Colonial Massachusetts* (Chapel Hill, N.C., 1995), chap. 1.

ferred before the things of God. In this respect, the interest of New England seemeth to be changed. We differ from other outgoings of our nation, in that it was not any worldly consideration that brought our fathers into this wilderness, but religion, even that so they might build a sanctuary unto the Lord's Name; whenas now, religion is made subservient unto worldly interests. Such iniquity causeth war to be in the gates, and cities to be burnt up. Judg. 8:5, Matt. 22:5, 7. Wherefore, we cannot but solemnly bear witness against that practice of settling plantations without any ministry amongst them, which is to prefer the world before the gospel. . . . Moreover, that many are under the prevailing power of the sin of worldliness is evident,

1. From that oppression which the land groaneth under. There are some traders, who sell their goods at excessive rates, day-laborers and mechanics are unreasonable in their demands; yea, there have been those that have dealt deceitfully and oppressively towards the heathen amongst whom we live, whereby they have been scandalized and prejudiced against the Name of Christ. The Scripture doth frequently threaten judgments for the sin of oppression, and in special the oppressing sword cometh as a just punishment for that evil. Ezek. 7:11 and 22:15, Prov. 28:8, Isa. 5:7. . . .

XIII. There are sins against the gospel, whereby the Lord hath been provoked. Christ is not prized and embraced in all his offices and ordinances as ought to be. Manna hath been loathed, the pleasant land despised, Ps. 106:24. Though the gospel and covenant of grace call upon men to repent, yet there are multitudes that refuse to repent, when the Lord doth vouchsafe them time and means. No sins provoke the Lord more than impenitency and unbelief Jer. 8:6, Zech. 7:11–13, Heb. 3:17–18, Rev. 2:21–22. There is great unfruitfulness under the means of grace, and that brings the most desolating judgments, Isa. 5:4–5, Matt. 3:10 and 21:43. . . .

QUESTION II. What is to be done that so these evils may be reformed.[9]

. . . VIII. Solemn and explicit renewal of the covenant is a scripture expedient for reformation. We seldom read of any solemn reformation but it was accomplished in this way, as the Scripture doth abundantly declare and testify. And as the judgments which befell the Lord's people of old are recorded for our admonition, 1 Cor. 10:11. So the course which they did (according to God) observe in order to reformation and averting those judgments, is recorded for our imitation; and this was an explicit renovation of covenant. And that the Lord doth call us to this

---

[9] Twelve recommendations follow, among them providing ministers a better maintenance, having the magistrates execute the laws against drinking and selling "strong drink," and more attention to schools.

work, these considerations seem to evince. 1. If implicit renewal of covenant be an expedient for reformation, and to divert impending wrath and judgment, then much more an explicit renewal is so. But the first of these is indubitable. In prayer, and more especially on days of solemn humiliation before the Lord, there is an implicit renewal of covenant, and yet the very dictates of natural conscience put men upon such duties, when they are apprehensive of a day of wrath, approaching. If we may not renew our covenants with God, for fear lest men should not be true and faithful in doing what they promise, then we must not observe days of fasting and prayer; which none will say. . . . 5. Men are hereby brought under a stronger obligation, unto better obedience. There is an awe of God upon the consciences of men when so obliged. As it is in respect of oaths, they that have any conscience in them, when under such bonds, are afraid to violate them. Some that are but legalists and hypocrites, yet solemn covenants with God, have such an awe upon conscience, as to enforce them unto an outward reformation, and that doth divert temporal judgments. And they that are sincere, will thereby be engaged unto a more close and holy walking before the Lord, and so become more eminently blessings unto the societies and places whereto they do belong. 6. This is the way to prevent (and therefore also to recover out of) apostasy. In this respect, although there were no visible degeneracy amongst us, yet this renovation of covenant, might be of singular advantage. There was no public idolatry (nor other transgression) allowed of in the days of Joshua. Judg. 2:7, Josh. 23:8. Yet did Joshua persuade the children of Israel, to renew their covenant; doubtless, that so he might thereby restrain them from future idolatry and apostasy. Josh. 24:25. Lastly, the churches which have lately and solemnly attended this scripture expedient, for reformation, have experienced the presence of God with them, signally owning them therein; how much more might a blessing be expected, should there be a general concurrence in this matter?

Source: [Increase Mather], *The Necessity of Reformation With the Expedients subservient thereunto, asserted* (Boston, 1679).

PART V

Dissenters

Dissenters

The Puritan movement was never monolithic. Some within the movement were moderates, others radical or conservative in how they wanted to remodel the church and refashion society. The radicals who called for the abolition of the episcopacy in the *Admonition to Parliament* (1572) were succeeded by "Separatists" who condemned the Church of England as "unlawful." In the early seventeenth century a few radicals abandoned orthodox Calvinism and affirmed a Holy Spirit–centered "spiritism." When Parliament asserted itself against Charles I in 1640 and allowed state censorship of the press to lapse in 1641, "Familists," "Anabaptists," "Antinomians," and "Seekers," all angrily described (and their dangers exaggerated) in heresiographies such as the Presbyterian Thomas Edwards's *Gangraena: Or a Catalogue and Discovery of many of the Errours, Heresies, Blasphemies and pernicious Practices of the Sectaries* (London, 1646), were suddenly free to publicize their denunciations of the ordained clergy, the system of tithes used to support them, and the authority of the civil state to regulate matters of conscience. Commonly, these groups extolled the "liberty of the Spirit" and denounced all forms of instituted worship. Commonly, too, these radicals viewed the present moment through the lens of apocalypticism, prophesying that a great spiritual transformation was about to occur. The most sizable of these groups and, apart from the Baptists, the only one to survive to our own day, were the "Friends" or "Quakers" who emerged out of this ferment in the early 1650s.

Some of this ferment had already appeared in the colonies. Shortly after he arrived in 1631, Roger Williams became a Separatist, a Baptist, and a Seeker (although he did not call himself this). Other Baptists were present almost from the outset. Although the first such congregation was not organized in Massachusetts until 1665, orthodox ministers were constantly under pressure to defend infant baptism.

The most disruptive episode of dissent was the Antinomian controversy of 1636–1638. It was provoked by the preaching of John Cotton and the spiritual counsel offered by Anne Hutchinson, a member of his congregation. A longer-lasting issue was whether the colonists would insist on uniformity or tolerate some differences of opinion. The colonists arrived sharing the same insistence on uniformity that almost every national church in the Reformed tradition had as its policy and that the Puritan movement within the Church of England also took for granted. Quite unexpectedly, opinion in England changed with the outbreak of war between the king and Parliament in 1642 and the summoning of the Westminster Assembly. The Congregational faction in the Assembly, which was dominated by Presbyterians, began to argue against uniformity, as did left-wing Puritans, including Roger Williams, who was a pioneer in this regard (see chap. 20 below). Three Baptists in New England initiated a confrontation with the Massachusetts government in 1651 that led to an exchange of arguments about liberty of conscience, with John Cotton defending what once had been the orthodox position (see chap. 22 below). The colonies continued to reject a policy of toleration until it was finally imposed on them by the English government toward the end of the century. The Quaker "invasion" of New England inaugurated another phase of conflict. Quaker missionaries, both men and women, engaged in astonishing feats of evangelism to the West Indies, the southern colonies, and New England. The willingness of the early Quakers to endure punishment by the civil state led to the execution in Massachusetts of four missionaries in 1659–1660, one of them Mary Dyer, who had sympathized with Anne Hutchinson in the 1630s.

Despite the harsh treatment of Baptists and Quakers, it is misleading to cast dissent as the other side of a repressive, intolerant orthodoxy. Far too often this is how the story is told, the few dissenters cast as protodemocrats and the orthodox as backward-looking. Yet most of the dissenters in England and New England emerged from the ranks of the Puritan movement and "dissented" in the sense of exaggerating some aspect of the Puritan program. Moreover, the orthodox disagreed among themselves over such questions as baptismal policy and the limits of congregational autonomy.

Bibliography

Miller (1933) on the commitment of the colonists to uniformity; Haller (1955) on the emergence of arguments for liberty of conscience; Gura (1984), the fullest survey; McLoughlin (1971); Chu (1985); Pestana (1991); Louise Breen (2001); Nuttall (1946) on radical uses of the Holy Spirit; Hill (1972) on the English side of the story; Endy (1986), indispensable for rethinking the history of radicalism.

Chapter 20

Roger Williams
Separatist, Baptist, "Seeker"

Canonized in the nineteenth century as a prophet of religious liberty, Roger Williams (1603–1683), a graduate of Cambridge University and former house chaplain in Essex, England, began to challenge the practices of the founders of Massachusetts almost from the moment he arrived in the colony in February 1631. No one expected him to do so, for in England he was an acquaintance of John Cotton and John Winthrop, connections that account for his being invited by the newly organized congregation in Boston to become its "teacher." He refused on the grounds that he "durst not officiate to an unseparated people," the first sign of his Separatist understanding of the true church. Soon he was voicing other opinions that put him at odds with his fellow ministers and the magistrates: that the royal patent from Charles I did not lawfully entitle the colonists to the land they were occupying; that women should wear veils over their heads in church; that the Cross of Saint George should be cut out of the royal flag; and that the clergy should not gather together in regular meetings since doing so threatened congregational independence. In early July 1635, the General Court cited four other "dangerous opinions," the most telling of them that "the magistrate ought not to punish the breach of the first table" — that is, the first four of the Ten Commandments, which specify the right worship of God. The following winter, the Court lost its patience when it learned he was continuing publicly to voice his opinions and ordered him returned to England. Learning of this order before it was enforced, Williams made his way in January 1636 to Plymouth, moving shortly thereafter to territory that lay beyond its boundaries, where he helped found the town of Providence and eventually a new colony, Rhode Island. He never resumed the ministry but became a trader, political leader, and negotiator or go-between with the local Indians.

Theologically Williams was an orthodox Calvinist in almost every respect. But like other radical Puritans before him, he wanted to free himself completely from the corruptions of the Church of England and to repent his complicity with those corruptions. A primitivist, he questioned the scriptural basis for infant baptism and in 1639 had himself rebaptized. Like other Congregationalists, he believed that with the coming of Christ the "national" church of the Jews had been abolished; more unusually, he went on to argue that the "types" of Old Testament kings and law were irrelevant to the fashioning of the true church under Christ: nation and church were no longer identical, one consequence being that the civil state had no authority over the church, or vice versa. A close reader of Scripture, and especially of the book of Revelation, he concluded on the basis of passages such as Jeremiah 27 that the visible church had fallen into apostasy and that no form of ministry was presently valid, the corollary argument being that the church would be raised out of its "wilderness" condition only when Christ commissioned a new priesthood. Summing up Williams's thinking in this regard, John Cotton recalled how Williams "first renounced communion with them all [the churches in New England] . . . and then fell off from his ministry, and then from all church fellowship, and then from his Baptism (and was himself baptized again), and then from the Lord's Supper and from all ordinances of Christ dispensed in any church way, till God shall stir up himself, or some other new apostles, to recover and restore the ordinances and churches of Christ out of the ruins of anti-Christian apostasy."[1] Other radicals in England who shared his thinking became known as Seekers, although Williams seems never to have described himself this way.[2]

Building on the standard Puritan distinction between "spiritual" and "temporal" spheres, Williams began to argue in the 1630s that civil officers could not regulate the church or impose their authority in matters of conscience. As various scholars have observed, his "conception of conscience did not differ significantly in most respects from that of orthodox Puritans," to whom it signified "an awareness of a divine rule of law shared by all members of a group."[3] That conscience would necessarily err in the fallen state of humankind was not, for Williams, a reason for the civil state to intervene. His position on the discontinuity of the Old and New Testaments, together with his assertion that the church was lost in apostasy, also entered into his defense of liberty of conscience. As another historian has pointed out, Williams "deconstructed the argument for civil jurisdiction over religious matters."[4] While in England in the early 1640s, Williams began to publish his

---

[1] *The Complete Writings of Roger Williams*, ed. Perry Miller, 7 vols. (New York, 1963), 2:11.
[2] Garrett (1970), chap. 7.
[3] LaFantasie (1988), 1:349, citing several scholars.
[4] Timothy L. Hall, *Separating Church and State: Roger Williams and Religious Liberty* (Urbana, 1998), 85.

opinions, with John Cotton as his foil. The two engaged in a long-range debate that extended throughout the 1640s, and Williams continued to publish his views on these issues into the early 1650s, when he published the second of his extended responses to Cotton, *The Bloudy Tenent Yet more bloudy By Mr. Cottons endeavor to wash it White in the Blood of the Lambe* (1652). Parliament ordered the first of his books, *The Bloudy Tenent of Persecution for Cause of Conscience* (1644), publicly burned.

Bibliography

Rosenmeier (1968); Garrett (1970); Gilpin (1979); LaFantasie (1988), with superb summaries of the scholarship in the headnotes and annotations, and including Cotton's initial letter challenging Williams's reasoning.

FROM JOHN WITHROP'S

🍃 *History of New England* 🍃

[April 12, 1631] At a Court holden at Boston (upon information to the governor that they of Salem had called Mr. Williams to the office of a teacher) a letter was written from the Court to Mr. Endicott,[5] to this effect that whereas Mr. Williams had refused to join with the congregation at Boston because they would not make a public declaration of their repentance for having communion with the churches of England while they lived there, and besides had declared his opinion that the magistrate might not punish the breach of the Sabbath nor any other offence as it was a breach of the first table.[6]

[Early November 1633] The ministers in the Bay and Saugus, did meet once a fortnight at one of their houses by course, where some question of moment was debated: Mr. Skelton the pastor of Salem[7] and Mr. Williams who was removed from Plymouth thither (but not in any office though he exercised by way of prophesy) took some exception against it, as fearing it might grow in time to a presbytery or superintendency, to the prejudice of the church's liberties: but this fear was without cause, for they were all clear in that point that no church or person can have power over another church. . . .

---

[5] John Endicott (1589?–1665) arrived in 1628 at Salem; he was an assistant (magistrate) in the General Court.

[6] The first four of the Ten Commandments.

[7] Samuel Skelton (1593–1634), an ordained minister in the Church of England; hired by the Massachusetts Bay Company, he emigrated in 1629.

[December 27, 1633] The governor and assistants met at Boston, and took into consideration a treatise which Mr. Williams (then of Salem) had sent to them, and which he had formerly written to the governor and council of Plymouth wherein among other things, he disputes their right to the lands they possessed here: and concluded that claiming by the king's grant they could have no title: nor otherwise except they compounded with the natives: for this taking advice with some of the most judicious ministers (who much condemned Mr. Williams's error and presumption) they gave order that he should be convented at the next Court, to be censured, etc.: There were three passages chiefly whereat they were much offended. 1: for that he chargeth King James to have told a solemn public lie: because in his patent he blessed God that he was the first Christian prince that had discovered this land. 2: for that he chargeth him and others with blasphemy for calling Europe Christendom or the Christian world: 3: for that he did personally apply to our present King Charles these three: places in the Revelation viz:[8]

. . . Mr. Williams also wrote to the governor and also to him and the rest of the council, very submissively: professing his intent to have been only to have written for the private satisfaction of the governor, etc.: of Plymouth without any purpose to have stirred any further in it. . . . At the next Court he appeared privately and gave satisfaction of his intention and loyalty[9] so it was left and nothing done in it.

[January 24, 1634] The governor and council met again at Boston to consider of Mr. William's letter, etc. when with the advice of Mr. Cotton and Mr. Wilson, and weighing his letter, and further considering of the aforesaid offensive passages in his book (which being written in very obscure and implicate phrases, might well admit of doubtful interpretation) they found the matters not to be so evil as at first they seemed: whereupon they agreed that upon his retractation, etc.: and taking an oath of allegiance to the king it should be passed over.

[November 27, 1634] It [the government] was likewise informed that Mr. Williams of Salem had broken his promise to us in teaching publicly against the king's patent and our great sin in claiming right thereby to this country, etc.: and for usual[ly] terming the churches of England Antichristian we granted summons to him for his appearance at the next Court.

[April, 30 1635] The governor and assistants sent for Mr. Williams. The occasion was for that he had taught publicly that a magistrate ought not to tender an oath to an unregenerate man: for that we

[8] The three places he cited were Rev. 16:13–14, 17:12–14, and 18:9. *Winthrop Papers* 3:147–48.

[9] The phrase "and loyalty" in Winthrop (1908) reads "his loyalty" in Winthrop (1996).

thereby have communion with a wicked man in the worship of God: and cause him to take the name of God in vain: he was heard before all the ministers and very clearly confuted: Mr. Endicott was at first of the same opinion but he gave place to the truth.

[July 8, 1635] Mr. Williams of Salem was summoned and did appear. It was laid to his charge that being under question before the magistrates and churches for divers dangerous opinions viz. 1: that the magistrate ought not to punish the breach of the first table, otherwise than in such cases as did disturb the civil peace. 2: that he ought not to tender an oath to an unregenerate man. 3: that a man ought not to pray with such though wife child, etc. 4: that a man ought not to give thanks after the sacrament nor after meat, etc. . . . Much debate was about these things the said opinions were adjudged by all magistrates and ministers (who were desired to be present) to be erroneous and very dangerous: and the calling of him to office at that time was judged a great contempt of authority. . . . It being professedly declared by the ministers (at the request of the Court to give their advice) that he who should obstinately maintain such opinions (whereby a church might run into heresy, apostasy, or tyranny, and yet the civil magistrate could not intermeddle) were to be removed, and that the other churches ought to request the magistrate so to do.

[August 1635] Mr. Williams pastor of Salem being sick and not able to speak wrote to his church a protestation that he could not communicate with the churches in the Bay: neither would he communicate with them except they would refuse communion with the rest: but the whole church was grieved herewith.

[November 1, 1635] At this General Court Mr. Williams the teacher in Salem was again convented, and . . . he was charged with the said two letters, that to the churches to complaining of the magistrates for injustice, extreme oppression, etc.: and the other to his own church, to persuade them to renounce communion with all the churches in the Bay, as full of Antichristian pollution, etc.: he justified both these letters, and maintained all his opinions: and . . . he chose to dispute presently, so Mr. Hooker[10] was appointed to dispute with him, but could not reduce him from any of his errors: so the next morning the Court sentenced him to depart out of our jurisdiction within six weeks all the ministers save one approving the sentence and his own church had him under question also for the same cause and he at his return home refused communion with his own church. . . .

[10] Thomas Hooker (1586–1647), who had known Williams in England, wrote "Touchinge ye Crosse in ye Banners," *Proceedings of the Massachusetts Historical Society*, 3d ser., 42 (1909): 272–80.

[January 1636] The governor and assistants met at Boston to consult about Mr. Williams, for that they were credibly informed, that notwithstanding the injunction laid upon him (upon the liberty granted him to stay till the spring) not to go about to draw others to his opinions, he did use to entertain company in his house and to preach to them, even of such points as he had been censured for: and it was agreed, to send him into England by a ship then ready to depart: the reason was because he had drawn above twenty persons to his opinion and they were intended to erect a plantation about the Narragansett Bay, from whence the infection would easily spread into these churches (the people being many of them much taken with the apprehension of his godliness) whereupon a warrant was sent to him. . . .

Source: Winthrop (1908), 1:61–62, 112–13, 116–19, 149, 154, 157, 162–63, 168; compared with Winthrop (1996).

Chapter 21

Anne Hutchinson Defies the Magistrates and Ministers

Anne Hutchinson (1591–1643) was exiled from Massachusetts in 1638 for "being a woman not fit for our society." Hutchinson made herself unfit because she was theologically at odds with the clergy she labeled "legal preachers." Another reason she alarmed the authorities is that she was reputedly able to foretell events; in the climactic moment of her "examination" before the General Court she spoke apocalyptically of being "delivered" by God from her enemies. The daughter of Francis Marbury, a minister in the Church of England, she married William Hutchinson, a merchant and member of a prosperous and educated family, in 1612. The two had fourteen children, eight of whom accompanied the parents in 1634 to Boston. Anne Hutchinson was already an admirer of John Cotton, whom she regarded as one of the few ministers she could trust. She began to invite other women to her house for meetings or "conferences" to discuss the sermons they were hearing, an exercise known as prophesying. She was also serving as spiritual counselor to women undergoing childbirth; she was not a midwife, but according to John Cotton "did much good in our Town, in womans meeting at Childbirth-Travells [travails]," by talking with them about "their spiritual estates."[1]

Except for what John Cotton said about her in *The Way of Congregational Churches Cleared* (1648), everything we know about Mrs. Hutchinson and the "Familism" or "Antinomianism" for which she was blamed comes from documents written by her opponents. Recalling her role as a counselor, Cotton told her in March 1638, "You have bine helpfull to many to bring them of[f] from thear unsound Grounds and Principles and from buildinge thear good Estate upon thear owne duties and performances or upon any Righteousnes of the Law." Hutchinson and her admirers regarded any minister who emphasized "duties" as preaching a "covenant of works," not free grace. She insisted that the right way of "building a good estate" (assurance of salvation) was to rely on the "immediate witness of the holy Spirit," an argument that implicitly eliminated the intervening stages and steps — the "means of

[1] Hall (1968), 412.

grace," the self-examination prompted by "the law" — that candidates for membership in Cambridge and Chelmsford so often cited in their "confessions" (see chap. 11).

In December 1636 the ministers living in the vicinity of Boston met with Mrs. Hutchinson and two of her supporters, John Cotton and John Wheelwright, her brother-in-law and an ordained minister, to discuss the differences among them. In January Wheelwright preached a fast-day sermon in the Boston congregation calling on the "children of God" to fight "against the enimyes of the Lord" and warning that "if we do not strive, those under a covenant of works will prevaile."[2] In March 1637 the General Court convicted Wheelwright of encouraging "sedition." At a session of the General Court in November, numerous people were fined or banished for signing a petition in behalf of Wheelwright or for engaging in other kinds of protest. Then the Court examined Mrs. Hutchinson. She deflected the charges against her and embarrassed the ministers by questioning their account of the conversations held the previous December, a discussion she regarded as having been "private." Then, however, she described a spiritual quest triggered by the doubts she had begun to have about the legitimacy of Puritan clergy who remained in the Church of England. Was it possible that they were agents of the Antichrist? Wandering in a wilderness of "atheism," she found assurance of truth only after she heard a "voice" she interpreted as God speaking to her. Excommunicated from the Boston congregation in March 1638 and already under sentence of banishment by the Court, she and her family left for Rhode Island that year; subsequently, they moved to present-day Rye, New York, where in 1643 she was killed by Native Americans. Two reports survive of her "examination." The shorter version, published as part of *A Short Story of the rise, reign, and ruine of the Antinomians* (1644), follows, with references to the fuller version in the notes.

Bibliography

The crucial documents are printed in Hall (1968, repr. 1990), with the secondary scholarship listed in the 1990 edition; Norton (1996); and Winship (2002). The best history of the controversy is Winship (2002), a response to Foster (1984), among others. Stoever (1978), Gura (1984), Ditmore (2000), and Gordis (2003) cover theological issues; on prophesying, see Hall (1989), chap. 4. Koehler (1980), Westerkamp (1990), Porterfield (1992), and Norton (1996) analyze gendered aspects of the controversy.

---

[2] Ibid., 158; the entire sermon is in this collection. For the source of Cotton's remark to Hutchinson cited above, see 371.

JOHN WINTHROP AND THOMAS WELD

🐾 *A Short Story of the Rise, Reign,* 🐾 *and Ruin of the Antinomians*

The "Examination" of Anne Hutchinson

The Court had now to do with the head of all this faction (*Dux foemina facti*),[3] a woman had been the breeder and nourisher of all these distempers, one Mistress Hutchinson, the wife of Mr. William Hutchinson of Boston (a very honest and peaceable man of good estate) and the daughter of Mr. Marbury, sometimes a preacher in Lincolnshire, after of London, a woman of a haughty and fierce carriage, of a nimble wit and active spirit, and a very voluble tongue, more bold than a man, though in understanding and judgment, inferior to many women. This woman had learned her skill in England, and had discovered some of her opinions in the ship,[4] as she came over, which had caused some jealousy of her, which gave occasion of some delay of her admission, when she first desired fellowship with the church of Boston,[5] but she cunningly dissembled and colored her opinions, as she soon got over that block, and was admitted into the church, then she began to go to work, and being a woman very helpful in the times of child-birth, and other occasions of bodily infirmities, and well furnished with means for those purposes, she easily insinuated herself into the affections of many, and the rather, because she was much inquisitive of them about their spiritual estates, and in discovering to them the danger they were in, by trusting to common gifts and graces, without any such witness of the Spirit, as the Scripture holds out for a full evidence; whereby many were convinced that they had gone on in a covenant of works, and were much humbled thereby, and brought to inquire more after the Lord Jesus Christ, without whom all their gifts and graces, all their contributions, etc. would prove but legal, and would vanish: all this was well, and suited with the public ministry, which went along in the same way, and all the faithful embraced it, and blessed God for the good success that appeared from

[3] Virgil, *Aeneid*, bk. 1, line 364: the woman the leader in the act.

[4] A fellow passenger in 1634 testified that on the voyage "she did slight the ministers of the word of God" and their arguments "about the evidencing of a good estate, and among the rest about that place in John [1 John 3:4] concerning the love of the brethren." Hall (1968), 322.

[5] Mrs. Hutchinson was admitted in November 1634, nearly two months after arriving, although only a week after her husband. Hall (1968), 371 n.

this discovery.[6] But when she had thus prepared the way by such wholesome truths, then she begins to set forth her own stuff, and taught that no sanctification was any evidence of a good estate, except their justification were first cleared up to them by the immediate witness of the Spirit, and that to see any work of grace (either faith or repentance, etc.), before this immediate witness, was a covenant of works: whereupon many good souls, that had been of long approved godliness, were brought to renounce all the work of grace in them, and to wait for this immediate revelation: then sprung up also that opinion of the indwelling of the person of the Holy Ghost, and of union with Christ, and justification before faith, and a denying of any gifts or graces, or inherent qualifications, and that Christ was all, did all, and that the soul remained always as a dead organ: and other of those gross errors, which were condemned in the late assembly,[7] and whereof divers had been quashed, by the public ministry; but the main and bottom of all, which tended to quench all endeavor, and to bring to a dependence upon an immediate witness of the Spirit, without sight of any gift or grace, this stuck fast, and prevailed so, as it began to be opposed, and she being questioned by some, who marveled that such opinions should spread so fast, she made answer, that wherever she came they must and they should spread, and indeed it was a wonder upon what a sudden the whole church of Boston (some few excepted) were become her new converts, and infected with her opinions, and many also out of the church, and of other churches also, yea, many profane persons became of her opinion, for it was a very easy, and acceptable way to heaven, to see nothing, to have nothing, but wait for Christ to do all;[8] so that after she had thus prevailed, and had drawn some of eminent place and parts to her party (whereof some profited so well, as in a few months they outwent their teacher) then she kept open house for all comers, and set up two lecture days in the week, when they usually met at her house, threescore or fourscore persons, the pretence was to repeat sermons, but when that was done, she would comment upon the doctrines, and interpret all passages at her pleasure, and expound dark places of Scripture, so as whatsoever the letter held forth (for this was one of her tenets, that the whole Scripture in the letter of it held forth nothing but a covenant of works) she would be sure to make it serve her turn, for the confirming of her main principles, whereof this was another, that the darker our sanctification is, the clearer is our justification;[9] and indeed

[6] Language repeated in John Cotton, *The Way of Congregational Churches Cleared* (1648), repr. in Hall (1968), 412.

[7] The synod of September 1637.

[8] Summarizing her opponents' critique of the "free grace" position; see Stoever (1978).

[9] The meaning of these terms is indicated in Thomas Shepard's catechism (chap. 5).

most of her new tenets tended to slothfulness, and quench all endeavor in the creature: and now was there no speech so much in use, as of vilifying sanctification, and all for advancing Christ and free grace, and the whole pedigree of the covenant of works was set forth with all its complements, beginning at Cain [Gen. 4:7], *If thou dost well shalt thou not be accepted?* Then it is explained and ratified at Mount Sinai, and delivered in the two tables, and after sprinkled with the blood of Christ, Exod. 24 and so carried on in the letter of the Scripture, till it be complete, as the covenant of grace by the Spirit, seals forgiveness of sins, one of the venters whereon Christ begets children, etc. and in the end wherefore is all this ado, but that having a more cleanly way, to lay all that opposed her (being near all the elders and most of the faithful Christians in this country) under a covenant of works, she might with the more credit, disclose and advance her masterpiece of immediate revelations, under the fair pretence of the covenant of free grace; wherein she had not failed of her aim, to the utter subversion both of churches and civil state, if the most wise and merciful providence of the Lord had not prevented it by keeping so many of the magistrates, and elders, free from the infection: for upon the countenance which it took from some eminent persons,[10] her opinions began to hold up their heads, in church assemblies, and in the court of justice, so as it was held a matter of offence to speak any thing against them in either assembly: thence sprang all that trouble to the pastor of Boston, for his free and faithful speech in the Court,[11] though required and approved: thence took Mr. Wheelwright courage to inveigh in his sermon against men in a covenant of works (as he placed them) and to proclaim them all enemies to Christ, scribes and pharisees, etc.[12] whereas before he was wont to teach in a plain and gentle style, and though he would sometimes glance upon these opinions, yet it was modestly and reservedly, not in such a peremptory and censorious manner, as he did then and after; for they made full account the day had been theirs. But blessed be the Lord, the snare is broken, and we are delivered, and this woman who was the root of all these troubles, stands now before the seat of justice, to be rooted out of her station, by the hand of authority, guided by the finger of divine providence, as the sequel will show.

When she appeared, the Court spake to her to this effect.

[10] Probably an allusion to Henry Vane; for his role and subsequent career as a radical Puritan in England, see Winship (2002).

[11] In December 1636, the pastor of Boston Church, John Wilson, "made a very sad speech of the condition of our churches" at the Court that Cotton and some members took "very ill." Winthrop (1996), 203–4.

[12] Matt. 23:23, a text John Wheelwright cited in his sermon of January 1637. Hall (1968), 165.

Mistress Hutchinson. You are called hither as one of those who have had a great share in the causes of our public disturbances, partly by those erroneous opinions which you have broached and divulged amongst us, and maintaining them, partly by countenancing and encouraging such as have sowed seditions amongst us, partly by casting reproach upon the faithful ministers of this country, and upon their ministry, and so weakening their hands in the work of the Lord, and raising prejudice against them, in the hearts of their people, and partly by maintaining weekly and public meetings in your house, to the offence of all the country, and the detriment of many families, and still upholding the same, since such meetings were clearly condemned in the late general assembly.[13]

Now the end of your sending for, is, that either upon sight of your errors, and other offences, you may be brought to acknowledge, and reform the same, or otherwise that we may take such course with you as you may trouble us no further.

We do desire therefore to know of you, whether you will justify and maintain what is laid to your charge or not?

Mistress Hutchinson. I am called here to answer to such things as are laid to my charge, name one of them.

Court. Have you countenanced, or will you justify those seditious practices which have been censured here in this Court?

Hutch. Do you ask me upon point of conscience?

Court. No, your conscience you may keep to yourself, but if in this cause you shall countenance and encourage those that thus transgress the law, you must be called in question for it, and that is not for your conscience, but for your practice.

Hutch. What law have they transgressed? the law of God?

Court. Yes, the Fifth Commandment, which commands us to honor father and mother, which includes all in authority, but these seditious practices of theirs, have cast reproach and dishonor upon the fathers of the commonwealth.

Hutch. Do I entertain, or maintain them in their actions, wherein they stand against any thing that God hath appointed?

---

[13] The synod of 1637 had resolved "that though women might meet (some few together) to pray and edify one another; yet such a set assembly (as was then in practice in Boston), where sixty or more did meet every week," with one woman offering commentary, was "disorderly, and without rule." Winthrop (1996), 234. But according to the "Body of Liberties" of 1641, the first code of law in the colony, "Wee allowe private meetings for edification in religion amongst Christians of all sortes of people. So it be without just offence for number, time, place, and other circumstances." *The Colonial Laws of Massachusetts . . . containing, also, The Body of Liberties of 1641,* ed. William H. Whitmore (Boston, 1889), 57.

Court. Yes, you have justified Mr. Wheelwright his sermon, for which you know he was convict[ed] of sedition, and you have likewise countenanced and encouraged those that had their hands to the petition.

Hutch. I deny it, I am to obey you only in the Lord.

Court. You cannot deny but you had your hand in the petition.[14]

Hutch. Put case, I do fear the Lord, and my parent do not, may not I entertain one that fears the Lord, because my father will not let me? I may put honor upon him as a child of God.

Court. That's nothing to the purpose, but we cannot stand to dispute causes with you now, what say you to your weekly public meetings? Can you shew a warrant for them?

Hutch. I will shew you how I took it up, there were such meetings in use before I came, and because I went to none of them, this was the special reason of my taking up this course, we began it but with five or six, and though it grew to more in future time, yet being tolerated at the first, I knew not why it might not continue.

Court. There were private meetings indeed, and are still in many places, of some few neighbors, but not so public and frequent as yours, and are of use for increase of love, and mutual edification, but yours are of another nature, if they had been such as yours they had been evil, and therefore no good warrant to justify yours; but answer by what authority, or rule, you uphold them.

Hutch. By Titus 2[:3–4], where the elder women are to teach the younger.

Court. So we allow you to do, as the Apostle there means, privately, and upon occasion, but that gives no warrant of such set meetings for that purpose; and besides, you take upon you to teach many that are elder than yourself, neither do you teach them that which the Apostle commands, viz. to keep at home.

Hutch. Will you please to give me a rule against it, and I will yield?

Court. You must have a rule for it, or else you cannot do it in faith, yet you have a plain rule against it; *I permit not a woman to teach* [1 Tim. 2:12].

Hutch. That is meant of teaching men.

Court. If a man in distress of conscience or other temptation, etc. should come and ask your counsel in private, might you not teach him?

Hutch. Yes.

Court. Then it is clear, that it is not meant of teaching men, but of teaching in public.

---

[14] A petition protesting the conviction of Wheelwright for sedition, presented to the Court in March 1637. The fuller version has Mrs. Hutchinson saying, "But I had not my hand to the petition," the implied point being that men signed, but no women. Hall (1968), 313.

Hutch. It is said [Acts 2:17], *I will pour my Spirit upon your daughters, and they shall prophesy,* etc. If God give me a gift of prophecy, I may use it.[15]

Court. First, the Apostle applies that prophecy unto those extraordinary times, and the gifts of miracles and tongues were common to many as well as the gift of prophecy. Secondly, in teaching your children, you exercise your gift of prophecy, and that within your calling.

Hutch. I teach not in a public congregation: The men of Berea are commended for examining Paul's doctrine; we do no more but read the notes of our teacher's sermons,[16] and then reason of them by searching the Scriptures.

Court. You are gone from the nature of your meeting, to the kind of exercise, we will follow you in this, and shew you your offence in them, for you do not as the Bereans search the Scriptures for their confirming in the truths delivered, but you open your teacher's points, and declare his meaning, and correct wherein you think he hath failed, etc. and by this means you abase the honor and authority of the public ministry, and advance your own gifts, as if he could not deliver his matter so clearly to the hearers' capacity as yourself.

Hutch. Prove that, that anybody doth that.

Court. Yes, you are the woman of most note, and of best abilities, and if some other take upon them the like, it is by your teaching and example, but you shew not in all this, by what authority you take upon you to be such a public instructor (after she had stood a short time, the Court gave her leave to sit down, for her countenance discovered some bodily infirmity).

Hutch. Here is my authority, Aquila and Priscilla, took upon them to instruct Apollo, more perfectly, yet he was a man of good parts, but they being better instructed might teach him [Acts 18:26].

Court. See how your argument stands, Priscilla with her husband, took Apollo home to instruct him privately, therefore Mistress Hutchinson without her husband may teach sixty or eighty.

Hutch. I call them not, but if they come to me, I may instruct them.

Court. Yet you shew us not a rule.

Hutch. I have given you two places of scripture.

Court But neither of them will suit your practice.

Hutch. Must I shew my name written therein?

---

[15] Within local Puritanism in England, and again in New England, prophesying was a form of public teaching, often involving the explication of Scripture or sermons, in conferences, private meetings, and church services. Less commonly, it involved predictions of future events. James (1999), 37.

[16] John Cotton, who held the office of "teacher."

Court. You must shew that which must be equivalent, seeing your ministry is public, you would have them receive your instruction, as coming from such an ordinance.

Hutch. They must not take it as it comes from me, but as it comes from the Lord Jesus Christ, and if I took upon me a public ministry, I should break a rule, but not in exercising a gift of prophecy, and I would see a rule to turn away them that come to me.

Court. It is your exercise which draws them, and by occasion thereof, many families are neglected, and much time lost, and a great damage comes to the commonwealth thereby, which we that are betrusted with, as the fathers of the commonwealth, are not to suffer. Divers other speeches passed to and fro about this matter, the issue was, that not being able to bring any rule to justify this her disordered course, she said she walked by the rule of the Apostle, Gal. [3] which she called the rule of the new creature, but what rule that was, she would not, or she could not tell, neither would she consent to lay down her meetings, except authority did put them down, and then she might be subject to authority.

Then the Court laid to her charge, the reproach she had cast upon the ministers, and ministry in this country, saying that none of them did preach the covenant of free grace, but Master Cotton, and that they have not the seal of the Spirit, and so were not able ministers of the New Testament: she denied the words, but they were affirmed by divers of the ministers, being desired by the Court to be present for that end. The matter was thus, it being reported abroad that Mistress Hutchinson did slight them and their ministry in their common talk, as if they did preach nothing but a covenant of works, because they pressed much for faith and love, etc. without holding forth such an immediate witness of the Spirit as she pretended, they advised with Master Cotton about it, and a meeting was appointed at his house, and she being sent for, and demanded the reason why she had used such speeches, at first she would not acknowledge them, but being told that they could prove them by witnesses, and persuaded to deal freely and truly therein, she said that the fear of man was a snare, and therefore she was glad she had this opportunity to open her mind, and thereupon she told them, that there was a wide difference between Master Cotton's ministry and theirs, and that they could not hold forth a covenant of free grace, because they had not the seal of the Spirit, and that they were not able ministers of the New Testament.

It was near night, so the Court brake up, and she was enjoined to appear again the next morning. When she appeared the next day, she objected that the ministers had spoken in their own cause, and that they ought not to be informers and witnesses both, and required that they might be sworn to what they had spoken: to which the Court answered, that if it were needful, an oath should be given them: but because the whole Court (in a manner man by man) did declare themselves to be fully satisfied of the truth of their testimonies, they being six or seven men of long approved godliness, and sincerity in their course, and for that it was also generally observed, that those of her party did look at their ministry (for the most part) as a way of the covenant of works, and one had been punished about half a year before, for reporting the like of them. The Court did pause a while at it, whereupon she said that she had Mr. Wilson's notes of that conference, which were otherwise than they had related: the Court willed her to shew them, but her answer was she had left them at home: whereupon Mr. Wilson (with the leave of the Court) said, that if she brought forth his notes, they should find written at the foot of them, that he had not written down all that was spoken, but being often interrupted, he had omitted divers passages; then she appealed to Mr. Cotton, who being called, and desired to declare what he remembered of her speeches, said, that he remembered only that which took impression on him, for he was much grieved that she should make such comparison between him and his brethren, but yet he took her meaning to be only of a gradual difference, when she said that they did not hold forth a covenant of free grace, as he did, for she likened them to Christ's disciples, and their ministry, before his ascension, and before the Holy Ghost was come down upon them; and when she was asked by some of them, why they could not preach a covenant of free grace, she made answer, because they had not the seal of the Spirit: upon this the Court wished her to consider, that Mr. Cotton did in a manner agree with the testimony of the rest of the elders: and as he remembered only so much as at present took most impression in him, so the rest of the elders had reason to remember some other passages, which he might not hear, or not so much observe as they whom it so nearly and properly concerned; all this would not satisfy Mistress Hutchinson, but she still called to have them sworn, whereupon the Court being weary of the clamor, and that all mouths might be stopped, required three of the ministers to take an oath, and thereupon they confirmed their former testimony.

Upon this she began to speak her mind, and to tell of the manner of God's dealing with her, and how he revealed himself to her, and made her know what she had to do; the governor perceiving whereabout she went, interrupted her, and would have kept her to the matter in hand, but seeing her very unwilling to be taken off, he permitted her to proceed. Her speech was to this effect.

Mistress Hutchinson.

When I was in old England, I was much troubled at the constitution of the churches there, so far, as I was ready to have joined to the Separation,[17] whereupon I set apart a day for humiliation by myself, to seek direction from God, and then did God discover unto me the unfaithfulness of the churches, and the danger of them, and that none of those ministers could preach the Lord Jesus aright, for he had brought to my mind, that in the 1 John 4:3, *Every spirit that confesseth not, that Jesus Christ is come in the flesh, is the spirit of Antichrist*; I marveled what this should mean, for I knew that neither Protestants nor papists did deny that Christ was come in the flesh; and are the Turks then the only Antichrists?[18] Now I had none to open the scripture to me, but the Lord, he must be the prophet, then he brought to my mind another scripture [Heb. 9:16–17]; he that denies the testament, denies the death of the testator; from whence the Lord did let me see, that everyone that did not preach the new covenant, denies the death of the testator; then it was revealed to me that the ministers of England were these Antichrists, but I knew not how to bear this, I did in my heart rise up against it, then I begged of the Lord that this atheism might not be in my heart: after I had begged this light, a twelve month together, at last he let me see how I did oppose Christ Jesus, and he revealed to me that place in Isa. 46:12–13 and from thence shewed me the atheism of my own heart, and how I did turn in upon a covenant of works, and did oppose Christ Jesus; from which time the Lord did discover to me all sorts of ministers, and how they taught, and to know what voice I heard, which was the voice of Moses, which of John Baptist, of Christ; the voice of my beloved, from the voice of strangers; and thenceforth I was the more careful whom I heard, for after our teacher Mr. Cotton, and my brother Wheelwright were put down,[19] there was none in England that I durst hear. Then it pleased God to reveal himself to me in that of Isa. 30:20, *Though the Lord give thee the bread of adversity, etc. yet thine eyes shall see thy teachers*; after this the Lord carrying Mr. Cotton to New England (at which I was much troubled) it was revealed to me, that I must go thither also, and that there I should be persecuted and suffer much trouble. I will give you another scripture, Jer. 46[:28],

---

[17] The name for radical Puritans who left the Church of England.

[18] Her dilemma was hermeneutical, whom to identify as the contemporary embodiments or agents of Antichrist. She came to a startling conclusion. For the context, see Christianson (1978).

[19] That is, Cotton and Wheelwright were deprived of their offices of ministry in England.

Fear not Jacob my servant, for I am with thee, I will make a full end of all the nations, etc. then the Lord did reveal himself to me, sitting upon a throne of justice, and all the world appearing before him, and though I must come to New England, yet I must not fear nor be dismayed. The Lord brought another scripture to me, Isa. 8:11, *The Lord spake this to me with a strong hand, and instructed me that I should not walk in the way of this people*, etc. I will give you one place more which the Lord brought to me by immediate revelations, and that doth concern you all, it is in Dan. 6[:4]. When the presidents and princes could find nothing against him, because he was faithful, they sought matter against him concerning the law of his God, to cast him into the lion's den; so it was revealed to me that they should plot against me, but the Lord bid me not to fear, for he that delivered Daniel, and the three children, his hand was not shortened. And see this scripture fulfilled this day in mine eyes, therefore take heed what ye go about to do unto me, for you have no power over my body, neither can you do me any harm, for I am in the hands of the eternal Jehovah my Savior, I am at his appointment, the bounds of my habitation are cast in heaven, no further do I esteem of any mortal man, than creatures in his hand, I fear none but the great Jehovah, which hath foretold me of these things, and I do verily believe that he will deliver me out of [y]our hands, therefore take heed how you proceed against me; for I know that for this you go about to do to me, God will ruin you and your posterity, and this whole state.

When she had thus vented her mind, the Court demanded of her, how she expected to be delivered, whether by miracle as Daniel was, to which she answered, yes, by miracle as Daniel was. Being further demanded how she did know that it was God that did reveal these things to her, and not Satan? she answered, how did Abraham know that it was the voice of God, when he commanded him to sacrifice his son?[20]

Mr. Cotton being present, and desired by the Court to deliver his judgment about Mistress Hutchinson her revelations, answered, there be two sorts of revelations, some are without or besides Scripture, those I look at as satanical, and tending to much danger, other are such as the Apostle speaks of, Eph. 1[:17] where he prayeth for a spirit of revelation to be given them, those are never dispensed but according to the Word of God, though the word revelation be uncouth, yet in Scripture sense I think it not lawful so to express it, and whenever it comes, it

[20] "Mr. Nowell. How do you know that that was the spirit? Mrs. H. How did Abraham know that it was God that bid him offer his son . . . ? Dept. Gov. By an immediate voice. Mrs. H. So to me by an immediate revelation. Dept. Gov. How! an immediate revelation." Hall (1968), 337.

comes with the ministry of the Word. Being again desired to express himself particularly concerning her revelations, he demanded of her (by the leave of the Court) whether by a miracle she doth mean a work beyond the power of nature, or only above common providence? for if (as you say) you expect deliverance from this Court beyond the power of nature, then I should suspect such a revelation to be false. To this she answered, you know when it comes, God doth not describe the way. Mr. Cotton asked her again, whether (when she said she should be delivered) she meant a deliverance from the sentence of the Court, or from the calamity of it? She answered, yes, from the calamity of it. Mistress Hutchinson having thus freely and fully discovered her self, the Court and all the rest of the assembly (except those of her own party) did observe a special providence of God, that (while she went about to cover such offences as were laid to her charge, by putting matters upon proof, and then quarrelling with the evidence) her own mouth should deliver her into the power of the Court, as guilty of that which all suspected her for, but were not furnished with proof sufficient to proceed against her, for here she hath manifested, that her opinions and practice have been the cause of all our disturbances, and that she walked by such a rule as cannot stand with the peace of any state; for such bottomless revelations, as either came without any Word, or without the sense of the Word (which was framed to human capacity), if they be allowed in one thing, must be admitted a rule in all things; for they being above reason and Scripture, they are not subject to control: Again, she hath given a reason why she hath so much slighted the faithful ministers of Christ here, why? It was revealed to her long since in England, that all the pack of them were Antichristians, so as she durst hear none of them, after Mr. Cotton and Mr. Wheelwright were once gone; for they could not preach Christ and the new covenant (as she affirms), why, but they did preach somewhat, and if they could not hold forth Christ in a covenant of free grace, then must they needs hold him forth in a covenant of works, then are they not able ministers of the New Testament, nor sealed by the Spirit; for the servants of God, who are come over into New England, do not think themselves more spiritual than other of their brethren whom they have left behind, nor that they can or do hold forth the Lord Jesus Christ in their ministry, more truly than he was held forth in England, and seeing their ministry was a most precious sweet savor to all the saints before she came hither, it is easy to discern from what sink that ill vapor hath risen, which hath made so many of her seduced party to loathe now the smell of those flowers which they were wont to find sweetness in: yet this is not all (though it be too vile) she can fetch a revelation that shall reach the magistrates and the whole Court, and the succeeding generations, and she hath scripture for it also, Daniel must be a type[21] of Mistress Hutchinson, the lion's den of the court of justice, and the presidents and princes of the reverend elders here, and all must sort to this conclusion, she must be delivered by miracle, and all we must be ruined; see the impudent boldness of a proud dame, that Athaliah-like makes havoc of all that stand in the way of her ambitious spirit; she had boasted before that her opinions must prevail, neither could she endure a stop in her way, as appeared once upon a slight occasion when her reputation being a little touched upon a mistake, yet so carried as she could not get the party upon that advantage which she expected, she vented her impatience with so fierce speech and countenance, as one would hardly have guessed her to have been an antitype of Daniel, but rather of the lions after they were let loose. The like appeared in her, when she could not have her will against her faithful pastor[22] for his opposing her opinions, as she apprehended, so as neither reason, nor Scripture, nor the judgment and example of such as she reverenced could appease her displeasure. So that the Court did clearly discern, where the fountain was of all our distempers, and the tragedy of Munster[23] (to such as had read it) gave just occasion to fear the danger we were in, seeing (by the judgment of Luther writing of those troublous times) we had not to do with so simple a devil, as managed that business, and therefore he had the less fear of him; but Satan seemed to have commission now to use his utmost cunning to undermine the kingdom of Christ here (as the same Luther foretold, he would do, when he should enterprise any such innovation under the clear light of the gospel) so as the like hath not been known in former ages, that ever so many wise, sober, and well grounded Christians, should so suddenly be seduced by the means of a woman, to stick so fast to her, even in some things wherein the whole current of Scripture goeth against them, and that notwithstanding that her opinions and practice have been so gross in some particulars, as their knowledge and sincerity would not suffer them to approve, yet such interest hath she gotten in their hearts, as they seek cloaks to cover the nakedness of such deformities, as in the meantime they are ashamed to behold.

The Court saw now an inevitable necessity to rid her away, except we would be guilty, not only of our own ruin, but also of the gospel, so in

[21] The meaning of "type" is explained in the introduction to part VII.

[22] John Wilson.

[23] Munster, the German city taken over in 1534 by apocalyptically radical Anabaptists who subsequently were besieged and slaughtered by orthodox Protestant forces; possibly referring to a play or story.

the end the sentence of banishment was pronounced against her, and she was committed to the Marshall, till the Court should dispose of her.

Source: [John Winthrop and Thomas Weld], *A Short Story of the Rise, reign, and ruine of the Antinomians, Familists & Liberties, that infected the Churches of New-England* (London, 1644).

Chapter 22

The Baptists Plead for Freedom of Conscience

A gesture of defiance by three Baptists in 1651 against the policies of the Massachusetts government led to an exchange of arguments over the rights of conscience. This exchange began with two letters criticizing the Massachusetts government, one from Roger Williams to Governor John Endicott, a second from Sir Richard Saltonstall, a leading Puritan and former colonist, to the ministers John Cotton and John Wilson. The Baptists published a short book narrating what had happened to them and arguing in favor of liberty of conscience. John Cotton wrote Saltonstall defending the colonists' policies.[1]

In mid-July 1651 John Clarke, Obadiah Holmes, and John Crandall traveled to Massachusetts in defiance of a Massachusetts law (1645) providing for the banishment of "Anabaptists" who, after "due time & means of conviction," continued to "openly condemn or oppose the baptizing of infants . . . or shall purposely depart the congregation at the administration of the ordinance, or shall deny the ordinance of magistracy, or their lawful right or authority . . . to punish the outward breaches of the first table."[2] After having held a service and baptized a man living in the town of Lynn, the three were arrested, sent to Boston, tried, and convicted, the penalty being either to be "well whipped" or to pay a fine. Clarke and Crandall were released after others paid their fines; Holmes, whose fine was by far the largest, refused this option and was publicly whipped in early September. John Clarke described these events in *Ill Newes from New-England* (1652). The title page announced "That while old England is becoming new, New-England is become Old," a reference to the policy of toleration recently adopted by the English government under Oliver Cromwell. The book included a long, firsthand testimonial by Holmes, who told of being tempted by Satan on the evening before his whipping until a "voice from heaven" resolved his confusion. Emulating the martyrs described by John Foxe,

---

[1] Thomas Cobbet of Lynn wrote another reply, *The Civil Magistrates Power in matters of Religion . . . Together with A brief Answer to a certain Slanderous Pamphlet called Ill Newes from New-England* (London, 1653).

[2] Shurtleff (1853–1854), 2:85.

he celebrated the triumph of his "weak flesh," supposedly remarking to the magistrates once the whipping ended that "you have struck me with Roses."

John Clarke's case against the uniformity of church and state combined Christian primitivism with the well-established distinction within Puritan theories of church and state between two kinds of authority or power: the "spiritual" authority of Christ as contrasted with the "temporal" or "civil" power of the civil state. In *Ill Newes* Clarke insisted at great length that Christ was the sole head of the church; that the church must contain only those whom Christ had redeemed (hence the error of administering baptism to infants prior to their having faith); that because the true church was always a suffering, persecuted body, it should not persecute others; and that coercive action by the civil state would ruin true religion by encouraging hypocrisy. Clarke acknowledged, however, that civil magistrates had a responsibility to regulate moral conduct. Saltonstall agreed with Clarke that the colonists' "practice of compelling any in matters of worship to do that whereof they are not fully persuaded, is to make them sin" or become hypocrites; he also urged that the magistrates and ministers "not assume to yourselves infallibilitie of judgment . . . for God is light, and no further than he doth illuminate us can we see." John Cotton's position on church and state was consistent with "magisterial" Protestantism: civil magistrates were empowered by God to punish blasphemy, heresy, and idolatry. Cotton insisted that the gathered church always contained hypocrites and that allowing heresy to flourish — the inevitable consequence of allowing toleration — was not what God expected of the magistrates. Cotton noted that in practice the orthodox colonists allowed for more variety than their critics were willing to acknowledge.

Clarke (1609–1672), a physician by training, emigrated to Massachusetts in 1637, moved to Rhode Island in 1638, and helped found Newport in 1639. "In or about" 1644, he organized a church in Newport founded on the repudiation of infant baptism; he also practiced rebaptism. Obadiah Holmes (1607?–1682) arrived in Massachusetts in 1638, settling in Salem and joining the church, where he had his children baptized. In 1645 he moved to Rehoboth, in Plymouth Colony. Difficulties arose between him and the town minister, and by 1650 he and others in the town had become Baptists; for this and other offences he was excommunicated from the town church.

Bibliography

McLoughlin (1971); Gaustad (1978), containing Obadiah Holmes's spiritual autobiography; James (1999).

JOHN CLARKE

Ill Newes from New-England

The testimony of John Clarke, Obadiah Holmes, and John Crandall, prisoners at Boston in New-England, concerning the faith and order of the gospel of Christ Jesus the Lord, as the same was laid down in four conclusions, and proffered to be openly and publicly defended against all gainsayers; when none would come forth thus to oppose it: now again by the aforesaid John Clarke reviewed, particularly, and strictly examined by the Word of God, and testimony of Jesus, and thereby (as is here at large to be seen) confirmed and justified.

[The First Conclusion]

[I testify that Jesus of Nazareth, whom God hath raised from the dead, is made both Lord and Christ] you may see this testimony clearly, and plentifully witnessed and confirmed by the scriptures of truth; for first, that God raised him from the dead, appears by the testimony of twelve chosen witnesses, Acts 2:24, 32. This Jesus, say they, hath God raised up, whereof we are witnesses; so also chap. 3:15. And being alive again he was seen of above 500 brethren at once being faithful witnesses, children that will not lie, see 1 Cor. 15:6. And last of all he was seen of Paul, whom he sent to the Gentiles, see 1 Cor. 15:8, Acts 22:18, 21. And this is laid by Paul as the foundation of the hope of the Israel of God, that they shall be raised, and shall share in that glory that shall then be revealed; yea it is that word of truth (as Peter witnesseth) by which the Father of mercies doth again beget such as had sinned and fallen short of the glory of God, and were without hope, unto a lively hope of the glory of God, in *an inheritance, incorruptible and undefiled, that fadeth not away, and is reserved in heaven for them*, see 1 Pet. 1:3–4. . . .

[The True Church as a Spiritual Body]

And that there is none to him by way of commanding and ordering with respect to the worship of God, the household of faith, will evidently appear if the nature of the household of faith, the worship of God, and the commanding and ordering power that suits therewith, be considered with respect unto him. For the nature of the household of faith, they are a company of faithful ones, that are bought with the price of his blood, knit together in one by his Spirit, founded wholly upon himself, built up by him to be a holy habitation of God, and therefore not in the least measure to be defiled with the inventions and commandments of men, from whence it is that they are still with their eye fixed upon him whom they look upon to be as well the finisher as the author of their faith, still in their hearts calling on him that hath bought them, and saying, Lord what wilt thou have me to do, and still standing upon their watch to hearken what this Lord will speak, for the voice of a stranger they will not hear; so that by this it evidently appears, that there is none that hath so much right unto this household of faith by way of ordering it, nor yet freedom in it by way of commanding, as hath Christ Jesus the Lord; and from the nature of the worship which is spiritual, to be performed by a spiritual worshipper, and after or in that true manner that the Father of spirits hath appointed, it will as evidently appear, that there is none to him by way of commanding and ordering in this matter. . . . And if the nature of the commanding and ordering power, that suits both with the worship, and with the worshippers, which the Father of spirits seeks for be also considered, which is not a law of a carnal commandment seconded with carnal weapons, or an arm of flesh: but a spiritual law, or as the Apostle calls it, Rom. 8[:2], a *law of the Spirit of life from Christ Jesus*, spoken unto, or rather written in the heart of a Christian by the Spirit of Christ, by reason whereof he obeys from the heart, readily, willingly and cheerfully that form of doctrine which is engraven and laid up therein, Heb. 8:10, 2 Cor. 3:3, Rom. 6:17. If this I say be considered, that the worship is spiritual, such as must begin in, spring up, and rise from the heart and the spirit, and so be directed to the Father of spirits, and so the commanding power that suits herewith, must speak to the heart and spirit of a man, then is there no lord in this matter to Christ Jesus the Lord, who speaks to the heart in the Spirit, and his words are as commands from the head to the members, which convey together spirit and life to obey them, by reason of which his commands are not grievous, for *where the Spirit of this Lord is, there is liberty*, and they by beholding the glory of the Lord, are transformed into the same image, from glory unto glory, by the Spirit of the Lord, 2 Cor. 3:17–18. . . .

When our Lord was about to be gone, he gave order unto his apostles, whom he made stewards in his house of the mysteries of God, to make him disciples of all nations, and that such as were so made should then be baptized, and so visibly planted into Christ, and put on Christ, and having so received him, should walk in him, observing all things whatsoever he had commanded, the first thing whereof as touching order was, to be added or joined one to another in the fellowship of the gospel by a mutual professed subjection to the scepter of Christ, and being a company thus called out of the world, from worldly vanities, and worldly worships, after Christ Jesus the Lord (which is the proper English of these words the church of Christ, and is in other terms called the household of faith) should steadfastly continue together in the Apostle's doctrine, *sci.* the consolation, reproof, and instruction thereof, in fellowship, *sci.* mutual support both inward and outward; in breaking of bread, thereby remembering the death of our Lord, whose soul was made an offering for sin, as his flesh is meat indeed, and his blood drink indeed, by the help of the Spirit, to nourish our souls and spirits up unto eternal life, and in prayer, one with and for another; and that this is the absolute order which the Lord hath appointed in his last will and testament, doth evidently appear both by his own precept, and command, and by the practice of such as first trusted in him, and if so, then neither infants of days, nor yet such as profess themselves, to be believers in Jesus, but refuse as a manifestation thereof, according to the practice of such as first trusted in Christ, to yield up themselves to be planted into the death, burial, and resurrection of Christ, and so visibly to put Christ on, as did the Christians of old, I say such have no visible right to enter into, or walk in the order of the gospel of Christ; and to conclude the point, the argument stands thus. They, and they only, have visible right to enter into, and walk in the visible order of Christ's house, and so to wait for his coming, whom Christ Jesus himself being the Lord of the house, hath appointed, and his apostles being his stewards, have approved of; but such as first have been taught and made disciples or scholars of Jesus, and believers in Christ, and afterwards have been baptized or dipped and thereby visibly and lively planted into the death, burial, and resurrection of Christ, are they, and they only, whom Christ hath appointed and the apostles have approved of. See his commission, peruse their practice; ergo they, and they only, have visible right to enter into, and walk in the order of Christ's house, and so to wait for his coming the second time, in the form of a king, with his glorious kingdom, according to promise. See for a farther confirmation of the last clause, in the first epistle to the Corinthians 1:7, 1 Thess. 1:10, 2 Thess. 3:5.

[Freedom of Conscience]

And thirdly, consider, the words were spoken by the Apostle Paul, who would have us to know (as he declares it, 2 Cor. 10:4) that the weapons of his warfare were not carnal, he was not wont to strive with them that opposed themselves with carnal weapons, and therefore if he speaks to such persons as these Galatians were (that had received such power from the Lord) touching a cutting off, which is a business that belongs to a sword, it would be too carnal an understanding of the place to conceive that this should be done by any other sword, than by the sword of the Spirit, which is the Word of God, and can reach to their spirits, and is the only offensive weapon the saints are to take in such cases as this against their spiritual opposers. . . .

3. Argument. The third argument [in favor of freedom of conscience] standeth thus. If Christ Jesus the Lord instructed his servants to be meek, lowly, and gentle, yea, kind and courteous to all; sent forth the chiefest of them, and told them that they should be as lambs in the midst of wolves; yea, holds them and us, and all that shall reign with Christ, when he shall appear with his kingdom, in a continual expectation of a persecuted and afflicted condition in this present evil world, then it cannot be expected that they should have any such liberty, much less authority, from him thus to persecute, prosecute, or enforce others.

But the first is true. See Matt. 11:29, 1 Cor. 13:4, Eph. 4:34, 1 Pet. 3:8, Matt. 10, 2 Tim. 3:12, *All that will live godly in Christ Jesus* (saith Paul, who well discerned the spirit that was abroad, and that which should remain and increase in the world) *shall suffer persecution*, and the servant is not greater than his Lord, saith Christ, Matt. 10:24–25. So that by this it appears, that the first is true, and therefore the second which is this, that no servant of Christ can expect any such liberty or authority from his Lord thus to persecute, prosecute, or enforce others.

A fourth argument against forcing men against their consciences, in the things, and worship of God, is taken from the nature of the conscience of man, and of the worship of God, which are both spiritual; and it standeth thus.

4. Argument. That which the Lord hath reserved in his own hand, and hath intended to manage as part of his own kingdom by his own power or Spirit, and by another manner of ministry, and sword, than that which is put forth in the kingdoms of men, his being such as suits with the understanding and conscience of man, as it is a spiritual thing, and with the worship of God, which is also spiritual, that, I say, can no servant of Christ have authority from him, by another sword, or arm of flesh, to undertake, manage, or think to effect.

But the Lord hath reserved this great work of ordering the understanding, and conscience, which is the spirit of man, by way of constraint, or restraint; and also the outward man, with respect to the worship of God, I say, he hath reserved this great work, in his own hand, and in the hand of the Spirit, and hath intended to manage it as a part of his kingdom, by his own Spirit, and by another manner of ministry, than that which is put forth in the kingdoms of men. . . .

The fifth argument against forcing men's consciences, or rather the outward man for conscience sake in the worship of God, standeth thus.

5. Argument. That which presupposeth one man to have dominion over another man's conscience, and is but a forcing of servants, and worshippers upon the Lord, at the least, which he seeks not for, and is the ready way to make men dissemblers and hypocrites before God and man, which wise men abhor, and to put men upon the profaning the Name of the Lord, that can no servant of Christ Jesus have any liberty, much less authority, from his Lord to do. But by outward force to seek to constrain, or restrain another's conscience in the worship of God, etc. doth presuppose one man to have dominion over another man's conscience, and is but to force servants, and worshippers upon the Lord, which he seeks not for, and is the ready way to make men dissemblers and hypocrites, and to put them upon the profaning the Name of the Lord.

Source: John Clarke, *Ill Newes from New-England; Or, a Narrative of New-Englands Persecution* (London, 1652), 39–68. Reprinted in *Collections of the Massachusetts Historical Society*, 4th ser., 2 (1854).

ROGER WILLIAMS

To the Governor of Massachusetts *protesting the Baptists' treatment*

. . . I say (I desire to say it, tremblingly and mournfully) I know not which way he will please to raise his glory only I know my duty, my conscience, my love, all which enforce me to knock, to call to cry at the gate of heaven, and at yours, and to present you with this loving, though loud and faithful noise and sound of a few grounds of deeper examination of both our souls and consciences uprightly and impartially at the holy and dreadful tribunal of him that is appointed the judge of all the living and the dead.

Be pleased then (honored sir) to remember that that thing which we call conscience is of such a nature (especially in Englishmen) as once a pope of Rome at the suffering of an Englishman in Rome, himself observed that although it be groundless, false, and deluded, yet it is not by any arguments or torments easily removed.

I speak not of the stream of the multitude of all nations, which have their ebbings and flowings in religion (as the longest sword, and strongest arm of flesh carries it)[.] But I speak of conscience, a persuasion fixed in the mind and heart of a man, which enforceth him to judge (as Paul said of himself a persecutor) and to do so and so, with respect to God, his worship, etc.

This conscience is found in all mankind, more or less, in Jews, Turks, papists, Protestants, pagans, etc. . . . But sir, your principles and conscience bind you, not to respect Romish or English, saints or sinners . . . you are bound by your conscience to punish (and it may be) to hang or burn, if they transgress against your conscience, and that because according to Mr. Cotton's monstrous distinction (as some of his chief brethren to my knowledge have called it) not because they sin in matters of conscience (which he denies the magistrate to deal in) but because they sin against their conscience.[3]

Secondly, it is so notoriously known, that the consciences of the most holy men, zealous for God and his Christ to death and admiration, yea even in our own country, and in Queen Mary's days especially, have been so grossly misled by mistaken consciences in matters concerning the worship of God, the coming out of the Antichristian Babel, and the rebuilding of the spiritual Jerusalem . . . I say, who they were that lived and died (five in the flames) zealous for their bishoprics,[4] yea and some too zealous for their popish ceremonies, against the doubting consciences of their brethren: at which and more, we that now have risen in our fathers' stead, wonder and admire how such piercing eyes could be deceived, such watchmen blinded and deluded. . . .

The maker and searcher of our hearts knows with what bitterness I write, as with bitterness of soul I have heard such language as this to proceed from yourself and others, who formerly have fled from (with crying out against) persecutors! "You will say, this is your conscience: You will say, you are persecuted, and you are persecuted for your conscience: No, you are conventiclers, heretics, blasphemers, seducers: You deserve to be hanged, rather than one shall be wanting to hang him I will hang him myself: I am resolved not to leave a heretic in the country. . . ." Oh Sir, you cannot forget what language and dialect this is, whether not the same unsavory, and ungodly, blasphemous and bloody, which the Gardiners and Bonners[5] both formerly and later used. . . .

---

[3] Cotton made this distinction in *The Bloudy Tenent Washed* (London, 1647), 9–10, a reference I owe to LaFantasie (1988), 348.

[4] A reference to the five Church of England bishops put to death during the reign of Mary Tudor (1553–1558), the point being that even those martyrs did not fully grasp the true nature of the church.

[5] Stephen Gardiner and Edmund Bonner, two bishops during the reign of the Catholic Mary Tudor, deeply resented for persecuting Protestants; earlier in this sentence, Williams was recalling the complaints of Puritans in England against the Church of England hierarchy.

Sir, I must be humbly bold to say, that 'tis impossible for any man or men to maintain their Christ by the sword, and to worship a true Christ! [August/September 1651].

Source: R[oger] Williams, *The Bloody Tenent Yet More Bloody* (London, 1652), 303–13. Reprinted in LaFantasie (1988), 1: 340–44, with notes identifying the scriptural allusions.

 SIR RICHARD SALTONSTALL TO JOHN COTTON
AND JOHN WILSON

Reverend and dear friends, whom I unfainedly love and respect,

It doth not a little grieve my spirit to hear what sad things are reported daily of your tyranny and persecutions in New England, as that you fine, whip and imprison men for their consciences. First, you compel such to come into your assemblies as you know will not join with you in your worship, and when they shew their dislike thereof or witness against it, then you stir up your magistrates to punish them for such (as you conceive) their public affronts. Truly, friends, this your practice of compelling any in matters of worship to do that whereof they are not fully persuaded, is to make them sin, for so the Apostle (Rom. 14 and 23) tells us, and many are made hypocrites thereby, conforming in their outward man for fear of punishment. We pray for you and wish you prosperity every way, hoped the Lord would have given you so much light and love there, that you might have been eyes to God's people here, and not to practice those courses in a wilderness, which you went so far to prevent. These rigid ways have laid you very low in the hearts of the saints. I do assure you I have heard them pray in the public assemblies that the Lord would give you meek and humble spirits, not to strive so much for uniformity as to keep the unity of the Spirit in the bond of peace [Eph. 4:3].

When I was in Holland about the beginning of our wars, I remember some Christians there that then had serious thoughts of planting in New England, desired me to write to the governor thereof to know if those that differ from you in opinion, yet holding the same foundation in religion, as Anabaptists, Seekers, Antinomians, and the like, might be permitted to live among you, to which I received this short answer from your then governor Mr. Dudley, God forbid (said he) our love for the truth should be grown so cold that we should tolerate errors, and when (for satisfaction of myself and others) I desired to know your grounds, he referred me to the books written here between the Presbyterians and

Independents, which if that had been sufficient, I needed not have sent so far to understand the reasons of your practice, I hope you do not assume to yourselves infallibility of judgment, when the most learned of the apostles confesseth he knew but in part and saw but darkly as through a glass [1 Cor. 13:12], for God is light, and no further than he doth illuminate us can we see, be our parts and learning never so great. Oh that all those who are brethren, though yet they cannot think and speak the same things might be of one accord in the Lord. Now the God of patience and consolation grant you to be thus minded towards one another, after the example of Jesus Christ our blessed Savior, in whose everlasting arms of protection he leaves you who will never leave to be Your truly and much affectionate friend in the nearest union,

Richard Saltonstall. [late 1651–early 1652]

Source: [Thomas Hutchinson], *A Collection of Original Papers relative to the History of the Colony of Massachusetts-Bay* (Boston, 1769), 401–2.

JOHN COTTON TO SIR RICHARD SALTONSTALL

Honored and dear Sir,

My brother Wilson and self do both of us acknowledge your love, as otherwise formerly, so now in the late lines we received from you, that you grieve in spirit to hear daily complaints against us, it springeth from your compassion of our afflictions therein, wherein we see just cause to desire you may never suffer like injury yourself, but may find others to compassionate and condole with you. For when the complaints you hear of are against our tyranny and persecutions in fining, whipping and imprisoning men for their consciences, be pleased to understand we look at such complaints as altogether injurious in respect of ourselves, who had no hand or tongue at all to promote either the coming of the persons you aim at into our assemblies, or their punishment for their carriage there. Righteous judgment will not take up reports, much less reproaches, against the innocent. The cry of the sins of Sodom was great and loud, and reached up to heaven; yet the righteous God (giving us an example what to do in the like case) he would first go down to see whether their crime were altogether according to the cry, before he would proceed to judgment, Gen. 18:20–21 and when he did find the truth of the cry, he did not wrap up all alike promiscuously in the judgment, but spared such as he found innocent; we are amongst those whom (if you knew us better) you would account of (as the matron of

Abel spake of herself) peaceable in Israel, 2 Sam. 20:19. Yet neither are we so vast in our indulgence or toleration as to think the men you speak of suffered an unjust censure. For one of them (Obadiah Holmes) being an excommunicate person himself, out of a church in Plymouth patent, came into this jurisdiction and took upon him to baptize, which I think himself will not say he was compelled here to perform. And he was not ignorant that the rebaptizing of an elder person, and that by a private person out of office and under excommunication, are all of them manifest contestations against the order and government of our churches established (we know) by God's law, and (he knoweth) by the laws of the country. And we conceive we may safely appeal to the ingenuity of your own judgment, whether it would be tolerated in any civil state, for a stranger to come and practice contrary to the known principles of their church estate? As for his whipping, it was more voluntarily chosen by him than inflicted on him. His censure by the court was to have paid (as I know) thirty pounds or else to be whipt, his fine was offered to be paid by friends for him freely; but he chose rather to be whipt; in which case, if his suffering of stripes was any worship of God at all, surely it could be accounted no better than will-worship. The other (Mr. Clarke) was wiser in that point and his offence was less, so was his fine less, and himself (as I hear) was contented to have it paid for him, whereupon he was released. The imprisonment of either of them was no detriment. I believe they fared neither of them better at home, and I am sure Holmes had not been so well clad of many years before.

But be pleased to consider this point a little further. You think to compel men in matter of worship is to make men sin, according to Rom. 14:23. If the worship be lawful in itself, the magistrate compelling him to come to it compelleth him not to sin, but the sin is in his will that needs to be compelled to a Christian duty. Josiah compelled all Israel, or (which is all one) made to serve the Lord their God, 2 Chron. 34:33 yet his act herein was not blamed but recorded amongst his virtuous actions. For a governor to suffer any within his gates to prophane the Sabbath, is a sin against the Fourth Commandment, both in the private householder and in the magistrate; and if he requires them to present themselves before the Lord, the magistrate sinneth not, nor doth the subject sin so great a sin as if he did refrain to come. If the magistrate connive at his absenting himself from Sabbath duties the sin will be greater in the magistrate than can be in the other's passive coming. Naaman's passive going into the house of Rimmon did not violate the peace of his conscience, 2 Kings 5:18–19. Bodily presence in a stewes,[6] forced to behold the lewdness of whoredoms there committed, is no

---

[6] Brothel.

whoredom at all. No more is it spiritual whoredom to be compelled by force to go to mass.

But (say you) it doth but make men hypocrites, to compel men to conform the outward man for fear of punishment. If it did so, yet better to be hypocrites than profane persons. Hypocrites give God part of his due, the outward man, but the profane person giveth God neither outward nor inward man.

Your prayers for us we thankfully accept, and we hope God hath given us so much light and love (which you think we want) that if our native country were more zealous against horrid blasphemies and heresies than we be, we believe the Lord would look at it as a better improvement of all the great salvations he hath wrought for them than to set open a wide door to all abominations in religion. Do you think the Lord hath crowned the state with so many victories that they should suffer so many miscreants to pluck the crown of sovereignty from Christ's head? Some to deny his godhead, some his manhood; some to acknowledge no Christ, nor heaven, nor hell, but what is in a man's self? Some to deny all churches and ordinances, and so to leave Christ no visible kingdom upon earth? And thus Christ by easing England of the yoke of a kingdom shall forfeit his own kingdom among the people of England. Now God forbid, God from heaven forbid, that the people and state of England should so ill requite the Lord Jesus. You know not, if you think we came into this wilderness to practice those courses here which we fled from in England. We believe there is a vast difference between men's inventions and God's institutions; we fled from men's inventions, to which we else should have been compelled; we compel none to men's inventions.

If our ways (rigid ways as you call them) have laid us low in the hearts of God's people, yea and of the saints (as you style them) we do not believe it is any part of their saintship. Michal had a low esteem of David's zeal, but he was never a whit lower in the sight of God, nor the higher.

What you wrote out of Holland to our then governor Mr. Dudley, in behalf of Anabaptists, Antinomians, Seekers, and the like, it seemeth, met with a short answer from him, but zealous; for zeal will not bear such mixtures as coldness or lukewarmness will, Rev. 2:2, 14–15, 20. Nevertheless, I tell you the truth, we have tolerated in our church some Anabaptists, some Antinomians, and some Seekers, and do so still at this day; though Seekers of all others have least reason to desire toleration in church fellowship. For they that deny all churches and church ordinances since the apostasy of Antichrist, they cannot continue in church fellowship but against their own judgment and conscience; and therefore four or five of them who openly renounced the church fellowship which they had long enjoyed, the church said amen to their act, and (after serious debate with them till they had nothing to answer) they were removed from their fellowship. Others carry their dissent more privately and inoffensively, and so are borne withal in much meekness. We are far from arrogating infallibility of judgment to ourselves or affecting uniformity; uniformity God never required, infallibility he never granted us. We content ourselves with unity in the foundation of religion and of church order: Superstructures we suffer to vary; we have here Presbyterian churches as well as Congregational, and have learned (through grace) to keep the unity of the spirit in the bond of peace; only we are loath to be blown up and down (like chaff) by every wind of new notions.

You see how desirous we are to give you what satisfaction we may to your loving expostulation, which we pray you to accept with the same spirit of love wherewith it is endited. The Lord Jesus guide and keep your heart forever in the ways of his truth and peace. So humbly commending our due respect and hearty affection to your worship, we take leave and rest. [1652]

Source: [Hutchinson], *Collection*, 403–7. Fully annotated in Bush (2001).

PART VI

Encountering the Native Americans

The Native Americans who were living in New England when the colonists arrived posed two challenges: who were they, and how should the newcomers behave toward these people? In the course of the seventeenth century the colonists answered the first of these questions several different ways, drawing as they did so on Scripture, deep-rooted assumptions about "civilization" and "degeneracy," and the reports that reached them of encounters between Europeans and "savages" elsewhere in the New World.[1] The second must be answered by taking into account an extraordinary range of interactions, three of which are described in the texts that follow: the Pequot War of 1637, when a force of colonists, allied with some Native Americans, came close to exterminating the Pequots; the effort, initiated in the mid-1640s, to convert the Native Americans to Christianity; and King Philip's War of 1675–1676.

That the Native Americans, called Indians by the Puritan colonists, were sons and daughters of Adam and therefore shared a common humanity with the colonists was certain, as was their "degenerated" condition at the time of encounter. In the eyes of the colonists, the signs of this degenerate condition were the Indians' ignorance of the Christian message and their "lapse into inevitable depravity" and "Barbarism." The colonists speculated on the genealogy of the Indians. Roger Williams declared, "From Adam and Noah that they spring, it is granted on all hands," but from which of Noah's two rebellious sons, Ham and Shem, did they descend? Or were they a branch of the Ten Lost Tribes who somehow found their way to America? Alternatively, were they an Asian people, probably the "Tartars, or Scythian"? A more extreme possibility, widely voiced by English explorers in the early seventeenth century, was that devil had claimed the New World as his domain. According to this scenario, the Indians were a people drawn there to serve him in his

---

[1] For such stories, and a comparative perspective, see Edmund S. Morgan, *American Slavery, American Freedom: The Ordeal of Colonial Virginia* (New York, 1975).

private kingdom.[2] When the colonists described the Indians as devil wor-
shipers and the powwows, or shamans, as witches who intended malice,
they were alluding to this scenario. In point of fact the shamans, who
figure prominently in Thomas Mayhew Jr.'s account of Native American
religion on Martha's Vineyard, called upon a variety of spirits, none of
which were "satanic" as this term was understood by Europeans.[3]

Each of these theories accounted for the degeneracy of the Indians;
each prompted the colonists to declare that a principal reason for coming to the New World was to raise the Indians out of darkness by bringing them the gospel. According to William Bradford, the Leiden Separatists justified their emigration as providing "some good foundation . . .
for the propagating and advancing the gospel of the kingdom of Christ
in those remote parts of the world," though in his next sentence he
voiced the more frightening expectation that the New World contained
"only savage and brutish men, which range up and down little otherwise than the wild beasts of the same."[4] The founders of the Massachusetts Bay Company commissioned a seal showing a Native American
uttering the "Macedonian plea": "come over and help us" (Acts 16:9).[5]

All this was utterly conventional, and perhaps mere window dressing.
Indeed, in the 1620s and 1630s nothing was done to provide this "help."
Instead, the immediate goal of the colonists was to ensure their security
from Indian attacks of the kind that, in 1622, had nearly eliminated the
English colony in Virginia. Steps were taken in Plymouth and Massachusetts to intimidate the local tribes and to place them in a situation of
political, military, and economic dependence on the colonists. Simultaneously the colonists asserted that the land was "empty" and therefore belonged to them, justifying such a claim by pointing to the absence of "settled habitation" or any other signs of European practices
among the Indians.[6] Such claims were also linked to a sharp decline in
the numbers of Native Americans because of new diseases introduced
by the Europeans. Thousands of Indians in southern New England died
from an epidemic of uncertain nature in 1616–1618. Thousands more
died in 1633 from an epidemic of smallpox, and still others died in the
1640s, as Mayhew notes in describing the situation on the Vineyard.

Another aspect of political and military affairs was a multisided
rivalry among the New England colonies and between them and the

---

[2] Canup (1990), chap. 3, 64–65; Cave (1996), chap. 1.

[3] Cave (1996), 23–26.

[4] Arber (1897), 267.

[5] "The missionary idealism enshrined in the Massachusetts charter . . . clearly reflected
a regnant convention in the literature of colonization rather than the central priority for
the leading planters." Cogley (1999), 2.

[6] Carroll (1969), 13–14. Negotiations, exchanges, and treaties regarding land were also
a feature of Indian-white relations.

Dutch in New Netherlands for control of the river ways in Connecticut, key arteries in the fur trade and the best means of access to the riverside towns of Windsor, Wethersfield, and Hartford, founded by emigrants from Massachusetts in the mid-1630s. In turn these rivalries became entangled with conflicts between different tribes of Indians and rivalries for leadership. The Algonquins were divided between groups that we name "tribes," among them the Massachusett, the Nipmuc, the Wampanoags, the Narragansetts, the Pequots, and the Mohegans. The political situation among the Indians, and especially those living in or bordering on Connecticut, was characterized by shifting allegiances, murders of chiefs, conflict over trade goods, and, among the colonists, a determination to establish the upper hand, come what may.

The Pequot War of 1637 arose out of these dynamics. The Pequots, a tribe that controlled much of the coast of Connecticut, sent a delegation to Boston in 1634 to negotiate an alliance with the Massachusetts government. Grievances began to mount on both sides: a party of Dutch murdered Tatobem, the chief sachem of the Pequots, and the colonists blamed (unjustly) the killing of an English trader on the Pequots. In early 1637 some Pequots began to harass and kill parties of colonists outside Saybrook and upriver, in Wethersfield. A dissatisfied Pequot-Mohegan sachem named Uncas offered his help to the colonists, as did some Narragansetts, a traditional enemy of the Pequots who lived in present-day Rhode Island. A force of Connecticut men, aided by a few Indians and, eventually, by soldiers from other colonies, attacked the Pequots in late May 1637, and another battle followed in June.[7] The more that historians have closely studied the reasons for this war and its outcome, the more they have questioned the colonists' justifications for it, disputing, in particular, the argument that the Pequots had "invaded" Connecticut.[8]

That, in general, the colonists depended on the Native Americans when they first arrived (the Pilgrims' encounter with Samoset and Squanto is a famous example of learning from the Indians); and that, once assured of survival, they exploited the Native Americans, is certain. No less certain is that many Native Americans resented the policies of the colonists and tried to preserve their independence. Long-accumulating resentments led in 1675–1676 to another war, known as "King Philip's" after the leader of the Narragansetts. Far more extensive and devastating than the Pequot War, this conflict ended the autonomy and power of the Narragansetts, the only substantial tribe to remain in southern New England.

In the mid-1640s the first efforts at missionary outreach were con-

---

[7] It is frequently said or implied that the Pequots were exterminated (e.g., Melville in *Moby Dick*); but see *The Pequots in Southern New England: The Fall and Rise of an American Indian Nation*, ed. Laurence M. Hauptman and James D. Wherry (Norman, Okla., 1990).

[8] Cave (1996) reviews interpretations.

ducted by the minister of Roxbury, Massachusetts, John Eliot (1604–1690), who employed a Native teacher to learn Algonquian, and gradually became able to preach in one of its dialects. The timing was linked to specific circumstances: in 1644 six sachems submitted to the General Court, and in January 1647 another group of sachems living near Concord agreed to abide by a series of moral and social rules, one of which mandated that there "be no more powwowing amongst the Indians."[9] Once the missionary enterprise was finally under way the orthodox colonists publicized it in a series of reports published in England. In the fifth of this series, *Tears of Repentance* (1653), Eliot described the attempt in 1652 to form a Native congregation in Natick.

Another missionary project was initiated in the 1640s on the island of Martha's Vineyard, lying to the southeast of Massachusetts. In 1641 Thomas Mayhew Sr., a merchant who had moved to New England, received a patent to the entire island and in 1642 settled there with a group of English families. The island was already inhabited by some two to three thousand Wapanoags, among whom the English remained in the minority until the eighteenth century. Mayhew's son Thomas Jr. (1621–1657), who had received some training for the ministry, began to offer instruction in Christianity, aided by the first convert, Hiacoomes, who was ordained in 1670 as a minister. Eventually this mission encompassed most of the Indians on the island. Mayhew died in a shipwreck en route to England in 1657.

The missionary enterprise on the mainland, which by 1674 included two Native churches and fourteen "praying towns" where Christian Indians lived together, was severely disrupted by King Philip's War. The hostility Mary Rowlandson expressed in her captivity narrative toward the Christian Indians was widely shared, and although some of them served as soldiers in the allied army, many were badly mistreated. A few colonists, notably the magistrate Daniel Gookin (1612–1687), defended the Christian Indians.

Bibliography

Historians debate whether the colonists were intentionally coercive and whether the missionary enterprise was unjust because it led to race suicide. Jennings (1975), Simmons (1979), Salisbury (1974), and Simmons (1981) criticize the colonists; Vaughan (1965; see also the rev. ed., 1995), and Cogley (1999) offer a measured defense, with Cogley's the best description of the Eliot mission. The Martha's Vineyard mission is sympathetically described in Ronda (1981) and Cogley (1999), chap. 7.

[9] Thomas Shepard, *The Day-Breaking* (1648), repr. in *Works of Thomas Shepard*, ed. John Albro, 3 vols. (Boston, 1853), 3:459.

Chapter 23

The Pequot "War" of 1637

The colonists rapidly learned how to exploit the rivalries that divided the tribes inhabiting southern New England. These rivalries were especially intense in eastern Connecticut, where the Pequots were constantly at odds with the Narragansetts. The resentment some of the Indians felt as parties of colonists built forts and trading posts along the Connecticut coast and founded towns in the interior led to killings that prompted Massachusetts and Connecticut to send an expeditionary force into the territory of the Pequots in 1637 and, as one eighteenth-century historian rightly observed, "attempt their entire destruction."[1] One rationale for this effort was the reputation of the Pequots for aggression, although whether this reputation was warranted is debatable. Led by John Underhill of Massachusetts and John Mason of Connecticut, the combined force, which also included Indians disaffected with the sachem of the Pequots, attacked on the morning of May 26, 1637, a Pequot "fort" on the present-day site of Groton, Connecticut. The fort contained several hundred men, women, and children, almost all of whom died once Mason set a wigwam on fire and the entire fort went up in flames. Although the colonists were outnumbered, they had firearms, the Indians only bows and arrows and hatchets. In June another force of colonists pursued the remaining group of Pequots as they attempted to escape to the west, catching up with them at a swamp near present-day Southport. This time most of the Pequots surrendered or were taken captive; some were sold into slavery in the West Indies and others were incorporated into local tribes. The colonists insisted that the survivors abandon their tribal name.[2] Entangled though it was in local and intercolonial politics, the war came to occupy a significant place in the historical memory of the colonists.

According to the most recent historian of the war, it "inspired the earliest expressions of the idea that Indian wars were providentially or-

---

[1] Thomas Hutchinson, *The History of the Colony and Province of Massachusetts Bay*, ed. L. S. Mayo, 3 vols. (Cambridge, Mass., 1936), 1:67.

[2] See, e.g., the request of Israel Stoughton, commander of the second attack, for captives: *Winthrop Papers* (1929–), 3:435.

dained events intended to test and chastise God's people."[3] The war was considered just for another reason, that God sanctioned violence and the shedding of blood, as the Old Testament so often indicates. Four accounts of the war were written in the seventeenth century, three by colonists and a fourth by Philip Vincent, an English minister. John Underhill's *News from America* was published in London in 1638, as was Vincent's *True Relation of The late Battell fought in New-England.* John Mason's "Brief History of the Pequot War" remained in manuscript until Increase Mather incorporated it into *A Relation Of the Troubles which have hapned in New-England, By reason of the Indians there* (Boston, 1677); the first complete printing occurred in 1736, arranged by the Boston minister Thomas Prince. The fourth account, by Lyon Gardiner, was not printed until 1833. Mason (1600–1672) was involved in military affairs in Massachusetts before moving with most of the townspeople of Dorchester to found Windsor, Connecticut, in 1635; after the Pequot War, he resided at Saybrook and held a number of important posts in the civil government of Connecticut. It seems likely that he knew of Underhill's narrative.

Bibliography

Jennings (1975), who accuses Mason of duplicity (220–22); Salisbury (1982), chap. 7; Cave (1996), who reviews interpretations of the war and defends Mason's veracity (see esp. 209–10). The four narratives are reprinted in Orr (1897) with useful notes.

JOHN MASON

A Brief History of the Pequot War

In the beginning of May 1637 there were sent out by Connecticut Colony ninety men under the command of Captain John Mason against the Pequots, with Uncas an Indian sachem living at Mohegan,[4] who was newly revolted from the Pequots; being shipped in one pink, one pinnace, and one shallop; who sailing down the river of Connecticut fell several times a ground, the water being very low: The Indians not being wonted to such things with their small canoes, and also being impatient

---

[3] Cave (1996), 171.

[4] Possibly descended from two Pequot sachems and married to a daughter of Tatobem, the Pequot grand sachem murdered in 1634 by the Dutch, Uncas was "a physically imposing, strong-willed, and ambitious politician" (Cave [1996], 67) who competed with Sassacus and other leaders to become grand sachem; he frequently lived among Narragansetts. Mason spelled his name as Onkos.

of delays, desired they might be set on shore, promising that they would meet us at Saybrook; which we granted: They hastening to their quarters, fell upon thirty or forty of the enemy near Saybrook Fort, and killed seven of them outright . . . which we looked at as a special providence; for before we were somewhat doubtful of his [Uncas's] fidelity. . . .

In the morning [May 25] there came to us several of Miantonimi[5] his men, who told us, they were come to assist us in our expedition, which encouraged divers Indians of that place to engage also; who suddenly gathering into a ring, one by one, making solemn protestations how gallantly they would demean themselves, and how many men they would kill.

On the Thursday about eight of the clock in the morning, we marched thence towards Pequot, with about five hundred Indians: But through the heat of the weather and want of provisions, some of our men fainted: And having marched about twelve miles, we came to Pawcatuck River, at a ford where our Indians told us the Pequots did usually fish; there making an halt,[6] we stayed some small time: The Narragansett Indians manifesting great fear, in so much that many of them returned, although they had frequently despised us, saying, That we durst not look upon a Pequot, but themselves would perform great things; though we had often told them that we came on purpose and were resolved, God assisting, to see the Pequots, and to fight with them before we returned, though we perished. I then inquired of Uncas, what he thought the Indians would do? Who said, the Narragansetts would all leave us, but as for himself he would never leave us: and so it proved: For which expressions and some other speeches of his, I shall never forget him. Indeed he was a great friend, and did great service.

And after we had refreshed ourselves with our mean commons, we marched about three miles, and came to a field which had lately been planted with Indian corn: There we made another [h]alt, and called our council, supposing we drew near to the enemy: and being informed by the Indians that the enemy had two forts almost impregnable; but we were not at all discouraged, but rather animated, in so much that we were resolved to assault both their forts at once. But understanding that one of them was so remote that we could not come up with it before midnight, though we marched hard; whereat we were much grieved, chiefly because the greatest and bloodiest sachem there resided, whose name was Sassacus:[7] We were then constrained, being exceedingly spent

---

[5] Usually called Miantonimo, the great sachem of the Narragansett Indians, he was killed in 1643, with the approval of the colonists, by Uncas. Cave (1996), chap. 4.

[6] Spelled "alta" in the 1736 printing.

[7] Succceded Tatobem as grand sachem; escaped the second swamp fight, described below, only to be killed by Mohawks shortly thereafter.

in our march with extreme heat and want of necessaries, to accept of the nearest.

We then marching on in a silent manner, the Indians that remained fell all into the rear, who formerly kept the van (being possessed with great fear); we continued our march till about one hour in the night: and coming to a little swamp between two hills, there we pitched our little camp; much wearied with hard travel, keeping great silence, supposing we were very near the fort as our Indians informed us; which proved otherwise: The rocks were our pillows; yet rest was pleasant: The night proved comfortable, being clear and moon light: We appointed our guards and placed our sentinels at some distance; who heard the enemy singing at the fort, who continued that strain until midnight, with great insulting and rejoicing, as we were afterwards informed: They seeing our pinnaces sail by them some days before, concluded we were afraid of them and durst not come near them; the burthen of their song tending to that purpose. In the morning, we awaking and seeing it very light, supposing it had been day, and so we might have lost our opportunity, having purposed to make our assault before day; roused the men with all expedition, and briefly commended ourselves and [our] design to God, thinking immediately to go to the assault; the Indians shewing us a path, told us that it led directly to the fort. We held on our march about two miles, wondering that we came not to the fort, and fearing we might be deluded: But seeing corn newly planted at the foot of a great hill, supposing the fort was not far off, a champian[8] country being round about us; then making a stand, gave the word for some of the Indians to come up: At length Uncas and one Wequash[9] appeared; we demanded of them, Where was the fort? They answered, On the top of that hill: Then we demanded, Where were the rest of the Indians? They answered, Behind, exceedingly afraid: We wished them to tell the rest of their fellows, that they should by no means fly, but stand at what distance they pleased, and see whether Englishmen would now fight or not. Then Captain Underhill[10] came up, who marched in the rear; and commending ourselves to God, divided our men: There being two entrances into the fort, intending to enter both at once: Captain Mason leading up to that on the north east side; who approaching within one rod, heard a dog bark and an Indian crying *Owanux*! *Owanux*! Which is Englishmen! Englishmen! We called up our forces with all expedition, gave fire upon them through the palisado; the Indians being in a dead indeed their last sleep: Then we wheeling off fell upon the main entrance, which was blocked up with bushes about breast high, over

---

[8] An expanse of level ground; open country (OED).

[9] Like Uncas, he lost out to Sassacus in the struggle to succeed Tatobem.

[10] John Underhill (1597?–1672) emigrated to Massachusetts in 1630 after having been a soldier in the Netherlands.

which the captain passed, intending to make good the entrance, encouraging the rest to follow. Lieutenant Seeley endeavored to enter; but being somewhat cumbered, stepped back and pulled out the bushes and so entered, and with him about sixteen men: We had formerly concluded to destroy them by the sword and save the plunder.

Whereupon Captain Mason seeing no Indians, entered a wigwam; where he was beset with many Indians, waiting all opportunities to lay hands on him, but could not prevail. At length William Heydon espying the breach in the wigwam, supposing some English might be there, entered; but in his entrance fell over a dead Indian; but speedily recovering himself, the Indians some fled, others crept under their beds: The captain going out of the wigwam saw many Indians in the lane or street; he making towards them, they fled, were pursued to the end of the lane, where they were met by Edward Pattison, Thomas Barber, with some others; where seven of them were slain, as they said. The captain facing about, marched a slow pace up the lane he came down, perceiving himself very much out of breath; and coming to the other end near the place where he first entered, saw two soldiers standing close to the palisado with their swords pointed to the ground: The captain told them that we should never kill them after that manner: The captain also said, We must burn them; and immediately stepping into the wigwam where he had been before, brought out a firebrand, and putting it into the mats with which they were covered, set the wigwam on fire.[11] Lieutenant Thomas Bull and Nicholas Omsted beholding, came up; and when it was thoroughly kindled, the Indians ran as men most dreadfully amazed.

And indeed such a dreadful terror did the Almighty let fall upon their spirits, that they would fly from us and run into the very flames, where many of them perished. And when the fort was thoroughly fired, command was given, that all should fall off and surround the fort; which was readily attended by all; only one Arthur Smith being so wounded that he could not move out of the place, who was happily espied by Lieutenant Bull, and by him rescued.

The fire was kindled on the northeast side to windward; which did swiftly overrun the fort, to the extreme amazement of the enemy, and great rejoicing of ourselves. Some of them climbing to the top of the palisado; others of them running into the very flames; many of them gathering to windward, lay pelting at us with their arrows; and we repaid them with our small shot: Others of the stoutest issued forth, as we did guess, to the number of forty, who perished by the sword.

What I have formerly said, is according to my own knowledge, there being sufficient living testimony to every particular.

[11] "Myself set fire on the south end with a train of powder." John Underhill, *Newes from America* (1638), in Orr (1897), 80.

But in reference to Captain Underhill and his parties acting in this assault, I can only intimate as we were informed by some of themselves immediately after the fight, thus they marching up to the entrance on the southwest side, there made some pause; a valiant, resolute gentleman, one Mr. Hedge, stepping towards the gate, saying, If we may not enter, wherefore came we here;[12] and immediately endeavored to enter; but was opposed by a sturdy Indian which did impede his entrance; but the Indian being slain by himself and Sergeant Davis, Mr. Hedge entered the fort with some others; but the fort being on fire, the smoke and flames were so violent that they were constrained to desert the fort.

Thus were they now at their wits' end, who not many hours before exalted themselves in their great pride, threatening and resolving the utter ruin and destruction of all the English, exulting and rejoicing with songs and dances: But God was above them, who laughed his enemies and the enemies of his people to scorn, *making them as a fiery oven* [Ps. 21:9]: Thus were the stouthearted spoiled, having slept their last sleep, and none of their men could find their hands: Thus did the Lord judge among the heathen, filling the place with dead bodies!

And here we may see the just judgment of God, in sending even the very night before this assault, one hundred and fifty men from their other fort, to join with them of that place, who were designed as some of themselves reported to go forth against the English, at that very instant when this heavy stroke came upon them, where they perished with their fellows. So that the mischief they intended to us, came upon their own pate: They were taken in their own snare, and we through mercy escaped. And thus in little more than one hour's space was their impregnable fort with themselves utterly destroyed, to the number of six or seven hundred, as some of themselves confessed. There were only seven taken captive and about seven escaped.

Of the English, there were two slain outright, and about twenty wounded: Some fainted by reason of the sharpness of the weather, it being a cool morning and the want of such comforts and necessaries as were needful in such a case; especially our chirurgeon was much wanting, whom we left with our barks in Narragansett Bay, who had order there to remain until the night before our intended assault. . . .

And when we had taken order for the safe conduct of the Narragansett Indians, we repaired to the place of our abode: where we were entertained with great triumph and rejoicing and praising God for his goodness to us, in succeeding our weak endeavors, in crowning us with

---

[12] In *A True Relation* Philip Vincent quotes Underhill as saying, "What! Shall we enter? Said Captain Underhill. What come we for else? Answered one Hedge. . . ." Orr (1897), 103; disputed by Underhill in *Newes*, 79.

success, and restoring of us with so little loss. Thus was God seen in the mount, crushing his proud enemies and the enemies of his people: They who were ere while a terror to all that were round about them, who resolved to destroy all the English and to root their very name out of this country, should by such weak means, even seventy seven (there being no more at the fort) bring the mischief they plotted, and the violence they offered and exercised, upon their own heads in a moment: burning them up in the fire of his wrath, and dunging the ground with their flesh: It was the Lord's doings, and it is marvelous in our eyes! It is he that hath made his work wonderful, and therefore ought to be remembered.

Immediately the whole body of Pequots repaired to that fort where Sassacus the chief sachem did reside; charging him that he was the only cause of all the troubles that had befallen them; and therefore they would destroy both him and his: But by the entreaty of their counselors they spared his life; and consulting what course to take, concluded there was no abiding any longer in their country, and so resolved to fly into several parts. The greatest body of them went towards Manhatance:[13] And passing over Connecticut, they met with three Englishmen in a shallop going for Saybrook, whom they slew: The English fought very stoutly, as themselves [the Pequots] confessed, wounding many of the enemy.

About a fortnight after our return home, which was about one month after the fight at Mystic, there arrived in Pequot River several vessels from the Massachusetts, Captain Israel Stoughton being commander in chief;[14] and with him about one hundred and twenty men; being sent by that colony to pursue the war against the Pequots: The enemy being all fled before they came, except some few stragglers, who were surprised by the Moheags[15] and others of the Indians, and by them delivered to the Massachusetts soldiers.

Connecticut Colony being informed hereof, sent forthwith forty men, Captain Mason being chief commander; with some other gentlemen, to meet those of the Massachusetts, to consider what was necessary to be attended respecting the future: Who meeting with them of the Massachusetts in Pequot harbor; after some time of consultation, concluded to pursue those Pequots that were fled towards Manhatance, and so forthwith marched after them, discovering several places where they rendezvoused and lodged not far distant from their several removes; making but little haste, by reason of their children, and want of provision;

[13] I suppose this the same which is sometimes called Manhatan or Manhatoes; which is since called New York. (Note by Thomas Prince in the 1736 printing).

[14] Of Dorchester, Massachusetts; he held local and colonial offices.

[15] Mohegans.

being forced to dig for clams, and to procure such other things as the wilderness afforded: Our vessels sailing along by the shore. In about the space of three days we all arrived at New Haven harbor, then called Quinnipiac. And seeing a great smoke in the woods not far distant, we supposing some of the Pequots our enemies might be there; we hastened ashore, but quickly discovered them to be Connecticut Indians. Then we returned aboard our vessels, where we stayed some short time, having sent a Pequot captive upon discovery, we named him Luz; who brought us tidings of the enemy, which proved true: so faithful was he to us, though against his own nation. Such was the terror of the English upon them; that a Moheage Indian named Jack Eatow going ashore at that time, met with three Pequots, took two of them and brought them aboard.

We then hastened our march towards the place where the enemy was: And coming into a corn field, several of the English espied some Indians, who fled from them: They pursued them; and coming to the top of an hill, saw several wigwams just opposite, only a swamp intervening, which was almost divided in two parts. Sergeant Palmer hastening with about twelve men who were under his command to surround the smaller part of the swamp, that so he might prevent the Indians flying; Ensign Danport,[16] Sergeant Jeffries, etc. entering the swamp, intended to have gone to the wigwams, were there set upon by several Indians, who in all probability were deterred by Sergeant Palmer. In this skirmish the English slew but few; two or three of themselves were wounded: The rest of the English coming up, the swamp was surrounded.

Our council being called, and the question propounded, How we should proceed, Captain Patrick advised that we should cut down the swamp; there being many Indian hatchets taken, Captain Traske concurring with him; but was opposed by others: Then we must palisado the swamp; which was also opposed: Then they would have a hedge made like those of Gotham; all which was judged by some almost impossible, and to no purpose, and that for several reasons, and therefore strongly opposed. But some others advised to force the swamp, having time enough, it being about three of the clock in the afternoon: But that being opposed, it was then propounded to draw up our men close to the swamp, which would much have lessened the circumference; and with all to fill up the open passages with bushes, that so we might secure them until the morning, and then we might consider further about it. But neither of these would pass; so different were our apprehensions; which was very grievous to some of us, who concluded the Indians would make an escape in the night, as easily they might and did: We

[16] Correctly, Davenport.

keeping at a great distance, what better could be expected? Yet Captain Mason took order that the narrow in the swamp should be cut through; which did much shorten our leaguer. It was resolutely performed by Sergeant Davis.

We being loath to destroy women and children, as also the Indians belonging to that place; whereupon Mr. Thomas Stanton a man well acquainted with Indian language and manners,[17] offered his service to go into the swamp and treat with them: To which we were somewhat backward, by reason of some hazard and danger he might be exposed unto: But his importunity prevailed: Who going to them, did in a short time return to us, with near two hundred old men, women and children; who delivered themselves to the mercy of the English. And so night drawing on, we beleaguered them as strongly as we could. About half an hour before day, the Indians that were in the swamp attempted to break through Captain Patrick's quarters; but were beaten back several times; they making a great noise, as their manner is at such times, it sounded round about our leaguer: Whereupon Captain Mason sent Sergeant Stares to inquire into the cause, and also to assist if need required; Capt. Traske coming also into their assistance: But the tumult growing to a very great height, we raised our siege; and marching up to the place, at a turning of the swamp the Indians were forcing out upon us; but we sent them back by our small shot.

We waiting a little for a second attempt; the Indians in the meantime facing about, pressed violently upon Captain Patrick, breaking through his quarters, and so escaped. They were about sixty or seventy as we were informed. We afterwards searched the swamp, and found but few slain. The captives we took were about one hundred and eighty; whom we divided, intending to keep them as servants, but they could not endure that yoke; few of them continuing any considerable time with their masters.

Thus did the Lord scatter his enemies with his strong arm! The Pequots now became a prey to all Indians. Happy were they that could bring in their heads to the English: Of which there came almost daily to Windsor, or Hartford. But the Pequots growing weary hereof, sent some of the chief that survived to mediate with the English; offering that if they might but enjoy their lives, they would become the English vassals, to dispose of them as they pleased. Which was granted them. Whereupon Uncas and Miantonimi were sent for; who with the Pequots met at Hartford. The Pequots being demanded, How many of them were then living? Answered, about one hundred and eighty, or two hundred. There were then given to Uncas, sachem of Monheag, eighty; to Mian-

---

[17] A trader whose language abilities enabled him to review John Eliot's translations.

tonimi, sachem of Narragansett, eighty; and to Ninigret, twenty, when he should satisfy for a mare of Edward Pomroye's killed by his men. The Pequots were then bound by covenant, that none should inhabit their native country, nor should any of them be called Pequots any more, but Moheags and Narragansetts forever. Shortly after, about forty of them went to Moheag; others went to Long Island; the rest settled at Pawcatuck, a place in Pequot country, contrary to their late covenant and agreement with the English.

Source: John Mason, *A Brief History of the Pequot War: Especially Of the memorable Taking of their Fort at Mistick in Connecticut In 1637* (Boston, 1736).

Chapter 24

Forming Native American Congregations

In 1646 John Eliot traveled to Nonantum (present-day Newton, Massachusetts) and preached in the Massachusetts dialect of Algonquian to an audience of Indians. Thus began the first sustained missionary outreach to the Indians in Massachusetts. Meanwhile, on the island of Martha's Vineyard, where Indians far outnumbered the few colonists, Thomas Mayhew Jr., son of the island's proprietor, was instructing some of them in Christianity. After the first of these ventures was publicized in England in a tract written by Thomas Shepard and published in 1647, both were described in another tract (1649) by Edward Winslow (1595–1655), a colonist who returned home to represent the interests of the Massachusetts government. Parliament responded by passing in July 1649 "An Act for the Promoting and Propagating the Gospel of Jesus Christ in New England." It created a charitable corporation empowered to solicit donations, the President and Society for the Propagation of the Gospel in New England. In ten years' time the New England Company, as it was usually called, raised some £16,500, most of which was invested in England in order to provide a steady income to support the missionary program—in particular, a printer and printing press in Cambridge, Massachusetts, together with any other costs related to printing books for the Indians in Algonquian.

To encourage the flow of donations, Eliot and his allies continued to write accounts of the missionary enterprise.[1] From Eliot's perspective, the first task was to instruct the Indians in the basic principles of Christianity, as revealed in Scripture. To this end he wrote a catechism in Algonquian that was distributed in handwritten copies before being printed in 1654; the Indians' narratives frequently cite or quote doctrinal statements it contained.[2] By 1653 or 1654, Eliot began the monumental task of translating the Bible into Algonquian with the aid of an Indian helper. A trial version of Genesis (fig. 2) was printed in 1655,

---

[1] All of these are reprinted in the *Collections of the Massachusetts Historical Society*, 3d ser., 4 (1834).

[2] A second catechism, "turned into the Narragansett or Pequott language," was written by Abraham Pierson, minister in Branford, Connecticut, and printed in 1658.

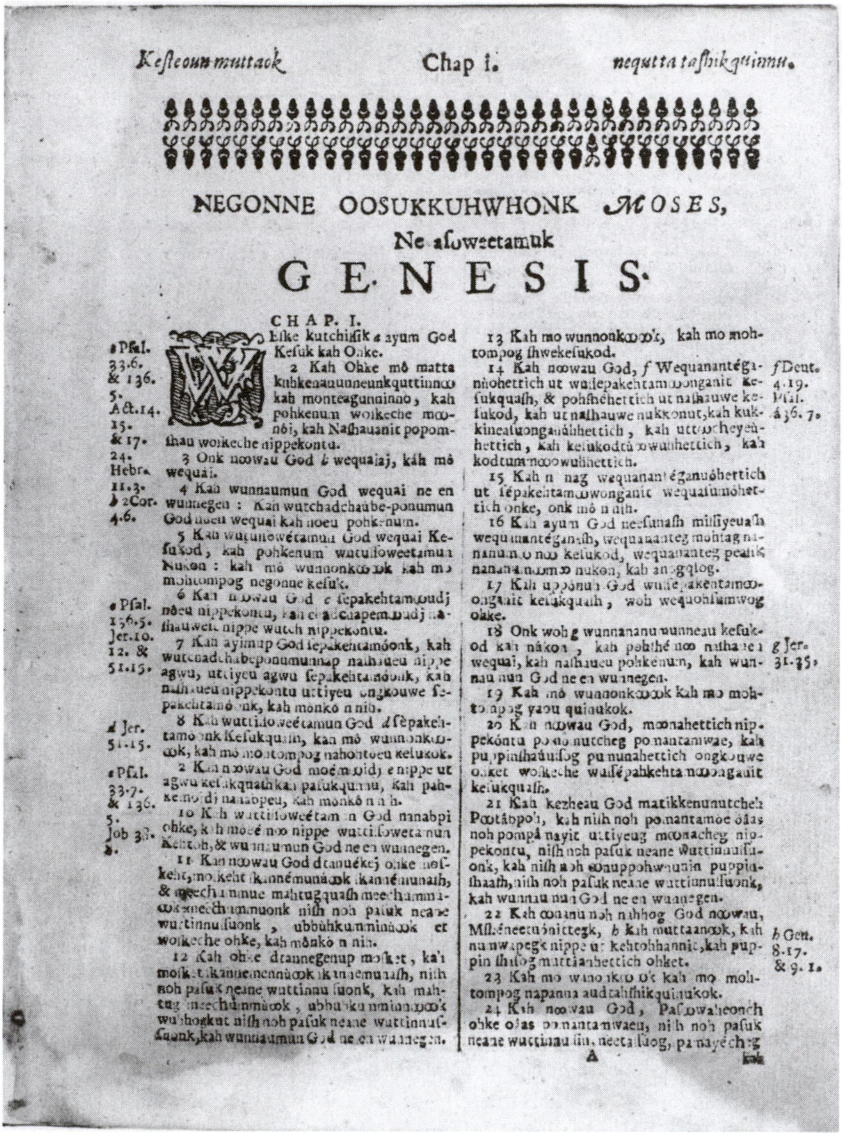
Kesteoum muttaok Chap I. *nequtta tashikquinnu.*

NEGONNE OOSUKKUHWHONK *MOSES,*

Ne asoweetamuk

GENESIS.

CHAP. I.

Figure 2. Genesis 1:1–13: the opening passages in John Eliot's translation of the Bible into Algonquian (Cambridge, Mass. 1661–1663). Courtesy of the American Antiquarian Society another followed of Matthew, the entire New Testament was printed in 1661, and the Bible as a whole was completed in 1663. Eliot and his Indian coworkers continued the work of translation, adding, among others, abridgments of Shepard's *Sincere Convert* and Lewis Bayley's *Practice of Piety*, two classics of "practical divinity."

Eliot wanted the Nonantum Indians to "live in an orderly way among us" on a tract of land assigned by the government for this purpose, a town that became known as Natick. Here and in similar enclaves the Indians were required to practice moral and social rules that were new to them: ending polygamous marriages, replacing wigwams with houses, staying put instead of shifting around with the seasons, cutting their hair short. These rules followed from the belief, not unique to Eliot, that "civility" and Christianity went hand in hand, the first being a necessary prerequisite of the second. He also reasoned that proximity to the colonists would persuade the Indians that they should remodel their lives, an assumption that one historian has termed the "affective" theory of missions.[3]

Eliot was a millenarian who came under the influence of the English theorist Thomas Brightman, famous in his day for arguing that the Second Coming of Christ would be preceded by a "Middle Advent," a phase of redemption history that marked the beginning of the recovery of true Christianity. The English Civil War, which culminated in the execution of Charles I in 1649, persuaded Eliot that "Christ . . . gloriously breaks forth in the brightness of his coming."[4] The letter to Oliver Cromwell that prefaces his section of *Tears of Repentance* (below) is charged with prophetic fervor. One practical consequence of this fervor was his attempt to organize the civil government of the Natick community on the basis of Exodus 18:21–22. During the 1650s, Eliot also believed that the Indians were a remnant of one of the lost tribes, a theory of their origins he ceased to mention by the 1660s.[5]

Eliot's final goal was to establish churches among the Indians, using the same requirements for church membership that the colonists themselves followed. He had some fifteen of the Indians do a trial run of confessions in the summer of 1652. In October, some of these same men offered relations of the work of grace in their own language, with Eliot struggling to translate, before an audience of ministers, magistrates, and others. The ministers who were present decided that the converts had made "a hopeful beginning" but had not yet achieved "a full and thorough conversion." Not until 1659 were eight Indians admitted to the

---

[3] Cogley (1999); the effort to educate boys and young men at Harvard is described in Morison (1936), chap. 17.

[4] Cogley (1999), 79.

[5] Ibid., chap. 4.

Roxbury church after offering further narratives, but by 1660 these and other converts were worshipping in an independent church in Natick.

The texts that follow are a selection of the narratives delivered at the October 1652 meeting, together with Mayhew's letter updating the English donors on the Vineyard mission and describing the natives' cultural and religious practices. The relations published in *Tears of Repentance* reiterate the importance of the Ten Commandments, the distinction between inward and outward aspects of Christianity, and the emphasis on sin that were so central to Puritan piety, but as Charles L. Cohen has pointed out, the narrators also "truncated and muted the affective cycle Puritans underwent, lopping off the joys of sanctification and mitigating the horrors of humiliation."[6]

Bibliography

Cogley (1999), with a full guide to the previous literature.

JOHN ELIOT AND THOMAS MAYHEW

 *Tears of Repentance (1653)*

To the much honored corporation in London, chosen to place of public trust for the promoting of the work of the Lord among the Indians in New-England.

[Mayhew's Report]

When the Lord first brought me to these poor Indians on the Vineyard, they were mighty zealous and earnest in the worship of false gods, and devils; their false gods were many, both of things in heaven, earth, and sea: And there they had their men-gods, women-gods, and children-gods, their companies, and fellowships of gods, or divine powers, guiding things amongst men, besides innumerable more feigned gods belonging to many creatures, to their corn, and every color of it: The devil also with his angels had his kingdom among them, in them; account him they did, the terror of the living, the god of the dead, under whose cruel power and into whose deformed likeness they conceived themselves to be translated when they died; for the same word they have for *devil,* they use also for a *dead man,* in their language: by him they were often hurt in their bodies, distracted in their minds, wherefore they had

[6] Cohen in Bremer (1993), 254.

many meetings with their powwows (who usually had a hand in their hurt),[7] to pacify the devil by their sacrifice, and get deliverance from their evil; I have sometimes marveled to see the vehemence of their spirits, which they acted with no less bodily violence therein. The powwows counted their imps their preservers, had them treasured up in their bodies, which they brought forth to hurt their enemies, and heal their friends; who when they had done some notable cure, would shew the imp in the palm of his hand to the Indians, who with much amazement looking on it, deified them, then at all times seeking to them for cure in all sicknesses, and counsel in all cases: This diabolical way they were in, giving heed to a multitude of heathen traditions of their gods, and many other things, under the observation whereof, they with much slavery were held, and abounding with sins, having only an obscure notion of a god greater than all, which they call Mannit,[8] but they knew not what he was, and therefore had no way to worship him.

What an entrance I had at first amongst these miserable heathen, how called thereunto, and what success God blessed us with, hath been in some measure already published,[9] which will I hope through the dew of God's blessing from heaven, have such a gracious increase, that the blossoming and budding time shall at least be acknowledged, and by many more God blessed for it, in the growth of the fruit to more maturity; since it hath pleased God to send his Word to these poor captivated men (bondslaves to sin and Satan) he hath through mercy brought two hundred eighty three Indians (not counting young children in the number) to renounce their false gods, devils, and powwows, and publicly in set meetings, before many witnesses, have they disclaimed the divinity of their formerly adored multitude, defied their tyrannical destroyer the devil, and utterly refused the help of the powwows in any case; neither have they at any time, either by threatenings or flatteries been drawn thereto, although their lives have been in hazard; yea, eight of their powwows have forsaken their devilish craft, and profitable trade as they accounted it, for to embrace the Word and way of God. The Indians which do pray to God, were not compelled thereto by power, neither also could they be allured by gifts, who received nothing for about seven years time, much less that which counterpoise their troubles, and exceed to the drawing of them from the beloved ways of their own worships: Surely it were great uncharitableness, and derogatory from

---

[7] Powwows were shamans or spiritual leaders; contrary to allegations by Europeans, these healers were not allied with any figure or powers approximating those of the devil.

[8] In other accounts, the name of this god (or better, power) is "Manitou." Cave (1996), 28.

[9] Descriptions of the missionary enterprise on the Vineyard had previously appeared in a series of tracts written by Thomas Shepard, Edward Winslow, and Henry Whitfield.

the glory of God, to think that none of these are truly changed, and that God himself by his Word and Spirit, hath not in mercy prevailed in their hearts against these evils; nay, may we not hope and be persuaded by this, and some other appearances of God amongst them, that some of them are truly turned to God from idols, to serve the living and true God? Serve him, through mercy they do in some hopeful reformations, walking inoffensively and diligently in their way, which I hope will more plainly appear when they are in a way more hopeful (by the blessing of God to their further well-being) which I hope will be in the best time. . . .

From the Vineyard the 22nd of October, 1652

[Eliot's Report]

Christian Reader,

I know thy soul longeth to hear tidings of God's grace poured out upon these goings down of the sun, because the Spirit of God by the word of prophecy, useth to raise up and draw forth such actings of faith, as accord with the accomplishment of those prophecies, when the time of their accomplishment is come. When *Israel* was to return from *Babylon,* the Spirit by the word of prophecy, raised up such actings of faith, as were put forth in the exercise of all gifts necessary for the accomplishment thereof. *Daniel* prayeth. *Zerubbabel* hath a spirit of ruling, the peoples' affections are loose from their dwellings, and have a spirit of traveling. *Ezra, Nehemiah*, and all the rest of the worthies of the Lord, are raised at that time to accomplish what is prophesied. In these times the prophesies of Antichrist his downfall are accomplishing.[10] And do we not see that the Spirit of the Lord, by the word of prophecy, hath raised up men, instruments in the Lord's hand, to accomplish what is written herein. And the spirit of prayer, and expectation of faith is raised generally in all saints, by the same word of prophecy. In like manner the Lord having said, *that the gospel shall spread over all the earth, even to all the ends of the earth; and from the rising to the setting sun; all nations shall become the nations, and kingdoms of the Lord and of his Christ.*[11] Such words of prophecy hath the Spirit used to stir up the servants of the Lord to make out after the accomplishment thereof: and hath stirred up a mighty spirit of prayer, and expectation of faith for the conversion both of the Jews (yea all *Israel*),[12] and of the *Gentiles* also, over all the world. For this cause I know every believing

[10] Eliot's eschatology is carefully described in Cogley (1999).

[11] Language derived from Romans 10:18.

[12] Like many other Protestants of his day, Eliot expected the conversion of the Jews to Christianity to occur as the "end times" of Christian history approached.

heart, awakened by such scriptures, longeth to hear of the conversion of our poor *Indians*, whereby such prophecies are in part begun to be accomplished. Yea, the design of Christ being to erect his own kingdom, in the room of all those dominions, which he doth, and is about to overturn: You shall see a Spirit by such words of prophecy poured forth upon the saints (into whose hands Christ will commit the managing of his kingdom on earth) that shall carry them forth to advance Christ to rule over men in all affairs, by the word of his mouth, and make him their only lawgiver, and supreme judge, and king.

It is a day of small things with us: and that is God's season to make the single beauty of his humbling grace, to shine in them, that are the veriest ruins of mankind that are known on earth; as Mr. Hooker[13] was wont to describe the forlorn condition of these poor Indians. I see evident demonstrations that God's Spirit by his Word hath taught them, because their expressions, both in prayer, and in the confessions which I have now published, are far more, and more full, and spiritual, and various, than ever I was able to express unto them; in that poor broken manner of teaching which I have used among them. . . .

A brief relation of the proceedings of the Lord's work among the *Indians*, in reference unto their church-estate; the reasons of the not accomplishing thereof at present: With some of their *confessions;* whereby it may be discerned in some measure, how far the Lord hath prepared among them fit matter for a *church*.

These Indians (the better and wiser sort of them) have for some years inquired after church-estate, baptism, and the rest of the ordinances of God, in the observation whereof they see the godly English to walk. I have from time to time, delayed them upon this point, that until they were come up unto civil cohabitation, government, and labor, which a fixed condition of life will put them upon, they were not so capable to be betrusted with that treasure of Christ, lest they should scandalize the same, and make it of none effect, because if any should through temptation fall under censure, he could easily run away (as some have done) and would be tempted so to do, unless he were fixed in an habitation, and had some means of livelihood to lose, and leave behind him: such reasons have satisfied them hitherunto. But now being come under civil order, and fixing themselves in habitations, and bending themselves to labor, as doth appear by their works of fencings, buildings, etc. and especially in building, without any English workman's help, or direction, a very sufficient meeting-house, of fifty foot long twenty-five foot broad, near twelve foot high betwixt the joints, well sawn, and framed

---

[13] Thomas Hooker (1586–1647) organized the Newtown (Cambridge) church and then settled in Hartford, Connecticut, where he was pastor until his death.

(which is a specimen, not only of their singular ingenuity, and dexterity, but also of some industry) I say this being so, now my argument of delaying them from entering into church-estate, was taken away. Therefore in way of preparation of them thereunto, I did this summer call forth sundry of them in the days of our public assemblies in God's worship; sometimes on the Sabbath when I could be with them, and sometimes on lecture days, to make confession before the Lord of their former sins, and of their present knowledge of Christ, and experience of his grace; which they solemnly doing, I wrote down their confessions: which having done, and being in my own heart hopeful that there was among them fit matter for a church, I did request all the elders about us to hear them read, that so they might give me advice what to do in this great, and solemn business; which being done on a day appointed for the purpose, it pleased God to give their confessions such acceptance in their hearts, as that they saw nothing to hinder their proceeding, to try how the Lord would appear therein. Whereupon, after a day of fasting and prayer among ourselves, to seek the Lord in that behalf, there was another day of fasting and prayer appointed, and public notice thereof, and of the names of Indians [who] were to confess, and enter into covenant that day, was given to all the churches about us, to seek the Lord yet further herein, and to make solemn confessions of Christ his truth and grace, and further to try whether the Lord would vouchsafe such grace unto them, as to give them acceptance among the saints, into the fellowship of church-estate, and enjoyment of those ordinances which the Lord hath betrusted his churches withal. That day was the thirteenth of the eighth month.

When the assembly was met,[14] the first part of the day was spent in prayer unto God, and exercise in the Word of God; in which, myself first; and after that, two of the Indians did exercise; and so the time was spent till after ten, or near eleven of the clock. Then addressing ourselves unto the further work of the day, I first requested the reverend elders (many being present) that they would ask them questions touching the fundamental points of religion, that thereby they might have some trial of their knowledge, and better that way, than if themselves should of themselves declare what they believe, or than if I should ask them questions in these matters: After a little conference hereabout, it was concluded, that they should first make confession of their experience in the Lord's work upon their hearts, because in so doing, it is like something will be discerned of their knowledge in the doctrines of religion: and if after those confessions there should yet be cause to inquire further touching any point of religion it might be fitly done at last.

[14] The meeting took place on October 13, 1652, in Natick.

Whereupon we so proceeded, and called them forth in order to make confession. It was moved in the assembly by Reverend Mr. Wilson,[15] that their former confessions also, as well as these which they made at present, might be read unto the assembly, because it was evident that they were daunted much to speak before so great and grave an assembly as that was, but time did not permit it so to be then: yet now in my writing of their confessions I will take that course, that so it may appear what encouragement there was to proceed so far as we did; and that such as may read these their confessions, may the better discern of the reality of the grace of Christ in them.

The first which was called forth is named Totherswamp, whose former confession read before the elders, was as followeth: Before I prayed unto God, the English, when I came unto their houses, often said unto me, Pray to God; but I having many friends who loved me, and I loved them, and they cared not for praying to God, and therefore I did not: But I thought in my heart, that if my friends should die, and I live, I then would pray to God; soon after, God so wrought, that they did almost all die, few of them left; and then my heart feared, and I thought, that now I will pray unto God, and yet I was ashamed to pray; and if I eat and did not pray, I was ashamed of that also; so that I had a double shame upon me: Then you came unto us, and taught us, and said unto us, *Pray unto God;* and after that, my heart grew strong, and I was no more ashamed to pray, but I did take up praying to God; yet at first I did not think of God, and eternal life, but only that the English should love me, and I loved them: But after I came to learn what sin was, by the commandments of God, and then I saw all my sins, lust, gaming, etc. (he named more). You taught, that Christ knoweth all our hearts, and seeth what is in them, if humility, or anger, or evil thoughts, Christ seeth all that is in the heart; then my heart feared greatly, because God was angry for all my sins; yea, now my heart is full of evil thoughts, and my heart runs away from God, therefore my heart feareth and mourneth. Every day I see sin in my heart; one man brought sin into the world, and I am full of that sin, and I break God's Word every day. I see I deserve not pardon, for the first man's sinning; I can do no good, for I am like the devil, nothing but evil thoughts, and words, and works. I have lost all likeness to God, and goodness, and therefore every day I sin against God, and I deserve death and damnation: The first man brought sin first, and I do every day add to that sin, more sins; but Christ hath done for us all righteousness, and died for us because of our sins, and Christ teacheth us, that if we cast away our sins, and trust in Christ, then God will pardon all our sins; this I believe Christ hath

---

[15] John Wilson (1588–1667), pastor of the Boston church.

done, I can do no righteousness, but Christ hath done it for me; this I believe, and therefore I do hope for pardon. When I first heard the commandments, I then took up praying to God, and cast off sin. Again, when I heard, and understood redemption by Christ, then I believed Jesus Christ to take away my sins: every commandment taught me sin, and my duty to God. When you ask me, why do I love God? I answer, Because he giveth me all outward blessings, as food, clothing, children, all gifts of strength, speech, hearing; especially that he giveth us a minister to teach us, and giveth us government; and my heart feareth lest government should reprove me: but the greatest mercy of all is Christ, to give us pardon and life.

Totherswamp, *the confession which he made on the fast day before the great assembly, was as followeth:*

I confess in the presence of the Lord, before I prayed, many were my sins, not one good word did I speak; not one good thought did I think not one good action did I do: I did act all sins, and full was my heart of evil thoughts: when the English did tell me of God, I cared not for it. I thought it enough if they loved me: I had many friends that loved me, and I thought if they died, I would pray to God: and afterward it so came to pass; then was my heart ashamed, to pray I was ashamed, and if I prayed not, I was ashamed; a double shame was upon me: when God by you taught us, very much ashamed was my heart; then you taught us that Christ knoweth all our hearts: therefore truly he saw my thoughts, and I had thought, if my kindred should die I would pray to God; therefore they dying, I must now pray to God: and therefore my heart feared, for I thought Christ knew my thoughts: then I heard you teach, *The first man God made was named* Adam, *and God made a covenant with him, Do and live, thou and thy children; if thou do not thou must die, thou and thy children:*[16] And we are children of *Adam* poor sinners, therefore we all have sinned, for we have broke God's covenant, therefore evil is my heart therefore God is very angry with me, we sin against him every day; but this great mercy God hath given us, he hath given us his only Son, and promiseth, that whosoever believeth in Christ shall be saved [John 3:16–17]: for Christ hath died for us in our stead, for our sins, and he hath done for us all the words of God, for I can do no good act, only Christ can, and only Christ hath done all for us; Christ have deserved pardon for us, and risen again, he hath ascended to God, and doth ever pray for us; therefore all believers' souls shall go to heaven to Christ. But when I heard that word of

[16] Almost certainly, he was quoting the catechism Eliot wrote for the Native Americans.

Christ, Christ said *Repent and believe* [Mark 1:15], and Christ seeth *who repenteth*, then I said, dark and weak is my soul, and I am one in darkness, I am a very sinful man, and now I pray to Christ for life. Hearing you teach that word that the scribes and pharisees said *Why do thy disciples break the tradition of the fathers?* Christ answered, *Why do ye make void the commandments of God* [Matt. 15:2–3]? Then my heart feared that I do so, when I teach the Indians, because I cannot teach them right, and thereby make the Word of God vain. Again, Christ said *If the blind lead the blind they will both fall into the ditch* [Matt. 15:14]; therefore I feared that I am one blind, and when I teach other Indians I shall cause them to fall into the ditch. This is the love of God to me, that he giveth me all mercy in this world, and for them all I am thankful; but I confess I deserve hell; I cannot deliver my self, but I give my soul and my flesh to Christ and I trust my soul with him for he is my Redeemer, and I desire to call upon him while I live.

This was his confesssion which ended, Mr. Allin[17] further demanded of him this question, How he found his heart, now in the matter of repentance. His answer was; I am ashamed of all my sins, my heart is broken for them and melteth in me, I am angry with myself for my sins, and I pray to Christ to take away my sins, and I desire that they may be pardoned. But it was desired that further question might be forborne, lest time would be wanting to hear them all speak.

Monequassun, *The confession which he made on the fast day before the great assembly was as followeth.*

I confess my sins before the Lord, and before men this day: a little while since I did commit many sins, both in my hands and heart; lusts thefts, and many other sins, and that every day: and after I heard of praying to God, and that others prayed to God, my heart did not like it, but hated it, yea and mocked at it; and after they prayed at Cohannet I still hated it, and when I heard the Word I did not like of it, but thought of running away, because I loved sin: but I loved the place of my dwelling, and therefore I thought I will rather pray to God, and began to do it; a little I desired to learn the Ten Commandments of God, and other points of catechism; and then a little I repented, but I was quickly weary of repentance, and fell again to sin, and full of evil thoughts was my heart: and then I played the hypocrite, and my heart was full of sin: I learned some things, but did not do what God commanded, but I sinned and played the hypocrite; some things I did before man, but not before God.

---

[17] John Allin (1596?–1671) was pastor of the church in Dedham and helped John Eliot with his missionary work.

But afterward I feared because of my sins, and feared punishment for my sins, therefore I thought again I would run away; yet again I loving the place, would not run away, but would pray to God: and I asked a question at the lecture, which was this, *How I should get wisdom?* The answer made me a little to understand: but afterward I heard the word *If any man lack wisdom, let him ask it of God, who giveth liberally to all that ask, and upbraideth none* [James 1:5]. But then I did fear God's anger, because of all my sins, because they were great. Afterward hearing that word, that Christ is named *Jesus,* because he redeemeth us from all our sins [Matt. 1:21]: I thought Christ would not save me, because I repent not, for he saveth only penitent believers; but I am not such an one, but still a daily sinner. Afterward hearing that word, *Blessed are they that hunger and thirst after righteousness, for they shall be filled* [Matt. 5:6]: then I thought I am a poor sinner, and poor is my heart: then I prayed to God to teach me to do that which he requireth, and to pray aright. Afterward hearing that word, *Who ever looks upon a woman to lust after her, hath already committed adultery with her in his heart* [Matt. 5:28]; then I thought I had done all manner of sins in the sight of God, because he seeth lust in the heart, and knoweth all the evil thoughts of my heart; and then I did pray unto God, *Oh! give me repentance and pardon.* Afterwards when I did teach among the Indians, I was much humbled because I could not read right, and that I sinned in it; for I saw that when I thought to do a good work, I sinned in doing it, for I knew not what was right, nor how to do it. In the night I was considering of my sins, and could not find what to do: three nights I considered what to do, and at last God shewed me mercy, and shewed me what I should do. And then I desired to learn to read God's Word, and hearing that if we ask wisdom of God, he will give it, then I did much pray to God, that he would teach me to read. After a year's time, I thought I did not rightly seek, and I thought I sinned, because I did not rightly desire to read God's Word, and I thought my praying was sinful, and I feared, how should I, my wife, and child be clothed, if I spend my time in learning to read; but then God was merciful to me, and shewed me that word, *Say not, What shall I eat, or drink, or wherewith shall I be clothed* [Matt. 6:31–32], *wicked men seek after these;* but *first seek the kingdom of heaven, and these things shall be added to you* [Luke 12:29–31]; then I prayed God to teach me this word, and that I might do it: and then I desired to read God's Word, whatever I wanted. Afterward hearing that we must make a town, and gather a church at Natick, my heart disliked that place; but hearing that word, that *Christ met two fishers, and said, follow me, and I will make you fishers of men, and they presently left all and followed him* [Matt. 4:18–19]; hearing this, I was much troubled, because I had not believed

Christ, for I would not follow him to make a church, nor had I done what he commanded me, and then I was troubled for all my sins. Again hearing that word, that the blind man called after Christ, *saying, thou Son of David have mercy on me*; Christ asked him what he would have him do, he said, *Lord open my eyes* [Matt. 20:30, 32–33]; and presently Christ gave him sight, and he followed Christ: then again my heart was troubled, for I thought I still believe not, because I do not follow Christ, nor hath he yet opened mine eyes: then I prayed to Christ to open my eyes, that I might see what to do, because I am blind and cannot see how to follow Christ, and do what he commandeth, and I prayed to Christ, teach me Lord what to do, and to do what thou sayest; and I prayed that I might follow Christ: and then I thought I will follow Christ to make a church. All this trouble I had to be brought to be willing to make a church: and quickly after, God laid upon me more trouble, by sickness and death; and then I much prayed to God for life, for we were all sick, and then God would not hear me, to give us life; but first one of my children died, and after that my wife; then I was in great sorrow, because I thought God would not hear me, and I thought it was because I would not follow him, therefore he hears not me: then I found this sin in my heart, that I was angry at the punishment of God: but afterward I considered, I was a poor sinner, I have nothing, nor child, nor wife, I deserve that God should take away all mercies from me; and then I repented of my sins, and did much pray, and I remembered the promise to follow Christ, and my heart said, I had in this sinned, that followed not Christ, and therefore I cried for pardon of this sin: and then hearing of this word, Whoever believeth in Christ, his sins are pardoned, he believing that Christ died for us;[18] and I believed. Again hearing that word, *If ye be not converted, and become as a little child you cannot go to heaven* [Matt. 18:3]; then my heart thought, I do not this, but I deserve hell fire for ever; and then I prayed Christ, Oh! turn me from my sin, and teach me to hear thy Word; and I prayed to my Father in heaven: and after this, I believed in Christ for pardon. Afterward I heard that word, that it is a shame for a man to wear long hair [1 Cor. 11:14], and that there was no such custom in the churches: at first I thought I loved not long hair, but I did, and found it very hard to cut it off; and then I prayed God to pardon that sin also: Afterward I thought my heart cared not for the Word of God: but then I thought I would give myself up unto the Lord, to do all his Word. Afterward I heard that word, *If thy right foot offend thee, cut it off, or thy right hand, or thy right eye; it's better to go to heaven with one foot, or hand, or eye, than having both to go to hell* [Matt. 5:29–30]; then I thought

[18] Drawing on John 3:16.

my hair had been a stumbling to me, therefore I cut it off, and grieved for this sin, and prayed for pardon. After hearing that word, *Come unto me all ye that are weary and heavy laden with your sins, and I will give rest to your souls* [Matt. 11:28]; then my heart thought that I do daily hate my sins, Oh! that I could go to Christ! and Christ looketh I should come unto him, therefore I will go unto him, and therefore then I prayed, Oh! Christ help me to come unto thee: and I prayed because of all my sins that they may be pardoned. For the first man was made like God in holiness, and righteousness, and God gave him his covenant; but Adam sinned, believing the Devil, therefore God was angry, and therefore all we children of Adam are like the Devil, and daily sin, and break every law of God, full of evil thoughts, words, and works, and only Christ can deliver us from our sins, and he that believeth in Christ is pardoned; but my heart of myself cannot believe: Satan hath power in me, but I cry to God, Oh! give me faith, and pardon my sin, because Christ alone can deliver me from hell; therefore I pray, Oh! Jesus Christ deliver me. Christ hath provided the new covenant to save believers in Christ, therefore I desire to give my soul to Christ, for pardon of all my sins: the first covenant is broke by sin, and we deserve hell; but Christ keepeth for us the new covenant, and therefore I betrust my soul with Christ. Again, I desire to believe in Christ, because Christ will come to judgment, and all shall rise again, and all believers in this life shall then be saved; therefore I desire to believe Christ, and mortify sin as long as I live; and I pray Christ to help me to believe: and I thank God for all his mercies every day: and now I confess before God that I loathe myself for my sins and beg pardon.

Thus far he went in his confession; but they being slow of speech, time was far spent and a great assembly of English understanding nothing he said, only waiting for my interpretation, many of them went forth, others whispered, and a great confusion was in the house and abroad: and I perceived that the graver sort thought the time long, therefore knowing he had spoken enough unto satisfaction (at least as I judged) I here took him off. Then one of the elders asked, if I took him off, or whether had he finished? I answered, that I took him off. So after my reading what he had said, we called another. . . . By such time as this man had finished, the time was far spent, and he was the fifth in number, their speeches being slow, and they were the more slow at my request, that I might write what they said; and oft I was forced to inquire of my interpreter (who sat by me) because I did not perfectly understand some sentences. . . . Wherefore the magistrates, elders, and grave men present, advised together what to do, and the conclusion was, not to proceed any further at present, yet so to carry the matter, as that the

Indians might in no wise be discouraged, but encouraged. . . . And so was the work of that day, with prayers unto God, finished; the accomplishment being referred to a fitter season.

Source: John Eliot and Thomas Mayhew Jr., *Tears of Repentance; or, A further Narrative of the Progress of the Gospel Amongst the Indians in New-England* . . . (London, 1653).

Chapter 25

The Martha's Vineyard Mission

In 1727 Experience Mayhew (1673–1758), the great-grandson of Thomas Mayhew Sr., published in London a collection of 126 biographies of Indians on Martha's Vineyard who had become Christians. Two of these biographies follow: that of Hiacoomes, the first Native American on the island to convert, and that of Margaret Osooit, of a later generation. Growing up on the island amid the Native American community, Experience learned the local dialect orally. In 1694 he began to preach to the several Native congregations. He was supported by the New England Company and, at their behest, resumed the project of translating religious books into Algonquian. Eventually, the mission came under the sponsorship of the Society for the Propagation of the Gospel, a charitable wing of the Church of England.

But by the late seventeenth and early eighteenth centuries the Christian community on Martha's Vineyard had passed "fully into the hands of native pastors, ruling elders, home-devotion leaders, catechists, and musicians."[1] Native American women, many of whom achieved literacy, were active in sustaining the family-centered worship of this intergenerational community. The political, economic, and social pressures that accompanied the Christianizing of Native Americans on the mainland were, for the most part, absent on the Vineyard, though epidemics played a part in the success of the missionary enterprise.

Bibliography

Clifford K. Shipton and John L. Sibley, *Biographical Sketches of the Graduates of Harvard College*, 18 vols. (Boston, 1873–   ), 7:632–39; Kellaway (1961); Simmons (1979) on Hiacoomes' conversion; Ronda (1981); Monaghan (1990) on women's literacy.

EXPERIENCE MAYHEW

Indian Converts

This Hiacoomes was an Indian of Great Harbor, now Edgartown, where a few English families first settled in the year 1642.

---

[1] Ronda (1981), 380 and passim.

His descent was but mean, his speech but slow, and his countenance not very promising. He was therefore by the Indian sachems, and others of their principal men, looked on as but a mean person, scarce worthy of their notice or regard: However, living near the English, some of them visited him in his wigwam, and were courteously entertained by him; these endeavored to discourse a little with him about the way of the English, and the man seemed to hearken to them, and in a little time began to pay them visits again, going frequently to some of their houses: And it was thought that he was trying to learn something of them that might be for his advantage. About the same time he went also to the English meeting, and observed what was done there.

This was soon observed by the Reverend Mr. Thomas Mayhew, who was then minister to the few English inhabitants in that new plantation, and was at the same time contriving what might be done in order to the salvation of the miserable Indians round about him, whom he, with compassion, saw perishing for lack of vision [Prov. 29:18].

But now, observing in this Hiacoomes a disposition to hear and receive instruction; observing also, that his countenance was grave and sober, he resolved to essay in the first place what he could do with him, and immediately took an opportunity to discourse him; and finding encouragement to go on in his endeavors to instruct and enlighten him, he invited him to come to his house every Lord's-day evening, that so he might then more especially have a good opportunity to treat with him about the things of GOD, and open the mysteries of his kingdom to him.

Hiacoomes accepting this kind invitation, Mr. Mayhew used his utmost endeavors to enlighten him. And Hiacoomes seemed as eagerly to suck in the instructions given him, as if his heart had been before prepared by God, and made good ground, in order to a due reception of his Word sown in it: And thus *as a newborn babe, desiring the sincere milk of the Word, that he might grow thereby* [1 Pet. 2:2], he increased daily in knowledge; and so far as could appear, grew in grace also.

But Hiacoomes's thus conversing with, and hearkening to the English, was soon noised about among the Indians; and the news of it coming to the sachems, and powwows of the island, they were, as obscure a person as Hiacoomes was, much alarmed at it: and some of them endeavored with all their might, to discourage him from holding communication with the English, and from receiving any instructions from them. But all that these could say or do to this end, was to no purpose; for it seems that God, by whom *not many wise men after the flesh, nor many mighty, nor many noble are called* [1 Cor. 1:26], had by his special grace effectually *called him out of darkness into his marvelous light* [1 Pet. 2:9]: and having now had a taste of that knowledge of God and Christ, which is life eternal, he was resolved that nothing should hinder him from laboring after still higher attainments in it. . . .

There was this year 1643 a very strange disease among the Indians, they ran up and down as if delirious, till they could run no longer; they would make their faces as black as a coal, and snatch up any weapon, as though they would do mischief with it, and speak great swelling words, but yet they did no harm.

Many of these Indians were by the English seen in this condition. Now this, and all other calamities which the Indians were under, they generally then attributed to the departure of some of them from their own heathenish ways and customs; but Hiacoomes being built on that foundation that standeth sure, and being one of those whom God had set apart for himself [Ps. 4:3], and knew to be his, none of these things moved him; but the things which he had heard and learned he held fast: And that he might be in a way to learn more than he had done, he now earnestly desired to learn to read; and having a primer given him, he carried it about with him, till, by the help of such as were willing to instruct him, he attained the end for which he desired it.

A while after, in the year 1644, Hiacoomes going to an Indian's house where there were several Indians met together, they laughed and scoffed at him, saying, Here comes the Englishman. At this his old enemy Pah-kehpunnassoo then asleep in the house, awaked, and, joining with the other Indians, said to him, "I wonder that you that are a young man, and have a wife and two children, should love the English and their ways, and forsake the powwows; what would you do if any of you were sick? whither would you go for help? If I were in your case, there should nothing draw me from our gods and powwows." To this Hiacoomes at present answered nothing, perhaps foreseeing that, if he should answer, it would only put the man into a rage, as formerly: However, he soon after told a friend of his, that he then thought in his heart, that the God of heaven did hear and know all the evil words that Pahkehpunnassoo said: And he was further confirmed in this, when a little after the said Pahkehpunnassoo was by the just hand of God terribly smitten with thunder, and fell down in appearance dead, with one leg in the fire, then in the house where he was, the same being grievously burned before any of the people present were (it being in the night and dark) aware of it, and could *pluck the brand out of the fire* [Zech. 3:2]. . . .

In this and the following year 1645, Mr. Mayhew went on with his design of instructing his Hiacoomes, and several others of the Indians, as he had opportunity; and now Hiacoomes begins to be so far from needing to be taught *the first principles of the oracles of God* [Heb. 5:12], that he becomes a teacher of others; communicating to as many as he could the knowledge he himself had attained: And some there were that now began to hearken to him, yet seemed not to be duly affected with the truths taught by him, and many utterly rejected them; but God now sending a general sickness among them, it was observed by the Indians themselves, that such as had but given a hearing to the things by Hiacoomes preached among them, and shewed any regard to them, were far more gently visited with it than others were; but Hiacoomes and his family in a manner not at all. At this many of the Indians were much affected, for they evidently saw that he, who, for the sake of the truth, exposed himself to the rage of his enemies, and such as adhered to him, fared better than those that opposed both him and that.

And being thus affected, many of the people desired to be instructed by him; and some persons of quality, such as before despised him, sent for him (as Cornelius for Peter) to come and instruct them, and those about them: so in particular did one Miohqsoo afterwards to be mentioned.

And now the Indians began not only to give some credit to the truth by Hiacoomes brought to them, but were also awakened by what they heard and believed, so as humbly to confess their sins, and be concerned how they should obtain the pardon of them, and also to renounce their own gods and powwows, and promise to serve the true God only: and Hiacoomes could now tell Mr. Mayhew, that this was the first time that ever he saw the Indians sensible of their sins.

Hitherto the Indians had not any public preaching to them; but now (in the year 1646) Tawanquatuck, one of the chief sachems of the island, invited both Mr. Mayhew and Hiacoomes to preach to himself and such of his people as would hear them, and Hiacoomes was from this time forward heard as a public preacher by a considerable number of the Indians, and God gave him not only light, but courage also for this work: and the Indians then said of him, that though formerly he had been a harmless man among them, yet he had not been at all accounted of, and therefore they wondered that he that had nothing to say in all their meetings formerly, was now become the teacher of them all.

The powwows, and those that adhered to them, observing those things, and seeing two meetings of the praying Indians set up, in opposition to that way which themselves and their fathers had long walked in, were very much disturbed and enraged: and now they thought to terrify Hiacoomes, and the rest of the praying Indians, by threatening to destroy them by witchcraft.

To this end several Indians went to a meeting of the praying Indians, and there told many stories of the great hurt which the powwows had in this way done to many, a thing of which these Indians could not be ignorant, and which seemed above anything else to discourage them from embracing the true religion now preached to them. Then this question was asked by one that was on the powwows' side, Who is there that does not fear the powwows? To which another of them answered, There is no man that is not afraid of them; which said, he looked upon Hiacoomes, who protested most against them, and told him the powwows could kill him: but he answered, that they could not; for, said he, I believe in God, and put my trust in him, and therefore all the powwows can do me no hurt. The Indians then wondering to hear Hiacoomes speak thus so openly, divers of them said one to another, that though they were before afraid of the powwows, yet now because they heard Hiacoomes's words, they did not fear them, but believed in God too.

A while after this, on a Lord's day after meeting was done, where Hiacoomes had been preaching, there came in a powwow very angry, and said, I know all the Meeting Indians are liars, you say you don't care for the powwows. Then calling two or three of them by name, he railed at them, and told them they were deceived; for the powwows could kill all the Meeting Indians if they set about it. But Hiacoomes then told him, that he would be in the midst of all the powwows on the island that they could procure, and they should do the utmost they could against him; and when they should do their worst by their witchcraft to kill him, he would without fear set himself against them, by remembering Jehovah: He told them also he did put all the powwows under his heel, pointing to it. By which answer he put the powwows to silence, so that they had nothing to say, but that none but Hiacoomes was able to do so. Such was the faith of this good man! nor were these powwows ever able to do the Christian Indians any hurt, though others were frequently hurt and killed by them. . . .

The piety of our Hiacoomes did further appear in that which here followeth. None of the praying Indians or their children, having died until the year 1650, as if God would on purpose in this way distinguish them from the rest of their neighbors, it now pleased him to begin with Hiacoomes, as being the best able to make a good use of such a providence, and carry well under it; God now by death took a young child from him, and he had grace to shew an excellent example under this trial, and so did his wife also, who by the way was a very pious woman. At the funeral there were no black faces or goods buried, or howling over the dead, as the manner of the Indians in those times was; but instead thereof a patient resignation of the child to him that gave it. At the funeral Mr. Mayhew made a speech concerning the resurrection of the godly, and their children, to life eternal at the last day: which great truth these good people believing, mourned not as those that had no hope were wont to do.

What I have hitherto related concerning this Hiacoomes being mostly extracted from some of Mr. Mayhew's letters concerning the Indians' affairs, I shall add this testimony concerning him, in one of them dated 1650: he says, "I must needs give him this testimony after some years' experience of him, that he is a man of a sober spirit, and good conversation; and as he hath, as I hope, received the Lord Jesus in truth, so I look upon him to be faithful, diligent, and constant in the work of the Lord, for the good of his own soul and his neighbors with him."[2]

To this testimony of Mr. Mayhew, let me add one of the Reverend Mr. Henry Whitfield's, who was once pastor to a church of Christ in New England. This Mr. Whitfield in his voyage to Boston, and so to England, was, by reason of contrary winds, stopped at Martha's Vineyard about ten days; in which time he conversed frequently with Hiacoomes, and in a book[3] which he published after his return to England, he says, "I had speech with some of the Indians (Mr. Mayhew being my interpreter), above the rest I desired to speak with the Indian that now preacheth to them twice every Lord's day, his name is Hiacoomes; he seemed to be a man of prompt understanding, of a sober and moderate spirit, and a man well reported of for his conversation, both by English and Indians. I thought him to be about thirty years of age; with this man I had often speech, and I asked him many questions about the Christian religion, and about his own estate before God: as 1. Whether he had found sorrow for sin as sin? 2. Whether he had found sorrow for his sins as they had pierced Christ? 3. Whether he had found the Spirit of God as an inward comforter to him? Unto all which he gave me very satisfactory and Christian answers."

As Hiacoomes was a good Christian, so he was doubtless a good minister, and herein his being a godly man was yet more evident. If any man might say, *I believed, therefore have I spoken* [Ps. 116:10], with respect to his entering on the ministry, it seems our Hiacoomes might truly do so. As soon as he came to understand and believe the great truths of the Christian religion, he began to publish and declare them to his countrymen; nor could he be hindered from doing so by all that the powwows, and their wretched instruments could do or say, to discourage him from it: And as he daily increased in knowledge under the instructions of Mr. Mayhew, to whom he continually resorted for that end, so he went on to prophesy, i.e. to preach to his neighbors, *according to the measure of the gift of Christ* [Eph. 4:7] which he had re-

---

[2] Henry Whitfield, ed., *The Light appearing more and more towards the perfect Day* (London, 1651; repr. *Collections of the Mass. Historical Society*, 1834), 3d ser., 4:112. Whitfield (d. 1659) emigrated to New England in 1639, founded Guilford, Conn., and returned to England in 1650.

[3] Ibid., 107.

ceived; and it pleased the Lord abundantly to succeed his endeavors for the good of these miserable creatures, to whom he sent him.

For three years after his conversion, this good man only instructed his neighbors in private, as he had opportunity: but after they were prepared and disposed to give him public audience, viz. in the year 1646, with what zeal and boldness did he preach to them? He then not only declared and opened the great mysteries of religion to them, as that of the Trinity, the covenant of works by God made with man, man's fall and apostasy by Adam's first transgression, and the wretched condition which mankind was thereby brought into, and the way of redemption which God has in and by his Son Jesus Christ provided for them, etc. I say, he not only instructed them in these things, but boldly charged them with the sins and abominations in which they daily lived; especially with their worshipping of false gods, and adhering to the powwows or wizards, and giving that honor to creatures that was due to Jehovah only.

Thus as Hiacoomes had God's Word, so he spake it faithfully, and God did abundantly own this his servant in the work to which he had called him: For when he reckoned up the sins of the people to them, instead of being provoked at him for it, they would many of them, with tears, confess their guilt, and promise to turn to the true God, and serve him only, and seek for the pardon of them through the blood of his Son, the only Savior of sinners.

This good man was a humble one, and in this, as well as in other things, his piety did much appear. Though God blessed his ministry, giving him much success in it, yet did he not at all appear to be exalted or lifted up therewith; nor did he thereupon think himself sufficient for the work of his ministry, but thought he still needed the continual help and instructions of Mr. Mayhew, by whom God had *called him out of darkness into his marvelous light* [1 Pet. 2:9]. To him therefore he frequently still resorted, that he might be yet more taught and illuminated by him; and in particular, on the day before the Sabbath he constantly did so, and that in order to his being the better prepared for the duties and service of that holy day.

This course Hiacoomes held, till, to his great grief, he lost Mr. Mayhew in the year 1657; which was indeed a very heavy stroke on these poor Indians, and exceedingly lamented by them. However, this good man went on still in the faithful discharge of his duty; and God so succeeded the labors of this, and some other servants of his, that most of the Indians here, were in a few years brought to an acknowledgement of the great truths of religion; and it is to be hoped, that many of them were effectually called.

However, there was no Indian church here completely formed and organized till the year 1670, when the Reverend Mr. John Eliot, and Mr. John Cotton,[4] came and ordained our Hiacoomes, and another Indian named Tackanash, pastor and teacher of an Indian church on this island.

After he was ordained, he went on steadily and faithfully in the work to which he was called, till he arrived to so great an age, that he was not able to attend the public ministry any longer. He survived his colleague before-mentioned, made a grave speech at his funeral, and laid hands on, and gave the charge to Mr. Japhet at his ordination; who succeeded the said Tackanash in his office in the year 1683. . . .

I saw him frequently when I was a youth, and still remember him, the gravity of his countenance, speech, and deportment: He seemed always to speak with much thought and deliberation, and I think very rarely smiled. I was present when he laid hands on Mr. Japhet, prayed, and gave the charge to him: which service he performed with great solemnity; and, as I have heard my father say, with very pertinent and suitable expressions. He was, by both the English and the Indians, looked upon as a man of a very blameless conversation. In his last sickness, he breathed forth many pious expressions, and gave good exhortations to all about him, and so went into eternal rest.

Margaret Osooit, commonly called by the Indians Meeksishqune, who died at the Gayhead December the fifth 1723.

This woman was a daughter of a petty sachem of Tisbury, called by the English Josiah, and by the Indians Keteanomin; but of him I can give no very good character. Her mother's name was Sianum, a daughter of Noquittompane, formerly mentioned; the same being esteemed a good woman, in some of the last years of her life.

But whatever the father or mother of this person was, it is much to be hoped she herself was *a woman that feared the Lord* [Prov. 31:30], and served him with integrity and uprightness of heart.

She was happy in this, that she was, while young, taught to read very well; and God gave her a heart afterwards to make a good use of this advantage, wherewith in his good providence he favored her, as we shall have further occasion to observe.

She was, so far as I can learn, while a maid, of a sober conversation, and free from any moral scandal whatsoever; but I do not know that she was religious while a young woman, though 'tis probable that she was so.

She was, after she had been some time a woman-grown, married to

---

[4] John Cotton (1639–1698), son of the first-generation minister of the same name; he preached on the island before moving to Plymouth as its minister.

Zachariah Osooit, an Indian of the Gayhead; and lived with him about thirty-three years, and did bear many children to him.

As soon as she became a wife, she began to discover such things as gave some grounds to hope that she had the fear of God in her; for it then appeared that she often read the Word of God, and such other books of piety as were so long ago published in the Indian tongue: She also then excited her husband to pray to God in his house, and prevailed with him so to do; and whereas he was very apt to follow after strong drink, she used her utmost endeavor to restrain him from that way of wickedness, and would have no fellowship with him in it.

Only she was once guilty of great folly this way; for being vexed with the intemperance of her husband, and having some rum ready at hand which she might drink of if she pleased, Satan tempted her to taste the liquor, and to take so plentifully of it, that she might see how good a thing it was to be drunk as many others were: and drunk she was to some purpose, so that falling down on the earthen floor of her house, and sleeping some time there, she at length awaked so sick and out of frame, that she thought it no good thing to be drunk; and was yet more sick at the thoughts of her sin and folly, in trying the wicked experiment by which she had made such a beast of herself as she had done: And it pleased God, that instead of now becoming in love with the liquor by which she had so basely fallen, her aversion to it was abundantly increased, and she never more returned to that folly of which she had been guilty: Nay, she could hardly be persuaded to taste of that liquor again as long as she lived; and she grew more earnest with others to refrain from the excessive use of it.

As she appeared to fear God and eschew evil, so she made conscience of worshipping God, and calling upon his Name. When her husband was gone from home, as he too often was, she constantly prayed with her children; nor did she pray in her family only, but frequently went into secret places to call upon the Name of the Lord: at which devotion she was sometimes accidentally surprised, by her relations and neighbors.

As her children became capable of receiving instruction, she endeavored to *train them up in the way in which they should go* [Prov. 22:6]: several of them have with tears told me what pains she used to take with them, as by teaching them their catechisms, and also reading the Scriptures to them, and pressing them to the duties mentioned in them, and warning them against the sins therein forbidden. Her husband and neighbors do likewise give the same testimony concerning her.

She was often grieved at her husband's erring through strong drink, and was unwearied in her endeavors to persuade him to refrain from that sin: but alas! she had not the success in it which she desired; and such were the hardships which she was by this means brought under, that it must be confessed, it made her sometimes speak unadvisedly, which she would readily confess and lament: but considering how much poverty and grief she underwent, it is more to be admired that her patience held out as it did, than that she sometimes shewed some infirmity.

She was looked upon as a person so well qualified for communion with the church of Christ, that many wondered that she did not ask an admission thereunto; and some discoursed with her about the matter, but she had such apprehensions concerning the holiness required of those who are admitted to fellowship with God in his ordinances, that she could not be persuaded that she was herself qualified for so high privileges, and would declare how grievously God was dishonored by such as had given up themselves to him, and yet did not walk worthy of the vocation wherewith they were called.

When she discoursed on these things, she used to take her Bible, to which she was no stranger, and turn to and read such places in it as she apprehended to intimate what holiness was required to be in such as so drew nigh to God, as particularly Psalms 15 and 24:3–4 and many other places.

She seldom went abroad, unless there were some special occasion that called for it; and indeed while her children were young, it was thought by some she did not go to meeting so often as she should have done: but others have alleged in her favor, that the miserable condition which she and her children were in, rendered it almost impossible that she should frequently leave her own house and go to God's, which they judge she would have otherwise gladly done. She was herself most miserably clothed, and her children were not better of it; nor had she ordinarily, while they were small, anybody to leave with them: and the diligence with which she afterwards attended God's public worship, when her children were grown more able to help themselves, gave grounds to think that she did not stay from public ordinances for want of an heart to attend them.

She mightily delighted in *The Practice of Piety*,[5] a book which our Indians have in their own language, and would scarce pass a day without reading something in it.

As she grew in years, she seemed to grow in grace, and in the knowledge of her Lord and Savior Jesus Christ; which many ways appeared to those that observed her.

She often confessed and lamented the sins of her heart and life, and talked much of that way of redemption by the Son of God which is revealed in the gospel, magnifying the grace of God therein manifested to sinners.

---

[5] Eliot's translation of Lewis Bayley's devotional classic, *The Practice of Piety*.

She complained often of the sins of the times, and mourned for them, particularly the sin of drunkenness, of which she knew many of her neighbors were frequently guilty; and that any in public stations were in this way faulty, seemed to her intolerable.

She frequently dealt with persons privately for their sins, especially with those of her own sex; and if they were persons who had made a public profession of religion, she would declare to them the solemn obligations they lay under to live to God, and to depart from all iniquity: And when she had begun to deal with any for their miscarriages, she would not willingly leave them till she had brought them to a confession of their faults, sometimes with tears, and to engage to endeavor to reform what was amiss in them.

After she had been supposed to have been several years past childbearing, and was, I suppose, upwards of fifty years old, she brought forth a son, who is still living; but not long after this she grew unhealthy, and was grievously exercised with a sore breast, which in the issue put an end to her life.

She was for some time towards the beginning of her illness in *much heaviness through manifold temptations* [1 Pet. 1:6], complaining of her sins as a burden too heavy for her to bear, and mourning under the weight of them; yet God did not suffer her to despair of his mercy, but enabled her to believe the gospel of his Son, and endeavor to obtain reconciliation to God through him, and a sense of his loving kindness to her soul. She herself cried earnestly to God for his mercy, and she called others to help her by their prayers in that time of her trouble, and she now declared, that she utterly disregarded everything in this world, and was only concerned that she might not fall short of the favor of God, without which nothing else could give rest and comfort to her soul: nor did God deny the humble requests of this his poor handmaid, but did graciously *lift up the light of his countenance upon her*, giving her peace in believing, and that joy of faith which passeth all understanding [Num. 6:26].

She was now not only willing to die, whenever it should please God that she should so do, but even longed for that happy hour; and yet said, that she was content still to bear more affliction, if her heavenly father saw it needful that she should.

She was wonderfully carried out in her endeavors to affect the hearts of her relations and neighbors, with a sense of the necessity and excellency of religion, and did with all possible earnestness press them to engage thoroughly in the great duties of it, and to avoid everything that might bring the displeasure of God on them.

To this end she not only spake to them all jointly, but having first spoken to her husband giving him the best counsel she could, and committing the care of her children to him, earnestly desiring him to *bring them up in the nurture and admonition of the Lord* [Eph. 6:4]; she called her children, all one by one, giving such advice to them as she thought they respectively most needed, and telling them she had often instructed and exhorted them, but that being now to leave them, that was the last time that she should ever speak to them.

She also declared before she died, that she saw the error she had been in, in not joining to the church of Christ, as she ought to have done; and she lamented this fault.

Some Christians that were with her when she was dying, having at her desire commended her to God by prayer, and sung a psalm of praises to him, she manifested a desire to be gone, and intimated, that the messengers of heaven were already come to receive her: and two persons that were then abroad, near the house where she lay a dying, do affirm, that they then plainly heard a melodious singing in the air, over the house where this woman lay; but whether that be a mistake or not, there is reason to believe that she died well, and that she is gone to the *innumerable company of angels, and to the spirits of just men made perfect* [Heb. 12:22–23].

Source: Experience Mayhew, *Indian Converts: or, Some Account of the Lives and Dying Speeches of a considerable Number of the Christianized Indians of Martha's Vineyard* (London, 1727), 1–12, 197–201.

Chapter 26

Mary Rowlandson

A CAPTIVE BECAUSE OF GOD'S PROVIDENCE

Mary (White) Rowlandson was the first colonist to write a "captivity narrative," a genre others would employ after her. The purpose of *The Sovereignty & Goodness of God* was to answer a question of theodicy: why did God cause her to undergo so much suffering? For modern readers, her narrative is also a revealing description of the most destructive of the wars between the seventeenth-century colonists and the Native Americans, "King Philip's War" of 1675–1676.

Rowlandson, who was probably born in England, moved to Lancaster, Massachusetts, in 1653 with several siblings and her mother and father. John White, her father, was a well-to-do proprietor (landowner) of the town, which changed its name that year from Nashaway. In 1656 she married Joseph Rowlandson, who arrived in the town two years after graduating from Harvard College in 1652 to minister to the townspeople. The community was small in numbers, and Rowlandson was so poorly paid that in 1658 he threatened to leave. Not until 1672 was Lancaster officially incorporated as a town. Mary and her husband had four children; the first died within a year, but the other three, Joseph (b. 1661), Mary (b. 1665), and Sarah (b. 1669), were in the family's "garrison house" when the town was attacked in February 1676. Taken captive with her children, Mrs. Rowlandson remained with the Indians eleven weeks and five days before being ransomed in early May and brought back to Boston, where she rejoined her husband and, eventually, her two surviving children. In the spring of 1677 the family moved to Wethersfield, Connecticut, where Joseph resumed his ministry. He died in November 1678; Mary remarried the following year and may have lived into the early eighteenth century.

It is almost certain she wrote out the story of her "captivity" before Joseph died, probably while the family was living in Wethersfield. When her narrative was published, an anonymous "friend"[1] wrote a preface extolling her modesty and justifying the publication of a woman's story,

---

[1] Frequently assumed to be Increase Mather, but Diebold (1972) proposes a convincing alternative, Benjamin Woodbridge.

written only for "private" use, on the grounds of its broader merit. Rowlandson tells us in her own voice (the "Eighth Remove") why she wrote, to "declare the works of the Lord, and his wonderful power in carrying us along, preserving us in the wilderness, while under the enemies' hand, and returning of us in safety again." In spite of all she suffered, she commemorated God's "goodness in bringing to my hand so many comfortable and suitable Scriptures in my distress." The narrative is modeled in part on biblical stories of people who are "delivered" from captivity and wander in a wilderness. At another level the narrative reflects the debate among the leaders of Massachusetts about "declension" and its causes,[2] with Rowlandson arguing that the success of the Indians at evading an English army indicated God was not yet satisfied with the work of reformation (see, e.g., the "Fifth Remove"). Her contempt for the "Praying Indians" was also, in context, a political statement. Nonetheless, the narrative remains a unique source on Native American ceremonies, even though she reiterated the argument that the Natives were allies of Satan.

Bibliography

Diebold (1972) on the history of the text; its later history is described in Derounian (1988); Slotkin (1973) on narrative patterns; Marvin (1879); Lepore (1998); Leach (1961) on the chronology of her captivity; Leach (1958) on the war itself. Other contemporary accounts of the war are collected in Richard Slotkin and James Folsom, eds., *So Dreadfull a Judgment: Puritan Responses to King Philip's War, 1676–1677* (Middletown, Conn., 1978).

MARY ROWLANDSON

❧ *The Sovereignty & Goodness of God* ❧

On the tenth of February 1675,[3] came the Indians with great numbers upon Lancaster: Their first coming was about sun-rising. Hearing the noise of some guns, we looked out; several houses were burning, and the smoke ascending to heaven. There were five persons taken in one house, the father, and the mother and a sucking child they knocked on the head; the other two they took and carried away alive. There were

[2] Hall (1972), chap. 10; Increase Mather, in *A Brief History of the Warr* (Boston, 1676), argued that victories and defeats coincided with the fluctuating spiritual condition of the colonists.

[3] Old style, with the new year beginning in March and the calendar ten days behind; the equivalent new-style date is February 20, 1676.

two others, who being out of their garrison upon some occasion were set upon; one was knocked on the head, the other escaped: Another there was who running along was shot and wounded, and fell down; he begged of them his life, promising them money (as they told me) but they would not hearken to him but knocked him in head, stript him naked, and split open his bowels. Another seeing many of the Indians about his barn, ventured and went out, but was quickly shot down. There were three others belonging to the same garrison who were killed; the Indians getting up upon the roof of the barn, had advantage to shoot down upon them over their fortification. Thus these murtherous wretches went on, burning, and destroying before them.

At length they came and beset our own house,[4] and quickly it was the dolefulest day that ever mine eyes saw. The house stood upon the edge of a hill; some of the Indians got behind the hill, others into the barn, and others behind anything that would shelter them; from all which places they shot against the house, so that the bullets seemed to fly like hail; and quickly they wounded one man among us, then another, and then a third. About two hours (according to my observation, in that amazing time) they had been about the house before they prevailed to fire it (which they did with flax and hemp, which they brought out of the barn, and there being no defense about the house, only two flankers at two opposite corners, and one of them not finished) they fired it once and one ventured out and quenched it, but they quickly fired it again, and that took. Now is that dreadful hour come, that I have often heard of (in the time of the war, as it was the case of others) but now mine eyes see it. Some in our house were fighting for their lives, others wallowing in their blood, the house on fire over our heads, and the bloody heathen ready to knock us on the head, if we stirred out. Now might we hear mothers and children crying out for themselves, and one another, Lord, What shall we do? Then I took my children (and one of my sisters, hers) to go forth and leave the house: but as soon as we came to the door and appeared, the Indians shot so thick that the bullets rattled against the house, as if one had taken an handful of stones and threw them, so that we were fain to give back. We had six stout dogs belonging to our garrison, but none of them would stir, though another time, if an Indian had come to the door, they were ready to fly upon him and tear him down. The Lord hereby would make us the more to acknowledge his hand, and to see that our help is always in him. But out we must go, the fire increasing, and coming along behind us, roaring, and

---

[4] The Rowlandson house contained thirty-seven persons, including Mrs. Rowlandson and her three children; her two sisters, Hannah White Divoll and Elizabeth White Kerley, with their families; and several neighboring families.

the Indians gaping before us with their guns, spears and hatchets to devour us. No sooner were we out of the house, but my brother-in-law (being before wounded, in defending the house, in or near the throat)[5] fell down dead, whereat the Indians scornfully shouted, and hallowed, and were presently upon him, stripping off his clothes. The bullets flying thick, one went through my side, and the same (as would seem) through the bowels and hand of my dear child in my arms. One of my elder sister's children, named William, had then his leg broken, which the Indians perceiving, they knockt him on head. Thus were we butchered by those merciless heathen, standing amazed, with the blood running down to our heels. My eldest sister being yet in the house, and seeing those woeful sights, the infidels haling mothers one way, and children another, and some wallowing in their blood: and her elder son telling her that her son William was dead, and myself was wounded, she said, And, Lord, let me die with them; which was no sooner said, but she was struck with a bullet, and fell down dead over the threshold. I hope she is reaping the fruit of her good labors, being faithful to the service of God in her place. In her younger years she lay under much trouble upon spiritual accounts, till it pleased God to make that precious scripture take hold of her heart, 2 Cor. 12:9, *And he said unto me, my grace is sufficient for thee.* More than twenty years after I have heard her tell how sweet and comfortable that place was to her. But to return: the Indians laid hold of us, pulling me one way, and the children another, and said, Come go along with us: I told them they would kill me: they answered, If I were willing to go along with them, they would not hurt me.

Oh the doleful sight that now was to behold at this house! *Come, behold the works of the Lord, what desolations he has made in the earth* [Ps. 46:8]. Of thirty-seven persons who were in this one house, none escaped either present death, or a bitter captivity, save only one, who might say as he, Job 1:15, *And I only am escaped alone to tell the news.* There were twelve killed, some shot, some stabb'd with their spears, some knock'd down with their hatchets. When we are in prosperity, oh the little that we think of such dreadful sights, and to see our dear friends and relations lie bleeding out their heart-blood upon the ground! There was one who was chopp'd into the head with a hatchet, and stripped naked, and yet was crawling up and down. It is a solemn sight to see so many Christians lying in their blood, some here, and some there, like a company of sheep torn by wolves. All of them stript naked by a company of hell-hounds, roaring, singing, ranting and in-

---

[5] Ensign John Divoll, husband of Mrs. Rowlandson's youngest sister and commander of the garrison.

sulting, as if they would have torn our very hearts out; yet the Lord by his almighty power preserved a number of us from death, for there were twenty-four of us taken alive and carried captive.

I had often before this said, that if the Indians should come, I should choose rather to be killed by them than taken alive, but when it came to the trial my mind changed; their glittering weapons so daunted my spirit, that I chose rather to go along with those (as I may say) ravenous bears, than that moment to end my days. And that I may the better declare what happened to me during that grievous captivity, I shall particularly speak of the several removes we had up and down the wilderness.

The First Remove.

Now away we must go with those barbarous creatures, with our bodies wounded and bleeding, and our hearts no less than our bodies. About a mile we went that night, up upon a hill within sight of the town, where they intended to lodge. There was hard by a vacant house (deserted by the English before, for fear of the Indians). I asked them whether I might not lodge in the house that night? to which they answered, what will you love English men still? This was the dolefulest night that ever my eyes saw. Oh the roaring, and singing and dancing, and yelling of those black creatures in the night, which made the place a lively resemblance of hell. And as miserable was the waste that was there made, of horses, cattle, sheep, swine, calves, lambs, roasting pigs, and fowls (which they had plundered in the town) some roasting, some lying and burning, and some boiling to feed our merciless enemies; who were joyful enough though we were disconsolate. To add to the dolefulness of the former day, and the dismalness of the present night, my thoughts ran upon my losses and sad bereaved condition. All was gone, my husband gone (at least separated from me, he being in the Bay; and to add to my grief, the Indians told me they would kill him as he came homeward) my children gone, my relations and friends gone, our house and home and all our comforts within door, and without, all was gone (except my life), and I knew not but the next moment that might go too.

There remained nothing to me but one poor wounded babe, and it seemed at present worse than death, that it was in such a pitiful condition, bespeaking compassion, and I had no refreshing for it, nor suitable things to revive it. Little do many think, what is the savageness and brutishness of this barbarous enemy! even those that seem to profess more than others among them, when the English have fallen into their hands.

Those seven that were killed at Lancaster the summer before upon a

Sabbath day, and the one that was afterward killed upon a week day, were slain and mangled in a barbarous manner, by One-ey'd John, and Marlborough's Praying Indians,[6] which Capt. Moseley brought to Boston, as the Indians told me.[7]

The Second Remove.

But now (the next morning) I must turn my back upon the town, and travel with them into the vast and desolate wilderness, I know not whither. It is not my tongue, or pen can express the sorrows of my heart, and bitterness of my spirit, that I had at this departure: But God was with me, in a wonderful manner, carrying me along, and bearing up my spirit, that it did not quite fail. One of the Indians carried my poor wounded babe upon a horse: it went moaning all along, I shall die, I shall die. I went on foot after it, with sorrow that cannot be exprest. At length I took it off the horse, and carried it in my arms, till my strength failed, and I fell down with it: Then they set me upon a horse, with my wounded child in my lap, and there being no furniture[8] upon the horse back, as we were going down a steep hill, we both fell over the horse's head, at which they like inhuman creatures laught, and rejoiced to see it, though I thought we should there have ended our days, as overcome with so many difficulties. But the Lord renewed my strength still, and carried me along, that I might see more of his power, yea, so much that I could never have thought of, had I not experienced it.

After this it quickly began to snow, and when night came on, they stopt: and now down I must sit in the snow (by a little fire, and a few boughs behind me) with my sick child in my lap; and calling much for water, being now (through the wound) fallen into a violent fever. My own wound also growing so stiff, that I could scarce sit down or rise up; yet so it must be, that I must sit all this cold winter night upon the cold snowy ground, with my sick child in my arms, looking that every

[6] That is, those Christianized Indians who were most vehement in their professions of faith.

[7] One-eyed John, or Monoco, or Apequinash, was executed in Boston September 26, 1676. The "Praying Indians" of Marlborough, Massachusetts, did not in fact participate in this raid. But in August 1675 Captain Samuel Mosely, a Jamaican privateer and ship captain who organized an independent military company, seized and brought to Boston a number of them. Captain Mosely was the most brutal of the colonial military leaders. His mistreatment of Christianized Indians in this and later episodes of the war is described in Daniel Gookin, "An Historical Account of the Doings and Sufferings of the Christian Indians in New England," *Archaeologia Americana: Transactions and Collections of the American Antiquarian Society* 2 (1836): 443–44 and passim. See also the letters printed in *New England Historic Genealogical Register* 37 (1883): 179–80.

[8] No saddle.

hour would be the last of its life; and having no Christian friend near me, either to comfort or help me. Oh, I may see the wonderful power of God, that my spirit did not utterly sink under my affliction; still the Lord upheld me with his gracious and merciful Spirit, and we were both alive to see the light of the next morning.

The Third Remove.

The morning being come, they prepared to go on their way: One of the Indians got up upon a horse, and they set me up behind him, with my poor sick babe in my lap. A very wearisome and tedious day I had of it; what with my own wound, and my child's being so exceeding sick, and in a lamentable condition with her wound. It may easily be judged what a poor feeble condition we were in, there being not the least crumb of refreshing that came within either of our mouths, from Wednesday night to Saturday night, except only a little cold water. This day in the afternoon, about an hour by sun, we came to the place where they intended, viz. an Indian town called Wenimesset,[9] northward of Quabaug.[10] When we were come, oh the number of pagans (now merciless enemies) that there came about me, that I may say as David, Ps. 27:13, *I had fainted, unless I had believed*, etc.[11] The next day was the Sabbath: I then remembered how careless I had been of God's holy time: how many Sabbaths I had lost and misspent, and how evilly I had walked in God's sight; which lay so close upon my spirit, that it was easy for me to see how righteous it was with God to cut off the thread of my life, and cast me out of his presence forever. Yet the Lord still shewed mercy to me, and upheld me; and as he wounded me with one hand, so he healed me with the other. This day there came to me one Robert Pepper (a man belonging to Roxbury), who was taken in Captain Beers his fight,[12] and had been now a considerable time with the Indians; and up with them almost as far as Albany to see King Philip, as he told me, and was now very lately come with them into these parts. Hearing I say that I was in this Indian town, he obtained leave to come and see me. He told me he himself was wounded in the leg at Captain Beers his fight; and was not able sometime to go, but as they carried him, and that he took oaken leaves and laid to his wound, and through

[9] Now New Braintree, Mass.

[10] Now Brookfield, Mass.

[11] "I had fainted, unless I had believed to see the goodness of the Lord in the land of the living."

[12] Captured in September 1675. King Philip was near Albany seeking gunpowder and an alliance with the Mohawks. Captain Richard Beers and half of his company of soldiers died in a fight near Northfield on September 4, 1675 (n.s.).

the blessing of God, he was able to travel again. Then I took oaken leaves and laid to my side, and with the blessing of God it cured me also: yet before the cure was wrought, I may say, as it is in Ps. 38:5–6, *My wounds stink and are corrupt, I am troubled, I am bowed down greatly, I go mourning all the day long*. I sat much alone with a poor wounded child in my lap, which moaned night and day, having nothing to revive the body, or cheer the spirits of her: but instead of that, sometimes one Indian would come and tell me, one hour, and your master will knock your child in the head, and then a second, and then a third, your master will quickly knock your child in the head.

This was the comfort I had from them, *miserable comforters are ye all*, as he said [Job 16:2]. Thus nine days I sat upon my knees, with my babe in my lap, till my flesh was raw again: my child being even ready to depart this sorrowful world, they bade me carry it out to another wigwam (I suppose because they would not be troubled with such spectacles). Whither I went with a very heavy heart, and down I sat with the picture of death in my lap. About two hours in the night, my sweet babe like a lamb departed this life, on February 18, 1675, it being about six years and five months old. It was nine days (from the first wounding) in this miserable condition, without any refreshing of one nature or other, except a little cold water. I cannot but take notice, how at another time I could not bear to be in the room where any dead person was, but now the case is changed: I must and could lie down by my dead babe, side by side, all the night after. I have thought since of the wonderful goodness of God to me, in preserving me so in the use of my reason and senses, in that distressed time, that I did not use wicked and violent means to end my own miserable life. In the morning, when they understood that my child was dead, they sent for me home to my master's wigwam (by my master in this writing, must be understood Quanopin, who was a sagamore, and married King Philip's wife's sister; not that he first took me, but I was sold to him by another Narragansett Indian, who took me when first I came out of the garrison). I went to take up my dead child in my arms to carry it with me, but they bid me let it alone: there was no resisting, but go I must and leave it. When I had been a while at my master's wigwam, I took the first opportunity I could get, to go look after my dead child: when I came I asked them what they had done with it? They told me it was upon the hill: then they went and shewed me where it was, where I saw the ground was newly digged, and there they told me they had buried it: There I left that child in the wilderness, and must commit it, and myself also in this wilderness condition, to him who is above all. God having taken away this dear child, I went to see my daughter Mary, who was at this same Indian town, at a wigwam not very far off, though we had little liberty or opportunity to see one another: she was about ten years old, and taken from the door at first by a Praying Indian, and afterward sold for a gun. When I came in sight she would fall a weeping; at which they were provoked, and would not let me come near her, but bade me be gone: which was a heart-cutting word to me. I had one child dead, another in the wilderness, I knew not where, the third they would not let me come near to: *Me* (as he said) *have ye bereaved of my children, Joseph is not, and Simeon is not, and ye will take Benjamin also, all these things are against me* [Gen. 42:36]. I could not sit still in this condition, but kept walking from one place to another. And as I was going along, my heart was even overwhelmed with the thoughts of my condition, and that I should have children, and a nation which I knew not ruled over them. Whereupon I earnestly entreated the Lord, that he would consider my low estate, and shew me a token for good, and if it were his blessed will, some sign and hope of some relief. And indeed quickly the Lord answered, in some measure, my poor prayer: for as I was going up and down mourning and lamenting my condition, my son came to me, and asked me how I did? I had not seen him before, since the destruction of the town: and I knew not where he was, till I was informed by himself, that he was amongst a smaller parcel of Indians, whose place was about six miles off; with tears in his eyes, he asked me whether his sister Sarah was dead? and told me he had seen his sister Mary; and prayed me, that I would not be troubled in reference to himself. The occasion of his coming to see me at this time, was this: There was, as I said, about six miles from us, a small plantation of Indians, where it seems he had been during his captivity: and at this time, there were some forces of the Indians gathered out of our company, and some also from them (among whom was my son's master) to go to assault and burn Medfield.[13] In this time of the absence of his master, his dame brought him to see me. I took this to be some gracious answer to my earnest and unfeigned desire. The next day, viz. to this, the Indians returned from Medfield (all the company, for those that belonged to the other smaller company, came through the town that now we were at). But before they came to us, Oh! the outrageous roaring and hooping that there was! They began their din about a mile before they came to us. By their noise and hooping they signified how many they had destroyed (which was at that time twenty-three). Those that were with us at home, were gathered together as soon as they heard the hooping, and every time that the other went over their number, these at home gave a shout, that the very earth rang again. And thus they continued till those that had been upon the expedition were come up to the sagamore's wigwam; and then, Oh, the hideous insulting and triumphing that there was over some Englishmen's

---

[13] Medfield was attacked and burned on February 21, 1676.

scalps that they had taken (as their manner is) and brought with them. I cannot but take notice of the wonderful mercy of God to me in those afflictions, in sending me a Bible. One of the Indians that came from Medfield fight and had brought some plunder, came to me, and asked me, if I would have a Bible, he had got one in his basket. I was glad of it, and asked him, whether he thought the Indians would let me read? He answered, yes: So I took the Bible, and in that melancholy time, it came into my mind to read first the 28 chapter of Deuteronomy which I did, and when I had read it, my dark heart wrought on this manner, that there was no mercy for me, that the blessings were gone, and the curses came in their room, and that I had lost my opportunity. But the Lord helped me still to go on reading till I came to chapter 30 the seven first verses, where I found there was mercy promised again, if we would return to him by repentance: and though we were scattered from one end of the earth to the other, yet the Lord would gather us together, and turn all those curses upon our enemies. I do not desire to live to forget this scripture, and what comfort it was to me.[14]

Now the Indians began to talk of removing from this place, some one way, and some another. There were now besides myself nine English captives in this place (all of them children, except one woman). I got an opportunity to go and take my leave of them; they being to go one way, and I another. I asked them whether they were earnest with God for deliverance; they all told me, they did as they were able; and it was some comfort to me, that the Lord stirred up children to look to him. The woman, viz. Goodwife Joslin told me, she should never see me again, and that she could find in her heart to run away: I wisht her not to run away by any means, for we were near thirty miles from any English town, and she very big with child and had but one week to reckon: and another child in her arms, two years old, and bad rivers there were to go over, and we were feeble with our poor and coarse entertainment. I had my Bible with me, I pulled it out; and asked her, whether she would read; we opened the Bible and lighted on Ps. 27 in which psalm we especially took notice of that, *ver. ult.* [14], *Wait on the Lord, be of good courage, and he shall strengthen thine heart, wait I say on the Lord.*

The Fourth Remove.

And now must I part with that little company that I had. Here I parted from my daughter Mary (whom I never saw again till I saw her in Dorchester, returned from captivity), and from four little cousins and

[14] These three chapters, 28–30, describe the consequences of obedience and disobedience, and promise the restoration of those who are captives.

neighbors, some of which I never saw afterward, the Lord only knows the end of them. Amongst them also was that poor woman before mentioned, who came to a sad end, as some of the company told me in my travel: she having much grief upon her spirit, about her miserable condition, being so near her time, she would be often asking the Indians to let her go home; they not being willing to that, and yet vexed with her importunity, gathered a great company together about her, and stript her naked, and set her in the midst of them: and when they had sung and danced about her (in their hellish manner) as long as they pleased, they knockt her on the head, and the child in her arms with her: when they had done that, they made a fire and put them both into it, and told the other children that were with them, that if they attempted to go home, they would serve them in like manner: The children said she did not shed one tear, but prayed all the while.[15] But to return to my own journey; we traveled about half a day or a little more, and came to a desolate place in the wilderness, where there were no wigwams or inhabitants before: we came about the middle of the afternoon to this place; cold and wet, and snowy, and hungry, and weary, and no refreshing (for man) but the cold ground to sit on, and our poor Indian cheer.

Heart-aching thoughts here I had about my poor children, who were scattered up and down among the wild beasts of the forest: my head was light and dizzy (either through hunger, or hard lodging, or trouble, or all together) my knees feeble, my body raw by sitting double night and day, that I cannot express to man the affliction that lay upon my spirit, but the Lord helped me at that time to express it to himself. I opened my Bible to read, and the Lord brought that precious scripture to me, Jer. 31:16, *Thus saith the Lord, refrain thy voice from weeping, and thine eyes from tears, for thy work shall be rewarded, and they shall come again from the land of the enemy.* This was a sweet cordial to me, when I was ready to faint; many and many a time have I sat down, and wept sweetly over this scripture. At this place we continued about four days.

The Fifth Remove.

The occasion (as I thought) of their moving at this time, was, the English army, its being near and following them: For they went as if they

---

[15] Ann Joslin, whose husband had died in the attack on Lancaster. The contemporary historian William Hubbard, noting her death in *A Narrative of the Troubles with the Indians* (Boston, 1677), added, "No Credit is to be given to any other Reports of Cruelty towards any English Woman in that Part of the Country." Quoted in Diebold (1972), 102.

had gone for their lives, for some considerable way; and then they made a stop, and chose out some of their stoutest men, and sent them back to hold the English army in play whilst the rest escaped: And then like Jehu they marched on furiously, with their old, and with their young: some carried their old decrepit mothers, some carried one, and some another. Four of them carried a great Indian upon a bier; but going through a thick wood with him they were hindered, and could make no haste; whereupon they took him upon their backs, and carried him, one at a time, till we came to Bacquaug River.[16] Upon a Friday a little after noon we came to this river. When all the company was come up, and were gathered together, I thought to count the number of them, but they were so many, and being somewhat in motion, it was beyond my skill. In this travel, because of my wound, I was somewhat favored in my load; I carried only my knitting work and two quarts of parched meal: Being very faint I asked my mistress to give me one spoonful of the meal, but she would not give me a taste. They quickly fell to cutting dry trees, to make rafts to carry them over the river: and soon my turn came to go over: By the advantage of some brush which they had laid upon the raft to sit on, I did not wet my foot (when many of themselves at the other end were mid-leg deep), which cannot but be acknowledged as a favor of God to my weakened body, it being a very cold time. I was not before acquainted with such kind of doings or dangers. *When thou passeth through the waters I will be with thee, and through the rivers they shall not overflow thee*, Isa. 43:2. A certain number of us got over the river that night, but it was the night after the Sabbath before all the company was got over. On the Saturday they boiled an old horse's leg (which they had got), and so we drank of the broth, as soon as they thought it was ready, and when it was almost all gone, they filled it up again.

The first week of my being among them, I hardly ate any thing: the second week, I found my stomach grow very faint for want of something; and yet 'twas very hard to get down their filthy trash: but the third week (though I could think how formerly my stomach would turn against this or that, and I could starve and die before I could eat such things, yet) they were pleasant and savory to my taste. I was at this time knitting a pair of white cotton stockings for my mistress: and I had not yet wrought upon the Sabbath-day; when the Sabbath came they bade me go to work; I told them it was the Sabbath-day, and desired them to let me rest, and told them I would do as much more tomorrow; to which they answered me, they would break my face. And here I cannot but take notice of the strange providence of God in preserving the hea-

[16] Miller's River; the crossing was in Orange, Mass.

then: They were many hundreds, old and young, some sick and some lame, many had papooses at their backs, the greatest number (at this time with us) were squaws, and they traveled with all they had, bag and baggage, and yet they got over this river aforesaid; and on Monday they set their wigwams on fire, and away they went: On that very day came the English army after them to this river, and saw the smoke of their wigwams, and yet this river put a stop to them. God did not give them courage or activity to go over after us; we were not ready for so great a mercy as victory and deliverance: if we had been, God would have found out a way for the English to have passed this river, as well as for the Indians with their squaws and children, and all their luggage: *Oh, that my people had hearkened to me, and Israel had walked in my ways, I should soon have subdued their enemies, and turned my hand against their adversaries*, Ps. 81:13–14.

The Sixth Remove.

On Monday (as I said) they set their wigwams on fire, and went away. It was a cold morning, and before us there was a great brook with ice on it; some waded through it, up to the knees and higher, but others went till they came to a beaver dam, and I amongst them, where through the good providence of God, I did not wet my foot. I went along that day, mourning and lamenting, leaving farther my own country, and traveling into the vast and howling wilderness, and I understood something of Lot's wife's temptation, when she looked back: we came that day to a great swamp, by the side of which we took up our lodging that night. When I came to the brow of the hill, that looked toward the swamp, I thought we had been come to a great Indian town (though there were none but our own company) the Indians were as thick as the trees: it seemed as if there had been a thousand hatchets going at once: if one looked before one, there was nothing but Indians, and behind one, nothing but Indians, and so on either hand: I myself in the midst, and no Christian soul near me, and yet how hath the Lord preserved me in safety! Oh the experience that I have had of the goodness of God, to me and mine!

The Seventh Remove.

After a restless and hungry night there, we had a wearisome time of it the next day. The swamp by which we lay was, as it were, a deep dungeon, and an exceeding high and steep hill before it. Before I got to the top of the hill, I thought my heart and legs and all would have broken, and failed me. What through faintness and soreness of body, it was a grievous day of travel to me. As we went along, I saw a place where English cattle had been: that was comfort to me, such as it was: quickly after that we came to an English path, which so took with me, that I thought I could there have freely lain down and died. That day, a little after noon, we came to Squakheag,[17] where the Indians quickly spread themselves over the deserted English fields, gleaning what they could find; some pickt up ears of wheat that were crickled down, some found ears of Indian corn, some found ground nuts, and others sheaves of wheat that were frozen together in the shock, and went to threshing of them out. My self got two ears of Indian corn, and whilst I did but turn my back, one of them was stolen from me, which much troubled me. There came an Indian to them at that time, with a basket of horse liver. I asked him to give me a piece: What (says he) can you eat horse liver? I told him, I would try, if he would give a piece, which he did: and I laid it on the coals to roast; but before it was half ready they got half of it away from me, so that I was fain to take the rest and eat it as it was, with the blood about my mouth, and yet a savory bit it was to me: *For to the hungry soul, every bitter thing is sweet* [Prov. 27:7]. A solemn sight methought it was, to see whole fields of wheat and Indian corn forsaken and spoiled: and the remainders of them to be food for our merciless enemies. That night we had a mess of wheat for our supper.

The Eighth Remove.

On the morrow morning we must go over the river, i.e. Connecticut, to meet with King Philip; two canoes full, they had carried over, the next turn I myself was to go; but as my foot was upon the canoe to step in, there was a sudden outcry among them, and I must step back; and instead of going over the river, I must go four or five miles up the river farther northward. Some of the Indians ran one way, and some another. The cause of this rout was, as I thought, their espying some English scouts, who were thereabout.

In this travel up the river, about noon the company made a stop, and sat down; some to eat, and others to rest them. As I sat amongst them, musing of things past, my son Joseph unexpectedly came to me: we asked of each other's welfare, bemoaning our doleful condition, and the change that had come upon us: We had husband and father, and children and sisters, and friends and relations, and house and home, and many comforts of this life: but now we might say, as Job, *Naked came I*

[17] In the vicinity of Northfield, Mass.

out of my mother's womb, and naked shall I return: The Lord gave, and the Lord hath taken away, Blessed be the Name of the Lord [Job 1:21]. I asked him whether he would read? he told me, he earnestly desired it. I gave him my Bible, and he lighted upon that comfortable scripture, Ps. 118:17–18, *I shall not die but live, and declare the works of the Lord: the Lord hath chastened me sore, yet he hath not given me over to death.* Look here, mother (says he), did you read this? And here I may take occasion to mention one principal ground of my setting forth these few lines: even as the Psalmist says, To declare the works of the Lord, and his wonderful power in carrying us along, preserving us in the wilderness, while under the enemies' hand, and returning of us in safety again. And his goodness in bringing to my hand so many comfortable and suitable scriptures in my distress. But to return. We traveled on till night; and in the morning we must go over the river to Philip's crew. When I was in the canoe, I could not but be amazed at the numerous crew of pagans, that were on the bank on the other side. When I came ashore, they gathered all about me, I sitting alone in the midst: I observed they asked one another questions, and laughed, and rejoiced over their gains and victories. Then my heart began to fail: and I fell a weeping; which was the first time to my remembrance, that I wept before them. Although I had met with so much affliction, and my heart was many times ready to break, yet could I not shed one tear in their sight: but rather had been all this while in a maze, and like one astonished; but now I may say as, Ps. 137:1, *By the rivers of Babylon, there we sat down: yea, we wept when we remembered Zion.* There one of them asked me, why I wept; I could hardly tell what to say: yet I answered, they would kill me: No, said he, none will hurt you. Then came one of them, and gave me two spoonfuls of meal (to comfort me) and another gave me half a pint of peas; which was more worth than many bushels at another time. Then I went to see King Philip, he bade me come in, and sit down, and asked me whether I would smoke it (a usual compliment nowadays amongst saints and sinners). But this no way suited me. For though I had formerly used tobacco, yet I had left it ever since I was first taken. It seems to be a bait, the devil lays to make men lose their precious time: I remember with shame, how formerly, when I had taken two or three pipes, I was presently ready for another, such a bewitching thing it is: But I thank God, he has now given me power over it; surely there are many who may be better employed, than to lie sucking a stinking tobacco pipe.

Now the Indians gather their forces to go against Northampton: overnight one went about yelling and hooting to give notice of the design. Whereupon they fell to boiling of ground nuts, and parching of corn (as many as had it) for their provision: and in the morning away they went.

During my abode in this place, Philip spake to me to make a shirt for his boy, which I did, for which he gave me a shilling: I offered the money to my master, but he bade me keep it: and with it I bought a piece of horse flesh. Afterwards he asked me to make a cap for his boy, for which he invited me to dinner: I went, and he gave me a pancake, about as big as two fingers; it was made of parched wheat, beaten, and fried in bear's grease, but I thought I never tasted pleasanter meat in my life. There was a squaw who spake to me to make a shirt for her sannup,[18] for which she gave me a piece of bear. Another asked me to knit a pair of stockings, for which she gave me a quart of peas. I boiled my peas and bear together, and invited my master and mistress to dinner, but the proud gossip, because I served them both in one dish, would eat nothing, except one bit that he gave her upon the point of his knife. Hearing that my son was come to this place, I went to see him, and found him lying flat upon the ground: I asked him how he could sleep so? He answered me, that he was not asleep, but at prayer; and lay so, that they might not observe what he was doing. I pray God, he may remember these things now he is returned in safety. At this place (the sun now getting higher) what with the beams and heat of the sun, and the smoke of the wigwams, I thought I should have been blind: I could scarce discern one wigwam from another. There was here one Mary Thurston of Medfield, who seeing how it was with me, lent me a hat to wear: but as soon as I was gone, the squaw (who owned that Mary Thurston) came running after me, and got it away again. Here there was the squaw who gave me one spoonful of meal. I put it in my pocket to keep it safe: yet notwithstanding somebody stole it, but put five Indian corns in the room of it: which corns were the greatest provision I had in my travel for one day.

The Indians returning from Northampton, brought with them some horses and sheep, and other things which they had taken: I desired them, that they would carry me to Albany upon one of those horses, and sell me for powder: for so they had sometimes discoursed. I was utterly hopeless of getting home on foot, the way that I came. I could hardly bear to think of the many weary steps I had taken, to come to this place.

The Ninth Remove.

But instead of going either to Albany or homeward, we must go five miles up the river, and then go over it. Here we abode a while. Here lived a sorry Indian, who spake to me to make him a shirt, when I had

---

[18] Her husband.

done it, he would pay me nothing. But he living by the river side, where I often went to fetch water, I would often be putting of him in mind, and calling for my pay: at last he told me if I would make another shirt, for a papoos not yet born, he would give me a knife, which he did when I had done it. I carried the knife in, and my master asked me to give it him, and I was not a little glad that I had any thing that they would accept of, and be pleased with. When we were at this place, my master's maid came home, she had been gone three weeks into the Narragansett country, to fetch corn, where they had stored up some in the ground: she brought home about a peck and half of corn. This was about the time that their great captain (Naananto) was killed in the Narragansett country.[19]

My son being now about a mile from me, I asked liberty to go and see him, they bade me go, and away I went: but quickly lost myself, traveling over hills and through swamps, and could not find the way to him. And I cannot but admire at the wonderful power and goodness of God to me, in that, though I was gone from home, and met with all sorts of Indians, and those I had no knowledge of, and there being no Christian soul near me; yet not one of them offered the least imaginable miscarriage to me. I turned homeward again, and met with my master; he shewed me the way to my son. When I came to him I found him not well: and withal he had a boil on his side, which much troubled him: We bemoaned one another a while, as the Lord helped us, and then I returned again. When I was returned, I found myself as unsatisfied as I was before. I went up and down mourning and lamenting: and my spirit was ready to sink, with the thoughts of my poor children: my son was ill, and I could not but think of his mournful looks, and no Christian friend was near him, to do any office of love for him, either for soul or body. And my poor girl, I knew not where she was, nor whether she was sick, or well, or alive, or dead. I repaired under these thoughts to my Bible (my great comforter in that time) and that scripture came to my hand, *Cast thy burden upon the Lord, and he shall sustain thee,* Ps. 55:22.

But I was fain to go and look after something to satisfy my hunger, and going among the wigwams, I went into one, and there found a squaw who shewed herself very kind to me, and gave me a piece of bear. I put it into my pocket, and came home; but could not find an opportunity to broil it, for fear they would get it from me, and there it lay all that day and night in my stinking pocket. In the morning I went to the same squaw, who had a kettle of ground nuts boiling: I asked her to let me boil my piece of bear in her kettle, which she did, and gave me

[19] Naananto or Canonchet, captured April 1676 in Rhode Island and executed the next day.

some ground nuts to eat with it: and I cannot but think how pleasant it was to me. I have sometime seen bear baked very handsomely amongst the English, and some liked it, but the thought that it was bear, made me tremble: but now that was savory to me that one would think was enough to turn the stomach of a brute creature.

One bitter cold day, I could find no room to sit down before the fire: I went out, and could not tell what to do, but I went into another wigwam where they were also sitting round the fire: but the squaw laid a skin for me, and bid me sit down, and gave me some ground nuts, and bade me come again: and told me they would buy me, if they were able, and yet these were strangers to me that I never knew before.

The Tenth Remove.

That day a small part of the company removed about three quarters of a mile, intending farther the next day. When they came to the place where they intended to lodge, and had pitched their wigwams, being hungry I went again back to the place we were before at, to get something to eat: being encouraged by the squaw's kindness, who bade me come again; when I was there, there came an Indian to look after me: who when he had found me, kickt me all along: I went home and found venison roasting that night, but they would not give me one bit of it. Sometimes I met with favor, and sometimes with nothing but frowns.

The Eleventh Remove.

The next day in the morning they took their travel, intending a day's journey up the river. I took my load at my back, and quickly we came to wade over a river: and passed over tiresome and wearisome hills. One hill was so steep, that I was fain to creep up upon my knees, and to hold by the twigs and bushes to keep myself from falling backward. My head also was so light, that I usually reeled as I went; but I hope all those wearisome steps that I have taken, are but a forewarning to me of the heavenly rest. *I know, O Lord, that thy judgments are right, and that thou in faithfulness hast afflicted me,* Ps. 119:75.

The Twelfth Remove.

It was upon a Sabbath-day morning, that they prepared for their travel. This morning I asked my master whether he would sell me to my husband? he answered *Nux*,[20] which did much rejoice my spirit. My mis-

---

[20] Yes.

tress, before we went, was gone to the burial of a papoos, and returning, she found me sitting and reading in my Bible: she snatched it hastily out of my hand, and threw it out of doors; I ran out and catcht it up, and put it into my pocket, and never let her see it afterward. Then they packed up their things to be gone, and gave me my load: I complained it was too heavy, whereupon she gave me a slap in the face, and bade me go; I lifted up my heart to God, hoping that redemption was not far off: and the rather because their insolence grew worse and worse.

But the thoughts of my going homeward (for so we bent our course) much cheered my spirit, and made my burden seem light, and almost nothing at all. But (to my amazement and great perplexity) the scale was soon turned: for when we had gone a little way, on a sudden my mistress gives out, she would go no further, but turn back again, and said, I must go back again with her, and she called her sannup, and would have had him gone back also, but he would not, but said, he would go on, and come to us again in three days. My spirit was upon this (I confess) very impatient, and almost outrageous. I thought I could as well have died as went back: I cannot declare the trouble that I was in about it; but yet back again I must go. As soon as I had an opportunity, I took my Bible to read, and that quieting scripture came to my hand, Ps. 46:10, *Be still, and know that I am God.* Which stilled my spirit for the present: But a sore time of trial I concluded I had to go through. My master being gone, who seemed to me the best friend that I had of an Indian, both in cold and hunger, and quickly so it proved. Down I sat, with my heart as full as it could hold, and yet so hungry that I could not sit neither: but going out to see what I could find, and walking among the trees, I found six acorns, and two chestnuts, which were some refreshment to me. Towards night I gathered me some sticks for my own comfort, that I might not lie a-cold: but when we came to lie down they bade me go out, and lie somewhere else, for they had company (they said) come in more than their own: I told them, I could not tell where to go, they bade me go look; I told them, if I went to another wigwam they would be angry, and send me home again. Then one of the company drew his sword, and told me he would run me through if I did not go presently. Then was I fain to stoop to this rude fellow, and to go out in the night, I knew not whither. Mine eyes have seen that fellow afterwards walking up and down in Boston, under the appearance of a friend-Indian, and several others of the like cut. I went to one wigwam, and they told me they had no room. Then I went to another, and they said the same; at last an old Indian bade me come to him, and his squaw gave me some ground nuts; she gave me also something to lay under my head, and a good fire we had: and through the good providence of God, I had a comfortable lodging that night. In the morning, another Indian bade me come at night, and he would give me six ground nuts, which I did. We were at this place and time about two miles from Connecticut River. We went in the morning (to gather ground nuts) to the river, and went back again at night. I went with a great load at my back (for they when they went, though but a little way, would carry all their trumpery with them) I told them the skin was off my back, but I had no other comforting answer from them than this, that it would be no matter if my head were off too.

The Thirteenth Remove.

Instead of going toward the Bay (which was that I desired) I must go with them five or six miles down the river into a mighty thicket of brush: where we abode almost a fortnight. Here one asked me to make a shirt for her papoos, for which she gave me a mess of broth, which was thickened with meal made of the bark of a tree, and to make it the better, she had put into it about a handful of peas, and a few roasted ground nuts. I had not seen my son a pretty while, and here was an Indian of whom I made inquiry after him, and asked him when he saw him: he answered me, that such a time his master roasted him, and that himself did eat a piece of him, as big as his two fingers, and that he was very good meat: But the Lord upheld my spirit, under this discouragement; and I considered their horrible addictedness to lying, and that there is not one of them that makes the least conscience of speaking the truth. In this place on a cold night, as I lay by the fire, I removed a stick which kept the heat from me, a squaw moved it down again, at which I lookt up, and she threw a handful of ashes in my eyes: I thought I should have been quite blinded, and have never seen more: but lying down, the water run out of my eyes, and carried the dirt with it, that by the morning, I recovered my sight again. Yet upon this, and the like occasions, I hope it is not too much to say with Job, *Have pity upon me, have pity upon me, O ye my friends, for the hand of the Lord has touched me* [Job 19:21]. And here I cannot but remember how many times sitting in their wigwams, and musing on things past, I should suddenly leap up and run out, as if I had been at home, forgetting where I was, and what my condition was: But when I was without, and saw nothing but wilderness, and woods, and a company of barbarous heathen; my mind quickly returned to me, which made me think of that, spoken concerning Sampson, who said, *I will go out and shake myself as at other times, but he wist not that the Lord was departed from him* [Judges 16:20]. About this time, I began to think that all my hopes of restoration would come to nothing. I thought of the English army, and hoped for their coming, and being retaken by them, but that failed. I hoped to be carried to Albany, as the Indians had discoursed, but that failed also. I thought of being sold to my husband, as my master spake, but instead of that, my master himself was gone, and I left behind, so that my spirit was now quite ready to sink. I asked them to let me go out and pick up some sticks, that I might get alone, *and pour out my heart unto the Lord* [Ps. 62:8]. Then also I took my Bible to read, but I found no comfort here neither, which many times I was wont to find: So easy a thing it is with God to dry up the streams of Scripture comfort from us. Yet I can say, that in all my sorrows and afflictions, God did not leave me to have my impatience work towards himself, as if his ways were unrighteous. But I knew that he laid upon me less than I deserved. Afterward, before this doleful time ended with me, I was turning the leaves of my Bible, and the Lord brought to me some scriptures, which did a little revive me, as that Isa. 55:8, *For my thoughts are not your thoughts, neither are your ways my ways, saith the Lord*. And also that, Ps. 37:5, *Commit thy way unto the Lord, trust also in him, and he shall bring it to pass*.

About this time they came yelping from Hadley, having there killed three Englishmen, and brought one captive with them, viz. Thomas Read. They all gathered about the poor man, asking him many questions. I desired also to go and see him; and when I came, he was crying bitterly, supposing they would quickly kill him. Whereupon I asked one of them, whether they intended to kill him? he answered me, they would not: He being a little cheered with that, I asked him about the welfare of my husband, he told me he saw him such a time in the Bay, and he was well, but very melancholy. By which I certainly understood (though I suspected it before) that whatsoever the Indians told me respecting him was vanity and lies. Some of them told me, he was dead, and they had killed him: some said he was married again, and that the governor wished him to marry; and told him he should have his choice, and that all persuaded him I was dead. So like were these barbarous creatures to him who was a liar from the beginning.

As I was sitting once in the wigwam here, Philip's maid came in with the child in her arms, and asked me to give her a piece of my apron, to make a flap for it, I told her I would not: then my mistress bade me give it, but still I said no: the maid told me, if I would not give her a piece, she would tear a piece off it: I told her I would tear her coat then: with that my mistress rises up, and takes up a stick big enough to have killed me, and struck at me with it, but I stept out, and she struck the stick into the mat of the wigwam. But while she was pulling of it out, I ran to the maid and gave her all my apron, and so that storm went over.

Hearing that my son was come to this place, I went to see him, and told him his father was well, but very melancholy: he told me he was as much grieved for his father as for himself; I wondered at his speech, for I thought I had enough upon my spirit in reference to myself, to make me mindless of my husband and everyone else: they being safe among their friends. He told me also, that a while before, his master (together with other Indians) were going to the French for powder; but by the way the Mohawks met with them, and killed four of their company which made the rest turn back again,[21] for which I desired that myself and he may bless the Lord; for it might have been worse with him, had he been sold to the French, than it proved to be in his remaining with the Indians.

I went to see an English youth in this place, one John Gilbert of Springfield. I found him lying without doors, upon the ground; I asked him how he did? He told me he was very sick of a flux, with eating so much blood: They had turned him out of the wigwam, and with him an Indian papoos, almost dead (whose parents had been killed), in a bitter cold day, without fire or clothes: the young man himself had nothing on, but his shirt and waistcoat. This sight was enough to melt a heart of flint. There they lay quivering in the cold, the youth round like a dog, the papoos stretcht out, with his eyes and nose and mouth full of dirt, and yet alive, and groaning. I advised John to go and get to some fire: he told me he could not stand, but I persuaded him still, lest he should lie there and die. And with much ado I got him to a fire, and went myself home. As soon as I was got home, his master's daughter came after me, to know what I had done with the Englishman? I told her I had got him to a fire in such a place. Now had I need to pray Paul's prayer, 2 Thess. 3:2, *That we may be delivered from unreasonable and wicked men.* For her satisfaction I went along with her, and brought her to him; but before I got home again, it was noised about, that I was running away and getting the English youth, along with me: that as soon as I came in, they began to rant and domineer: asking me where I had been? and what I had been doing? and saying they would knock me on the head: I told them, I had been seeing the English youth, and that I would not run away: they told me I lied, and taking up a hatchet, they came to me, and said they would knock me down if I stirred out again; and so confined me to the wigwam. Now may I say with David, 2 Sam. 24:14, *I am in a great strait.* If I keep in, I must die with hunger, and if I

---

[21] The alliance that King Philip hoped to create with the Mohawks foundered on the long-lasting hostililty of the Mohawks toward the New England tribes.

go out, I must be knockt in the head. This distressed condition held that day, and half the next; and then the Lord remembered me, whose mercies are great. Then came an Indian to me with a pair of stockings which were too big for him, and he would have me ravel them out, and knit them fit for him. I shewed myself willing, and bid him ask my mistress, if I might go along with him a little way; she said yes, I might, but I was not a little refresht with that news, that I had my liberty again. Then I went along with him, and he gave me some roasted ground nuts, which did again revive my feeble stomach.

Being got out of her sight, I had time and liberty again to look into my Bible: Which was my guide by day, and my pillow by night. Now that comfortable scripture presented itself to me, Isa. 54:7, *For a small moment have I forsaken thee, but with great mercies will I gather thee.* Thus the Lord carried me along from one time to another, and made good to me this precious promise, and many others. Then my son came to see me, and I asked his master to let him stay a while with me, that I might comb his head, and look over him, for he was almost overcome with lice. He told me, when I had done, that he was very hungry, but I had nothing to relieve him; but bid him go into the wigwams as he went along, and see if he could get anything among them. Which he did, and (it seems) tarried a little too long; for his master was angry with him, and beat him, and then sold him. Then he came running to tell me he had a new master, and that he had given him some ground nuts already. Then I went along with him to his new master, who told me he loved him: and he should not want. So his master carried him away, and I never saw him afterward, till I saw him at Piscataqua in Portsmouth.

That night they bade me go out of the wigwam again: my mistress's papoos was sick, and it died that night, and there was one benefit in it, that there was more room. I went to a wigwam, and they bade me come in, and gave me a skin to lie upon, and a mess of venison and ground nuts, which was a choice dish among them. On the morrow they buried the papoos, and afterward, both morning and evening, there came a company to mourn and howl with her: though I confess, I could not much condole with them. Many sorrowful days I had in this place: often getting alone; *like a crane, or a swallow, so did I chatter: I did mourn as a dove, mine eyes fail with looking upward. Oh, Lord, I am oppressed; undertake for me,* Isa. 38:14. I could tell the Lord as Hezekiah, [Isa. 38] v. 3, *Remember now, O Lord, I beseech thee, how I have walked before thee in truth.* Now had I time to examine all my ways: my conscience did not accuse me of unrighteousness toward one or other: yet I saw how in my walk with God, I had been a careless creature. As David said, *Against thee, thee only have I sinned* [Ps. 51:4]: and I might say with the poor publican, *God be merciful unto me a sinner* [Luke 18:13]. On the Sabbath-days, I could look upon the sun and think how people were going to the house of God, to have their souls refresht; and then home, and their bodies also: but I was destitute of both; and might say as the poor prodigal, *He would fain have filled his belly with the husks that the swine did eat, and no man gave unto him*, Luke 15:16. For I must say with him, *Father I have sinned against heaven, and in thy sight*, v. 21. I remembered how on the night before and after the Sabbath, when my family was about me, and relations and neighbors with us; we could pray and sing, and then refresh our bodies with the good creatures of God; and then have a comfortable bed to lie down on: but instead of all this, I had only a little swill for the body and then like a swine, must lie down on the ground. I cannot express to man the sorrow that lay upon my spirit, the Lord knows it. Yet that comfortable scripture would often come to my mind, *For a small moment have I forsaken thee, but with great mercies will I gather thee* [Isa. 54:7].

The Fourteenth Remove.

Now must we pack up and be gone from this thicket, bending our course toward the Bay-towns. I having nothing to eat by the way this day, but a few crumbs of cake, that an Indian gave my girl, the same day we were taken. She gave it me, and I put it into my pocket: there it lay till it was so moldy (for want of good baking) that one could not tell what it was made of; it fell all to crumbs, and grew so dry and hard, that it was like little flints; and this refreshed me many times, when I was ready to faint. It was in my thoughts when I put it into my mouth; that if ever I returned, I would tell the world what a blessing the Lord gave to such mean food. As we went along, they killed a deer, with a young one in her: they gave me a piece of the fawn, and it was so young and tender, that one might eat the bones as well as the flesh, and yet I thought it very good. When night came on we sat down; it rained, but they quickly got up a bark wigwam, where I lay dry that night. I looked out in the morning, and many of them had lain in the rain all night, I saw by their reeking. Thus the Lord dealt mercifully with me many times: and I fared better than many of them. In the morning they took the blood of the deer, and put it into the paunch, and so boiled it; I could eat nothing of that: though they ate it sweetly. And yet they were so nice[22] in other things, that when I had fetcht water, and had put the dish I dipt the water with, into the kettle of water which I brought, they

---

[22] That is, fastidious.

would say, they would knock me down; for they said, it was a sluttish trick.

The Fifteenth Remove.

We went on our travel. I having got one handful of ground nuts, for my support that day, they gave me my load, and I went on cheerfully (with the thoughts of going homeward) having my burden more on my back than my spirit: we came to Baquaug River again that day, near which we abode a few days. Sometimes one of them would give me a pipe, another a little tobacco, another a little salt: which I would change for a little victuals. I cannot but think what a wolvish appetite persons have in a starving condition: for many times when they gave me that which was hot, I was so greedy, that I should burn my mouth, that it would trouble me hours after; and yet I should quickly do the same again. And after I was thoroughly hungry, I was never again satisfied. For though sometimes it fell out, that I got enough, and did eat till I could eat no more, yet I was as unsatisfied as I was when I began. And now could I see that scripture verified (there being many scriptures which we do not take notice of, or understand till we are afflicted) Mic. 6:14, *Thou shalt eat and not be satisfied.* Now might I see more than ever before, the miseries that sin hath brought upon us: Many times I should be ready to run out against the heathen, but that scripture would quiet me again, Amos 3:6, *Shall there be evil in the city, and the Lord hath not done it?* The Lord help me to make a right improvement of his Word, and that I might learn that great lesson, Mic. 6:8–9, *He hath showed thee (O man) what is good, and what doth the Lord require of thee, but to do justly, and love mercy, and walk humbly with thy God? Hear ye the rod, and who hath appointed it.*

The Sixteenth Remove.

We began this remove with wading over Baquag River. The water was up to the knees, and the stream very swift, and so cold that I thought it would have cut me in sunder. I was so weak and feeble, that I reeled as I went along, and thought there I must end my days at last, after my bearing and getting through so many difficulties. The Indians stood laughing to see me staggering along, but in my distress the Lord gave me experience of the truth and goodness of that promise, Isa. 43:2, *When thou passeth through the waters, I will be with thee, and through the rivers, they shall not overflow thee.* Then I sat down to put on my stockings and shoes, with the tears running down mine eyes, and many sorrowful thoughts in my heart: but I gat up to go along with them. Quickly there came up to us an Indian, who informed them, that I must go to Wachuset to my master: for there was a letter come from the Council to the sagamores, about redeeming the captives, and that there would be another in fourteen days, and that I must be there ready. My heart was so heavy before that I could scarce speak, or go in the path; and yet now so light, that I could run. My strength seemed to come again, and to recruit my feeble knees, and aching heart: yet it pleased them to go but one mile that night, and there we stayed two days. In that time came a company of Indians to us, near thirty, all on horseback. My heart skipt within me, thinking they had been Englishmen at the first sight of them: for they were dressed in English apparel, with hats, white neckcloths, and sashes about their waists, and ribbons upon their shoulders: but when they came near, there was a vast difference between the lovely faces of Christians, and the foul looks of those heathens, which much damped my spirit again.

The Seventeenth Remove.

A comfortable remove it was to me, because of my hopes. They gave me my pack, and along we went cheerfully: but quickly my will proved more than my strength; having little or no refreshing, my strength failed, and my spirits were almost quite gone. Now may I say as David, Ps. 109:22–24, *I am poor and needy, and my heart is wounded within me. I am gone like the shadow when it declineth: I am tossed up and down like the locust; my knees are weak through fasting, and my flesh faileth of fatness.* At night we came to an Indian town, and the Indians sat down by a wigwam discoursing, but I was almost spent, and could scarce speak. I laid down my load, and went into the wigwam, and there sat an Indian boiling of horses' feet (they being wont to eat the flesh first, and when the feet were old and dried, and they had nothing else, they would cut off the feet and use them): I asked him to give me a little of his broth, or water they were boiling in: he took a dish, and gave me one spoonful of samp,[23] and bid me take as much of the broth as I would. Then I put some of the hot water to the samp, and drank it up, and my spirit came again. He gave me also a piece of the ruff or ridding of the small guts, and I broiled it on the coals; and now may I say with Jonathan, *See, I pray you, how mine eyes have been enlightened, because I tasted a little of this honey,* 1 Sam. 14:29. Now is my spirit revived again: though means be never so inconsiderable, yet if the

[23] Corn, ground and turned into porridge.

Lord bestow his blessing upon them, they shall refresh both soul and body.

The Eighteenth Remove.

We took up our packs, and along we went. But a wearisome day I had of it. As we went along, I saw an Englishman stript naked, and lying dead upon the ground, but knew not who it was. Then we came to another Indian town, where we stayed all night. In this town, there were four English children, captives; and one of them my own sister's. I went to see how she did, and she was well, considering her captive-condition. I would have tarried that night with her, but they that own her would not suffer it. Then I went to another wigwam, where they were boiling corn and beans, which was a lovely sight to see, but I could not get a taste thereof. Then I went into another wigwam, where there were two of the English children: the squaw was boiling horses' feet, then she cut me off a little piece and gave one of the English children a piece also. Being very hungry I had quickly eat up mine: but the child could not bite it, it was so tough and sinewy, but lay sucking, gnawing, chewing and slobbering of it in the mouth and hand, then I took it of the child, and eat it myself, and savory it was to my taste.

Then I may say as Job 6:7, *The things that my soul refused to touch, are as my sorrowful meat*. Thus the Lord made that pleasant and refreshing, which another time would have been an abomination. Then I went home to my mistress's wigwam: and they told me I disgraced my master with begging: and if I did so any more, they would knock me in [the] head: I told them, they had as good knock me in [the] head, as starve me to death.

The Nineteenth Remove.

They said, when we went out, that we must travel to Wachuset this day. But a bitter weary day I had of it, traveling now three days together, without resting any day between. At last, after many weary steps, I saw Wachuset hills, but many miles off. Then we came to a great swamp: through which we traveled up to the knees in mud and water, which was heavy going to one tired before. Being almost spent, I thought I should have sunk down at last, and never get out; but I may say, as in Ps. 94:18, *When my foot slipped, thy mercy, O Lord, held me up*. Going along, having indeed my life, but little spirit, Philip (who was in the company) came up, and took me by the hand, and said, Two weeks more and you shall be mistress again. I asked him, if he spake true? He answered, Yes, and quickly you shall come to your master again: who had been gone from us three weeks. After many weary steps we came to Wachuset, where he was; and glad I was to see him. He asked me, When I washt me? I told him not this month; then he fetcht me some water himself, and bid me wash, and gave me the glass to see how I lookt; and bid his squaw give me something to eat. So she gave me a mess of beans and meat, and a little ground nut cake. I was wonderfully revived with this favor shewed me, Ps. 106:46, *He made them also to be pitied, of all those that carried them captives.*

My master had three squaws: living sometimes with one, and sometimes with another. One, this old squaw, at whose wigwam I was, and with whom my master had been those three weeks. Another was Wettimore,[24] with whom I had lived and served all this while. A severe and proud dame she was; bestowing every day in dressing herself near as much time as any of the gentry of the land: powdering her hair and painting her face, going with her necklaces, with jewels in her ears, and bracelets upon her hands: When she had dressed herself, her work was to make girdles of wampum and beads. The third squaw was a younger one, by whom he had two papooses. By that time I was refresht by the old squaw, with whom my master was, Wettimore's maid came to call me home, at which I fell a weeping; then the old squaw told me, to encourage me, that if I wanted victuals, I should come to her, and that I should lie there in her wigwam. Then I went with the maid, and quickly came again and lodged there. The squaw laid a mat under me, and a good rug over me; the first time I had any such kindness shewed me. I understood that Wettimore thought, that if she should let me go and serve with the old squaw, she would be in danger to lose not only my service, but the redemption pay also. And I was not a little glad to hear this; being by it raised in my hopes, that in God's due time there would be an end of this sorrowful hour. Then [in] came an Indian, and asked me to knit him three pair of stockings, for which I had a hat, and a silk handkerchief. Then another asked me to make her a shift, for which she gave me an apron.

Then came Tom and Peter,[25] with the second letter from the Council, about the captives. Though they were Indians, I gat them by the hand, and burst out into tears; my heart was so full that I could not speak to them: but recovering myself, I asked them how my husband did? and all

---

[24] Usually spelled Weetamoo; she was the widow of King Philip's brother Wamsutta and, at the war's end, drowned attempting to escape.

[25] The efforts to ransom Mrs. Rowlandson, using two Christian Indians, Tom Doublet (Nepanet) and Peter Conway (Tatatiquinea), from the praying town of Nashoba, are described in Gookin, "Historical Account," 502–8.

my friends and acquaintance? They said, they were well, but very melancholy. They brought me two biscuits, and a pound of tobacco. The tobacco I quickly gave away: when it was all gone, one asked me to give him a pipe of tobacco, I told him it was all gone; then began he to rant and threaten. I told him when my husband came, I would give him some: Hang him rogue (says he) I will knock out his brains, if he comes here. And then again in the same breath, they would say, that if there should come an hundred without guns, they would do them no hurt. So unstable and like mad men they were: So that fearing the worst, I durst not send to my husband, though there were some thoughts of his coming to redeem and fetch me, not knowing what might follow; for there was little more trust to them than to the master they served.[26] When the letter was come, the sagamores met to consult about the captives, and called me to them to inquire how much my husband would give to redeem me: when I came I sat down among them, as I was wont to do, as their manner is: Then they bade me stand up, and said, they were the General Court. They bid me speak what I thought he would give. Now knowing that all we had was destroyed by the Indians, I was in a great strait. I thought if I should speak of but a little, it would be slighted, and hinder the matter; if of a great sum, I knew not where it would be procured: yet at a venture, I said twenty pounds, yet desired them to take less; but they would not hear of that, but sent that message to Boston, that for twenty pounds I should be redeemed. It was a Praying Indian that wrote their letter for them. There was another Praying Indian, who told me, that he had a brother, that would not eat horse; his conscience was so tender and scrupulous (though as large as hell, for the destruction of poor Christians). Then he said, he read that scripture to him, 2 Kings 6:25, *There was a famine in Samaria, and behold they besieged it, until an asses head was sold for fourscore pieces of silver, and the fourth part of a kab of doves' dung, for five pieces of silver.* He expounded this place to his brother, and shewed him that it was lawful to eat that in a famine, which is not at another time. And now, says he, he will eat horse with any Indian of them all. There was another Praying Indian, who when he had done all the mischief that he could, betrayed his own father into the Englishes hands, thereby to purchase his own life. Another Praying Indian was at Sudbury fight,[27] though, as he deserved, he was afterward hanged for it. There was another Praying Indian, so wicked and cruel, as to wear a string about his neck, strung with Christian fingers. Another Praying Indian, when they went to Sudbury fight, went with them, and his squaw also with him, with her

---

[26] The devil, described in John 8:44 as the father of lies.
[27] Battle of April 18, 1676, an ambush that killed more than thirty colonists.

papoos at her back: before they went to that fight, they got a company together to powwow;[28] the manner was as followeth. There was one that kneeled upon a deerskin, with the company round him in a ring, who kneeled, striking upon the ground with their hands, and with sticks, and muttering or humming with their mouths. Besides him who kneeled in the ring, there also stood one with a gun in his hand: Then he on the deerskin made a speech, and all manifested assent to it; and so they did many times together. Then they bade him with the gun go out of the ring, which he did; but when he was out they called him in again; but he seemed to make a stand; then they called the more earnestly, till he returned again: Then they all sang. Then they gave him two guns, in either hand one: And so he on the deerskin began again; and at the end of every sentence in his speaking, they all assented, humming or muttering with their mouths, and striking upon the ground with their hands. Then they bade him with the two guns go out of the ring again: which he did a little way. Then they called him in again, but he made a stand; so they called him with greater earnestness: but he stood reeling and wavering, as if he knew not whether he should stand or fall, or which way to go. Then they called him with exceeding great vehemency, all of them, one and another: after a little while, he turned in, staggering as he went, with his arms stretched out, in either hand a gun. As soon as he came in, they all sang and rejoiced exceedingly a while. And then he upon the deerskin, made another speech, unto which they all assented in a rejoicing manner: and so they ended their business, and forthwith went to Sudbury fight. To my thinking they went without any scruple but that they should prosper and gain the victory. And they went out not so rejoicing, but they came home with as great a victory. For they said they had killed two captains, and almost an hundred men. One Englishman they brought alive with them; and he said, it was too true, for they had made sad work at Sudbury, as indeed it proved. Yet they came home without that rejoicing and triumphing over their victory, which they were wont to shew at other times: but rather like dogs (as they say) which have lost their ears. Yet I could not perceive that it was for their own loss of men: they said they had not lost above five or six: and I missed none, except in one wigwam. When they went, they acted as if the devil had told them that they should gain the victory: and now they acted, as if the devil had told them that they should have a fall. Whether it were so or no, I cannot tell, but so it proved: for quickly they began to fall, and so held on that summer, till they came to utter ruin. They came home on a Sabbath day, and the powwow that kneeled

---

[28] "Powwow" (spelled pawwaw in these texts), the name of shamans or healers, and also of assemblies.

upon the deerskin came home (I may say without abuse) as black as the devil. When my master came home, he came to me and bid me make a shirt for his papoos, of a holland-laced pillowbeer. About that time there came an Indian to me, and bid me come to his wigwam at night, and he would give me some pork and ground nuts. Which I did, and as I was eating, another Indian said to me, he seems to be your good friend, but he killed two Englishmen at Sudbury, and there lie their clothes behind you: I looked behind me, and there I saw bloody clothes, with bullet holes in them; yet the Lord suffered not this wretch to do me any hurt. Yea, instead of that, he many times refresht me: five or six times did he and his squaw refresh my feeble carcass. If I went to their wigwam at any time, they would always give me something, and yet they were strangers that I never saw before. Another squaw gave me a piece of fresh pork, and a little salt with it, and lent me her frying pan to fry it in: and I cannot but remember what a sweet, pleasant and delightful relish that bit had to me, to this day. So little do we prize common mercies when we have them to the full.

The Twentieth Remove.

It was their usual manner to remove, when they had done any mischief, lest they should be found out: and so they did at this time. We went about three or four miles, and there they built a great wigwam, big enough to hold an hundred Indians, which they did in preparation to a great day of dancing. They would say now amongst themselves, that the governor would be so angry for his loss at Sudbury, that he would send no more about the captives, which made me grieve and tremble. My sister being not far from the place where we now were, and hearing that I was here, desired her master to let her come and see me, and he was willing to it, and would go with her; but she being ready before him, told him she would go before, and was come within a mile or two of the place: Then he overtook her, and began to rant as if he had been mad, and made her go back again in the rain; so that I never saw her till I saw her in Charlestown. But the Lord requited many of their ill doings, for this Indian her master, was hanged afterward at Boston. The Indians now began to come from all quarters against their merry dancing day. Amongst some of them came one Goodwife Kettle: I told her my heart was so heavy that it was ready to break: so is mine too, said she, but yet said, I hope we shall hear some good news shortly. I could hear how earnestly my sister desired to see me, and I as earnestly desired to see her; and yet neither of us could get an opportunity. My daughter was also now but about a mile off, and I had not seen her in nine or ten weeks, as I had not seen my sister since our first taking. I earnestly desired them to let me go and see them: yea, I entreated, begged, and persuaded them, but to let me see my daughter: and yet so hard-hearted were they, that they would not suffer it. They made use of their tyrannical power whilst they had it: but through the Lord's wonderful mercy, their time was but short.

On a Sabbath day, the sun being about an hour high, in the afternoon, came Mr. John Hoar (the Council permitting him, and his own forward spirit inclining him), together with the two fore-mentioned Indians, Tom and Peter, with the third letter from the Council. When they came near, I was abroad: though I saw them not, they presently called me in, and bade me sit down, and not stir. Then they catched up their guns, and away they ran, as if an enemy had been at hand; and the guns went off apace. I manifested some great trouble, and they asked me what was the matter? I told them, I thought they had killed the Englishman (for they had in the meantime informed me that an Englishman was come) they said, No; they shot over his horse, and under, and before his horse; and they pusht him this way and that way, at their pleasure: shewing what they could do: Then they let them come to their wigwams. I begged of them to let me see the Englishman, but they would not. But there was I fain to sit their pleasure. When they had talked their fill with him, they suffered me to go to him. We asked each other of our welfare, and how my husband did? and all my friends? He told me they were all well, and would be glad to see me. Amongst other things which my husband sent me, there came a pound of tobacco: which I sold for nine shillings in money: for many of the Indians for want of tobacco, smoked hemlock, and ground ivy. It was a great mistake in any, who thought I sent for tobacco: for through the favor of God, that desire was overcome. I now asked them, whether I should go home with Mr. Hoar? They answered No, one and another of them: and it being night, we lay down with that answer: in the morning Mr. Hoar invited the sagamores to dinner: but when we went to get it ready, we found that they had stolen the greatest part of the provision Mr. Hoar had brought, out of his bags, in the night. And we may see the wonderful power of God, in that one passage, in that when there was such a great number of the Indians together, and so greedy of a little good food; and no English there, but Mr. Hoar and myself: that there they did not knock us in the head, and take what we had: there being not only some provision, but also trading cloth, a part of the twenty pounds agreed upon: But instead of doing us any mischief, they seemed to be ashamed of the fact, and said, it were some matchit Indians[29] that

---

[29] Bad Indian.

did it. Oh, that we could believe that there is nothing too hard for God! God shewed his power over the heathen in this, as he did over the hungry lions when Daniel was cast into the den. Mr. Hoar called them betime to dinner; but they ate very little, they being so busy in dressing themselves, and getting ready for their dance: which was carried on by eight of them, four men and four squaws; my master and mistress being two. He was dressed in his Holland shirt, with great laces sewed at the tail of it; he had his silver buttons, his white stockings, his garters were hung round with shillings, and he had girdles of wampum upon his head and shoulders. She had a kersey coat,[30] covered with girdles of wampum from the loins upward. Her arms from her elbows to her hands were covered with bracelets; there were handfuls of necklaces about her neck, and several sorts of jewels in her ears. She had fine red stockings, and white shoes, her hair powdered and her face painted red, that was always before black. And all the dancers were after the same manner. There were two other singing and knocking on a kettle for their music. They kept hopping up and down one after another, with a kettle of water in the midst, standing warm upon some embers, to drink of when they were dry. They held on, till it was almost night, throwing out wampum to the standers by. At night I asked them again, if I should go home? They all as one said No, except my husband would come for me. When we were lain down, my master went out of the wigwam, and by and by sent in an Indian called James the Printer,[31] who told Mr. Hoar, that my master would let me go home tomorrow, if he would let him have one pint of liquors. Then Mr. Hoar called his own Indians, Tom and Peter, and bid them all go and see whether he would promise it before them three: and if he would, he should have it; which he did, and had it. Then Philip smelling the business, called me to him, and asked me what I would give him, to tell me some good news, and to speak a good word for me, that I might go home tomorrow? I told him, I could not tell what to give him; I would anything I had, and asked him what he would have? He said, two coats and twenty shillings in money, and half a bushel of seed corn, and some tobacco. I thanked him for his love: but I knew the good news as well as that crafty fox. My master,

---

[30] Made of coarsely woven wool.

[31] James Printer, having learned English and mastered the Algonquian alphabet created by the missionary John Eliot, played a key role in setting type for the first translation of the Bible into Algonquian. After joining the war on the Indian side, he surrendered in the summer of 1676 and, unusually, was allowed to resume his work as compositor/translator. He may have set type for the Cambridge, Mass., 1682 printing of Rowlandson's book. See Increase Mather, *A Brief History of the Warr* (Boston, 1676), 89; Hugh Amory, *First Impressions: Printing in Cambridge, 1639–1989* (Cambridge, Mass., 1989), 41.

after he had had his drink, quickly came ranting into the wigwam again, and called for Mr. Hoar, drinking to him, and saying he was a good man; and then again he would say, Hang him, rogue: Being almost drunk, he would drink to him, and yet presently say he should be hanged. Then he called for me, I trembled to hear him, yet I was fain to go to him, and he drank to me, shewing no incivility. He was the first Indian I saw drunk all the while that I was amongst them. At last his squaw ran out, and he after her, round the wigwam, with his money jingling at his knees: But she escaped him; but having an old squaw, he ran to her: and so through the Lord's mercy, we were no more troubled with him that night. Yet I had not a comfortable night's rest: for I think I can say, I did not sleep for three nights together. The night before the letter came from the Council, I could not rest, I was so full of fears and troubles (God many times leaving us most in the dark, when deliverance is nearest), yea, at this time I could not rest night nor day. The next night I was overjoyed, Mr. Hoar being come, and that with such good tidings. The third night I was even swallowed up with the thoughts of things, viz. that ever I should go home again; and that I must go, leaving my children behind me in the wilderness; so that sleep was now almost departed from mine eyes.

On Tuesday morning they called their General Court (as they styled it) to consult and determine, whether I should go home or no: And they all as one man did seemingly consent to it, that I should go home: except Philip, who would not come among them.

But before I go any further, I would take leave to mention a few remarkable passages of providence, which I took special notice of in my afflicted time.

1. Of the fair opportunity lost in the long march, a little after the Fort-fight, when our English army was so numerous, and in pursuit of the enemy; and so near as to overtake several, and destroy them: and the enemy in such distress for food, that our men might track them by their rooting in the earth for ground nuts, whilst they were flying for their lives: I say, that then our army should want provision, and be forced to leave their pursuit, and return homeward: and the very next week the enemy came upon our town, like bears bereft of their whelps, or so many ravenous wolves, rending us and our lambs to death. But what shall I say? God seemed to leave his people to themselves, and ordered all things for his own holy ends. *Shall there be evil in the city and the Lord hath not done it? They are not grieved for the affliction of Joseph, therefore shall they go captive, with the first that go captive* [Amos 3:6, 6:6–7]. *It is the Lord's doing, and it should be marvelous in our eyes* [Ps. 118:23].

2. I cannot but remember how the Indians derided the slowness, and dullness of the English army, in its setting out. For after the desolations at Lancaster and Medfield, as I went along with them, they asked me when I thought the English army would come after them? I told them I could not tell: It may be they will come in May, said they. Thus did they scoff at us, as if the English would be a quarter of a year getting ready.

3. Which also I have hinted before; when the English army with new supplies were sent forth to pursue after the enemy, and they understanding it: fled before them till they came to Baquaug River, where they forthwith went over safely: that that river should be impassable to the English, I can but admire to see the wonderful providence of God in preserving the heathen for farther affliction to our poor country. They could go in great numbers over, but the English must stop: God had an overruling hand in all those things.

4. It was thought, if their corn were cut down, they would starve and die with hunger, and all their corn that could be found, was destroyed, and they driven from that little they had in store, into the woods, in the midst of winter; and yet how to admiration did the Lord preserve them for his holy ends, and the destruction of many still amongst the English! strangely did the Lord provide for them: that I did not see (all the time I was among them) one man, or woman, or child, die with hunger.

Though many times they would eat that, that a hog or a dog would hardly touch: yet by that God strengthened them to be a scourge to his people.

Their chief and commonest food was ground nuts: they ate also nuts and acorns, harty-choaks, lily roots, ground beans, and several other weeds, and roots, that I know not.

They would pick up old bones, and cut them in pieces at the joints, and if they were full of worms and maggots, they would scald them over the fire to make the vermin come out; and then boil them and drink up the liquor, and then beat the great ends of them in a mortar, and so eat them. They would eat horses' guts, and ears, and all sorts of wild birds which they could catch: also bear, venison, beaver, tortoise, frogs, squirrels, dogs, skunks, rattle-snakes: yea, the very bark of trees; besides all sorts of creatures, and provision which they plundered from the English. I can but stand in admiration to see the wonderful power of God, in providing for such a vast number of our enemies in the wilderness, where there was nothing to be seen, but from hand to mouth. Many times in a morning, the generality of them would eat up all they had, and yet have some further supply against they wanted. It is said, Ps. 81:13–14, *Oh, that my people had hearkened to me, and Israel had walked in my ways, I should soon have subdued their enemies, and turned my hand against their adversaries.* But now our perverse and evil carriages in the sight of the Lord, have so offended him, that instead of turning his hand against them, the Lord feeds and nourishes them up to be a scourge to the whole land.[32]

5. Another thing that I would observe is, the strange providence of God in turning things about when the Indians were at the highest, and the English at the lowest. I was with the enemy eleven weeks and five days; and not one week passed without the fury of the enemy, and some desolation by fire and sword upon one place or other. They mourned (with their black faces) for their own losses: yet triumphed and rejoiced in their inhumane (and many times devilish cruelty) to the English. They would boast much of their victories; saying, that in two hours time, they had destroyed such a captain, and his company, in such a place; and boast how many towns they had destroyed, and then scoff, and say, they had done them a good turn, to send them to heaven so soon. Again, they would say, this summer they would knock all the rogues in the head, or drive them into the sea, or make them fly the country: thinking surely, Agag-like, *The bitterness of death is past* [1 Sam. 15:32]. Now the heathen begin to think all is their own, and the poor Christians' hopes to fail (as to man) and now their eyes are more to God, and their hearts sigh heaven-ward: and to say in good earnest, *Help Lord, or we perish* [Matt. 8:25; Luke 8:24]; when the Lord had brought his people to this, that they saw no help in anything but himself; then he takes the quarrel into his own hand: and though they had made a pit (in their own imaginations) as deep as hell for the Christians that summer; yet the Lord hurl'd themselves into it. And the Lord had not so many ways before, to preserve them, but now he hath as many to destroy them.

But to return again to my going home: where we may see a remarkable change of providence: at first they were all against it, except my husband would come for me; but afterwards they assented to it, and seemed much to rejoice in it: some asking me to send them some bread, others some tobacco, others shaking me by the hand, offering me a hood and scarf to ride in: not one moving hand or tongue against it. Thus hath the Lord answered my poor desires, and the many earnest requests of others put up unto God for me. In my travels an Indian came to me, and told me, if I were willing, he and his squaw would run away, and go home along with me. I told him No: I was not willing to run away, but desired to wait God's time, that I might go home quietly, and without fear. And now God hath granted me my desire. O the wonderful power of God that I have seen, and the experiences that I have had! I have been in the midst of those roaring lions, and savage

[32] A partisan passage, in the context of debate among the colonists over the meaning of the war.

bears, that feared neither God, nor man, nor the devil, by night and day, alone and in company, sleeping all sorts together; and yet not one of them ever offered the least abuse of unchastity to me, in word or action.[33] Though some are ready to say, I speak it for my own credit; but I speak it in the presence of God, and to his glory. God's power is as great now, and as sufficient to save, as when he preserved Daniel in the lion's den; or the three children in the fiery furnace. I may well say, as he, Ps. 107:1–2, *Oh give thanks unto the Lord for he is good, for his mercy endureth for ever. Let the redeemed of the Lord say so, whom he hath redeemed from the hand of the enemy;* especially that I should come away in the midst of so many hundreds of enemies, quietly and peaceably, and not a dog moving his tongue. So I took my leave of them, and in coming along my heart melted into tears, more than all the while I was with them, and I was almost swallowed up with the thoughts that ever I should go home again. About the sun going down, Mr. Hoar, and myself, and the two Indians came to Lancaster, and a solemn sight it was to me. There had I lived many comfortable years amongst my relations and neighbors, and now not one Christian to be seen, nor one house left standing. We went on to a farmhouse that was yet standing, where we lay all night; and a comfortable lodging we had, though nothing but straw to lie on. The Lord preserved us in safety that night, and raised us up again in the morning, and carried us along, that before noon we came to Concord. Now was I full of joy, and yet not without sorrow: joy, to see such a lovely sight, so many Christians together, and some of them my neighbors: There I met with my brother, and my brother-in-law, who asked me, if I knew where his wife was? Poor heart! he had helped to bury her, and knew it not; she being shot down by the house, was partly burnt: so that those who were at Boston at the desolation of the town, and came back afterward, and buried the dead, did not know her. Yet I was not without sorrow, to think how many were looking and longing, and my own children amongst the rest, to enjoy that deliverance that I had now received; and I did not know whether ever I should see them again. Being recruited with food and raiment, we went to Boston that day: where I met with my dear husband, but the thoughts of our dear children, one being dead, and the other we could not tell where, abated our comfort each in other. I was not before so much hem'd in with the merciless and cruel heathen, but now as much with pitiful, tender-hearted and compassionate Christians. In that poor, and distressed, and beggarly condition I was received in, I was kindly entertained in several houses: so much love I received from several (some of whom I knew, and others I knew not), that I am not

---

[33] Possibly a response to the rumor she had married one of her captors.

capable to declare it. But the Lord knows them all by name: the Lord reward them seven fold into their bosoms of his spirituals for their temporals. The twenty pounds, the price of my redemption, was raised by some Boston gentlewomen, and M. Usher,[34] whose bounty and religious charity, I would not forget to make mention of. Then Mr. Thomas Shepard of Charlestown received us into his house, where we continued eleven weeks; and a father and mother they were to us. And many more tender-hearted friends we met with in that place. We were now in the midst of love, yet not without much and frequent heaviness of heart, for our poor children, and other relations, who were still in affliction.

The week following, after my coming in, the governor and Council sent forth to the Indians again; and that not without success: for they brought in my sister, and Goodwife Kettle: Their not knowing where our children were, was a sore trial to us still, and yet we were not without secret hopes that we should see them again. That which was dead lay heavier upon my spirit than those which were alive and amongst the heathen: thinking how it suffered with its wounds, and I was in no way able to relieve it: and how it was buried by the heathen in the wilderness, from among all Christians. We were hurried up and down in our thoughts; sometimes we should hear a report that they were gone this way, and sometimes that: and that they were come in, in this place or that: we kept inquiring and listening to hear concerning them, but no certain news as yet. About this time the Council had ordered a day of public thanksgiving: though I thought I had still cause of mourning; and being unsettled in our minds, we thought we would ride toward the eastward, to see if we could hear anything concerning our children. And as we were riding along (God is the wise disposer of all things) between Ipswich and Rowley we met with Mr. William Hubbard, who told us our son Joseph was come in to Major Waldren's and another with him, which was my sister's son. I asked him how he knew it? He said, the Major himself told him so. So along we went till we came to Newbury; and their minister being absent, they desired my husband to preach the thanksgiving for them; but he was not willing to stay there that night, but would go over to Salisbury, to hear farther, and come again in the morning; which he did, and preached there that day. At night, when he had done, one came and told him that his daughter was come in at Providence: here was mercy on both hands: Now hath God fulfilled that precious scripture, which was such a comfort to me in my distressed condition. When my heart was ready to sink into the earth (my children being gone I could not tell whither) and my knees trembled under me,

---

[34] Either Hezekiah or John Usher, merchants in Boston. The Cambridge 1682 version of the text reads, "gentlemen."

and I was walking through the valley of the shadow of death [Ps. 23:4]: then the Lord brought, and now has fulfilled that reviving word unto me: *Thus saith the Lord, Refrain thy voice from weeping, and thine eyes from tears, for thy work shall be rewarded, saith the Lord, and they shall come again from the land of the enemy* [Jer. 31:16]. Now we were between them, the one on the east, and the other on the west: our son being nearest, we went to him first, to Portsmouth, where we met with him, and with the Major also: who told us he had done what he could, but could not redeem him under seven pounds; which the good people thereabouts were pleased to pay. The Lord reward the Major, and all the rest, though unknown to me, for their labor of love. My sister's son was redeemed for four pounds, which the Council gave order for the payment of. Having now received one of our children, we hastened toward the other: going back through Newbury, my husband preached there on the Sabbath day: for which they rewarded him manifold.

On Monday we came to Charlestown, where we heard that the governor of Rhode Island had sent over for our daughter, to take care of her, being now within his jurisdiction: which should not pass without our acknowledgments. But she being nearer Rehoboth than Rhode Island, Mr. Newman[35] went over, and took care of her, and brought her to his own house. And the goodness of God was admirable to us in our low estate; in that he raised up compassionate friends on every side to us; when we had nothing to recompense any for their love. The Indians were now gone that way, that it was apprehended dangerous to go to her: but the carts which carried provision to the English army, being guarded, brought her with them to Dorchester, where we received her safe: blessed be the Lord for it, for *great is his power, and he can do whatsoever seemeth him good.* Her coming in was after this manner: she was traveling one day with the Indians, with her basket at her back: the company of Indians were got before her, and gone out of sight, all except one squaw: she followed the squaw till night, and then both of them lay down, having nothing over them but the heavens, nor under them but the earth. Thus she traveled three days together, not knowing whither she was going: having nothing to eat or drink but water, and green hirtleberries. At last they came into Providence, where she was kindly entertained by several of that town. The Indians often said, that I should never have her under twenty pounds: but now the Lord hath brought her in upon free cost, and given her to me the second time. The Lord make us a blessing indeed, each to others. Now have I seen that scripture also fulfilled, Deut. 30:4–7, *If any of thine be driven out to the*

---

[35] Noah Newman, minister in Rehoboth.

outmost parts of heaven, from thence will the Lord thy God gather thee, and from thence will he fetch thee. And the Lord thy God will put all these curses upon thine enemies, and on them which hate thee, which persecuted thee. Thus hath the Lord brought me and mine out of that horrible pit, and hath set us in the midst of tender-hearted and compassionate Christians. 'Tis the desire of my soul that we may walk worthy of the mercies received, and which we are receiving.

Our family being now gathered together (those of us that were living) the South Church in Boston hired an house for us: then we removed from Mr. Shepard's (those cordial friends) and went to Boston, where we continued about three quarters of a year: Still the Lord went along with us, and provided graciously for us. I thought it somewhat strange to set up housekeeping with bare walls; but, as Solomon says, *Money answers all things* [Eccles. 10:19]: and that we had through the benevolence of Christian friends, some in this town, and some in that, and others, and some from England, that in a little time we might look, and see the house furnished with love. The Lord hath been exceeding good to us in our low estate, in that when we had neither house nor home, nor other necessaries, the Lord so moved the hearts of these and those towards us, that we wanted neither food, nor raiment for ourselves or ours, Prov. 18:24, *There is a friend which sticketh closer than a brother.* And how many such friends have we found, and now living amongst! and truly such a friend have we found him to be unto us, in whose house we lived, viz. Mr. James Whitcomb, a friend unto us near hand, and afar off.

I can remember the time, when I used to sleep quietly without workings in my thoughts, whole nights together: but now it is otherwise with me. When all are fast about me, and no eye open, but his who ever waketh, my thoughts are upon things past, upon the awful dispensations of the Lord towards us: upon his wonderful power and might in carrying of us through so many difficulties, in returning us in safety, and suffering none to hurt us. I remember in the night season, how the other day I was in the midst of thousands of enemies, and nothing but death before me: it was then hard work to persuade myself, that ever I should be satisfied with bread again. But now we are fed with the finest of the wheat, and (as I may say) with *honey out of the rock* [Ps. 81:16]: instead of the husk, we have the fatted calf: the thoughts of these things in the particulars of them, and of the love and goodness of God towards us, make it true of me, what David said of himself, Ps. 6:6, *I watered my couch with my tears.* Oh the wonderful power of God that mine eyes have seen, affording matter enough for my thoughts to run in, that when others are sleeping mine eyes are weeping.

I have seen the extreme vanity of this world: one hour I have been in health, and wealth, wanting nothing: but the next hour in sickness, and wounds, and death, having nothing but sorrow and affliction.

Before I knew what affliction meant, I was ready sometimes to wish for it. When I lived in prosperity, having the comforts of this world about me, my relations by me, and my heart cheerful: and taking little care for any thing; and yet seeing many (whom I preferred before myself) under many trials and afflictions, in sickness, weakness, poverty, losses, crosses, and cares of the world, I should be sometimes jealous lest I should have my portion in this life, and that scripture would come to my mind, Heb. 12:6, *For whom the Lord loveth he chasteneth, and scourgeth every son whom he receiveth*: but now I see the Lord had his time to scourge and chasten me. The portion of some is to have their affliction by drops, now one drop and then another: but the dregs of the cup, the wine of astonishment, like a sweeping rain that leaveth no food, did the Lord prepare to be my portion. Affliction I wanted, and affliction I had, full measure (I thought) pressed down and running over: yet I see when God calls a person to anything, and through never so many difficulties, yet he is fully able to carry them through, and make them see and say they have been gainers thereby. And I hope I can say in some measure, as David did, *It is good for me that I have been afflicted* [Ps. 119:71]. The Lord hath shewed me the vanity of these outward things, that they are the vanity of vanities, and vexation of spirit; that they are but a shadow, a blast, a bubble, and things of no continuance; that we must rely on God himself, and our whole dependence must be upon him. If trouble from smaller matters begin to arise in me, I have something at hand to check myself with, and say, why am I troubled? It was but the other day, that if I had had the world, I would have given it for my freedom, or to have been a servant to a Christian. I have learned to look beyond present and smaller troubles, and to be quieted under them, as Moses said, Exod. 14:13, *Stand still and see the salvation of the Lord*.

Source: Mary Rowlandson, *The Sovereignty & Goodness of God* (based on the London printing of 1682, but modified in some accidentals). The many variations between printings are analyzed in Diebold (1972), who also provides more extensive annotation.

PART VII

Errand into the Wilderness

Errand into the Wilderness

The colonists relied on the Bible for understanding contemporary events. From it they learned that God had a master plan for history, to culminate in the return of Christ to earth and the restoration of his kingdom. The question the colonists asked themselves again and again was the same question Christians have asked since the days of the apostles: when will the history of redemption reach its end, as foretold in Scripture? No less urgently, the colonists wondered whether their "errand into the wilderness" had any special significance within God's master plan.

To understand how the colonists answered these questions we must return to the Protestant Reformation of the sixteenth century. The Reformers believed that their revolt against Catholicism fulfilled certain prophecies in Scripture. More specifically, some argued that it portended the overthrow of the Antichrist. Who or what was the Antichrist? Mentioned in the epistles of John as "deceivers" who deny that Christ was the Messiah,[1] the Antichrist was regarded by many Reformers as identical with the pope in Rome and the entire apparatus of Catholicism. The Antichrist was forever warring against the true church, a struggle the Reformers regarded as being resumed in their own quarrel with Rome. Exegetically, these Protestants linked the Pope with the "deceivers" of 1 John, the "Beast" evoked in Revelation 13, and the "Man of Sin" of 2 Thessalonians 2.[2] The Separatist Pilgrims carried these identifications one step further, identifying the Antichrist with the bishops of the Church of England who persecuted the remnant of saints (Bradford in chap. 1).

[1] 2 John 1:7, For many deceivers are entered into the world, men who confess not that Jesus Christ is come in the flesh. This is a deceiver and an antichrist. 1 John 2:18, ". . . as ye have heard that antichrist shall come, even now there are many antichrists; whereby we shall know it is the last time."

[2] Hill (1971), chap. 1; Christianson (1978), 9.

Scripture posed another challenge, how to interpret the thousand years ("millennium") described in the concluding book of the New Testament, Revelation. Did the Bible provide reliable clues as to when the millennium or another crucial event, the triumph of the saints at Armageddon, would occur? John Cotton, who preached on the end times in Boston in 1639–1640, accepted the end-times theory of the English theologian Thomas Brightman (d. 1607), who divided the resurrection of Christ at his Second Coming into two phases, a purely "spiritual" phase or "Middle Advent," a thousand-year period when the saints would reign, followed by Armageddon and the Second Coming, when all the dead would rise and the kingdom of Christ be fully established. Brightman took the daring step of connecting these events with his own times and the near future, thus contradicting a long-lasting exegetical tradition that placed the millennium in the past. Specifically, he argued that the Middle Advent had been initiated in the mid–sixteenth century with the reign of Elizabeth I, a step that allowed him to locate the triumph of the saints at the close of the seventeenth century.

Only if we heed these distinctions can we read Cotton's sermons as he intended them to be read. He too was speaking of a phase that preceded the fullness of the end times, a season of greater purity or "reformation" that fell short of the perfection of Christ's kingdom. Cotton also relied, as did Brightman, on the historical framework of Christian primitivism. Primitivists believed that the "first times" or "first beginnings" of the Christian church, the apostolic period, had established the normative pattern for the true church. When this pattern became corrupted with "humane inventions," which Protestant primitivists accused Catholics of having introduced into Christianity, it was imperative to restore the "purity" of the first times by cleansing the church of all such corruptions. The colonists regarded the "Congregational Way" they had created in the 1630s as doing exactly this — that is, restoring the ministry and sacraments and other rituals to their "lawful" form as designated in the New Testament. In sermons from the 1670s by Samuel Danforth and Increase Mather that follow, Christian primitivism reappears as the rationale for extolling the "errand" of the founders and lamenting "declension." Puritan radicals also relied on primitivism; Roger Williams was emphatically a primitivist, as were John Clarke and the early Baptists, who regarded the rite of infant baptism as a "humane invention."[3]

But the most pervasive framework for understanding history as embodying God's purposes was in terms of providence and covenant. The doctrine of providence is the assertion that God directs (governs) every-

[3] Bozeman (1988); Gilpin (1979).

thing that happens; a providential world is one without chance, luck, or fortune. For the godly, providence is always in the end a good thing, though even the saints are not spared adversity as part of God's plan for them, as Mary Rowlandson learned the hard way (chap. 26). Bradford celebrated God's providence in enabling the Pilgrims to overcome their enemies and survive in the "wilderness" of the New World; the founders of Massachusetts celebrated the safe passage of so many ships and victories over dangerous foes such as the Pequots; and John Winthrop recorded every possible indication of a favoring providence in the pages of his journal-history of New England.

Yet as Winthrop sometimes had to admit, God's intentions were not always easy to understand. Was God using "remarkable" providences such as comets, great storms, sudden deaths, sicknesses, droughts, and war to warn the colonists that they were not living up to their covenant with him? Could these events signify that he was punishing them for their sins, or perhaps on the verge of casting them off? As early as the 1640s some ministers were interpreting certain events in this vein and calling on the colonists to repent. The chief means of doing so was to stage a ritual known as the fast day. Dozens of fast days were held in New England, many of them designated by a colonial government, others by churches or towns.[4] By the 1660s and 1670s, the search for the meaning of providence and pleas to repent were intensifying as the second generation came of age and as conflicts among the colonists multiplied. Near the close of the century, Increase Mather's son Cotton (1663–1728) proposed that the outbreak of witchcraft in Salem Village was a sign of Satan's wrath as the end times approached. Yet even as the Mathers were voicing this apocalypticism and employing the traditional language of prodigies and "wonders," the scientific revolution of the late seventeenth century was beginning to curtail some of the possibilities for prophetic interpretation.

Using Scripture to understand the meaning of their own times involved the colonists in a method of interpretation known as typology. According to this method, "events, personages, ceremonies, and objects" in the Old Testament "foreshadow" and are "fulfilled . . . in Christ."[5] That is, the two parts of the Bible, "type" and "anti-type," are really one, united thematically and structurally around the fulfilling of prophecy: Christ's coming is anticipated in the Old Testament and completed in the New. The colonists extended this method of reading Scripture to the history of the Christian church, as Anne Hutchinson did in associating herself with Daniel in the lion's den (chap. 21). Despite what

[4] Bosco (1978); Love (1895) on fasts and thanksgivings.
[5] Lewalski (1979); quoted in Morrissey (2000), 49.

has been said by some modern historians, most English Protestants and the colonists limited the meaning of type to the church (the saints, or the elect) and did not extend it to encompass society (nation) as a whole.[6] Cotton's sermons refer to the church universal, not to nation or colony. Like others before them, however, the ministers in New England drew lavishly on Scripture, especially Deuteronomy, for the concept of a national covenant in which the colonists were participating. Assuming, too, that other Christian groups before them had been in covenant, they were constantly comparing events and situations in their own times with episodes in the history of Christianity. This covenantal framework allowed them to speak as though the colonies were a new Israel and to assume that events and situations in their own day were replays of previous episodes in Christian history. These comparisons may be characterized as "examples" as distinct from "types," the major difference being that examples did not directly recapitulate salvation history.[7]

Bibliography

The essential starting point is Bozeman (1988), together with Hill (1971), Christianson (1978), and Firth (1979). On the Mathers, Middlekauff (1971); Cogley (1999) is authoritative on Eliot. On providence, covenant, and the jeremiad: Bozeman (1988), chaps. 9–10; Stout (1986) on providence and covenant; Hall (1989), chap. 2, on prophecy and providence. Earlier studies should be treated with caution: Miller (1956); Bercovitch (1975); Bercovitch (1978). The emigrants' confusion is underlined in Delbanco (1989). See also Zakai (1994) and Bremer (1992), reviewing the issues. On the English side, Lamont (1969) and Walsham (1999), a magisterial study of providence.

[6] Christianson (1978), chap. 1, correcting Haller (1963) on "elect nation."
[7] Morrissey (2000), 43–59.

Chapter 27

John Cotton on the Millennium

The concluding book of the New Testament, Revelation or the "Apocalypse to John," opens with John declaring that Christ has shown him "things which must shortly come to pass." There follows an unfolding of "things which must be hereafter," many of them calamities, like the slaying of martyrs. Finally, however, John is assured that the martyrs will reign with Christ, although not until Satan and his agents cause further conflict that ends when Satan is cast into a pit, where he remains for a thousand years and Christ's kingdom flourishes (the millennium). Breaking free once again, Satan wages one last battle before he is defeated forever. The saints enter "a new heaven and a new earth," the holy city Jerusalem, which descends from heaven. The heavenly city is theirs to rule, in perfect obedience to Christ.

This vision of the triumph of the saints and martyrs at the "end times" has persistently comforted religious movements or communities that were being persecuted, as undoubtedly it comforted the earliest Christians when they suffered persecution and martyrdom. But after Christianity became established and then Reformed, the question arose, had the millennium already occurred? For most orthodox Protestants in the sixteenth century the answer was yes. The early-seventeenth-century English minister Thomas Brightman argued, however, that the millennium was yet to be accomplished. Relying especially on the reference in 2 Thessalonians 2:8 to the "Brightness of his coming," Brightman divided the return of Christ into two phases, both of which lay ahead: the first in brightness, when an extraordinary recovery of the true church would occur, and a second, his personal coming when the dead would be raised and ordinary history come to an end.

Brightman was therefore a "millenarian" who anticipated glorious times for the Christian church—from his perspective, a church purged of all "popery" and organized according to the principles of Puritanism. John Cotton came under Brightman's influence and preached a series of sermons in Boston in 1639–1640 that reproduce the core elements of Brightman's scheme. Great things are being accomplished, Cotton argues, as the Christian church enters a "new reformation" when both "outward" and "inward" change will occur. Cotton celebrates the Congregational churches in New England, with their membership of visible saints; here, he tells the colonists, we have "a greater face of reformation" than anywhere else. Yet he also warns against complacency, for the "first resurrection" is not yet complete. Never does he identify New England as the site of the New Jerusalem. Not until the end of the century, with the two Mathers, Increase and Cotton, and a few others, did millennialism reemerge as an important theme, though shorn of most of its radical possibilities.

Bibliography

Bozeman (1988), chaps. 6 and 7, noting much abuse of the term "millennial"; Cogley (1999), chap. 1; Middlekauff (1971).

JOHN COTTON

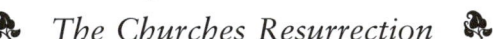 *The Churches Resurrection*

Rev. 20:5–6: But the rest of the dead lived not again, until the thousand years were finished: This is the first resurrection, etc.

These words are an amplification of the estate of the martyrs and confessors of Jesus after the destruction of Antichrist and Rome. . . .

[On When the Thousand-Years Rule by Saints Begins]

. . . Yet hitherto it is not given to the saints to rule. These thousand years therefore do most properly begin from the throwing down of Antichrist and the destruction of Rome; the Lord will then send such powerful ministers into the church, that by the power of the keys they shall take hold on Satan, that is to say, convince him and his instruments of all popish, and paganish religion and bind him by the chain that is to say the strong chain of God's ordinances Word and sacraments and censures . . . : So they shall restrain Satan for a thousand years after Antichrist is down: And in that time . . . men of the same spirit . . . shall reign in the church and have the judicature and government of the church together with these angels or messengers and ministers of God, . . . they shall execute spiritual judgment according to the will of Christ, *for a thousand years*: So that those that were branded before for Huguenots, and Lollards,[1] and heretics, they shall be thought the only men to be fit to have crowns upon their heads and independent government committed to them, together with the angels . . . Now in opposition to this, *The rest of the dead* (saith the text) *lived not again*, that is to say, the profest Catholics and wicked enemies of the church, they rose not again, either in their persons, or successors, that is to say, there was no room for any such to trouble the church any more, *till the thousand years should be fulfilled*, and then Satan shall trouble the world as much as before, though but for a season. . . .

Doctrine 1. First, that such nations and peoples as are not renewed, and restored in the first resurrection, upon the destruction of Antichrist and the ruin of Rome, they shall not recover the like liberty, either of reformation of themselves, or of persecution of the churches, for a thousand years after. . . .

Use 1. The use of this point is first a serious and strong warning unto all the people of God that shall live when Antichrist shall be abolished, and Rome ruinated: Take heed how you slip such opportunities of turning unto God: If men grow not more sincere and pure in seeking after God (whether they be public states or private persons): If men be not brought on, but will stand out such glorious reformation then, and such powerful providences then; if men stand out then, and not be awakened, it is to be feared they will not be awakened (nor men of their spirits) for a thousand years together.

You know what is done in our native country. . . . They live in their hypocrisy, in their ignorance and dote upon the Episcopacy, and in their hearts undermine all reformation as much as in them lies. . . . And let it be a warning to us also, forasmuch as we see the vanity of episcopacy, and all the inventions and usurpations of the sons of men, and plantations God hath not planted: God may bear with us a while, but if we be not brought on to this resurrection when we see these things before our eyes, and have all stumbling-blocks removed out of our ways that may hinder our reformation, and regeneration; if we do not now strike a fast covenant with our God to be his people, if we do not now abandon whatsoever savors of death in the world, of death in lust and passion, then we and ours will be of this dead hearted frame for a thousand years. . . .

[In the "first resurrection"] . . . So it was with churches; they had a time to be established by the apostles, and such as they appointed: afterward they grew to a dead frame. . . . And as they had a time of dying, that is to say, of deformation, of apostasy by the Catholic mother church, so afterward they came to a new reformation such a reforma-

---

[1] A proto-Protestant movement in fifteenth-century England, condemned as a heresy.

tion as doth not only reform the outward face of government in the church, and the outward face of worship and doctrine, but the inward frame of the members of the church, that they are reformed by a regenerating power; they arise from a state of formality to the power of godliness. . . .

But you will say, were not the churches reformed in the times of Luther, and Calvin, and Bucer, etc. in Germany, and England, and Scotland, etc. hath there not been a notable resurrection of churches then?

It is a difficult objection, I confess, but I shall leave it to your further consideration and shall tell you what I think the text holds forth: It is such a reformation as much deadness lies upon it to this day. This reformation is not risen to such a resurrection as the Holy Ghost should call it a resurrection if you speak of the churches . . . are not the greater part of the members (I reproach none) . . . dead in trespasses and sins? If you walk all through England (for aught I know) you will find a dead frame of the generality of church members.[2] If that be the state of their spirits, then wonder not, if the Holy Ghost say not they are come to their resurrection. . . .

For the use of this point, it is a strong warning to our churches here, that we be not deceived in our reformation, and deceived in our rules by which it is carried, for I am clear in that, and so I think are most of us, and it is our sins if we be not. That our reformation and rules of it are of God, neither do I doubt of the resurrection of many choice Christians throughout the country (the Lord increase their number). But I am afraid there is more reformation than resurrection. Therefore it is a holy warning from heaven to attend resurrection here also; here is a great reformation of churches, I think I may speak it without vanity and vainglory, and puffing up of the hearts of the sons of men, a greater face of reformation than in any churches are to be found: But this first resurrection in my text the first of these years is not begun. . . . Therefore let not New England be secure, and bless ourselves in our resurrection, because we have our part in this reformation. . . .

Source: John Cotton, *The Churches Resurrection, or the Opening of the Fifth and sixth verses of the 20th Chap. of the Revelation* (London, 1642), 1–21.

[2] Cotton also cited the churches of Germany and Scotland as suffering from deadness.

Chapter 28

Edward Johnson on New England's Newfound Prosperity

Even though the colonists imagined themselves living as pilgrims in a fallen world and lamented the symptoms of worldliness (see Bradford, chap. 1), they welcomed the economic prosperity that became visible by the second half of the 1640s. Properly understood, prosperity was a sign of God's favor and therefore something to celebrate. The lay historian Edward Johnson did so in *The Wonder-working Providence of Sions Saviour in New-England* (London, 1654 [1653]). Yet the colonists remained ambivalent about prosperity, as when the minister John Norton (1606–1663) warned that "the Glory is departed" if the colonists forget that "Originally they are a Plantation Religious, not a plantation of Trade," although simultaneously noting how "this vast Jeshenon" had been "converted into Corn-fields Orchards, streets inhabited, and a place of Merchandize."[1] Johnson (1599–1672), a person of means, arrived in Massachusetts in 1630, returned almost immediately to England, came back in 1636, and in 1642 moved to the town of Woburn, which he served in various public offices. Writing with an English audience in mind, and mixing the apocalyptic and the realistic, he described the civil and religious history of Massachusetts town by town while also noting events like the Antinomian controversy.

Bibliography

William Frederick Poole's introduction to *Wonder-working Providence* (repr., Andover, Mass., 1867); Sweet (2002); Gallagher and Werge (1976).

---

[1] John Norton, *The heart of N-England Rent* (Cambridge, Mass., 1659), 58.

EDWARD JOHNSON

🦋 *Wonder-working Providence of Sions Saviour* 🦋 *in New-England*

Of the Lord's wonder-working providence, in fitting
this people with all kind of manufactures, and the
bringing of them into the order of a commonwealth.

. . . [T]he Lord is pleased also to complete this commonwealth abundantly beyond all expectation in all sorts of needful occupations, it being for a long time the great fear of many, and those that were endued
with grace from above also, that this would be no place of continued
habitation, for want of a staple-commodity, but the Lord, whose promises are large to his Sion, hath blest his people's provision, and satisfied
her poor with bread, in a very little space, every thing in the country
proved a staple-commodity, wheat, rye, oats, peas, barley, beef, pork,
fish, butter, cheese, timber, mast, tar, soap, plank-board frames of houses,
clapboard, and pipe staves, iron and lead is like to be also; and those
who were formerly forced to fetch most of the bread they eat, and beer
they drink a hundred leagues by sea, are through the blessing of the
Lord so increased, that they have not only fed their elder sisters, Virginia, Barbados, and many of the Summer Islands that were preferred
before her for fruitfulness, but also the grandmother of us all, even the
fertile isle of Great Britain, beside Portugal hath had many a mouthful
of bread and fish from us, in exchange of their Madeira liquor, and also
Spain; nor could it be imagined, that this wilderness should turn a mart
for merchants in so short a space, Holland, France, Spain, and Portugal
coming hither for trade, shipping going on gallantly, till the seas became
so troublesome, and England restrained our trade, forbidding it with
Barbados, etc.[2] and Portugal stopped and took our ships; many a fair
ship had her framing and finishing here, besides lesser vessels, barques,
and ketches, many a master, beside common seamen, had their first
learning in this colony. Boston, Charlestown, Salem, and Ipswich, our
maritime towns began to increase roundly, especially Boston, the which
of a poor country village, in twice seven years is become like unto a
small city, and is in election to be mayor town suddenly,[3] chiefly increased by trade by sea . . . nor hath this colony alone been actors in
this trade of venturing by sea, but New Haven also, who were many of

---

[2] Because Barbados remained in the hands of Royalists after Charles I was executed,
Parliament in 1650 prohibited trade with the island.

[3] In 1650 Boston petitioned the General Court, unsuccessfully, to become an incorporated town.

them well experienced in traffic, and had good estates to manage it, Connecticut did not linger behind, but put forth to sea with the other; all other trades have here fallen into their ranks and places, to their great advantage; especially coopers and shoemakers, who had either of them a corporation granted, enriching themselves by their trades very much, coopers having their plenty of stuff at a cheap rate, and by reason of trade, with foreign parts abundance of work, as for tanners and shoemakers, it being naturalized into these occupations, to have a higher reach in managing their manufactures, than other men in N. E. are, having not changed their nature in this, between them both they have kept men to their stander hitherto, almost doubling the price of their commodities, according to the rate they were sold for in England, and yet the plenty of leather is beyond what they had, their counting the number of the people, but the transportation of boots and shoes into foreign parts hath vented all however: as for tailors, they have not come behind the former, their advantage being in the nurture of new fashions, all one with England; carpenters, joiners, glaziers, painters, follow their trades only; gunsmiths, locksmiths, blacksmiths, nailors, cutlers, have left the husbandmen to follow the plow and cart, and they their trades, weavers, brewers, bakers, costermongers, felt makers, braziers, pewterers, and tinkers, rope makers, masons, lime, brick, and tile makers, card makers[4] to work, and not to play, turners, pump makers, and wheelers, glovers, fellmongers, and furriers, are orderly turned to their trades, besides divers sorts of shopkeepers, and some who have a mystery beyond others, as have the vintners.

Thus hath the Lord been pleased to turn one of the most hideous, boundless, and unknown wildernesses in the world in an instant, as 'twere (in comparison of other work) to a well-ordered commonwealth, and all to serve his churches. . . .

Source: Edward Johnson, *The Wonder-working Providence of Sions Saviour in New-England*; the title page reads [anon.], *A History of New-England* (London, 1654), 207–10.

[4] Metal combs or cards for straightening wool.

Chapter 29

Samuel Danforth on Errand and Decline

Election-day sermons, preached annually in Connecticut and Massachusetts at the spring Court of Election, rapidly became a central ritual in the civil culture of early New England. Little is known of their contents before they began to be published in the 1660s. Some of these sermons were "jeremiads," so named by the literary historian Perry Miller. Organized around a "dialectic of decline and recovery,"[1] the jeremiad described a declining present contrasted with a better past, the days of the "fathers," and prophesied a better future to come. Recalling the original "errand," as jeremiads of the 1670s commonly did, was a means of rebuking the "present generation" for its sins. Itemizing the signs and causes of decline, the election-day preacher urged everyone, including the civil government, to resume the work of reformation in order to spare the colonists from further judgments. Such sermons complement and, indeed, anticipate *The Necessity of Reformation* issued by the synod of 1679 (see chap. 19).

How did the jeremiads and contemporary histories like Nathaniel Morton's *New-Englands Memoriall* (1669) characterize the "errand" of the emigrants? One way of answering this question is to note that the second-generation ministers who preached most of the jeremiads were struggling to make sense of three related circumstances: the collapse of magisterial Puritanism in England after the restoration of Charles II to the throne in 1660; the transition from emigrants who knew what it was like to be in the minority to a generation that grew up in a culture dominated by Puritan values; and the shrinking of the colonists' horizon of expectations. The founders had assumed that they were participating in the overthrow of the Antichrist and the restoration of the primitive church, but the second generation had to wonder if anyone on the other side of the Atlantic cared about the "Congregational Way."

The glowing picture these sermons paint of the first generation should be seen as a function of the confusion affecting the second. Historians have emphasized the prophetic and visionary qualities of the election-day sermons, arguing that, consistent with the "Deuteronomic formula"

[1] Miller (1953), 31.

found in the Old Testament (God warns a people, who humble them-selves and regain God's favor), these narratives of decline also contain a hugely optimistic promise of greater things to come should the colonists respond and renew their covenant.

Samuel Danforth, in his election sermon of 1670, *A Brief Recognition of New-England's Errand into the Wilderness,* catalogues the "decays and languishings" of the colonists more fully than anyone before him, decrying, in particular, the "eager pursuit . . . of private business."[2] Danforth (1626–1674) arrived in Massachusetts with his high-status father Nicholas in 1634. Educated at Harvard College, he joined John Eliot in 1650 as cominister in Roxbury.

Bibliography

Miller (1953), chap. 2; Miller (1956), chap. 1; Bercovitch (1975, 1978), empha-sizing, contrary to Miller, the optimism of the sermons; Middlekauff (1971) on the "invention of New England" (chap. 6); Bosco (1978), correcting Miller on genres and themes; Bozeman (1988); Stout (1986).

SAMUEL DANFORTH

❧ *A Brief Recognition of New-England's Errand* ❧ *into the Wilderness*

> *Matt. 11:7–9: What went ye out into the wilderness to see? A reed shaken with the wind? But what went ye out for to see? A man clothed in soft raiment? behold, they that wear soft clothing, are in kings' houses. But what went ye out for to see? A prophet? yea, I say unto you, and more than a prophet. . . .*

Doctrine. Such as have sometime left their pleasant cities and habita-tions to enjoy the pure worship of God in a wilderness, are apt in time to abate and cool in their affection thereunto: but then the Lord calls upon them seriously and thoroughly to examine themselves, what it was that drew them into the wilderness, and to consider that it was not the expectation of ludicrous levity, nor of courtly pomp and delicacy, but of the free and clear dispensation of the gospel and kingdom of God. . . .

Use 1. Of solemn and serious inquiry to us all in this general assem-bly, whether we have not in a great measure forgotten our errand into the wilderness. You have solemnly professed before God, angels and

---

[2] Bosco (1978), 1:xliii–lxiv.

men, that the cause of your leaving your country, kindred, and fathers' houses, and transporting yourselves with your wives, little ones and substance over the vast ocean into this waste and howling wilderness, was your liberty to walk in the faith of the gospel with all good conscience according to the order of the gospel, and your enjoyment of the pure worship of God according to his institution, without human mixtures and impositions. Now let us sadly consider whether our ancient and primitive affections to the Lord Jesus, his glorious gospel, his pure and spiritual worship and the order of his house, remain, abide and continue firm, constant, entire and inviolate. . . .

In our first and best times the kingdom of heaven brake in upon us with a holy violence, and every man pressed into it. What mighty efficacy and power had the clear and faithful dispensation of the gospel upon your hearts? How affectionately and zealously did you entertain the kingdom of God? How careful were you, even all sorts, young and old, high and low, to take hold of the opportunities of your spiritual good and edification? ordering your secular affairs (which were wreathed and twisted together with great variety) so as not to interfere with your general calling, but that you might *attend upon the Lord without distraction.* How diligent and faithful in preparing your hearts for the reception of the Word, laying apart all filthiness and superfluity of naughtiness, that you might receive with meekness the engrafted Word, which is able to save your souls; and purging out all malice, guile, hypocrisies, envies, and all evil speakings, and *as new-born babes, desiring the sincere milk of the Word, that ye might grow thereby* [1 Pet. 2:1–2] How attentive in hearing the everlasting gospel, watching daily at the gates of wisdom, and waiting at the posts of her doors, that ye might find eternal life, and obtain favor of the Lord? Gleaning day by day in the fields of God's ordinances, even among the sheaves, and gathering up handfuls, which the Lord let fall of purpose for you [Ruth 2:17], and at night going home and beating out what you had gleaned, by meditation, repetition, conference, and therewith feeding yourselves and your families. How painful were you in recollecting, repeating and discoursing of what you heard, whetting the Word of God upon the hearts of your children, servants and neighbors? How fervent in prayer to Almighty God for his divine blessing upon the seed sown, that it might take root and fructify? O what a reverent esteem had you in those days of Christ's faithful ambassadors, that declared unto you the Word of reconciliation! *How beautiful were the feet of them, that preached the gospel of peace, and brought the glad tidings of salvation* [Rom. 10:15]! you esteemed them highly in love for their works' sake. Their persons, names and comforts were precious in your eyes; you counted yourselves blessed in the enjoyment of a pious, learned and orthodox ministry: and

though you ate the bread of adversity and drank the water of affliction,
yet you rejoiced in this, *that your eyes saw your teachers,* they were not
removed into corners, and *your ears heard a word behind you, saying,
This is the way, walk ye in it, when you turned to the right hand and
when you turned to the left,* Isa. 30:20–21. What earnest and ardent
desires had you in those days after communion with Christ in the holy
sacraments? With desire you desired to partake of the seals of the covenant. You thought your evidences for heaven not sure nor authentic,
unless the broad seals of the kingdom were annexed. What solicitude
was there in those days to seek the Lord after the right order? What
searching of the holy scriptures, what collations among your leaders,
both in their private meetings and public councils and synods, to find
out the order, which Christ hath constituted and established in his
house? What fervent zeal was there then against sectaries and heretics,
and all manner of heterodoxies? . . . What holy endeavors were there in
those days to propagate religion to your children and posterity, training
them up in the nurture and admonition of the Lord, keeping them under the awe of government, restraining their enormities and extravagan-
cies; charging them to know the God of their fathers, and serve him
with a perfect heart and willing mind; and publicly asserting and maintaining their interest in the Lord and in his holy covenant, and zealously
opposing those that denied the same? . . .

But who is there left among you, that saw these churches in their first
glory, and how do you see them now? Are they not in your eyes in
comparison thereof, as nothing? *How is the gold become dim! how is
the most fine gold changed* [Lam. 4:1]! Is not the temper, complexion
and countenance of the churches strangely altered? Doth not a careless,
remiss, flat, dry, cold, dead frame of spirit, grow in upon us secretly,
strongly, prodigiously? They that have ordinances, are as though they
had none; and they that hear the Word, as though they heard it not; and
they that pray, as though they prayed not; and they that receive sacraments, as though they received them not; and they that are exercised in
the holy things, using them by the by, as matters of custom and ceremony, so as not to hinder their eager prosecution of other things which
their hearts are set upon. Yea and in some particular congregations
amongst us, is there not instead of a sweet smell, a stink? and instead of
a girdle, a rent? and instead of a stomacher, a girding with sackcloth?
and burning instead of beauty? yea the vineyard is *all overgrown with
thorns, and nettles cover the face thereof, and the stone wall thereof is
broken down,* Prov. 24:31. Yea, and that which is the most sad and
certain sign of calamity approaching, *iniquity aboundeth, and the love
of many waxeth cold,* Matt. 24:12. Pride, contention, worldliness, covetousness, luxury, drunkenness and uncleanness break in like a flood

upon us, and good men grow cold in their love to God and to one another. . . . What then is the cause of our decays and languishings? . . .

The ground and principal cause is our unbelief: We believe not the grace and power of God in Christ. Where is that lively exercise of faith, which ought to be, in our attendance upon the Lord in his holy ordinances? Christ came to Nazareth with his heart full of love and compassion, and his hands full of blessings to bestow upon his old acquaintance and neighbors, among whom he had been brought up, but their unbelief restrained his tender mercies, and bound his omnipotent hands, that he could not do any great or illustrious miracle amongst them. Matt. 13:58, Mark. 6:5–6. *He could do there no mighty work — and he marveled because of their unbelief.* Unbelief straitens the grace and power of Christ, and hinders the communication of divine favors and special mercies. *The Word preached profits not, when it is not mixed with faith in them that hear it*, Heb. 4:2. We may pray earnestly, but if we ask not in faith, how can we expect *to receive anything of the Lord?* James 1:6–7.

But though unbelief be the principal, yet it is not the sole cause of our decays and languishings: Inordinate worldly cares, predominant lusts, and malignant passions and distempers stifle and choke the Word, and quench our affections to the kingdom of God, Luke 8:14. The manna was gathered early in the morning, *when the sun waxed hot, it melted*, Exod. 16:21. It was a fearful judgment on Dathan and Abiram, that the earth opened its mouth and swallowed them up. How many professors of religion, are swallowed up alive by earthly affections? Such as escape the lime-pit of pharisaical hypocrisy, fall into the coal-pit of Sadducean atheism and epicurism. Pharisaism and Sadduceism do almost divide the professing world between them. Some split upon the rock of affected ostentation of singular piety and holiness, and others are drawn into the whirlpool, and perish in the gulf of sensuality and luxury. . . .

To what purpose then came we into the wilderness, and what expectation drew us hither? Was it not the expectation of the pure and faithful dispensation of the gospel and kingdom of God? The times were such that we could not enjoy it in our own land: and therefore having obtained liberty and a gracious patent from our sovereign, we left our country, kindred and fathers' houses, and came into these wild woods and deserts; where the Lord hath *planted us, and made us dwell in a place of our own, that we might move no more, and that the children of wickedness might not assist us anymore*, 2 Sam. 7:10. What is it that distinguisheth New England from other colonies and plantations in America? Not our transportation over the Atlantic Ocean, but the ministry of God's faithful prophets, and the fruition of his holy ordinances. . . .

How sadly hath the Lord testified against us, because of our loss of our first love, and our remissness and negligence in his work? Why hath the Lord smitten us with blasting and mildew now seven years together, superadding sometimes severe drought, sometimes great tempests, floods, and sweeping rains, that leave no food behind them? Is it not because the Lord's house lieth waste? Temple-work in our hearts, families, churches is shamefully neglected? What should I make mention of signs in the heavens and in the earth, blazing-stars,[3] earthquakes, dreadful thunders and lightnings, fearful burnings? What meaneth the heat of his great anger, in calling home so many of his ambassadors? In plucking such burning and shining lights out of the candlesticks; the principal stakes out of our hedges; the corner-stones out of our walls? In removing such faithful shepherds from their flocks, and breaking down our defensed cities, iron pillars, and brazen-walls? Seemeth it a small thing unto us, that so many of God's prophets (whose ministry we came into the wilderness to enjoy) are taken from us in so short a time? Is it not a sign that God is making a way for his wrath, when he removes his chosen out of the gap? Doth he not threaten us with a famine of the Word, the scattering of the flock, the breaking of the candlesticks, and the turning of the songs of the temple into howlings?

It is high time for us to remember whence we are fallen, and repent, and do our first works. *Wherefore let us lift up the hands that hang down, and strengthen the feeble knees, and make straight paths for our feet, lest that which is lame be turned out of the way, but let it rather be healed*, Heb. 12:12–13. Labor we to redress our faintings and swervings, and address ourselves to the work of the Lord. Let us arise and build, and the Lord will be with us, and from this day will he bless us.

Source: Samuel Danforth, *A Brief Recognition of New-England's Errand into the Wilderness* (Cambridge, Mass., 1671).

[3] Comets. See Hall (1989), chap. 2.

Chapter 30

Increase Mather on the Politics of Declension

When ministers urged the colonists to correct the "decays and languishings" that crept into their lives, what gave force to such exhortations was the warning that "if we should so frustrate and deceive the Lords Expectations, that his Covenant-interest in us, and the Workings of his Salvation be made to cease, then All were lost indeed; Ruine upon Ruine . . . would come, until one stone were not left upon another."[1] In sermons on this theme, the ministers usually evoked the social ethic of mutuality that Winthrop had sketched in the "Model of Christian Charity." In doing so, jeremiads rehearsed the Puritan vision of the godly society.

Increase Mather (1639–1723) took these themes and magnified them in *The Day of Trouble is near*, a fast-day sermon preached to his own Boston congregation in early 1674, filling it with themes his predecessors had already employed but adding an apocalyptic emphasis upon portents, prodigies, and the meaning of New England. The allusions to showers of blood and blazing stars are typical of the lore of wonders or prodigies that was widely employed in the seventeenth century.[2] Mather's litany of troubles extended from "oppression" and disobedience in families to church members who avoided participating in the Lord's Supper.[3] Like some of his predecessors, he played the rhetorical card of the founders and the special relationship they had enjoyed with God. What was unusual was the fervency of his apocalypticism and the suggestion that New England might possibly be the site of Christ's kingdom, the "New Jerusalem." Throughout his jeremiads of the 1670s he wrestled with the connections between the history of Israel, as told in the Old Testament, and the history of New England. Were the colonists following the pattern of reform and decay that the Jews had undergone, and would the cycle conclude with the same tragic consequences? Were the people of God a church or a nation? Could the tribulations of God's

[1] William Stoughton, *New-England's True Interest* (Cambridge, Mass., 1670), quoted in Bosco (1978), xliii.
[2] Hall (1989), chap. 2; Walsham (1999); see also Increase Mather, *An Essay for the Recording of Illustrious Providences* (1684).
[3] See Brown and Hall (1997).

people be regarded as signs, not of his disfavor, but of the approaching end times when the church would experience "a glorious issue and happy deliverance, of all these troubles"? Proposing that "here the Lord hath caused as it were New Jerusalem to come down from heaven," Mather employed apocalyptic and providential language both to threaten and to reassure the colonists, promising them in any case that "destruction shall not as yet be."

Bibliography

Middlekauff (1971), chap. 6; Bercovitch (1975); Bosco (1978); Foster (1991), chap. 5.

INCREASE MATHER

❧ *The Day of Trouble is near* ❧

Ezekiel 7:7, The day of trouble is near . . .

Doctrine. That God doth sometimes bring times of great trouble upon his own people. . . .

Use III. 1. . . . There is a day of trouble coming upon all the world; and such trouble too, as the like hath not been: for I am persuaded that Scripture is yet to be fulfilled, even that Dan. 12:1 where it is said, *There shall be a time of trouble, such as never was since there was a nation, to that same time.* We are in expectation of glorious times, wherein peace and prosperity shall run down like a river, and like a mighty stream over all the earth; but immediately before those days, there will be such horrible combustions and confusions, as the like never was. . . . We know that in Abraham's vision, *when the sun was going down, an horror of great darkness fell upon him*, Gen. 15:12. Why so? But to signify, that when the sun is going down, even in the end of the world, when Christ is ready to come and set up his kingdom, and judge the earth, there shall be great horror of darkness and misery upon the world: *Darkness shall then cover the earth, and gross darkness the people* [Isa. 60:2].

2. Our eyes see, and our ears hear of *the beginnings of sorrows* [Matt. 24:8; Mark 13:8]. That which Christ spake with immediate reference to the troubles preceding the destruction of the Jewish church and state, may be applied to the troubles of the last times, the former being a type of the latter, Matt. 24:6–8, *And ye shall hear of wars, and rumors of wars, see that you be not troubled, for all these things must come to pass, but the end is not yet: for nation shall rise against nation,*

*and kingdom against kingdom, and there shall be famines, and pesti-
lences, and earthquakes in divers places: All these are the beginnings of
sorrows.* What do we hear of at this day, but wars, and rumors of wars?
and nation rising up against nation, and kingdom against kingdom?
Now if these are the beginnings of sorrows, what, and where, and when
will the end be? There's an *overflowing scourge* [Isa. 28:15] breaking in
upon the world, even a judgment, that will not keep within ordinary
banks or bounds, but shall pass over into many lands. And how far will
it go? where will the tail of this storm fall at last, do we think? How if it
should fall upon America? Will not some drops at least light upon New
England? We may speak in the words of the prophet in my text, and
say, *The morning is come* [Ezek. 7:7], the day of trouble begins to dawn
upon the world. *Alas for this day, it is great, there is none like it*
[Jer. 30:7]. It is then high time for us to awake out of sleep.

3. To come nearer home; the fatal strokes which have been amongst
us speak ominously. Is not that a plain scripture, Isa. 57:1, *The righteous is taken away from the evil to come?* The Lord hath been taking
away many righteous ones from the midst of us; yea righteous ones,
that should have stood in the gap, now when the waters of many troubles are breaking in upon us, whereby *he hath made a way to his anger*,
Ps. 78:50. How many magistrates, and ministers especially, hath the
Lord bereaved us of? When kings call home their ambassadors,[4] it's a
sign they will proclaim war. God hath called home many of his ambassadors of late, and that's a sign that war is determined in heaven against
us. . . .

4. There are manifold transgressions, and mighty sins amongst us.
And here if I should leave off speaking, and we should all of us join
together in weeping and lamenting, it would be the best course that
could be taken. Brethren, what shall I say? As to matters of religion,
things are not as should be. There is a great decay as to the power of
godliness amongst us. Professors are many of them of a loose, carnal,
ungirt conversation. We can now see little difference between church
members and other men, as to their discourses, or their spirits, or their
walking, or their garb, but professors of religion fashion themselves according to the world. And what pride is there? Spiritual pride, in parts
and common gifts of the spirit, and in spiritual privileges; yea carnal,
shameful, foolish pride, in apparel, fashions, and the like. Whence is all
that rising up, and disobedience in inferiors toward superiors, in families, in churches, and in the commonwealth, but from the unmortified
pride which is in the hearts of the sons and daughters of men? And is
there not oppression amongst us? Are there no biting usurers in New

[4] A synonym for ministers.

England? Are there not those that *grind the faces of the poor* [Isa. 3:15]? A poor man cometh amongst you, and he must have a commodity whatever it cost him, and you will make him give whatever you please, and put what price you please upon what he has to give too, without respecting the just value of the thing.[5] Verily I am afraid, that the *oppressing sword* [Jer. 50:16] will come upon us, because of the oppressions and extortions which the eyes of the Lord's glory have seen amongst us. And are there not contentions and divisions amongst us? It is in vain for us to go about to palliate this matter, or to cover this sore, for the shame of our nakedness doth appear, so as that we are become a derision amongst our enemies. We are divided in our judgments; and if that were all, the matter were not much: but we are divided in our affections, divided in our prayers, divided in our counsels: And will not a house divided be brought to desolation? . . . And what a woeful worldly spirit is there in many? Hence God, and Christ, and heaven, and the concernments of men's own souls, are not minded: yea, duties of communion with the Lord are either totally neglected, or slubbered over. Some don't pray in their families above once a day: Why? They have not time, they say. Why not? how is your time taken up? Is it in doing public service for God or for his people? If it were so, we must have a care that it be not said to us, *Thou wast made the keeper of the vineyard, but thy own vineyard thou hast not kept* [Song of Sol. 1:6]. But that's not the reason why men neglect duty; no, it is because they have not time for their worldly occasions. O this world! this world! undoeth many a man, that thinks he shall go to heaven when he dieth. And in this respect our land is full of idolatry. What is like to come on us? Alas! we have changed our interest. The interest of New England was religion, which did distinguish us from other English plantations, they were built upon a worldly design, but we upon a religious design, whenas now we begin to espouse a worldly interest, and so to choose a new God, therefore no wonder that war is like to be in the gates. I cannot but admire the providence of God, that he should threaten to punish us with a generation of men that are notorious for that sin of worldliness, as if the Lord would make us see what our great sin is, in the instruments of our trouble. . . . And as for the *children of the covenant* [Acts 3:25], as the scripture calls them, are not they lamentably neglected? Methinks it is a very solemn providence, that the Lord should seem at this day to be numbering many of the rising generation for the sword; as if the Lord should say, I will bring a sword to avenge the quarrel of a neglected covenant. Churches have not so performed cove-

---

[5] For contrasting interpretations of "just price," a concept that John Cotton famously evoked in a case of church discipline in 1639, see Bailyn (1956) and Innes (1995).

nant duties towards their children, as should have been; and especially, the rising generation have many of them broken the covenant themselves, in that they do not endeavor to come up to that which their solemn vow in baptism doth engage them to before the Lord, even to *know and serve the Lord God of their fathers* [1 Chron. 28:9]. Yet again, how unfruitful have we been under precious means of grace? How hath the Lord been disappointed in his righteous and reasonable expectations concerning us? We have not in this our day known the things that do belong unto our peace, and therefore now things look as if the days of our peace were ended. It is not long since that scripture was opened and applied in the hearing of many of you, Luke 19:43–44, *The days shall come upon thee, that thine enemies shall keep thee in on every side, because thou knewest not the time of thy visitation.* How righteous is it, that the Lord should make us to know the difference that is between the service of the Lord, and the service of Shishak? 2 Chron. 12:8. O New England, *Because thou servedst not the Lord thy God with joyfulness, and with gladness of heart, for the abundance of all things*, therefore it is just with God to say, *Thou shalt serve thy enemies which the Lord shall send against thee, in hunger, and in thirst, and in nakedness, and in want of all things*, Deut. 28:47–48.

5. Signs have appeared in heaven and earth, presaging sad mutations to be at hand. By signs, I mean prodigies, which the Scripture calls signs. It is a celebrated saying, that God never brings great judgments upon any place, but he first giveth warning of it, by some portentous signs. So did the Lord deal by Egypt in the days of old: and so it was with Jerusalem, a few years before the Roman destruction. Therefore Christ said, Luke 21:11, *Fearful sights, and great signs shall there be from heaven.* Josephus doth relate at large, what terrible prodigies appeared before those miserable days.[6] The like also happened before the troubles under Antiochus, as the historiographers of that age have declared. "There appeared troops of horsemen in array, encountering and running one against another, with shaking of shields, and multitude of pikes, and drawing of swords, etc." Something like unto that, is said to have been amongst us. I confess I am very slow to give credit to reports of that nature: but it is credibly reported, that in sundry places volleys of small shot have been heard in the air, yea and great pieces of ordinance discharged, when there has been no such thing in reality. And I think God would not have us altogether slight that bloody prodigy which happened about this time twelve-month (as eye-witnesses have affirmed) in that neighboring place, which since is fallen into the hands

---

[6] *The Famous and Memorable Workes of Josephus* (London, 1620), contains his much cited account of the fall of Jerusalem. Hall (1989), 79.

of our enemies. However, it puts me in mind of what I have read, viz. that in York in England it rained blood, a little before the Danes' entrance into the land. Moreover, we have all seen and felt blazing stars, earthquakes, prodigious thunders, and lightnings, and tempests. We may here make use of that scripture, which though it have a spiritual meaning, yet some good interpreters do not reject a literal sense of the words, Isa. 29:6, *And thou shalt be visited of the Lord of hosts with thunder, and with earthquakes, and great noise, with storm, and tempest, and the flame of devouring fire.* Hath it not been so with us? . . .

7. Without doubt the Lord Jesus hath a peculiar respect unto this place, and for this people. This is Immanuel's land. Christ by a wonderful providence hath dispossessed Satan, who reigned securely in these ends of the earth, for ages the Lord knoweth how many, and here the Lord hath caused as it were New Jerusalem to come down from heaven; he dwells in this place: therefore we may conclude that he will scourge us for our backslidings. So doth he say, Rev. 3:19, *As many as I love, I rebuke and chasten.* It is not only true concerning particular persons, but as to churches (those words were spoken to a church) that if Christ hath a peculiar love unto them, then he will rebuke and chasten them, as there shall be cause for it. Indeed we may therefore hope that the Lord will not destroy us. Through the grace of Christ, I am not at all afraid of that. The Lord will not as yet destroy this place: Our fathers have built sanctuaries for his Name therein, and therefore he will not destroy us. The planting of these heavens, and the laying the foundations of this earth, is one of the wonders of this last age. As Moses said, *Ask now of the days that are past, ask from one side of heaven to the other, hath God essayed to go and take him a nation out of the midst of a nation?* Deut. 4:32–34. God hath culled out a people, even out of all parts of a nation, which he hath also had a great favor towards, and hath brought them by *a mighty hand, and an outstretched arm* [Deut. 26:8], over a greater than the Red Sea, and here hath he planted them, and hath caused them to grow up as it were into a little nation: And shall we think that all this is to destroy them within forty or fifty years? Destruction shall not as yet be. Nevertheless, the Lord may greatly afflict us, and bring us very low. It is a notable observation, which I remember a Jewish writer hath, who lived in the days of the second temple. "The dealings of God with our nation (saith he) and with the nations of the world, is very different: for other nations may sin and do wickedly, and God doth not punish them, until they have filled up the measure of their sins, and then he utterly destroyeth them; but if our nation forsake the God of their fathers never so little, God presently cometh upon us with one judgment or other, that so he may prevent our destruction." So let me say, neighboring plantations about us may possi-

bly sin grievously, and yet it may be long before the Lord taketh them to do, because it may be he'll reckon with them once for all at last; but if New England shall forsake the Lord, judgment shall quickly overtake us, because the God of our fathers is not willing to destroy us their children.

Source: Increase Mather, *The Day of Trouble is near* (Cambridge, Mass., 1674), 20–27.

Bibliography

BIBLIOGRAPHICAL NOTE

Scholarship on Puritanism in England and New England is abundant. For a selective bibliography of publications printed before 1963, see the annotated bibliography in Perry Miller and Thomas H. Johnson, *The Puritans* (1938; repr. with updated references, New York, 1963). See also the author bibliographies in Edward G. Gallagher and Thomas Werge, *Early Puritan Writers: A Reference Guide: William Bradford, John Cotton, Thomas Hooker, Edward Johnson, Richard Mather, Thomas Shepard* (Boston, 1976). Also useful are the endnotes in David Leverenz, *The Language of Puritan Feeling: An Exploration in Literature, Psychology, and Social History* (New Brunswick, N.J., 1980). The extensive bibliography in Charles L. Cohen, *God's Caress: The Psychology of Puritan Religious Experience* (New York, 1986), is the fullest guide to discussions of theology up to the time of its publication.

Other guides to recent scholarship: Michael McGiffert, "American Puritan Studies in the 1960's," *William and Mary Quarterly*, 3d ser., 27 (1970): 36–67; David D. Hall, "Understanding the Puritans," in Herbert Bass, ed., *The State of American History* (Chicago, 1970): 330–49; David D. Hall, "On Common Ground: The Coherence of American Puritan Studies," *William and Mary Quarterly*, 3d ser., 44 (1987): 193–229; Peter Lake, "Defining Puritanism — Again?" in Francis J. Bremer, ed., *Puritanism: Transatlantic Perspectives on a Seventeenth-Century Anglo-American Faith* (Boston, 1993): 3–29; David D. Hall, "Narrating Puritanism," in Harry S. Stout and D. G. Hart, eds., *New Directions in American Religious History* (New York, 1997): 51–83; Darren Staloff, *The Making of an American Thinking Class: Intellectuals and Intelligentsia in Puritan New England* (New York, 1998), app. B; Ann Hughes, "Anglo-American Puritanisms," *Journal of British Studies* 39 (2000): 1–7; and the essays in Francis J. Bremer and Lynn Botello, eds.,

The World of John Winthrop: England and New England, 1688–1649 (Boston, 2004).

Surveys of the history of Puritanism in England and New England: Larzer Ziff, *Puritanism in America: New Culture in a New World* (New York, 1973); Francis J. Bremer, *The Puritan Experiment: New England Society from Bradford to Edwards* (New York, 1976; rev. ed., Hanover, N.H., 1995); E. Brooks Holifield, *Era of Persuasion: American Thought and Culture, 1521–1680* (Boston, 1989); Michael Watts, *The Dissenters* (New York, 1978); John Spurr, *English Puritanism, 1603–1689* (New York, 1998). More substantial works, each indispensable, include Patrick Collinson, *The Elizabethan Puritan Movement* (London, 1967); Perry G. E. Miller, *The New England Mind: The Seventeenth Century* (New York, 1939) and *The New England Mind: From Colony to Province* (Cambridge, 1953); Stephen Foster, *The Long Argument: English Puritanism and the Shaping of New England Culture, 1570–1700* (Chapel Hill, N.C., 1991). The material culture of seventeenth-century New England is covered in Jonathan L. Fairbanks and Robert F. Trent, eds., *New England Begins: the Seventeenth Century*, 3 vols. (Boston, 1982).

WORKS CITED

Allen, David Grayson. 1981. *In English Ways: The Movement of Societies and the Transfer of English Local Law and Custom to Massachusetts Bay in the Seventeenth Century*. Chapel Hill, N.C.
———. 1986. "The Matrix of Motivation." *New England Quarterly* 59: 408–18.
Anderson, Douglas. 2003. *William Bradford's Books* Of Plimmoth Plantation, *and the Printed Word*. Baltimore.
Anderson, Virginia DeJohn. 1991. *New England's Generation: The Great Migration and the Formation of Society and Culture in the Seventeenth Century*. New York.
Andrews, Charles M. 1934–1938. *The Colonial Period in American History*. 4 vols. New Haven, Conn.
Arber, Edward. 1897. *The Story of the Pilgrim Fathers, 1606–1623 A.D.* London.
Axtell, James. 1985. *The Invasion Within: The Contest of Cultures in Colonial North America*. New York.
Bailyn, Bernard. 1955. *The New England Merchants in the Seventeenth Century*. Cambridge, Mass.
Beales, Ross W., Jr. 1985. "The Child in Seventeenth-Century America." In Joseph M. Hawes and N. Ray Hiner, eds., *American Childhood: A Research Guide and Historical Handbook*, 15–56. Westport, Conn.
Bercovitch, Sacvan. 1975. *The Puritan Origins of the American Self*. New Haven, Conn.
———. 1978. *The American Jeremiad*. Madison, Wis.

Bosco, Ronald A., ed. 1978. *The Puritan Sermon in America, 1630–1750.* 4 vols. Delmar, N.Y.

Bozeman, Theodore D. 1988. *To Live Ancient Lives: The Primitivist Dimension in Puritanism.* Chapel Hill, N.C.

Bradford, William. 1912. *History of Plymouth Plantation, 1620–1647,* ed. Worthington C. Ford. Boston.

Breen, Louise. 2001. *Transgressing the Bounds: Subversive Enterprises among the Puritan Elite in Massachusetts, 1630–1692.* New York.

Breen, Timothy H. 1970. *The Character of the Good Ruler: A Study of Puritan Political Ideas in New England, 1630–1730.* New Haven, Conn.

Bremer, Francis J. 1992. "To Live Exemplary Lives: Puritans and Puritan Communities as Lofty Lights." *The Seventeenth Century* 7: 27–39.

———. 2003. *John Winthrop: America's Forgotten Founding Father.* New York.

———. 1997. "The Heritage of John Winthrop: Religion along the Stour Valley, 1548–1630." *New England Quarterly* 70: 515–47.

———, ed. 1993. *Puritanism: Transatlantic Perspectives on a Seventeenth-Century Anglo-American Faith.* Boston.

Brown, Anne S, and David D. Hall. 1997. "'That Her Children Might Get Good': Family Strategies and Church Membership in Early New England." In David D. Hall, ed., *Lived Religion in America: Toward a History of Practice.* Princeton, N.J.

Brown, B. Katherine. 1954. "A Note on the Puritan Concept of Aristocracy." *Mississippi Valley Historical Review* 41: 105–12.

Bush, Sargent, Jr. 1980. *The Writings of Thomas Hooker: Spiritual Adventure in Two Worlds.* Madison, Wis.

———, ed. 2001. *The Correspondence of John Cotton.* Chapel Hill, N.C.

Caldwell, Patricia. 1983. *The Puritan Conversion Narrative: The Beginnings of American Expression.* New York.

Canup, John. 1990. *Out of the Wilderness: The Emergence of an American Identity in Colonial New England.* Middletown, Conn.

Carroll, Peter N. 1969. *Puritanism and the Wilderness: The Intellectual Significance of the New England Frontier, 1629–1700.* New York.

Cave, Alfred A. 1996. *The Pequot War.* Amherst, Mass.

Christianson, Paul. 1978. *Reformers and Babylon: English Apocalyptic Visions from the Reformation to the Eve of the Civil War.* Toronto.

Chu, Jonathan M. 1985. *Neighbors, Friends, or Madmen: The Puritan Adjustment to Quakerism in Seventeenth-Century Massachusetts Bay.* Westport, Conn.

Cogley, Richard W. 1999. *John Eliot's Mission to the Indians before King Philip's War.* Cambridge, Mass.

Cohen, Charles Lloyd. 1986. *God's Caress: The Psychology of Puritan Religious Experience.* New York.

———. 1993. "Conversion Among Puritans and Amerindians: A Theological and Cultural Perspective." In Frances J. Bremer, ed., *Puritanism: Transatlantic Perspectives on a Seventeenth-Century Anglo-American Faith,* 233–56. Boston.

Collinson, Patrick. 1967. *The Elizabethan Puritan Movement*. London.

———. 1980. "A Comment: Concerning the Name Puritan." *Journal of Ecclesiastical History* 31: 483–88.

———. 1982. *The Religion of Protestants: The Church in English Society, 1559–1625*. Oxford.

———. 1983. *Godly People: Essays on English Protestantism and Puritanism*. London.

Coolidge, John S. 1970. *The Pauline Renaissance in England: Puritanism and the Bible*. Oxford.

Cressy, David. 1987. *Coming Over: Migration and Communication between England and New England in the Seventeenth Century*. New York.

Crowley, John E. 1974. *This Sheba, Self: The Conceptualization of Economic Life in Eighteenth-Century America*. Baltimore.

Daly, Robert. 1978. *God's Altar: The World and the Flesh in Puritan Poetry*. Berkeley, Calif.

Dawson, Hugh J. 1991. "John Winthrop's Rite of Passage: The Origins of the 'Christian Charitie' Discourse." *Early American Literature* 26: 219–31.

———. 1998. "'Christian Charity' as Colonial Discourse: Rereading Winthrop's Sermon in Its English Context." *Early American Literature* 33: 117–48.

Delbanco, Andrew. 1989. *The Puritan Ordeal*. Cambridge, Mass.

Demos, John Putnam. 1970. *A Little Commonwealth: Family Life in Plymouth Colony*. New York.

———. 1982. *Entertaining Satan: Witchcraft and the Culture of Early New England*. New York.

Denholm, Andrew Thomas. 1961. "Thomas Hooker: Puritan Preacher, 1586–1647." Ph.D. diss., Hartford Seminary Foundation.

Derounian, Kathryn Zabelle. 1988. "The Publication, Promotion, and Distribution of Mary Rowlandson's Indian Captivity Narrative in the Seventeenth Century." *Early American Literature* 23: 239–61.

Dever, Mark. 2000. *Richard Sibbes: Puritanism and Calvinism in Late Elizabethan and Early Stuart England*. Macon, Ga.

Diebold, Robert K. 1972. "A Critical Edition of Mrs. Mary Rowlandson's Captivity Narrative." Ph.D. diss., Yale University.

Ditmore, Michael G. 2000. "A Prophetess in Her Own Country: An Exegesis of Anne Hutchinson's 'Immediate Revelation.'" *William and Mary Quarterly*, 3d ser., 57: 349–92.

Ellis, John Harvard. 1867. *The Works of Anne Bradstreet in Prose and Verse*. Charlestown, Mass.

Emerson, Everett. 1965. *John Cotton*. New York.

———. 1976. *Letters from New England: The Massachusetts Bay Colony, 1629–1638*. Amherst, Mass.

Endy, Melvin B. 1986. "Puritanism, Spiritualism, and Quakerism: An Historiographical Essay." In Richard S. and Mary M. Dunn, eds., *The World of William Penn*, 281–301. Philadelphia.

Ferrell, Lori, and Peter McCullough, eds. 2000. *The English Sermon Revised: Religion, Literature, and History, 1600–1750*. New York.

Fiering, Norman S. 1972. "Will and Intellect in the New England Mind." *William and Mary Quarterly*, 3d ser., 29: 515–58.

———. 1981. *Moral Philosophy at Seventeenth-Century Harvard*. Chapel Hill, N.C.

Firth, Katharine R. 1979. *The Apocalyptic Tradition in Reformation Britain, 1530–1645*. New York.

Foster, Stephen. 1971. *Their Solitary Way: The Puritan Social Ethic in the First Century of Settlement in New England*. New Haven, Conn.

———. 1981. "New England and the Challenge of Heresy, 1630 to 1660: The Puritan Crisis in Transatlantic Perspective." *William and Mary Quarterly*, 3d ser., 38: 624–60.

———. 1991. *The Long Argument: English Puritanism and the Shaping of New England Culture, 1570–1700*. Chapel Hill, N.C.

Foxe, John. 1837–1841. *The Acts and Monuments*, ed. Stephen R. Cattley. 8 vols. London.

Gallagher, Edward G., and Thomas Werge. 1976. *Early Puritan Writers: A Reference Guide: William Bradford, John Cotton, Thomas Hooker, Edward Johnson, Richard Mather, Thomas Shepard*. Boston.

Garrett, John. 1970. *Roger Williams: Witness beyond Christendom*. New York.

Gaustad, Edwin S., ed. 1978. *Baptist Piety: The Last Will & Testimony of Obadiah Holmes*. Grand Rapids, Mich.

Geddes, Gordon E. 1981. *Welcome Joy: Death in Puritan New England*. Ann Arbor, Mich.

Gilpin, W. Clark. 1979. *The Millenarian Piety of Roger Williams*. Chicago.

Godbeer, Richard. 1992. *The Devil's Dominion: Magic and Religion in Early New England*. New York.

Gordis, Lisa. 2003. *Bible Reading and Interpretive Authority in Puritan New England*. Chicago.

Green, Ian. 1996. *The Christian's ABC: Catechisms and Catechizing in England c. 1530–1740*. Oxford.

Greven, Philip J. 1970. *Four Generations: Population, Land, and Family in Colonial Andover, Massachusetts*. Ithaca, N.Y.

Gura, Philip. 1984. *A Glimpse of Sion's Glory: Puritan Radicalism in New England, 1620–1660*. Middletown, Conn.

Hall, David D. 1972. *The Faithful Shepherd: A History of the New England Ministry in the Seventeenth Century*. Chapel Hill, N.C.

———, ed. 1968. *The Antinomian Controversy, 1636–1638: A Documentary History*. Middletown, Conn.; repr., 1990.

———. 1989. *Worlds of Wonder, Days of Judgment: Popular Religious Belief in Early New England*. New York.

———. 1991. *Witch-Hunting in Seventeenth-Century New England: A Documentary History, 1638–1693*. Boston; rev. ed., 1999.

Haller, William. 1938. *The Rise of Puritanism*. New York.

———. 1955. *Liberty and Reformation in the Puritan Revolution*. New York.

———. 1963. *The Elect Nation: The Meaning and Relevance of Foxe's Book of Martyrs*. New York.

Hambrick-Stowe, Charles E. 1982. *The Practice of Piety: Puritan Devotional Disciplines in Seventeenth-Century New England*. Chapel Hill, N.C.

———, ed. 1988. *Early New England Meditative Poetry: Anne Bradstreet and Edward Taylor*. New York.

Haskins, George Lee. 1960. *Law and Authority in Early Massachusetts: A Study in Tradition and Design*. New York.

Hill, Christopher. 1971. *Antichrist in Seventeenth-Century England*. New York.

———. 1972. *The World Turned Upside Down: Radical Ideas during the English Revolution*. New York.

Holifield, E. Brooks. 1974. *The Covenant Sealed: The Development of Puritan Sacramental Theology in Old and New England, 1570–1720*. New Haven, Conn.

Howard, Alan B. 1971. "Art and History in Bradford's *Of Plymouth Plantation*." *William and Mary Quarterly*, 3d ser., 28: 237–66.

Hunt, William. 1983. *The Puritan Moment: The Coming of Revolution in an English County*. Cambridge, Mass.

Innes, Stephen. 1995. *Creating the Commonwealth: The Economic Culture of Puritan New England*. New York.

James, Sydney V. 1999. *John Clarke and His Legacies: Religion and Law in Colonial Rhode Island, 1638–1750*. University Park, Pa.

Jennings, Francis. 1975. *The Invasion of America: Indians, Colonialism, and the Cant of Conquest*. Chapel Hill, N.C.

Karlsen, Carol F. 1987. *The Devil in the Shape of a Woman*. New York.

Kellaway, William. 1961. *The New England Company, 1649–1776: Missionary Society to the American Indians*. London.

Knight, Janice. 1994. *Orthodoxies in Massachusetts: Rereading American Puritanism*. Cambridge, Mass.

Koehler, Lyle. 1980. *A Search for Power: The "Weaker Sex" in Seventeenth-Century New England*. Urbana, Ill.

Kupperman, Karen Ordahl. 1989. "Definitions of Liberty on the Eve of Civil War: Lord Saye and Sele, Lord Brooke, and the American Puritan Colonies." *Historical Journal* 32: 17–33.

LaFantasie, Glenn W., ed. 1988. *The Correspondence of Roger Williams*. 2 vols. Providence, R.I.

Lake, Peter. 1982. *Moderate Puritans and the Elizabethan Church*. Cambridge.

———. 1989. "The Impact of Early Modern Protestantism." *Journal of British Studies* 28: 293–303.

Lamont, William M. 1969. *Godly Rule: Politics and Religion, 1603–1660*. New York.

Laslett, Peter. 1965. *The World We Have Lost*. New York.

Leach, Douglas E. 1958. *Flintlock and Tomahawk: New England in King Philip's War*. New York.

———. 1961. "The 'Whens' of Mary Rowlandson's Captivity." *New England Quarterly* 34:352–63.

Lepore, Jill. 1998. *The Name of War: King Philip's War and the Origins of American Identity*. New York.

Levin, David. 1972. "William Bradford." In Everett Emerson, ed., *Major Writers of Early American Literature*, 11–31. Madison, Wis.

Lewalski, Barbara Kiefer. 1979. *Protestant Poetics and the Seventeenth-Century Religious Lyric*. Princeton, N.J.

Lockridge, Kenneth A. 1970. *A New England Town: The First Hundred Years, Dedham, Massachusetts, 1636–1736*. New York.

Love, William DeLoss. 1895. *The Fast and Thanksgiving Days of New England*. Boston.

Ludwig, Allan I. 1966. *Graven Images: New England Stonecarving and Its Symbols, 1650–1815*. Middletown, Conn.

McCarl, Mary R. 1991. "Thomas Shepard's Record of Relations of Religious Experience, 1648–1649." *William and Mary Quarterly*, 3d ser., 48: 432–66.

McElrath, Joseph R., Jr., and Allan P. Robb. 1981. *The Complete Works of Anne Bradstreet*. Boston.

McGee, J. Sears. 1976. *The Godly Man in Stuart England: Anglicans, Puritans, and the Two Tables, 1620–1670*. New Haven, Conn.

McGiffert, Michael P. 1972. *God's Plot: The Paradoxes of Puritan Piety; Being the Autobiography & Journal of Thomas Shepard*. Amherst, Mass.

McLoughlin, William G. 1971. *New England Dissent, 1630–1833: The Baptists and the Separation of Church and State*. 2 vols. Cambridge, Mass.

Martin, John F. 1991. *Profits in the Wilderness: Entrepreneurship and the Founding of New England Towns in the Seventeenth Century*. Chapel Hill, N.C.

Marvin, Abijah P. 1879. *History of the Town of Lancaster, Massachusetts: From the First Settlement to the Present Time, 1643–1879*. Lancaster, Mass.

Middlekauff, Robert. 1971. *The Mathers: Three Generations of Puritan Intellectuals, 1596–1728*. New York.

Miller, Perry. 1933. *Orthodoxy in Massachusetts, 1630–1650*. Cambridge, Mass.

———. 1939. *The New England Mind: The Seventeenth Century*. New York; repr., 1954.

———. 1943. "'Preparation for Salvation' in Seventeenth-Century New England." *Journal of the History of Ideas* 4: 253–86. Repr. in *Nature's Nation* (Cambridge, Mass., 1967): 50–77.

———. 1953. *The New England Mind: From Colony to Province*. Cambridge.

———. 1956. "The Marrow of Puritan Divinity." In Perry Miller, *Errand into the Wilderness*, 48–98. Cambridge, Mass.

Monaghan, E. Jennifer. 1990. "'She Loved to Read in Good Books': Literacy and the Indians of Martha's Vineyard, 1643–1725." *History of Education Quarterly* 30: 493–521.

Moran, Gerald F. 1980. "'Sisters' in Christ: Women and the Church in Seventeenth-Century New England." In Janet Wilson James, ed., *Women in American Religion*, 47–65. Philadelphia.

———, and Maris A. Vinovskis. 1982. "The Puritan Family and Religion: A Critical Reappraisal." *William and Mary Quarterly*, 3d ser., 39: 29–63.

Morgan, Edmund S. 1944. *The Puritan Family: Essays on Religion and Domestic Relations in Seventeenth-Century New England*. Boston; rev. and enl. ed., New York, 1966.

———. 1958. *The Puritan Dilemma: The Story of John Winthrop*. Boston.

———. 1961. "New England Puritanism: Another Approach." *William and Mary Quarterly*, 3d ser., 18: 236–242.

———. 1963. *Visible Saints: The History of a Puritan Idea*. New York.

Morison, Samuel Eliot. 1936. *Harvard College in the Seventeenth Century*. Cambridge, Mass.

———, ed. 1952. *Of Plymouth Plantation*, by William Bradford. New York.

Morrissey, Mary. 2000. "Elect Nations and Prophetic Preaching: *Types* and *Examples* in the Paul's Cross Jeremiad." in Lori Anne Ferrell and Peter McCullough, eds., *The English Sermon Revised: Religion, Literature and History, 1600–1750*, 43–58. New York.

Muller, Richard A. 1986. *Christ and the Decree: Christology and Predestination in Reformed Theology from Calvin to Perkins*. Durham, N.C.

Murrin, John M. 1984. "Magistrates, Sinners, and a Precarious Liberty: Trial by Jury in Seventeenth-Century New England." In David D. Hall et al., *Saints and Revolutionaries: Essays on Early American History* (New York, 1984), 99–137.

Newell, Margaret E. 1998. *From Dependency to Independence: Economic Revolution in Colonial New England*. Ithaca, N.Y.

Norton, Mary Beth. 1996. *Founding Mothers and Fathers: Gendered Power and the Forming of American Society*. New York.

Nuttall, Geoffrey F. 1946. *The Holy Spirit in Puritan Faith and Experience*. Oxford.

Orr, Charles, ed. 1897. *History of the Pequot War*. Cleveland.

Pestana, Carla Gardina. 1991. *Quakers and Baptists in Colonial Massachusetts*. New York.

Peterson, Mark A. 1997. *The Price of Redemption: The Spiritual Economy of Puritan New England*. Stanford, Calif.

Pope, Robert G. 1969. *The Half-Way Covenant: Church Membership in Puritan New England*. Princeton, N.J.

Porterfield, Amanda. 1992. *Female Piety in Puritan New England: The Emergence of Religious Humanism*. New York.

Reis, Elizabeth. 1997. *Damned Women: Sinners and Witches in Puritan New England*. Ithaca, N.Y.

Ronda, James P. 1981. "Generations of Faith: The Christian Indians of Martha's Vineyard." *William and Mary Quarterly*, 3d ser., 38: 369–94.

Rosenmeier, Jesper. 1968. "The Teacher and the Witness: John Cotton and Roger Williams." *William and Mary Quarterly*, 3d ser., 25: 408–31.

———. 1972. " 'With My Owne Eyes': William Bradford's *Of Plymouth Plantation*." in Savcan Bercovitch, ed., *Typology and Early American Literature*, 69–105. Amherst, Mass.

Rowe, Karen E. 1986. *Saint and Singer: Edward Taylor's Typology and the Poetics of Meditation*. New York.

Rutman, Darrett B. 1965. *Winthrop's Boston: A Portrait of a Puritan Town, 1630–1649.* Chapel Hill, N.C.

Salisbury, Neal. 1974. "Red Puritans: The 'Praying Indians' of Massachusetts Bay and John Eliot." *William and Mary Quarterly,* 3d ser., 31: 27–54.

———. 1982. *Manitou and Providence: Indians, Europeans, and the Making of New England, 1500–1643.* New York.

Schweitzer, Ivy. 1991. *The Work of Self-Representation: Lyric Poetry in Colonial New England.* Chapel Hill, N.C.

Shurtleff, Nathaniel E., ed. 1853–1854. *Records of the Governor and Company of the Massachusetts Bay in New England.* 5 vols. Boston.

Simmons, William S. 1979. "Conversion from Indian to Puritan." *New England Quarterly* 52: 197–218.

———. 1981. "Cultural Bias in the New England Puritans' Perception of Indians. *William and Mary Quarterly,* 3d ser., 38: 56–72.

Slater, Peter. 1977. *Children in the New England Mind: In Death and in Life.* Hamden, Conn.

Slotkin, Richard. 1973. *Regeneration through Violence: The Mythology of the American Frontier, 1600–1860.* Middletown, Conn.

Solberg, Winton. 1977. *Redeem the Time: The Puritan Sabbath in Early America.* Cambridge, Mass.

Staloff, Daren. 1998. *The Making of an American Thinking Class: Intellectuals and Intelligentsia in Puritan New England.* New York.

Stoever, William K. B. 1978. *"A Faire and Easie Way to Heaven": Covenant Theology and Antinomianism in Early Massachusetts.* Middletown, Conn.

Stout, Harry S. 1986. *The New England Soul: Preaching and Religious Culture in Colonial New England.* New York.

Sweet, Timothy. 2002. *American Georgics: Economy and Environment in Early American Literature.* Philadelphia.

Thompson, Roger. 1986. *Sex in Middlesex: Popular Mores in a Massachusetts County, 1649–1699.* Amherst, Mass.

———. 1994. *Mobility and Migration: East Anglian Founders of New England, 1629–1640.* Amherst, Mass.

Tipson, Lynn Baird, Jr. 1978. "The Routinized Piety of Thomas Shepard's Diary." *Early American Literature* 13: 64–80.

Torrance, Thomas F., ed. 1959. *The School of Faith: The Catechisms of the Reformed Church.* New York.

Ulrich, Laurel. 1982. *Good Wives: Image and Reality in the Lives of Women in Northern New England, 1650–1750.* New York.

Valeri, Mark. 1997. "Religious Discipline and the Market: Puritans and the Issue of Usury." *William and Mary Quarterly,* 3d ser., 54: 747–68.

Vaughan, Alden. 1965. *The New England Frontier: Puritans and Indians, 1620–1675.* Boston; rev. ed., 1995.

Vickers, Daniel. 1988. "Working the Fields in a Developing Economy: Essex County, Massachusetts, 1630–1675." In Stephen Innes, ed., *Work and Labor in Early America,* 49–69. Chapel Hill, N.C.

von Rohr, John. 1986. *The Covenant of Grace in Puritan Thought.* Athens, Ga.

Wakefield, Gordon S. 1957. *Puritan Devotion: Its Place in the Development of Christian Piety.* London.

Walker, Williston. 1893. *The Creeds and Platforms of Congregationalism.* New York.

Wall, Robert E. 1972. *Massachusetts Bay: The Crucial Decade, 1640–1650.* New Haven, Conn.

Wallace, Dewey D., Jr. 1982. *Puritans and Predestination: Grace in English Protestant Theology, 1525–1695.* Chapel Hill, N.C.

Walsham, Alexandra. 1999. *Providence in Early Modern England.* New York.

Webster, Tom. 1997. *Godly Clergy in Early Stuart England: The Caroline Puritan Movement, c. 1620–1643.* New York.

Westerkamp, Marilyn J. 1999. *Women and Religion in Early America, 1600–1850.* New York.

Williams, George H., et al., eds. 1975. *Thomas Hooker: Writings in England and Holland, 1626–1633.* Cambridge, Mass.

Winship, Michael P. 2001. "Weak Christians, Backsliders, and Carnal Gospelers: Assurance of Salvation and the Pastoral Origins of Puritan Practical Divinity in the 1580s." *Church History* 70: 462–81.

———. 2002. *Making Heretics: Militant Protestantism and Free Grace in Massachusetts, 1636–1641.* Princeton, N.J.

Winthrop, John. 1908. *Winthrop's Journal "History of New England," 1630–1649*, ed. James Kendall Hosmer. 2 vols. New York.

———. 1996. *The Journal of John Winthrop, 1630–1649*, ed. Richard S. Dunn, James Savage, and Laetitia Yeandle. Cambridge, Mass.

Winthrop Papers. 1929– . 7 vols. Boston.

Wrightson, Keith, and Levine, David. 1979. *Poverty and Piety in an English Village: Terling, 1525–1700.* New York; rev. ed., 1995.

Young, Alexander. 1841. *Chronicles of the Pilgrim Fathers of the Colony of Plymouth, from 1602–1625.* Boston.

Zakai, Avihu. 1994. *Theocracy in Massachusetts: Reformation and Separation in Early Puritan New England.* Lewiston.

Index